# IMPROVING LEARNING ENVIRONMENTS

# IMPROVING LEARNING ENVIRONMENTS

*School Discipline and Student Achievement in Comparative Perspective*

Edited by *Richard Arum and Melissa Velez*

STANFORD UNIVERSITY PRESS
STANFORD, CALIFORNIA

Stanford University Press
Stanford, California


Printed in the United States of America on acid-free, archival-quality paper

Library of Congress Cataloging-in-Publication Data

Improving learning environments : school discipline and student achievement in comparative perspective / edited by Richard Arum and Melissa Velez.
pages cm.—(Studies in social inequality)
Includes bibliographical references and index.
ISBN 978-0-8047-7803-9 (cloth : alk. paper)
1. School discipline. 2. Academic achievement.
3. Comparative education. I. Arum, Richard. II. Velez, Melissa.
LB3012.I49 2012
371.5—dc23 2011039932

Typeset by Newgen in 10/14 Sabon

CONTENTS

## CONTRIBUTORS

**Robert Andersen** is professor of sociology and political science at the University of Toronto. His general research interests are in political sociology (especially the relationship between inequality and politics), social stratification (especially with respect to the role of education and social class), and statistical methods. His research often explores the nature of contextual influences on behaviors and attitudes, and thus it is inherently comparative. Some of his recent work has appeared in the *American Sociological Review*, *American Journal of Political Science*, *Sociological Methodology*, *Public Opinion Quarterly*, and *Journal of Politics*. He has also written a monograph on *Modern Methods for Robust Regression* (Sage, 2008).

**Richard Arum** is professor of sociology and education at New York University and since 2005 has been the director of the Education Research Program at the Social Science Research Council. He received his doctorate in sociology in 1996 from the University of California, Berkeley. He is coauthor of *Academically Adrift: Limited Learning on College Campuses* (University of Chicago Press, 2011). He is coeditor of a comparative study on expansion, differentiation, and access to higher education in 15 countries (*Stratification in Higher Education: A Comparative Study*, Stanford University Press, 2007) and author of *Judging School Discipline: The Crisis of Moral Authority* (Harvard University Press, 2003), which analyzes variation in court decisions and how these judicial opinions have affected public school disciplinary practices across jurisdictions and over time. In 2007 he led the creation of the Research Partnership for NYC Schools, which facilitates rigorous data-driven research, analysis, and dissemination to improve public school performance.

**Paolo Barbieri** is associate professor in economic sociology at the University of Trento, Italy. His research interests include welfare states and labor markets in a comparative perspective and networks, social capital, and status attainment processes. He coordinates the doctoral program in sociology at Trento University. He has been a member of various national and international research teams and recently directed Economic Change, Quality of Life, and Social Cohesion (EQUALSOC) projects, within the European Union's Network of Excellence.

**Machteld Bergstra** is a junior researcher and junior lecturer at the Amsterdam Institute for Social Science Research (AISSR) and graduated from the Research Master's Social Sciences program of the Graduate School for Social Sciences at the University of Amsterdam.

**Carmel Blank** is a doctoral student in the sociology and anthropology department at Tel Aviv University and a fellow of the educational policy program at the Taub Center in Jerusalem. Her research interests focus on stratification and the sociology of education. Her previous work examined the effects of an affirmative action program for the promotion of Ethiopian immigrants in the Israeli police force. Currently, she is studying the relationship between school disciplinary climate, student discipline, and student scholastic achievements.

**Karly Ford** is a doctoral candidate in the Sociology of Education program at New York University. In the broadest sense, she is interested in the relationship between education and social stratification. Her current research focuses on educational homogamy and intermarriage among American college graduates. She is the recipient of an Institute of Education Sciences predoctoral interdisciplinary research and training fellowship. She also works on projects related to international education for the Education Statistics Services Institute at American Institutes for Research.

**Theodore P. Gerber** is professor of sociology at the University of Wisconsin, Madison. His research examines socioeconomic stratification, labor markets, demographic processes, public opinion, institutional change, HIV/AIDS, and science in contemporary Russia. His articles have appeared in such journals as *American Sociological Review*, *American Journal of Sociology*, *Social Forces*, *Foreign Affairs*, *International Security*, *Social Science Research*, *Sociology of Education*, *Contexts*, and *International Migration Review* and several edited volumes. Gerber has developed (in whole or in part) 20 large-sample surveys in Russia, Ukraine, and Estonia since 1998 and conducted numerous focus groups and in-depth interviews.

**Hiroshi Ishida** is professor of sociology at the Institute of Social Sciences, University of Tokyo. His research interests include comparative social mobility, school-to-work transitions, and social inequality over the life course. He served as editor in chief of *Social Science Japan Journal* (published by Oxford University Press) from 2005 to 2010 and currently directs the Japanese Life Course Panel Surveys. He is the author of *Social Mobility in Contemporary Japan* (Stanford University Press, 1993) and is the coeditor of *Social Class in Contemporary Japan* (Routledge, 2009).

**Satoshi Miwa** is associate professor of sociology at the Graduate School of Education, Tohoku University. His research interests include social stratification and mobility, sociology of education, longitudinal data analysis, and quantitative sociological methodology. He has contributed to several large-scale survey projects in Japan. He is the coeditor of *Kekkon no Kabe: Hikon, Bankon no Kozo* (Staying single and marrying late: Barriers to marriage) (Keiso Shobo, 2010).

**Alejandra Mizala** is professor of economics at the Department of Industrial Engineering at the University of Chile and director of the Center for Applied Economics. She is also academic director of the Center for Advanced Research in Education at the University of Chile. Her main research areas of interest are in economics of education, mainly the impact of institutional arrangements on the outcomes of the Chilean school choice system and its effects on students' achievement, and the socioeconomic distribution of achievement within and between schools. Her research also includes school performance evaluation and the introduction of incentives in the educational sector in Latin America and trade-offs in the generation of school-quality information. She has been president of the Chilean Economic Association (2004–2005) and a member of the Presidential Education Reform Council (2006).

**Hyunjoon Park** is a Korea Foundation Associate Professor of Sociology at the University of Pennsylvania. His research interests include sociology of education, social stratification, and family in cross-national comparative perspective, focusing on Korea and other east Asian countries. He has studied how the effects of family and school on student achievement vary across countries according to the institutional arrangements of educational systems. His current research examines causal effects of single-sex schools on students' educational outcomes in Korea (with Jere Behrman).

**Stefani Scherer** is an assistant professor of sociology at Trento University, Italy. Her research interests are in inequality and social stratification processes in international comparative perspective, the analysis of life course, family, and labor market dynamics.

**Yossi Shavit** is professor of sociology and director of the B. I. Cohen Institute for Public Opinion Research at Tel Aviv University. He also heads the educational policy program at the Taub Center in Jerusalem. His main areas of interest are social inequality and the sociology of education. He is especially interested in the differences between societies in processes of educational and social stratification. His work has appeared in the *American Sociological Review*, *Sociology of Education*, *European Sociological Review*, *American Journal of Sociology*, and other journals. His best-known works are *Persistent Inequality*, coedited with Hans-Peter Blossfeld (Westview Press, 1993); *From School to Work*, coedited with Walter Müller (Clarendon Press, 1998); and *Stratification in Higher Education: A Comparative Study*. (Stanford University Press, 2010), coedited with Richard Arum and Adam Gamoran.

**Florencia Torche** is an associate professor of sociology at New York University, faculty affiliate at the Steinhardt School of Education, NYU, and research affiliate at the Institute for Social and Psychiatric Initiatives—Research, Education and Services (InSPIRES), NYU School of Medicine. Her research interests are in stratification, education, and the dynamics of inequality over the life course. She uses demographic and econometric methods to examine the intergenerational reproduction of inequality in different domains, including intergenerational mobility, educational attainment, wealth transfers, marital sorting, and the early emergence of disadvantage.

**René Veenstra** is professor of sociology at the University of Groningen and at the Interuniversity Center for Social Science Theory and Methodology (ICS) in Groningen, the Netherlands. He is involved in TRAILS (Tracking Adolescents' Individual Lives Survey), a longitudinal study on the development of physical and mental health and social behavior from preadolescence into adulthood. This project started in 2001 and will continue until 2015. His published research includes temperament-by-environment interactions, disagreement among teachers and parents about children's prosocial and antisocial behavior, continuities and discontinuities in antisocial behavior during the transition from elementary to secondary education, and bullying and victimization. He is associate editor of *Journal of Research on Adolescence.*

**Melissa Velez** is a senior analyst in the Social and Economic Policy Division at Abt Associates. Her research interests focus on stratification and the sociology of education. Her previous collaborative work has examined the relationship between school disciplinary climate and academic achievement, the impact of adversarial legalism, and the longitudinal effects of education reform on urban school districts. Her professional experience includes conducting educational data analysis for MDRC, the Social Science Research Council, and the New York City Department of Education.

**Herman G. van de Werfhorst** is professor of sociology at the University of Amsterdam, the Netherlands. He leads the Amsterdam Centre for Inequality Studies (AMCIS) and is director of Institutions, Inequalities and Internationalisation, one of the sociology research programs of the Amsterdam Institute for Social Science Research (AISSR). He serves in the coordination teams of two large European research projects: Economic Change, Quality of Life, and Social Cohesion (EQUALSOC) and Growing Inequalities' Impacts (GINI). His interests are in the role of educational systems in inequality of opportunity, labor market preparation, and active civic engagement.

**David Zarifa** is assistant professor of sociology at Nipissing University and an adjunct research professor in Carleton University's Department of

Sociology and Anthropology, both in Canada. His main areas of interest are in sociology of education, social stratification, work, occupations, and quantitative methods and statistics. He has published on a broad range of topics, including postsecondary access, school-to-work transitions, literacy and skills, and the teaching profession. He recently completed an international research project with the Centre for Education Statistics at Statistics Canada and the Organization for Economic Cooperation and Development (OECD), which compared adult literacy trends in 11 countries.

# IMPROVING LEARNING ENVIRONMENTS

INTRODUCTION

# School Discipline, Student Achievement, and Social Inequality

*Richard Arum, Karly Ford, and Melissa Velez*

In a series of lectures at the beginning of the 20th century (1902–1903), Emile Durkheim (1973 [1925]) argued for the centrality of school discipline in the process of youth socialization. According to Durkheim, school confronts youth as the first nonfamilial social institution (other than in some cases religion) that teaches students that there are external social norms, values, and rules that structure social interaction. Youth who internalize these norms and values are more likely to demonstrate conventional behaviors associated with productive employment and citizenship as adults, whereas the failure of schools and families to instill these values and norms in children is associated with delinquency, crime, and other outcomes at odds with the goals of these social institutions. While school discipline plays a role in allowing learning to occur and permitting educators to teach in work settings that are safe and professionally conducive to teaching, Durkheim (1973 [1925]) argued that school discipline was "not a simple device for securing superficial peace in the classroom" but, more important, "an instrument—difficult to duplicate—of moral education" (148–49).

Sociologists in particular have been interested in the role of school disciplinary environments in shaping individual student outcomes. Although discipline has long been recognized as a central feature of successful schools, researchers in recent decades have given relatively scant attention to comparative studies on this critical topic. Comparative research on school discipline is especially important at this time because we need to know more about how schools vary systematically in their approaches to discipline and how youth development varies with respect to school context. Such knowledge gives policy makers a sound empirical basis for the formation of effective educational policies. This book provides the first systematic comparative cross-national study of school disciplinary climates and aspires to contribute to academic knowledge, public understanding, and educational policy formation.

School disciplinary climates are made up of multiple elements and are best conceptualized as joint functions of the actions of students and educators. First, administrators' and teachers' actions to maintain school order—that is, school discipline as *administrative regulation*, or social control—set the parameters within which student attitudes, behaviors, and subcultures in schools are expressed. Second, school discipline manifests itself not just in administrative actions but also in student behaviors, norms, and values—that is, school discipline as *peer environment*. A school's *disciplinary climate* thus can be conceptualized as a product of the actions of teachers and administrators, the cultural beliefs and behaviors of students, and the interactions between students and educators that shape the school's organizational culture. These school-level processes, of course, are embedded in and structured by larger institutional, social, and cultural contexts that constitute the organizational field in which schools are situated.

School disciplinary climates not only are potentially associated with academic achievement but also provide the institutional context in which student moral development occurs. Sociologists have focused on the potentially critical role school plays in shaping the attitudes and dispositions of youth. Following Durkheim's thinking, sociologists have understood the moral dimensions of schooling as those aspects primarily related to the capacity to shape youth attitudes and dispositions in a manner aligned with normative expectations.

This contrasts with other developmental approaches that have understood moral education in terms of growth in the capacity of individuals to apply abstract systems of moral reasoning to problems they confront in the world (e.g., Kohlberg 1981). For sociologists, moral education is considerably simpler; it can be understood as schooling—and particularly school discipline—that plays a potentially critical role in children's and adolescents' internalization of conventional social expectations and norms.

Although social scientists regard school disciplinary climate as central to school effectiveness and individual development, surprisingly little systematic empirical research has been focused on examining the causes and consequences of variation in these climates. An early exception to this lack of attention to school discipline is the work of James Coleman and his colleagues. In 1959 Coleman postulates in *Adolescent Society* that students' educational orientations and behaviors are the product of specific school organizational environments and that these behavioral orientations can shape educational outcomes. The 1966 "Coleman Report," *Equality of Educational Opportunity*, further develops this theme, demonstrating that, after controlling for students' social background, "differences between schools account for only a small fraction of differences in pupil achievement" (22). To the extent that schools do affect student outcomes, however, the most important characteristic of schools is not facilities, curriculum, or teacher quality but peer environment. Coleman notes that "a pupil's achievement is strongly related to the educational backgrounds of the other students in the school" (22) and maintains that

> a child's fellow-students provide challenges to achievement and distractions from achievement; they provide the opportunities to learn outside the classroom, through association and casual discussions. Indeed, when parents and educators think of a "good school" in a community, they most often measure it by the kind of student body it contains: college-bound and high achieving. (183)

Coleman and his colleagues extend this focus on peer environments in the United States with research using the High School and Beyond study, a national probability survey of students in the 1980s. Coleman's colleague Tom DiPrete (1981) and his associates find that students in school climates with stricter discipline in 10th grade have lower rates of 12th grade misbehavior. In subsequent work exploring differences between U.S. public and private school student outcomes, Coleman and Thomas Hoffer (1987) link student behavioral climate to growth in cognitive performance between 10th and 12th grades and to differences across school sectors. Coleman, Hoffer, and Sally Kilgore (1982, 171) find that high school sophomores' reports of other student misbehavior (i.e., peer absenteeism, cutting class, students fighting each other, and students threatening teachers) were less frequent in Catholic schools and account for 33 percent of the higher performance of Catholic students relative to public school students on standardized reading tests and 46 percent of the difference between them on standardized mathematics tests.

Additional research on U.S. schools highlights how misbehaving students have lower levels of educational achievement as measured by changes in grades and test scores (Myers et al. 1987). Consistent with this position, researchers such as Paul Barton, Richard Coley, and Harold Wenglinsky (1998) argue that stricter school disciplinary practices are associated with improved student behavior. Richard Arum (2003) highlights how students' perception of the fairness (or legitimacy) of school discipline has a greater impact on student outcomes than perceived strictness of school regulation and sanctions against students. Research on school behavioral climates often also draws on student-level victimization data. This research suggests that certain school factors, such as school size, student composition, and school location, are associated with variation in victimization rates (Gottfredson and Gottfredson 1985).

In recent decades, educational systems have increasingly monitored and assessed reports of victimization in efforts to reduce school violence and increase school safety. Social scientists have been integral to this development, organizing themselves through such collaborative efforts as the International Conference on School Violence and the *International Journal of School Violence* (Benbenishty and Astor 2008). While these efforts have typically focused on developing programmatic interventions to reduce violence and improve school climate in settings with high levels of victimization, they have only recently begun contributing to the advance of social scientific knowledge on the structural and organizational differences across countries that are associated with student disciplinary climates (Benbenishty and Astor 2008).

Only a few systematic efforts have been launched to identify and understand how school discipline is structured differently across modern industrial societies. Two strands of comparative research are exceptions to this lack of empirical work. In the first, a few comparative studies highlight cultural explanations for differences in school discipline between the United States and Asian countries (e.g., Stigler, Lee, and Stevenson 1987). While these studies are fascinating and informative, accounting for cross-national differences largely in terms of national cultures, they do not systematically map out or account for differences in school disciplinary climates in either structural or institutional terms. A second line of research takes advantage of cross-national datasets to identify variation in student victimization, but it fails to advance compelling structural and institutional accounts of these differences (e.g., Craig et al. 2009; Akiba et al. 2002). Wendy Craig and colleagues (2009) analyze the Health Behavior in School-Aged Children (HBSC) 2005–2006 survey of more than 200,000 students in 40 countries and conclude that adolescents in Baltic nations have higher rates of victimization. Motoko Akiba and colleagues (2002) find that student victimization is lower in countries with higher levels of economic development (measured by gross domestic product per capita) but is not influenced by the income inequality within a country or by the percentage of linguistic minorities as a share of the population.

In this book a group of leading international social science researchers addresses this dearth of studies with systematic comparative research on a set of nine strategically chosen national case studies. The goal of the project is to identify the institutional determinants of variation in school discipline and the association of these school contexts with student achievement. How do these countries vary in terms of population heterogeneity, organizational structure of the educational system (e.g., centralization, privatization, and tracking), legal rights of students, administration of school discipline, and other factors that could potentially account for differences in school disciplinary climates? Which structural and institutional factors at the country and school level are related to school disciplinary climates? And finally, how are associations between social background and academic achievement related to school discipline?

## RESEARCH FRAMEWORK AND COMPARATIVE METHODOLOGY

To address these questions, we employ a collaborative comparative methodology similar to that used by Yossi Shavit and Hans-Peter Blossfeld (1993), Shavit and Walter Müller (1998), Arum and Müller (2004), and Shavit, Arum, and Adam Gamoran (2007). Research teams in nine countries address the overarching research questions using a common theoretical and methodological framework, which allows comparison across countries. Figure I.1 highlights the conceptual framework adopted for the analysis. The authors of the country chapters begin their exploration of school discipline by providing a detailed description of four institutional dimensions of school disciplinary context theorized to have important implications for structuring student behavioral climates. These dimensions are defined as

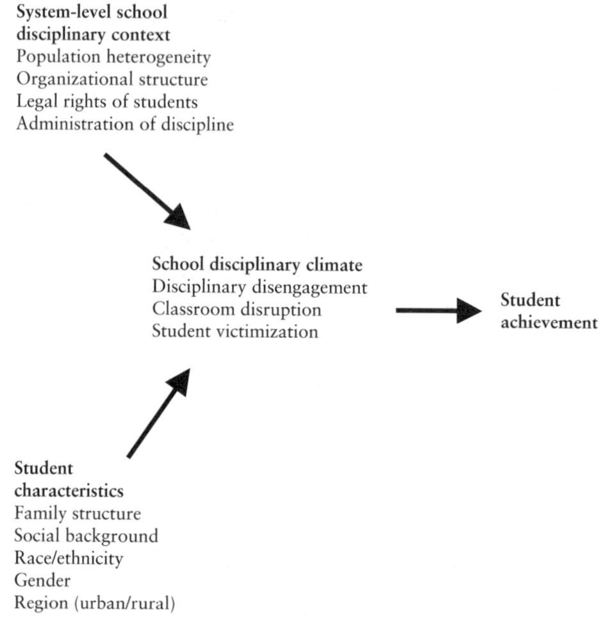


*Figure I.1.* Research design

(1) population heterogeneity and (2) organizational structure of educational systems, two components of national contexts that vary cross-nationally and that we quantitatively identify for this study, and (3) the legal rights of students and (4) the administration of discipline, two additional elements of national differences that we describe qualitatively.

*Population heterogeneity* is explored in terms of patterns of immigration and socioeconomic inequality that create pedagogical challenges and, often, public anxiety regarding assimilation, integration, or youth socialization. Previous social science scholarship suggests that student misbehavior can emerge from oppositional subcultures associated with these social differences (e.g., Ogbu 1978; Fordham and Ogbu 1986).

*Organizational structure* of educational systems is identified primarily in terms of school stratification (e.g., Müller and Shavit 1998), with particular focus on curricular tracking early in a student's academic career. School systems vary cross-nationally by whether they are stratified by curricular tracking, which separates youth at early ages on the basis of ability, academic performance, occupational orientations, and other factors, including such ascriptive characteristics as race, social class, and gender. In addition, where applicable for the educational systems of particular countries, we consider variation in school centralization (i.e., organization and administration from a central national bureaucratic authority) and privatization (i.e., private sector alternatives to publicly organized schooling). These institutional configurations are expected to affect student behavior through the sorting and segregation of students prone to misbehavior, individual assessments of the likelihood of success related to school persistence, and within-country variance of institutional characteristics.

*Legal rights of students* are examined and described qualitatively in terms of students' legal entitlements related to the administration of school discipline. We also explore court adjudication in student and parent disputes with school administrators over discipline issues. What formal legal rights are afforded to students in the country? Have formal definitions of the legal rights of students diffused internationally? Is there any evidence (e.g., media reports) that students and parents use the legal system to challenge school disciplinary practices (e.g., are educators ever sued for disciplining students)? Earlier research (Arum 2003) demonstrates how laws influence disciplinary practices and the perceived legitimacy of administrative efforts to sanction disruptive student behavior. Labor economist Philip Babcock (2009) further extends this line of research to highlight associations between legal environments, school disciplinary climate, and student behavior in the National Study of Adolescent Health[1] (Add Health), a study of adolescents in 132 schools, grades 7–12, across the United States. Babcock demonstrates that legal environments are associated with school disciplinary policies and that students attending schools with stricter discipline have lower truancy, greater likelihood of high school graduation, and improved employment outcomes.

*Administration of school discipline* is identified and described qualitatively in terms of the particular disciplinary forms and procedures employed by an educational system. We explore how schools impose discipline on students, to what extent school discipline is formalized, and how schools deal with minor and serious disciplinary problems. In the case of serious disciplinary issues, we pay particular attention to the use of mandatory school transfers, expulsion, and corporal punishment. Theoretically, these institutional practices should have direct effects on student behavioral climate.

Following descriptions of institutional variation in each country, authors assess within-country variation in school discipline and its association with individual student background characteristics and student achievement using 2003 Trends in International Mathematics and Science Study (TIMSS) data (Mullis et al. 2004). Analyses in each country explore the association between student background, school-level characteristics (i.e., student body composition in terms of student social background and heterogeneity), and school disciplinary climate. Researchers model the association between school disciplinary climate and student achievement on math and science tests and model how variation in school disciplinary climate mediates the effects of social background on student achievement. In many chapters, authors use other national data to supplement the comparative TIMSS analysis. This chapter provides details on the 2003 TIMSS data, measures, results from pooled analysis of all countries' data, and a summary of each country's results.

## TIMSS 2003 DATA

The TIMSS project, conducted by the International Association for the Evaluation of Educational Achievement (IEA), gathered data from fourth and eighth grade students,[2] teachers, and administrators in 49 countries, resulting in a dataset containing over 360,000 students, 25,000 teachers, and 12,000 principals. All participating countries employed a stratified multistage sampling design in which at least 150 schools were chosen at the first stage using probability-proportional-to-size sampling, and then one or two classes within each school were randomly selected at the second stage. This book includes TIMSS eighth grade data collected from Canada, Chile, Israel, Italy, Japan, South Korea, the Netherlands, Russia, and the United States.[3] Finally, two qualifications are worth noting. First, data on the United States and Canada were limited to specific states or provinces and thus are not nationally representative. Second, the United States did not ask students about individual victimization.

The primary goal of the TIMSS project was to measure trends in math and science achievement across countries. To that end TIMSS researchers in each country administered comprehensive math and science assessments near the end of the school year in each country. Countries whose school year ends in November or December administered the tests in October or November of 2002, while countries whose school year ends in June administered the tests in April, May, or June of 2003. In addition to the assessments, students filled out questionnaires on their attitude toward school, their home environment, and the school climate. Math and science teachers of sampled students provided information about their professional training and background, instructional practices, and curriculum. Principals (or headmasters) were also administered a questionnaire on school demographics, teacher support, school staffing and resources, and math and science course offerings. Student, teacher, and administrator surveys contained information pertinent to this book about school disciplinary climates, including questions about school violence, school safety, and student victimization.

## MEASUREMENT OF VARIABLES

### *Cognitive Performance: Math and Science Assessments*

Math and science assessments contained two dimensions, a content domain and a cognitive domain, administered in multiple-choice and open-ended formats. In math there were five content domains (numbers, algebra, measurement, geometry, and data) and four cognitive domains (knowing facts and procedures, using concepts, solving routine problems, and using reasoning). The science assessment had five content domains (life science, chemistry, physics, earth science, and environmental science) and three cognitive domains (factual knowledge, conceptual understanding, and reasoning and analysis). Because the extensive number of questions would have overburdened students, they were administered a subsection of items chosen using a matrix-sampling technique in which questions were chosen to create balanced designs containing math and science items. To create individual test scores, responses were scaled to derive estimates of what students would have scored if they had completed the entire test. Five imputed scores were provided for each student in the math and science subsections, respectively, each with an average of 500 and a standard deviation of 100. For this book, the math score is the average of the five imputed math scores, the science score is the average of the five imputed science scores, and the combined score is the sum of the averaged math and science scores.

*Student Characteristics*

Student background characteristics were drawn from student responses to the student questionnaire. Gender was measured using a dummy variable indicating a male student, a continuous age variable was calculated by TIMSS researchers using student reports of birth month and year, and immigrant status was measured using a dummy variable indicating that a student was not born in the country where the test was taken. Highest parental education was measured as the highest level of education completed by a student's mother (or stepmother or female guardian) or father (or stepfather or male guardian) and was standardized across countries into the following categories: did not go to school or did not finish primary school, finished primary school, finished lower secondary school, finished upper secondary school, finished postsecondary nontertiary education (e.g., vocational training), finished tertiary education designed to provide direct access to the labor market, finished tertiary education designed to prepare students for skilled work, and received beyond tertiary education. A categorical variable indicated the number of books students reported having in their household (none or very few, enough to fill one shelf, enough to fill one bookcase, enough to fill two bookcases, and enough to fill three or more bookcases), and a continuous variable indicated the number of people in the students' homes (two, three, four, five, six, seven, eight, or more). Finally, student expectations about educational attainment were measured using a dummy variable indicating that students expected to finish college.

*School and Community Characteristics*

School and community variables included principal reports of the school size (adjusted for skewness in the distribution with a logarithmic transformation), the school's highest grade level, and a categorical measure of the size of the community the school was located in (fewer than 3,000 people, 3,001 to 15,000 people, 15,001 to 50,000 people, 50,001 to 100,000 people, 100,001 to 500,000 people, and more than 500,000 people).

Because principal responses were not available for several school-level measures of interest, they were derived by taking the average of individual student measures. Specifically, the number of male students,[4] the number of immigrant students, and the highest level of parental education were identified by averaging the characteristics of sampled students by school.

The average numbers of males and immigrants in the school were then divided into categories based on an evaluation of the naturally occurring breaks in the distribution across countries. As a result, the average number of male students in a school was divided into categories of 0–45 percent male, 46–60 percent male, and more than 60 percent male. The average number of immigrant students in the school was divided into categories of 0 immigrants, 1–10 percent immigrants, and more than 10 percent immigrants. For our project, we calculate the school-level average of the highest level of parental education, and we create a measure of variation in parental education by dividing the school-level standard deviation of parental education by the mean of the highest parental education of the school.

### *School Disciplinary Climate*

School disciplinary climate was measured using principal, teacher, and student information collected from their respective questionnaires. Disciplinary disengagement was measured using principal responses to questions regarding how often arriving late at school, absenteeism, and skipping class occurred among eighth graders at their school (never, rarely, monthly, weekly, or daily).[5] If principals answered at least two of these questions, the responses were averaged to create the discipline disengagement index (Cronbach alpha is .76 for all schools; individual country alphas ranged from .67 to .87). Higher numbers on the index indicate more disciplinary disengagement in the school.

Frequency of classroom disruption was measured by a question administered to math and science teachers asking how often disruptive students limit how they teach their math or science class (not at all, a little, some, a lot). The school average of these responses was calculated separately for math and science teachers; those averages were then averaged to create one teacher average per school. Higher averages indicate more classroom disruption.

Student perceptions of disciplinary climate were captured using a student victimization index created by summing variables indicating whether students had reported that something of theirs was stolen, they had been hit or hurt by other students, or they had been made fun of or called names in school during the past month ($\alpha$ = .53 for all students; individual country $\alpha$'s ranged from .47 to .56).[6] A school-level student victimization measure was calculated by taking the school-level average of individual student measures.[7] Higher numbers on these indices indicate more victimization.

## METHODS

All chapters include descriptive statistics, school-level models predicting disciplinary climate, and student-level models predicting student outcomes. Some present additional TIMSS analyses or supplementary data from other sources. School-level models use ordinary least squares regression to examine the relationship between school-level characteristics and school-level disciplinary climate measures. Student-level analyses can take several forms but at a minimum include hierarchical linear models (HLMs) that examine the relationship between student-level measures, school-level characteristics, disciplinary climate, and math and science test scores. Some countries supplement the test score models with additional models examining students' college expectations or student victimization as outcomes.[8]

Using HLMs for the student-level outcomes is appropriate for these data because they adjust for the clustering of students within schools by calculating separate student- and school-level equations. In the student-level equation, an outcome Y for student *i* in school *j* is predicted by *k* student-level variables:

$$Y_{ij} = \beta_{0j} + \sum_{1}^{k} \beta_{kj} X_{kij} + r_{ij},$$

where $\beta_{0j}$ represents the average outcome of school *j* adjusted for student characteristics (X) included in the model and $r_{ij}$ is the student-specific error.

In school-level equations, the school average of the student outcome is predicted by

$$\beta_{0j} = \gamma_{00} + \sum_{1}^{k} \gamma_{0k} W_{kj} + u_{0j},$$

where school-level outcomes ($\beta_{0j}$) are predicted by the sum of the average intercept across groups ($\gamma_{00}$); a vector of school-level variables ($W_{kj}$), including school discipline measures; and a school-specific error ($u_{0j}$).

A second school-level equation indicates that the effects of the student-level variables are assumed not to vary across schools:

$$\beta_{kj} = \gamma_{k0}.$$

While our multilevel models control extensively for covariates that might affect estimates of relationships of interest, it is important for readers to recognize that our comparative project relies on cross-sectional observational data that limit the extent to which causal inferences can be drawn. In particular, disciplinary problems and student achievement are endogenous, and thus from cross-sectional observational data one would not want to assume causality. Nevertheless, descriptive modeling of how school discipline and its association with school inputs and outcomes vary within and across countries can still usefully contribute to sociological understandings and inform educational policy and practice by identifying how these factors covary with respect to other variables.

### WEIGHTS

For analyses to accurately reflect the populations of participating countries, we add sampling weights provided by TIMSS to the student- and school-level analyses. School-level analyses include a school-level weight that adjusts for a school's probability of selection and nonparticipation. Student-level analyses for individuals are weighted using a student-level weight, HOUWGT (house weight), that adjusts for the selection probability of schools, classrooms, and students and for school, classroom, and student nonparticipation. Student-level analyses conducted on the pooled sample of all countries in the project are weighted using a variation of the student-level weight, SENWGT (senate weight), that is adjusted so that each country contributes equally to the analyses regardless of population.

### MISSING DATA

Unless otherwise noted, authors use mean substitution to handle missing data.[9] All missing student- and school-level covariates are mean substituted with the exception of the disciplinary climate measures and student- and school-level gender measures. Missing data from continuous variables are replaced with the means from the sample, and missing-data dummy variables are created to flag observations with mean substitution. Missing data from categorical measures are set to 0 and then flagged using a missing-data dummy variable. The missing-data dummy variables are included in all multivariate analyses but not reported in the tables.

## QUANTITATIVE FINDINGS ON SCHOOL DISCIPLINE AND STUDENT ACHIEVEMENT

Table I.1 presents results of school-level regressions on our three measures of school disciplinary problems in pooled data from our case study countries. In our pooled analyses we add fixed effects at the country level to control for unmeasured differences. We find consistent evidence that students, teachers, and administrators in schools where immigrant students are concentrated report greater school disciplinary problems. Heterogeneity in a school's student population is thus related to increased disciplinary problems in the school. We also find consistent evidence that schools with greater concentrations of male students experience more disciplinary problems. In addition, we find some evidence that larger size of schools and communities is associated with school disciplinary problems. We do not find consistent evidence that parental education is related in a clear and simple way to our measures of school disciplinary climate.

The structure of TIMSS data allows us to move from an examination of school disciplinary problems at the school level to exploring one aspect of school disciplinary problems at the student level—individual victimization—in multilevel hierarchical models.[10] Table I.2 presents results from such an analysis and yields a set of additional intriguing findings. First, multilevel models suggest that the school-level finding that victimization increases with concentration of immigrant students is largely due to higher rates of victimization of immigrant students themselves rather than students in general. In the pooled analysis, the coefficient for a concentration of more than 10 percent immigrant students at a school is no longer significant in a model that includes student-level immigrant status. While immigrant students in Italy and Israel in particular report high levels of victimization, the multilevel regressions show that only in the Netherlands are students in general subject to higher rates of individual victimization in schools with higher concentrations of immigrants. In addition, the pooled analysis indicates that heterogeneity of parental education at the school level is associated with increased rates of student victimization.[11]

Multilevel modeling of student-level victimization indicates that boys and students in schools where boys are concentrated have higher levels of victimization. Eighth grade students who are younger than most of their classmates experience greater victimization. Interestingly, students from

## Table I.1

*Regression models predicting three indicators of discipline (nine project countries, school-level analysis, TIMSS 2003)*

| | *Disciplinary disengagement* | | *Classroom disruption* | | *School victimization* | |
|---|---|---|---|---|---|---|
| SCHOOL AND COMMUNITY CHARACTERISTICS | | | | | | |
| *School and community variables* | | | | | | |
| School size (log) | 0.433*** | CAN, CHL | 0.172*** | CHL, USA | 0.002 | |
| | (0.028) | JPN, RUS, USA | (0.024) | | (0.010) | |
| School highest grade level[a] | −0.022 | ITL | 0.045* | CAN | 0.003 | (CAN), JPN |
| | (0.023) | | (0.020) | | (0.008) | |
| Community size | 0.047*** | ISR, KOR, USA | −0.013 | CAN, NLD | 0.013** | CHL |
| | (0.014) | | (0.012) | | (0.005) | |
| *School-level student characteristics* | | | | | | |
| Average parental education | −0.182*** | ITL, KOR | −0.054 | ISR | 0.040*** | CAN, (CHL) |
| | (0.034) | NLD, RUS | (0.030) | | (0.010) | KOR, RUS |
| Variation in parental education | 0.156 | CAN, RUS | −0.975** | | 0.510*** | CAN, JPN |
| | (0.351) | | (0.307) | | (0.122) | KOR, RUS |
| STUDENT BODY CHARACTERISTICS | | | | | | |
| *Male* | | | | | | |
| 46%–60% | 0.102* | CHL, USA | 0.199*** | ISR, ITL | 0.087*** | CAN, CHL, ISR |
| | (0.048) | | (0.041) | | (0.015) | ITL, JPN |
| >60% | 0.166** | RUS | 0.407*** | ISR, NLD | 0.064*** | (NLD), USA |
| | (0.057) | | (0.050) | RUS, USA | (0.018) | |
| *Immigrants* | | | | | | |
| 1%–10% | 0.235*** | CHL, RUS | 0.090* | | −0.024 | (ISR), (NLD) |
| | (0.051) | (KOR) | (0.044) | | (0.016) | RUS |
| >10%[a] | 0.176** | CHL, RUS | 0.296*** | ISR, ITL | 0.049** | ISR, ITL, NLD |
| | (0.056) | | (0.049) | NLD, RUS | (0.018) | |
| Intercept | 0.768** | | 2.102*** | | 0.308*** | |
| | (0.306) | | (0.268) | | (0.086) | |
| $R^2$ | 0.247 | | 0.224 | | 0.405 | |
| *N* | 1,677 | | 1,700 | | 1,507 | |

NOTE: Models with all countries include country fixed effects. Standard errors in parentheses are adjusted for clustering of students within schools. Canada, Chile, Israel, Italy, Japan, South Korea, the Netherlands, Russia, and the United States are identified as CAN, CHL, ISR, ITL, JPN, KOR, NLD, RUS, and USA, respectively. Missing covariates (with the exception of gender variables) are mean substituted; dummy variables flagging missing covariates are included in the analyses but not shown. Analyses are adjusted using weights provided by TIMSS. Project countries in the table not in parentheses have statistically significant coefficients in the same direction as coefficients in the pooled analysis. Countries in parentheses indicate statistically significant findings in the opposite direction of coefficients in the pooled analysis.

[a] Models for Korea do not include a school's highest grade or the dummy variable indicating that a school contains more than 10% immigrant students. All Korean schools in the sample have a highest grade of nine and none are more than 10% immigrant.

* $p < .05$; ** $p < .01$; *** $p < .001$.

TABLE I.2

*Hierarchical linear models estimating the effects of student- and school-level characteristics on student reports of victimization (eight project countries—excluding the United States—individual-level analysis, TIMSS 2003)*

| | *Model 1* | *Model 2* | *Model 3* | *Countries* |
|---|---|---|---|---|
| STUDENT BACKGROUND | | | | |
| Male | 0.207*** | 0.197*** | 0.197*** | CAN, CHL, ISR JPN, KOR, NLD |
| | (0.009) | (0.009) | (0.009) | |
| Age | −0.036*** | −0.038*** | −0.039*** | CHL, ISR, KOR |
| | (0.009) | (0.009) | (0.009) | |
| Immigrant status | 0.081*** | 0.070*** | 0.071*** | ISR, ITL |
| | (0.018) | (0.018) | (0.018) | |
| Highest parental education | −0.002 | 0.003 | 0.003 | |
| | (0.003) | (0.003) | (0.003) | |
| Number of books in household | 0.023*** | 0.025*** | 0.026*** | CAN, JPN KOR, NLD |
| | (0.004) | (0.004) | (0.004) | |
| Household size | −0.006 | −0.008* | −0.008* | |
| | (0.004) | (0.004) | (0.004) | |
| SCHOOL AND COMMUNITY CHARACTERISTICS | | | | |
| *School and community variables* | | | | |
| School size (log) | | −0.014 | −0.022 | |
| | | (0.013) | (0.013) | |
| School highest grade level[a] | | −0.027*** | −0.027*** | CAN, (JPN) |
| | | (0.007) | (0.007) | |
| Community size | | 0.008 | 0.007 | CHL |
| | | (0.006) | (0.006) | |
| *School-level student characteristics* | | | | |
| Male students | | | | |
| 46%–60% | | 0.069*** | 0.060*** | ITL, JPN |
| | | (0.016) | (0.016) | |
| >60% | | 0.130*** | 0.120*** | CHL, KOR |
| | | (0.021) | (0.021) | |

| | | | | |
|---|---|---|---|---|
| Immigrant students | | | | |
| 1%–10% | | 0.043** | 0.040* | |
| | | (0.017) | (0.016) | |
| >10% | | 0.050* | 0.038 | NLD |
| | | (0.022) | (0.022) | |
| Average parental education | | −0.039*** | −0.032** | (CAN), CHL, ISR ITL, (KOR), (RUS) |
| | | (0.012) | (0.012) | |
| Variation in parental education | | 0.257* | 0.266* | CHL, KOR |
| | | (0.127) | (0.126) | |
| *Disciplinary climate* | | | | |
| Principal reports: frequency of disciplinary disengagement | | | 0.010 | |
| | | | (0.008) | |
| Teacher reports: frequency of classroom disruption | | | 0.044*** | CHL, JPN |
| | | | (0.010) | |
| Intercept | 1.088*** | 1.487*** | 1.353*** | |
| | (0.132) | (0.171) | (0.173) | |
| Pseudo $R^2$ | 0.010 | 0.011 | 0.011 | |
| Proportion of variance across schools | 0.059 | 0.054 | 0.053 | |
| $N$ | 39,447 | 39,447 | 39,447 | |

NOTE: Models with all countries include country fixed effects. Standard errors in parentheses are adjusted for clustering of students within schools. Students in the United States were not administered questions about victimization. Missing covariates (with the exception of gender and disciplinary climate measures) are mean substituted; dummy variables flagging missing covariates are included in the analyses but not shown. Analyses are adjusted using weights provided by TIMSS. Project countries in the table not in parentheses have statistically significant coefficients in the same direction as coefficients in the pooled analysis. Countries in parentheses indicate statistically significant findings in the opposite direction of coefficients in the pooled analysis.

[a] Models for Korea do not include a school's highest grade or the dummy variable indicating that a school contains more than 10% immigrant students. All Korean schools in the sample have a highest grade of nine, and none are more than 10% immigrant.

* $p < .05$; ** $p < .01$; *** $p < .001$.

households with greater numbers of books experience more victimization, whereas students from larger households, perhaps because of the presence of older siblings, experience less victimization. Model 3 in Table I.2 includes teacher and administrative assessments of school-level disciplinary problems in the model: teacher reports of school disciplinary problems are associated with greater levels of student victimization.

In Table I.3, we continue to use multilevel models of pooled TIMSS data on our case study countries to explore the association of student test scores with school disciplinary problems. *Our results indicate that all our measures of school disciplinary problems at the school level are consistently associated with lower student-level performance on combined math and science test scores.* These results remain even after controlling for school disciplinary problems at the student level (i.e., individual victimization). Differences in student performance are strongly associated with experiences of disruptive learning environments.

In addition, when examining change in the magnitude of coefficients from Model 2 to Model 3, we find evidence that school disciplinary problems account for a portion of the effects of school-level heterogeneity on student test scores. The coefficient for schools in which more than 10 percent of students are immigrants decreases by 25 percent, the coefficient for schools with fewer immigrants decreases by 29 percent, and the coefficient measuring variation at the school level in parental education decreases by 15 percent. Twenty-one percent of the negative coefficient for schools located in larger communities is accounted for in Model 3 by adding in the school disciplinary climate measures. An interesting pattern of change in coefficient magnitude is also seen on the measure of school size: the positive effect of large school size increases by 40 percent in Model 3 after school disciplinary climate is considered. Larger schools are associated with greater student achievement, although these benefits are muted by large schools' association with greater behavioral problems.

Coefficients measuring the association of student characteristics with test scores demonstrate a set of well-known findings: students from more privileged backgrounds score higher on the combined math and science test than students from less privileged backgrounds, and male students score higher than the average female student does. Students who are older than typical students in eighth grade (and have often been retained in a grade for limited achievement) score lower on this indicator, as do immigrant

TABLE I.3

*Hierarchical linear models estimating the effects of student- and school-level characteristics on test score (nine project countries, student-level analysis, TIMSS 2003)*

| | *Model 1* | *Model 2* | *Model 3* | *Countries* |
|---|---|---|---|---|
| STUDENT BACKGROUND | | | | |
| Male | 25.523*** | 25.865*** | 26.874*** | CAN, CHL, ISR, ITL, JPN |
| | (1.082) | (1.084) | (1.090) | KOR, NLD, RUS, USA |
| Age | −20.664*** | −20.121*** | −20.163*** | CAN, CHL, ISR, ITL, (JPN) |
| | (1.128) | (1.125) | (1.124) | (KOR), NLD, RUS, USA |
| Immigrant status | −27.883*** | −26.946*** | −26.636*** | CHL, ISR, ITL, JPN |
| | (2.180) | (2.183) | (2.182) | KOR, NLD, RUS, USA |
| Highest parental education | 10.281*** | 9.206*** | 9.223*** | CAN, CHL, ISR, ITL, JPN |
| | (0.387) | (0.390) | (0.389) | KOR, NLD, RUS, USA |
| Number of books in household | 21.290*** | 20.785*** | 20.896*** | CAN, CHL, ISR, ITL, JPN |
| | (0.469) | (0.469) | (0.469) | KOR, NLD, RUS, USA |
| Household size | −3.289*** | −3.094*** | −3.174*** | CAN, CHL, ITL, RUS, USA |
| | (0.444) | (0.443) | (0.443) | |
| SCHOOL AND COMMUNITY CHARACTERISTICS | | | | |
| *School and community variables* | | | | |
| School size (log) | | 7.584** | 10.621*** | CAN, CHL, (RUS) |
| | | (2.785) | (2.748) | |
| School highest grade level[a] | | 7.903*** | 7.027*** | CAN, JPN, NLD |
| | | (1.419) | (1.382) | |
| Community size | | −4.218*** | −3.318** | CAN, ITL, NLD |
| | | (1.202) | (1.165) | |
| *School-level student characteristics* | | | | |
| Male students | | | | |
| 46%–60% | | −5.555 | 1.000 | |
| | | (3.597) | (3.544) | |
| >60% | | −6.789 | 3.572 | ISR |
| | | (4.509) | (4.527) | |

(*continued*)

TABLE I.3 *(continued)*

| | *Model 1* | *Model 2* | *Model 3* | *Countries* |
|---|---|---|---|---|
| Immigrant students | | | | |
| 1%–10% | | −10.678** | −7.614* | USA |
| | | (3.637) | (3.524) | |
| >10% | | −22.071*** | −16.581*** | CAN, USA |
| | | (4.654) | (4.533) | |
| Average parental education | | 40.449*** | 36.834*** | CAN, CHL, ISR, ITL KOR, NLD, RUS, USA |
| | | (2.476) | (2.423) | |
| Variation in parental education | | −96.281*** | −81.852** | JPN, NLD |
| | | (27.500) | (26.663) | |
| *Disciplinary climate* | | | | |
| Principal reports: frequency of disciplinary disengagement | | | −8.762*** | ITL |
| | | | (1.709) | |
| Teacher reports: frequency of classroom disruption | | | −8.003*** | CAN, ISR, USA |
| | | | (2.156) | |
| Student reports | | | | |
| Victimization incidents, school level | | | −33.310*** | CAN, KOR, NLD |
| | | | (5.664) | |
| Victimization incidents, student level | | | −4.535*** | CAN, ISR, ITL, JPN, (NLD) |
| | | | (0.620) | |
| Intercept | 1,230.740*** | 925.320*** | 1,001.260*** | |
| | (16.755) | (28.718) | (29.209) | |
| Pseudo $R^2$ | 0.013 | 0.014 | 0.015 | |
| Proportion of variance across schools | 0.304 | 0.214 | 0.201 | |
| *N* | 39,447 | 39,447 | 39,447 | |

NOTE: Models with all countries include country fixed effects. Standard errors in parentheses are adjusted for clustering of students within schools. Students in the United States were not administered questions about victimization. Missing covariates (with the exception of gender and disciplinary climate measures) are mean substituted; dummy variables flagging missing covariates are included in the analyses but not shown. Analyses are adjusted using weights provided by TIMSS. Project countries in the table not in parentheses have statistically significant coefficients in the same direction as coefficients in the pooled analysis. Countries in parentheses indicate statistically significant findings in the opposite direction of coefficients in the pooled analysis.

[a] Models for Korea do not include a school's highest grade or the dummy variable indicating that a school contains more than 10% immigrant students. All Korean schools in the sample have a highest grade of nine, and none are more than 10% immigrant.

* $p < .05$; ** $p < .01$; *** $p < .001$.

students and children from large households. An important finding on the relationship between school disciplinary problems and student achievement is revealed by inspecting changes across models in the magnitude of the coefficients on the variables measuring student-level attributes. While some modest declines in the effects of social background appear between Models 1 and 2 (when school structural and compositional measures are added), suggesting that a small portion of the effects of social background on academic achievement work through sorting into schools, there is virtually no change in the magnitude of coefficients on the student-level variables between Models 2 and 3 (when school behavioral climate variables are added). This pattern suggests that *while variation in school disciplinary climates accounts for a relatively large portion of the association between school structural or compositional measures and test scores, school disciplinary climates have a much smaller role in accounting for the association of student-level attributes with test scores.*

In addition to examining school disciplinary problems and student achievement for our nine case study countries in school-level and multilevel models, we use TIMSS data to model these phenomena at the country level. This modeling exercise allows us to situate our case study countries in the larger context of variation across international school systems. We create indices for socioeconomic development, social heterogeneity, and school disciplinary problems to allow a parsimonious representation of these relationships given the limited number of countries with data available. We measure socioeconomic development with a composite index based on average parental education, number of books in household, and per capita gross national income (converted to international dollars using purchasing-power-parity rates).[12] Our measure of social heterogeneity is a composite index based on three standardized measures: each country's Gini coefficient of income inequality, percentage of students from immigrant backgrounds, and percentage of schools with more than 10 percent of students from immigrant backgrounds.[13] Our measure of school disciplinary problems is an index based on student, teacher, and administrator reports of school disciplinary problems in the TIMSS dataset. These three composite measures are standardized with a mean of 0 and a standard deviation of 1.[14]

Figure I.2 presents a scatter plot of the 49 countries in the TIMSS 2003 data along the dimensions of social heterogeneity and school disciplinary problems. There is a strong correlation (0.48) between these two measures,

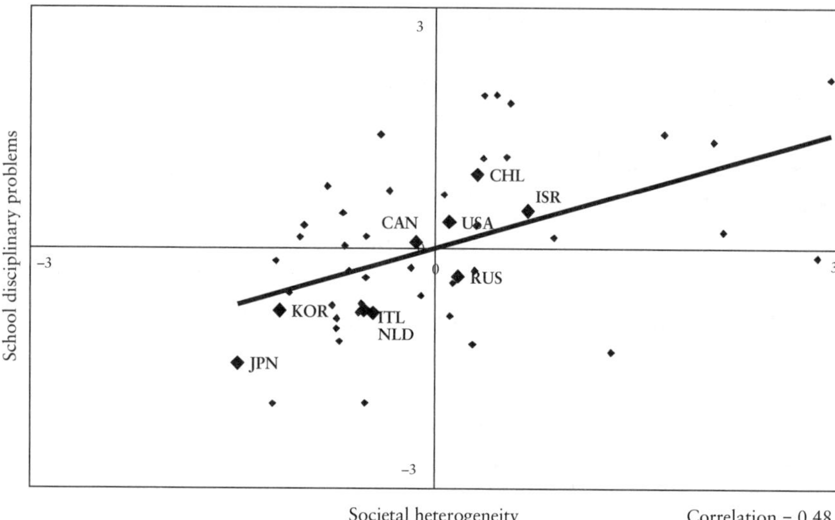


*Figure I.2.* Societal heterogeneity and school disciplinary problems (country-level analysis)

indicating that countries with greater social heterogeneity tend also to have higher levels of school disciplinary problems. Our nine case study countries are located fairly close to the plotted regression line in the scatter plot. Japan and South Korea, with lower levels of social heterogeneity and relatively low levels of school disciplinary problems, are in the far left of the lower quadrant. Israel, Chile, and the United States, with higher levels of both social heterogeneity and school disciplinary problems, are in the top right-hand quadrant of the scatter plot.

In Figure I.3 we contrast countries having less educational system stratification (a set that includes Canada and the United States) with countries having greater stratification. We operationalized stratification by adopting methodology used by the Organization for Economic Cooperation and Development (OECD) in classifying systems that are based on age of selection into distinct curricular tracks (see OECD 2005, 58).[15] Countries with low educational system stratification, operationalized here as the absence of significant curricular tracking before age 16, have greater levels of disciplinary problems in their schools. Although our measure of school disciplinary problems is taken in grade eight, often before sorting into these distinct curricular tracks in almost all countries, we believe that this measure

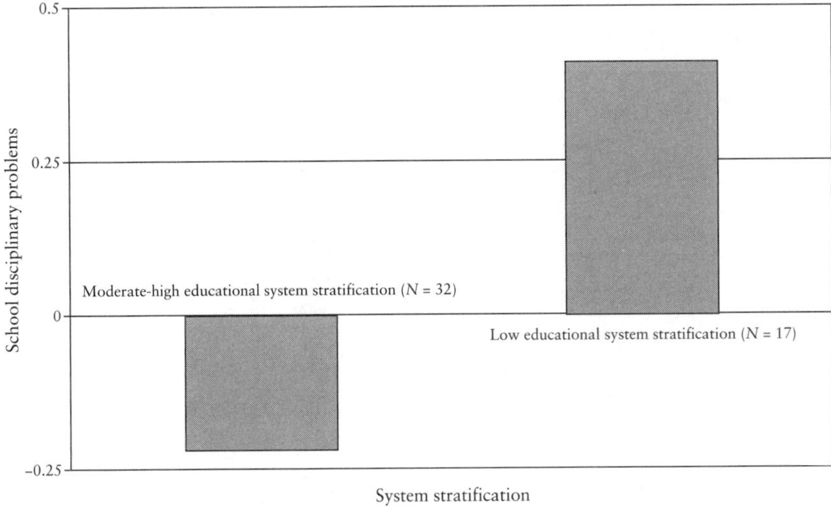


*Figure I.3.* School disciplinary problems by educational system stratification (country-level analysis)

nevertheless indicates a school system's embrace of a philosophy and practice of heterogeneous grouping. School systems with less stratification (i.e., less sorting of students at an earlier age) have higher levels of school disciplinary problems.

Figure I.4 shows the relationship of school disciplinary problems and student test scores across countries. The figure indicates that our two measures are correlated (−0.43), with greater levels of school disciplinary problems associated with lower test scores at the country level. Japan, Korea, and the Netherlands have relatively high test scores and low levels of school disciplinary problems and are at the top left side of the scatter plot. Of our nine case study countries, Chile is alone in the bottom right-hand quadrant of low test scores and higher levels of school disciplinary problems.

The bivariate relationships illustrated in our scatter plots, however, do not adjust for the influence of covariates. We move to a multivariate regression framework to identify these patterns of associations after taking into account covariates. Table I.4 presents results of country-level regressions of our measure of school disciplinary climate on socioeconomic and educational system characteristics. Model 1 considers how social heterogeneity is significantly associated with school disciplinary problems after accounting

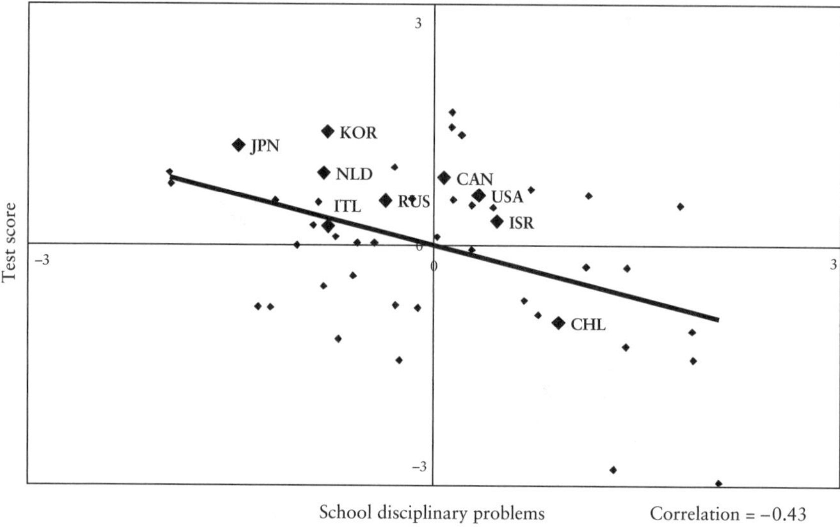


*Figure I.4.* School disciplinary problems and test scores (country-level analysis)

for the overall socioeconomic development of the country, which is not significantly related to this outcome. Model 2 adds a measure of educational system stratification to Model 1. Countries with low levels of educational system stratification, such as the United States and Canada, have higher levels of school disciplinary problems than other countries after accounting for social heterogeneity and socioeconomic development.

In Table I.5 we present a series of regressions that predict average combined math and science test scores in a country. Model 1 indicates that test scores are significantly higher in countries with more advanced levels of socioeconomic development; in addition, test scores are higher in countries whose populations are more homogeneous. Model 2 adds school disciplinary problems to Model 1, a factor that proves to be significantly related to test scores. Interestingly, the (42 percent) decline in magnitude of the coefficient on social heterogeneity suggests that the negative association of social heterogeneity on test scores is closely related to variation in school disciplinary climates—that is, *countries with greater social heterogeneity tend to have lower test scores because school disciplinary problems often accompany greater social heterogeneity.* Models 3 and 4 add educational system stratification to the earlier models but suggest that variation in

## TABLE I.4

*Country-level regression of school disciplinary climate on socioeconomic characteristics and educational system structure*

| | *Model 1* | *Model 2* |
|---|---|---|
| Socioeconomic development | −0.053 | −0.157 |
| | (0.138) | (0.141) |
| Social inequality or heterogeneity | 0.464** | 0.404** |
| | (0.138) | (0.139) |
| Low educational system stratification | | 0.678* |
| | | (0.321) |
| Moderate educational system stratification | | 0.121 |
| | | (0.314) |
| Intercept | −0.001 | −0.279 |
| | (0.127) | (0.228) |
| $R^2$ | 0.236 | 0.316 |
| *N* | 49 | 49 |

NOTE: Standard errors in parentheses are adjusted for clustering of students within schools.
* $p < .05$; ** $p < .01$.

## TABLE I.5

*Country-level regression of test score on socioeconomic characteristics, educational system structure, and school disciplinary climate*

| | *Model 1* | *Model 2* | *Model 3* | *Model 4* |
|---|---|---|---|---|
| Socioeconomic development | 0.627** | 0.615** | 0.666** | 0.633** |
| | (0.104) | (0.100) | (0.110) | (0.109) |
| Social inequality or heterogeneity | −0.251* | −0.145 | −0.246* | 0.161 |
| | (0.104) | (0.111) | (0.108) | (0.114) |
| Low educational system stratification | | | −0.325 | −0.183 |
| | | | (0.250) | (0.256) |
| Moderate educational system stratification | | | −0.226 | −0.201 |
| | | | (0.244) | (0.238) |
| School disciplinary climate | | −0.227* | | −0.209† |
| | | (0.107) | | (0.114) |
| Intercept | 0.009 | 0.009 | 0.201 | 0.142 |
| | (0.096) | (0.092) | (0.178) | (0.176) |
| $R^2$ | 0.568 | 0.608 | 0.585 | 0.615 |
| *N* | 49 | 49 | 49 | 49 |

NOTE: Standard errors in parentheses are adjusted for clustering of students within schools.
† $p < .10$; * $p < .05$; ** $p < .01$.

educational systems along this dimension is not significantly related to average student test score.

In sum, our quantitative analysis demonstrates that school disciplinary climates are significantly associated with student academic performance. While these disciplinary climates do not significantly account for the relationship between social background and test scores, they do in large part account for the negative association of school- or country-level heterogeneity and student academic performance. Heterogeneous environments are associated with lower student academic performance in that school disciplinary problems often become pronounced in such settings.

## NATIONAL CASE STUDIES—DESCRIPTIVE DIFFERENCES IN SCHOOL DISCIPLINE ADMINISTRATION AND INSTITUTIONAL CONTEXT

In addition to the country-level and multilevel findings we have identified, Table I.6 provides further elaboration on cross-national differences in the heterogeneity of societies, the structure of school systems, the legal environment of schools, and the administration of school discipline in our nine case study settings. While discussing these differences, we note how variation along these dimensions is associated with high, moderate, or low levels of school disciplinary problems. Identification of relationships with this form of qualitative data is speculative but suggests potential relationships to explore in future research.

### *Heterogeneity*

The countries in this study vary in heterogeneity of school composition. Korea and Japan have the lowest levels of heterogeneity, with less than 1 percent of their schools having student populations of more than 10 percent immigrant students. Israel, a country of immigrants, has 55 percent of schools with student bodies composed of more than 10 percent immigrant students. In the last 20 years, about one million people have emigrated from the former Soviet Union to Israel. Other sizable Israeli immigrant populations hail from Arabic-speaking Middle Eastern countries, Africa, and Europe. Chile and Italy have moderate levels of immigrant students with 13 percent and 16 percent, respectively, of their schools having student populations with more than 10 percent immigrant students. The majority

TABLE I.6

*Population heterogeneity, organizational structure of schools, legal rights of students, and distinctive features of school disciplinary administration*

| | POPULATION HETEROGENEITY | | | | |
|---|---|---|---|---|---|
| *Country* | *Gini coefficient* | *Schools with >10% immigrant students (%)* | *Organizational structure* | *Legal rights of students* | *Distinctive features of school discipline* |
| HIGH LEVELS OF SCHOOL DISCIPLINE PROBLEMS | | | | | |
| Chile | 0.549 | 13 | Three-tiered system is result of universal vouchers: municipal schools, voucher-subsidized private schools, and unsubsidized private schools. No tracking within schools. Separate vocational and academic track high schools. | Legislative expansion of students' legal protections in the late 1990s. Since 2000, about 24 cases of students litigating against schools have been filed. A small but growing trend. | Uniform is strictly enforced as a means to identify and monitor students inside and outside school. Demerits, parent-teacher interviews, and detention are common. Suspension and expulsion occasional. |
| MODERATE LEVELS OF SCHOOL DISCIPLINE PROBLEMS | | | | | |
| Canada | 0.326 | 30 | Decentralized system controlled by provinces. "Separate schools have religious orientations and are publicly funded. Rates of private schooling vary between provinces: from 4.3% in Ontario to 9.2% in Quebec. | Fewer court cases than the United States, but a sizable number since 1982 adoption of the Charter of Rights and Freedoms. Courts tend to "respect . . . discretionary decisions made by school authority."[a] | Zero tolerance policies for possession of weapons and drugs did not deter student misbehavior and seemed unnecessarily harsh. Now some provinces are introducing "progressive discipline,"[a] a program that emphasizes positive school climates and opportunities for penalized students to continue their education. |
| Israel | 0.392 | 55 | Moderately centralized, highly segregated system. Jewish students attend nonreligious public schools (70%), religious public schools (20%), and ultra-orthodox private schools (10%). Secondary school students choose between academic and vocational tracks. | Political and legislative interest in school discipline and violence. No reported cases of students suing schools. Media coverage features students' rights as the central issue. | Corporal punishment and exclusion of students from school activities or trips is prohibited. Very few students are expelled, suspended, or transferred because Israeli law makes this very difficult. |

*(continued)*

Table I.6 *(continued)*

| | POPULATION HETEROGENEITY | | | | |
|---|---|---|---|---|---|
| *Country* | *Gini coefficient* | *Schools with >10% immigrant students (%)* | *Organizational structure* | *Legal rights of students* | *Distinctive features of school discipline* |
| United States | 0.408 | 29 | Decentralized system controlled by states and local school boards; 89% public. Vocational programs declining. | Widespread legal challenges. Courts protect students' constitutional rights within schools. | Corporal punishment legal in many southern states. Random searches, metal detectors, and sniffer dogs are common policing strategies in schools. |
| LOW LEVELS OF SCHOOL DISCIPLINARY PROBLEMS | | | | | |
| Italy | 0.360 | 16 | Highly centralized, standardized curricula and state examinations. Secondary school tracks are differentiated; academic tracks lead to university and shorter vocational tracks lead to entry into the labor force. | Political and legislative interest in school discipline. Public school considered a public good, so private recourse such as suing teachers is unusual. | No formal means of legal or social control (school ID checks) or informal ones such as uniforms are present in Italian schools. Teachers are supported by school councils when dealing with severe misbehavior. |
| Japan | 0.249 | 1 | Highly centralized and standardized at the national level. Less than 1% of elementary school students and less than 10% of high school students attend private schools. | Political and legislative interest in school discipline. | Homeroom teachers provide guidance to students if delinquent behavior is detected and attempt rehabilitation. Discipline strictly enforced in high schools. Among misbehaving high school students, 80% were expelled, suspended, or given a home curfew, reprimand, or written warning. Only 5% of elementary and middle school students experienced such consequences. School uniform requirements regulate clothing, hairstyle, shoes, bags, and personal items and identify students throughout the day and on weekends. |

| | | | | | |
|---|---|---|---|---|---|
| Korea | 0.316 | 0 | Highly centralized and standardized at the national level. Curricula, materials, and exams are standard. Primary schooling dominated by public schools. However, for secondary schooling 50% of students attend private schools. Private schools are regulated by the government. 78% of students are randomly assigned to schools in their district. Of high schools, 25% are vocational. | Political and legislative interest in school discipline. Education and law are viewed as separate. Students' rights are considered an infringement on teacher authority. | Corporal punishment is ubiquitous—70% of high school students report it is used in their schools. School uniform requirements regulate clothing, hairstyle, shoes, bags, and personal items brought to school and identify students throughout the day. Students are kept in schools for long hours, as late as 10 p.m. at academic high schools. Students must secure special permission to enter and leave school during the day. Korean students view peers as competitors in highly selective university entry. Students comply with school rules in this distinctively competitive culture of peer group social control. |
| Netherlands | 0.309 | 29 | Highly centralized and standardized at the national level. Curricula, materials, and exams are standard. Highly stratified secondary school system. Government funds public and private schools. Paradoxically, a large number of private religious schools within this highly secular society. | Political and legislative interest in school discipline. Suspensions and expulsions must be reported to the Inspectorate of Education. Other than cases of suspension or expulsion, school discipline is not seen as a legal issue. | Students suspended for fights, drug and alcohol use, and possession of weapons or fireworks. Police contacted only in instances of burglary or theft. Warnings issued in cases of bullying and discriminatory acts. Parents contacted when students destroy school property. |
| Russia | 0.399 | 35 | Highly centralized national public schooling with a very small private sector. Students are not tracked. Vocational education an option for secondary school students. | Legal environment has no influence on school context. Citizens could not sue government officials during the Soviet era; as a result Russians have little experience with this mechanism for seeking redress. | Teachers are maternal and supportive toward students, cultivating a strong commitment to a classroom collective. Bad behavior and poor grades are viewed as letting the team down. Teachers contact parents when a student's behavior is inappropriate. Only in rare and extreme cases are students expelled or suspended. |

[a] See Chapter 1.

of Chile's immigrant students are from neighboring countries, and many arrived as native Spanish speakers, though some spoke indigenous languages and did not receive the benefit of instruction.

### *Structure of School Systems*

In many respects, the nations we study similarly structure their educational systems. Schooling is age graded, compulsory until midadolescence, and divided into elementary and secondary levels in all countries. Secondary schools provide academic preparation for university entrance, and most nations' educational systems structure options for access to a vocational track at this stage. While the public sector educates the majority of students, other organizational forms also exist, such as voucher-subsidized private schools in Chile, ultra-orthodox Hebrew schools in Israel, and publicly funded religious institutions in Canada known as "separate schools." These variations flourish alongside the public school sector. In Japan virtually all students attend public schools at the elementary level. Koreans demonstrate a similar commitment to public elementary education; however, at the secondary level, 50 percent of Korean students attend private schools.

School systems vary in degree of central control. Highly centralized systems, such as those in Italy, Japan, Korea, the Netherlands, and Russia, provide nationwide standardized funding, curricula, and exams. Teacher training, compensation, and school construction are also highly regulated and are remarkably similar throughout these countries. In the United States and Canada, control of school systems is decentralized, with educational decisions made at provincial, state, and district levels. Curricula, educational standards, and per pupil expenditure vary widely among American and Canadian states and provinces. Students surveyed in these two nations report the highest rates of misbehavior and bullying, suggesting an association between the level of centralization and the overall disciplinary climate.

The countries in our study differ on our measure of educational system stratification. Canada and the United States have low levels of stratification: typically students attend similar schools and programs until age 16, when there is some limited tracking into vocational programs. In Israel and the Netherlands, vocational tracking often occurs at age 14; in all other countries in the study, vocational tracking occurs around age 15.

*Legal Environment*

Only the United States and Canada, and to a lesser extent Chile, consider legal action an appropriate mechanism for recourse in disputes between students and schools. In the United States, where courts often rule in favor of students' rights, 38 percent of teachers and 51 percent of principals report personal contact with legal challenges related to school practices. In Canada, where courts hear fewer school-related suits, judges tend to support the discretionary decisions made by schools.

In Israel, Italy, the Netherlands, Russia, Japan, and Korea, parliamentary bodies have largely legislated decisions about students' rights, appropriate punishments, and procedures for school discipline. Political leaders have passed laws and constitutional amendments, and some have ratified the UN Convention on the Rights of the Child as a means of protecting students' rights in schools. However, this interest in monitoring school discipline is framed as a public policy issue and not as a private or personal matter. Suing a schoolteacher is not a common occurrence and is not perceived as appropriate behavior for students or families in these countries. In Korea, where public opinion supports protection of teachers' ability to maintain order over protection of students' rights, there is a clear separation between the role of the legal system and the daily workings of schools.

*Forms of Discipline*

Uniforms, dress codes, and strict policies about students' possessions and appearance are part of the Japanese, Korean, and Chilean school systems. Schools mandate specific requirements for the tidy appearance of students' uniforms, including a visible badge bearing the name of the school and the student. School administrators specify the length, color, and style of students' hair. Careful inspection of students and enforcement of these rules about appearance ensure that students are easily recognized and monitored by the community.

The United States does not enforce dress codes in most schools; however, students' behavior and possessions are strictly monitored and policed. About a quarter of schools in the United States use drug-sniffing dogs, metal detectors, random searches, or uniformed law enforcement officers to uphold school rules. Our other case study countries have not adopted policing practices to maintain order in schools.

Use of corporal punishment has diminished throughout the world, but it is still practiced in Korea, Japan, and parts of the southern United States. In these places, corporal punishment is reserved for instances of severe misbehavior and is thought to support teachers' legitimate authority over students. In Korea the instrument of corporal punishment is colloquially called the "stick of love"—a name that complicates simplistic framings of corporal punishment as solely punitive.

## OUTLINE OF THE BOOK

Chapter 1 describes the moderate association between school disciplinary climate and academic achievement in Canada. While the disciplinary climate of schools does play a role in predicting academic outcomes, the effect is less pronounced in Canada than in other countries. Canada's school disciplinary problems are moderate—mostly bullying and disorderly behavior and only rarely involving severe violence—therefore the weak relationship between academic performance and reports of school disciplinary climates are somewhat expected. In separate analyses of Quebec and Ontario, the authors uncover striking variation between provinces in terms of the effects of disciplinary climate on test scores. In Ontario, school disciplinary climate has no apparent effect on student academic performance. However, in Quebec, teacher reports of classroom disruption are strongly related to student performance on academic measures. On average, a one-unit increase in teacher reports of classroom disruption is associated with student test scores that are 19 points (or approximately 1.9 percent) lower.

The distinctive organizational structure of Chile's educational system is discussed in Chapter 2. The Chilean school system underwent an organizational transformation in 1981, from being centrally controlled by the national government to becoming a universal voucher system controlled by municipal governments. Currently, a socioeconomically stratified, three-tiered school system exists, with the poorest Chileans attending public schools, the slightly better off attending public voucher schools, and the elite attending private schools. Students in Chile report the highest levels of victimization at school in our comparative project. Chile's high student-victimization score may be related to pervasive bullying in Chilean schools, specifically because the student victimization index is particularly sensitive to bullying behaviors. The authors find a weak association between school socioeconomic composition and disciplinary climate. Although Chilean schools are dramatically segregated on class lines, schools that serve wealthier students are only slightly more orderly than schools that serve less affluent students. The authors find striking regional differences in the stratification of disciplinary climates—students attending Chile's rural schools report far less victimization than those attending urban schools.

In Chapter 3, the authors find a strong, significant association between a school's disciplinary climate and student achievement in Israel. Test scores are negatively associated with principals' reports of students' engagement and teachers' reports of classroom discipline. Reports of violence among students, and by students against teachers, have been common recently in the Israeli media. Israeli students receive mixed messages about obedience and deference. At school, Israeli students receive grades for their behavior in the same report as the one with their grades for core academic subjects, and they can be expelled if they fail to maintain satisfactory behavior grades. On the other hand, Israelis idealize *sabra* youth culture, which values defiant, rebellious, independent, and daring behavior. The romanticization of *sabra* culture may conflict with the maintenance of order in schools.

In Chapter 4, the authors find that high student victimization, on average, directly hinders academic performance for Italian students. The negative impact of high victimization is most acutely observed in the performance of immigrant students. Immigrant students are more likely to report being victimized than native-born Italian students and have lower scores on academic measures. Italy has seen a rapid growth of its immigrant population in the last few years. As of 2009, immigrants from non–European Union countries or their children account for 6.5 percent of the total population of Italy. Immigrants in Italy come from all over the world, with the largest populations arriving from Morocco, China, Romania, Ukraine, Moldova, India, and the Philippines. In addition to variation between immigrant and native-born students, the authors find dramatic regional variation between the north and south of Italy. The south, which has fewer financial resources than the north, trails the north in educational investment and all measures of academic achievement, enrollment, and attainment. In Italy's south, students, teachers, and principals report higher levels of disorder in schools than their counterparts in the north did.

Chapter 5 explores the low levels of disorder and delinquency in Japanese schools. Greater discipline in Japanese schools comes from comparatively high levels of parental expectations, institutional demands of employers, and hierarchically ordered secondary and postsecondary schools. Variations between levels of students' misbehavior in Japanese schools are not easily explained by school-level student population differences such as parental education or the ethnic and gender ratios of the school. In Japan, school disciplinary environment does not seem to directly influence student achievement. However, students' experiences of victimization significantly correlate with their test scores. Students who report having personally experienced victimization have lower test scores than those who do not.

In the Netherlands, school disciplinary climates only modestly affect student performance, independent of the effects of the composition of the student population. In Chapter 6, the authors suggest that the unique structure of the Dutch educational system explains the limited effects of school disciplinary climates on student performance. The educational system in the Netherlands is highly standardized; however, it leaves much room for school-level autonomy. The authors find dramatic variation in disciplinary climate by school type. Schools that offer academic tracks have higher levels of school safety than schools that offer both academic and prevocational tracks. In general, the Netherlands is known for demonstrating a high degree of cultural tolerance for adolescent and adult behavior that would be subject to sanctions and punishment in other societies. Simultaneously, Dutch people pride themselves on effectively regulating adolescent behavior through both informal and formal mechanisms, in which the behavior is tolerated and accommodated to be more effectively controlled (Schalet 2000).

The Russian educational system is, in principle, highly centralized and standardized, yet given Russia's vast territory, geographic diversity, and political and economic turmoil of the last several decades, school policies, resources, and curricula vary considerably across regions. The economic problems and institutional uncertainties of the Perestroika era (1985–1991) led to a downward drift in educational attainment, as did the chaos, dislocations, and economic crisis of the early post–Soviet era (Gerber 2000). Public opinion polls in the early 1990s pointed to a decline in the perceived value of education (Kitaev 1994). The author of Chapter 7 demonstrates that the disciplinary climates of Russian schools are associated with students' academic achievement and college expectations. Russian students who attend schools with fewer disciplinary problems perform better on combined math and science tests and are more likely to plan to attend college than are their peers at schools with more disciplinary problems. The author suggests that TIMSS survey questions are inherently subjective and may have overpredicted the extent of school disorder in Russia. Russian teachers hold their pupils to extremely high standards of behavior, in which slouching or speaking out of turn could be considered disruptive. In other contexts, teachers might tolerate this behavior and not report students as disorderly.

South Korea's high levels of student academic performance and relatively orderly school disciplinary climates are discussed in Chapter 8. The orderly disciplinary climates in Korean schools are often attributed to the standardized educational system, ethnically and linguistically homogeneous population, and the society's cultural emphasis on discipline, hard work, and respect for adult authority (Shin and Koh 2005). The author finds that schools with more student victimization incidents demonstrate worse average test scores than their counterparts, even after taking into account other school- and student-level characteristics.

Chapter 9 examines the moderately high levels of victimization in schools reported by students in the United States. For American students, school climate measures are strongly associated with student academic achievement, after accounting for social background, prior test score performance, and other factors. Striking differences exist between African American and white students' academic performance and exposure to school discipline environments. Differences in disciplinary climates explain the within-group variance between individual African American and white student learning gains. Specifically, in schools that have greater levels of discipline, African American students learn at rates comparable to whites (as assessed through longitudinal modeling of test score performance). Since the expansion of student rights in the late 1960s and early 1970s, forms of school discipline in the United States have changed. Teachers report that the threat of potential lawsuits affects how they discipline students in their classrooms. U.S. students have been afforded unparalleled explicit legal rights that constrain traditional forms of school discipline.

The significance of school disciplinary climate for student achievement throughout these chapters is demonstrated repeatedly and consistently. While it is often not a significant factor in accounting for differences in academic achievement related to social class background, it does account for a portion of the effects of school composition (particularly measures of heterogeneity) on student test scores in many settings. These findings are encouraging in that they point to concrete educational policies and practices that potentially could improve student academic outcomes. Reducing school-level disciplinary problems by adopting responsive, proactive, and appropriate administrative measures could improve learning environments and student outcomes for all.

## APPENDIX

*Country-level regression of test score and school disciplinary climate on socioeconomic and educational system characteristics*

| | *Student victimization reports* | *Teacher disruption reports* | *Principal disciplinary problem reports* | *Standardized test score* |
|---|---|---|---|---|
| SOCIOECONOMIC DEVELOPMENT | | | | |
| Parental education | 0.004 | −0.151† | 0.166 | 0.053 |
| | (0.060) | −0.086 | (0.123) | (0.189) |
| Number of books in household | −0.110 | 0.081 | 0.100 | 0.649† |
| | (0.108) | (0.154) | (0.221) | (0.330) |
| Purchasing power parity | −0.058 | 0.035 | −0.021 | 0.385** |
| | (0.043) | (0.063) | (0.089) | (0.134) |
| SOCIAL INEQUALITY OR HETEROGENEITY | | | | |
| Gini coefficient | 0.084* | 0.035 | 0.129 | −0.045 |
| | (0.040) | (0.057) | (0.082) | (0.128) |
| Immigrant students | 0.070† | 0.032 | 0.010 | −0.184 |
| | (0.036) | (0.052) | (0.074) | (0.112) |
| EDUCATIONAL SYSTEM STRATIFICATION | | | | |
| Low stratification | 0.112 | 0.111 | 0.300† | −0.107 |
| | (0.083) | (0.120) | (0.171) | (0.265) |
| Moderate stratification | −0.057 | 0.099 | 0.052 | −0.065 |
| | (0.085) | (0.121) | (0.174) | (0.258) |
| SCHOOL DISCIPLINARY CLIMATE | | | | |
| Student victimization reports | | | | −0.129 |
| | | | | (0.487) |
| Teacher disruption reports | | | | −0.353 |
| | | | | (0.343) |
| Principal disciplinary problem reports | | | | −0.402† |
| | | | | (0.232) |
| Intercept | 0.997 | 3.838 | 1.496 | 0.381 |
| | (0.268) | (0.384) | (0.550) | (1.581) |
| $R^2$ | 0.503 | 0.132 | 0.215 | 0.657 |
| N | 49 | 49 | 49 | 49 |

NOTE: Standard errors in parentheses are adjusted for clustering of students within schools.
† $p < .10$; * $p < .05$; ** $p < .01$; *** $p < .001$.

NOTES

For critical editorial assistance on this project, we would like to thank Esther Cho and Jeannie Kim at the Social Science Research Council, Rebecca Logan at Newgen North America, and Kate Wahl and Joa Sourez at Stanford University Press.

1. Add Health dataset is a longitudinal, nationally representative sample of middle and high school students from the 1994–1995 school year. The most recent wave of data collection occurred in 2008, when students in the sample were ages 24–32. For more information on the dataset see http://www.cpc.unc.edu/projects/addhealth.

2. Eighth grade students were defined as those in the upper of two adjacent grades with the largest percentage of 13-year-old students at the time of testing. This definition was intended to represent the grade level equivalent to eight years of schooling, counting from the first year of primary school. In most countries, this was the eighth grade.

3. The U.S. data rely on a benchmarking exercise confined to Indiana. Data from the Department of Education suggest that while Indiana is more white than the national average (76 percent compared to 55 percent), mostly because of fewer Asian Americans and Hispanics, it was otherwise fairly representative of U.S. student behavior, class background, and student achievement. Some 39 percent of students are eligible for free or reduced-price lunch relative to 40 percent nationally; in 1999, per capita income was $20,400 compared to $21,600 nationally; and the percentage of eighth grade students at or above proficiency in math was 36 percent compared to 33 percent nationally and in science was 29 percent compared to 27 percent nationally (see National Center for Education Statistics, State Profiles Application, CCD 2004–2005 data). Of Indiana high school students, 8.4 percent were threatened or injured with a weapon on school property between 2003 and 2007, compared to 8.3 percent nationally; 42 percent of Indiana teachers reported that student misbehavior interfered with teaching, and 36 percent reported that student tardiness and class cutting did, compared to 36 and 34 percent, respectively, nationally (see Dinkes, Kemp, and Baum 2009). In the U.S. chapter, analysis of TIMSS data is supplemented with analysis of nationally representative data from the National Educational Longitudinal Study.

4. This aggregation is problematic in schools that sampled all-boy or all-girl classrooms within a coeducational school.

5. Principals were also asked other questions about the school disciplinary climate (e.g., profanity, vandalism); however, on the basis of a factor analysis, the items included in the index were the ones most consistently and strongly linked across countries.

6. Similar to the principal disciplinary disengagement index, questions in the student victimization index were part of a larger battery of questions asked of students about school climate (e.g., additional items included questions about being left out of activities and being made to do something by other students).

However, we believed that the three items selected for the index were most theoretically linked to the school's *disciplinary* climate in particular.

7. Students in the United States were not administered questions about school climate and related analyses are thus missing the student victimization indices.

8. The college expectation outcome is a dummy variable; therefore, authors assess this outcome using logistical regression with robust standard errors or multilevel logit models.

9. Some authors chose to use listwise deletion to handle missing data.

10. The United States is not included in multilevel pooled analyses of victimization and test scores given the absence of TIMSS data on U.S. victimization.

11. Although higher average parental education at the school level in the pooled models is associated with lower rates of victimization, significant variation in these coefficients appears when regressions are done at the country level. In Chile, Israel, and Italy higher parental education at the country level is associated with lower rates of victimization; in Canada, Korea, and Russia the rates occur in the opposite direction.

12. Per capita GNI data are from UNESCO Institute for Statistics website's reports of World Bank, International Comparison Program database. http://stats.uis.unesco.org/unesco/tableviewer/document.aspx?ReportId=14.

13. The Gini coefficients are from the World Bank's *World Development Indicators* (2007). Gini coefficients are not calculated each year for every nation. The coefficients reported here were calculated between 1997 and 2007. The World Bank does not list Gini coefficients for Serbia, Scotland, Taiwan, Cyprus, and Palestine. The coefficients for these nations were found on their respective national government websites: Serbia, http://www.prsp.gov.rs/engleski/kolikoje.jsp; Scotland, http://www.scotland.gov.uk/Publications/2007/07/18083820/4; Taiwan, http://www.gio.gov.tw/info/taiwan-story/economy/edown/3-5.htm; Cyprus, http://www.cyprusnet.com/content.php?article_id=2816&subject=standalone; Palestine, http://www.pcbs.gov.ps/Portals/_pcbs/PressRelease/endyear2006_E.pdf.

14. All components of the indices were standardized before summing. The Cronbach alpha on the socioeconomic development measure is .83, and on the social heterogeneity measure it is .78. The Cronbach alpha on the school disciplinary problems index is only .21; we use the index nevertheless to represent the overall patterns in the data with respect to our theoretical concerns. The appendix to this chapter provides results with these measures disaggregated. For the country-level analysis, the percentage of schools with more than 10 percent of student immigrants was identified; to deal with the absence of victimization data for the United States in TIMSS, we used prior comparative analyses of victimization rates in the United States and Canada (see Craig et al. 2009). Supplementary analyses excluded Syria and Yemen because of data quality issues but yielded results similar to those reported.

15. For countries not reported in the OECD 2005 report, data were taken from Postlethwaite and Husén (1994) and Hörner (2007). Taiwan was classified as moderate stratification with tracking occurring at age 15.

## REFERENCES

Akiba, Motoko, Gerald K. LeTendre, David P. Baker, and Brian Goesling. 2002. "Student Victimization: National and School System Effects on School Violence in 37 Nations." *American Educational Research Journal* 39 (4): 829–53.

Arum, Richard. 2003. *Judging School Discipline: The Crisis of Moral Authority.* Cambridge, MA: Harvard University Press.

Arum, Richard, and Walter Müller, eds. 2004. *The Resurgence of Self-Employment: A Comparative Study of Self-Employment Dynamics and Social Inequality.* Princeton, NJ: Princeton University Press.

Babcock, Philip. 2009. "The Rational Adolescent: Discipline Policies, Lawsuits and Skill Acquisition." *Economics of Education Review* 28:551–60.

Barton, Paul, Richard Coley, and Harold Wenglinsky. 1998. *Order in the Classroom.* Princeton, NJ: Educational Testing Service.

Benbenishty, Rami, and Ron Astor. 2008. "School Violence in an International Context: A Call for Global Collaboration in Research and Prevention." *School Violence in an International Context* 7:59–80.

Coleman, James. 1959. *The Adolescent Society: The Social Life of the Teenager and Its Impact on Education.* Oxford: Free Press of Glencoe.

Coleman, James, Ernest Campbell, Carol Hobson, James McPartland, Alexander Mood, Frederic Weinfeld, and Robert York. 1966. *Equality of Educational Opportunity.* Washington, DC: Government Printing Office.

Coleman, James, and Thomas Hoffer. 1987. *Public and Private Schools: The Impact of Communities.* New York: Basic Books.

Coleman, James, Thomas Hoffer, and Sally Kilgore. 1982. *High School Achievement: Public, Catholic, and Private Schools Compared.* New York: Basic Books.

Craig, Wendy, Yossi Harel-Fisch, Haya Fogel-Grinvald, Suzanne Dostaler, Jorn Hetland, Bruce Simons-Morton, Michal Molcho, et al. 2009. "A Cross-National Profile of Bullying and Victimization among Adolescents in 40 Countries." *International Journal of Public Health* 54 (suppl. 2): 216–24.

Dinkes, R., J. Kemp, and K. Baum. 2009. *Indicators of School Crime and Safety: 2009.* Washington, DC: National Center for Education Statistics and Bureau of Justice Statistics. Available at http://nces.ed.gov/pubs2010/2010012.pdf.

DiPrete, Tom, Chandra Muller, and Nora Shaeffer. 1981. *Discipline and Order in American High Schools.* Washington, DC: National Center for Educational Statistics.

Durkheim, Emile. (1925) 1973. *Moral Authority: A Study in the Theory and Application of Sociology of Education*. New York: Macmillan.

Fordham, Signithia, and John Ogbu. 1986. "Black Students' School Success: Coping with the 'Burden of Acting White.'" *Urban Review* 18:176–206.

Gerber, Theodore P. 2000. "Educational Stratification in Contemporary Russia: Stability and Change in the Face of Economic and Institutional Crisis." *Sociology of Education* 73:219–46.

———. 2007. "Russia: Stratification in Postsecondary Education Since the Second World War." In *Stratification in Higher Education: A Comparative Study*, edited by Yossi Shavit, Richard Arum, and Adam Gamoran. Palo Alto, CA: Stanford University Press.

Gottfredson, Gary, and Denise Gottfredson. 1985. *Victimization in Schools*. New York: Plenum Press.

Kitaev, Igor V. 1994. "The Labor Market and Education in the Post-Soviet Era." In *Education and Society in the New Russia*, edited by Anthony Jones, 311–32. Armonk, NY: M. E. Sharpe.

Kohlberg, Lawrence. 1981. *Essays on Moral Development*. San Francisco: Harper and Row.

Müller, Walter, and Yossi Shavit. 1998. "The Institutional Embeddedness of the Stratification Process: A Comparative Study of Qualifications and Occupations in Thirteen Countries." In *From School to Work: A Comparative Study of Educational Qualifications and Occupational Destinations*, edited by Yossi Shavit and Walter Müller, 1–48. Oxford: Oxford University Press.

Mullis, Ina V. S., Michael O. Martin, Eugenio J. Gonzalez, and Steven J. Chrostowski. 2004. *TIMSS 2003 International Mathematics Report: Findings from IEA's Trends in International Mathematics and Science Study at the Fourth and Eighth Grade*. Chestnut Hill, MA: International Association for the Evaluation of Education Achievement.

Myers, David E., Ann M. Milne, Keith Baker, and Alan Ginsburg. 1987. "Student Discipline and High School Performance." *Sociology of Education* 60:18–33.

Ogbu, John U. 1978. *Minority Education and Caste: The American System in Cross Cultural Perspective*. New York: Academic Press.

Organization for Economic Cooperation and Development (OECD). 2005. *School Factors Related to Quality and Equity: Results from PISA 2000*. Paris: OECD.

Schalet, Amy T. 2000. "Raging Hormones, Regulated Love: Adolescent Sexuality and the Constitution of the Modern Individual in the United States of America and the Netherlands." *Body and Society* 6 (1): 75–105.

Shavit, Yossi, Richard Arum, and Adam Gamoran, eds. 2007. *Stratification in Higher Education: A Comparative Study*. Palo Alto, CA: Stanford University Press.

Shavit, Yossi, and Hans-Peter Blossfeld. 1993. *Persisting Barriers: Changes in Educational Opportunities in Thirteen Countries*. Boulder, CO: Westview Press.

Shavit, Yossi, and Walter Müller. 1998. *From School to Work: A Comparative Study of Educational Qualifications and Occupational Destinations*. Oxford: Oxford University Press.

Shin, S., and M. Koh. 2005. "Korean Education in Cultural Context." *Essays in Education* 14:1–10.

Stigler, James, Shin-ying Lee, and Harold W. Stevenson. 1987. "Mathematics Classrooms in Japan, Taiwan, and the United States." Special issue on schools and development, *Child Development* 58 (5): 1272–85.

World Bank. 2007. *World Development Indicators*. Washington, DC: World Bank. http://data.worldbank.org/data-catalog/world-development-indicators.

CHAPTER ONE

# Academic Performance and Expectations of Canadian Students

*Robert Andersen and David Zarifa*

This chapter explores the effect of school disciplinary climate on student performance in Canada. It makes two main contributions. First, this is the first Canadian study to systematically explore the general topic of school disciplinary climate, whether it affects academic performance and expectations, and how much it accounts for provincial differences in school performance and expectations. In terms of provincial differences, we focus on Ontario and Quebec because of data availability. General cultural differences—and related differences in immigration patterns and educational systems—between these two provinces make Canada an interesting context in which to explore the effects of school disciplinary climate. Second, by following a framework similar to the other chapters, it helps situate correlates of school disciplinary climate in cross-national perspective.

In contrast to the United States, research on the relationship between school discipline and academic performance in Canada is virtually nonexistent. Nonetheless, some U.S. studies may be particularly relevant to the Canadian situation. For example, research suggests that school performance in the United States is positively related to the level of strictness in the school disciplinary climate (Arum 2003; Barton, Coley, and Wenglinsky 1998; Myers et al. 1987; DiPrete, Muller, and Shaeffer 1981; Coleman et al. 1966). There is also research indicating differential effects of school disciplinary climates according to minority status. Research by Valerie Lee and Anthony Bryk (1989; see also Chapter 9) demonstrates that white and minority student achievement gaps in the United States are smaller in schools with effective and systematic disciplinary climates and policies. Other research suggests that the minority gap in achievement may be narrowed in Catholic schools, where students are more likely to exhibit deferential behavior and thus school climates are characterized by fewer disruptions, which is more conducive to learning (Coleman and Hoffer 1987; Coleman et al. 1982).

Although previous research has not specifically addressed the issue, it is possible that similar mechanisms are at work in Canada. For example, school disciplinary climate may explain differences in school performance between Ontario and Quebec students. It is also possible that disciplinary climate is useful in explaining school performance and achievement gaps between immigrants and nonimmigrants within the two provinces, especially since recent Canadian immigrants tend to be ethnic minorities (Chui, Tran, and Maheux 2007). The possibility of differential effects is further highlighted by the fact that the gap between immigrant and nonimmigrant school performance is generally smaller in Canada than it is in other Organization for Economic Cooperation and Development (OECD) countries, except in Quebec, where the difference resembles the OECD average (see Bussiere, Knighton, and Pennock 2007, 40).

In the following section we describe the school disciplinary climate in Canada using the common framework set out for individual country analyses by the larger project. We then proceed to our analysis of the role of school disciplinary climate in school performance in Canada. Consistent with the other chapters in this volume, our analysis draws on Canadian data collected as part of the Trends in International Mathematics and Science Study (TIMSS) in 2003.

## CANADIAN SCHOOL DISCIPLINARY CONTEXT

Following the overall comparative design for country-specific chapters in this volume, we explore four dimensions of the school disciplinary context. We start by discussing the heterogeneity of the Canadian population, with a particular emphasis on the role of immigration. We then outline the structure of the Canadian educational system and how educational institutions differ according to province, focusing primarily on Ontario and Quebec. We then consider the legal context of school discipline in Canada. In this regard, we give special attention to the roles of the Charter of Rights and Freedoms and the Supreme Court of Canada. Finally, we detail recent developments in Canadian policies regarding the administration of school discipline.

*Population Heterogeneity: The Role of Immigration*

Canada is an immigrant society. According to the 2006 Canadian census, 19.8 percent (more than six million) Canadians were born outside Canada. To put this number in perspective, immigrants constitute 12.5 percent of the population of the United States, and only Australia (with 22.2 percent immigrants) exceeds Canada's proportion of immigrants among Western nations (Chui, Tran, and Maheux 2007, 8). Immigrants are not equally distributed throughout Canada, however. Important to this study is the size difference between Quebec's and Ontario's immigrant populations. As of 2006 Ontario was home to 54.9 percent of Canada's immigrant population, which closely resembles its share of recent immigrants (52.3 percent). Quebec, on the other hand, had only 13.8 percent of Canada's immigrant population and slightly less than 18 percent of Canada's recent immigrants (Chui, Tran, and Maheux 2007). With respect to their own populations, Ontario contains approximately 28.2 percent immigrants, and Quebec contains only 11.5 percent immigrants (Statistics Canada 2008a).

In the last few decades, Canadian immigrants have become increasingly more likely to be visible minorities. In 1971 immigrants were generally European in origin (61.6 percent) and only a small minority came from Asia (12.1 percent). By 2006 Europeans dropped to the second-largest group, representing only 16.1 percent of recent immigrants, and emigrants from Asia (including the Middle East) represented approximately 58.3 percent of Canada's recent immigrants (Chui, Tran, and Maheux 2007). Just as the size of the immigrant populations differ by province, so do their ethnic compositions. In Ontario about 65 percent of immigrants arriving in Canada between 2001 and 2006 were from Asia or the Middle East, compared to only 28.8 percent in Quebec (Statistics Canada 2008b).

The increased diversity associated with recent immigration patterns has been accompanied by growing concern over the integration of immigrant youth into the Canadian educational system. Although second-generation immigrants typically do well in terms of school performance (Cortes 2006) and educational attainment (see Boyd 2002), first-generation immigrants continue to score lower in science, math, and reading tests (Gluszynski and Dhawan-Biswal 2008). Research by Patrick Bussiere, Tamara Knighton, and Dianne Pennock (2007) indicates that immigrant students tend to score lower on science tests than nonimmigrant students, but especially so in

Quebec, where nonimmigrant students scored more than 10 percent higher on average than first-generation immigrants. In Ontario the difference between these two groups was less than 5 percent.

One possible explanation for the larger performance gap between Quebec's immigrant and nonimmigrant students pertains to how well immigrants are integrated into the Quebec school system. Some critics argue that Quebec's intensive language program, *accueil*, focuses heavily on learning French and isolates students from the mainstream academic route, thus putting them a couple of years behind in the core subjects (e.g., science and history; Allen 2006). On the other hand, others claim that Quebec's French-language schools integrate the children of newly arrived immigrants and teach students the importance of respecting pluralism (see McAndrew 2003).

Aside from the language barrier to comprehension, immigrant integration into the larger Canadian society may also play a role in academic performance. Research on this topic is limited, but some argue that racial minorities and students from families whose parents lack the social capital to deal with school teachers or administrators—especially immigrants and students from low socioeconomic backgrounds—are most at risk for involvement in youth violence (see McMurtry and Curling 2008), which in turn could affect their performance in school. This is consistent with U.S. research that suggests minority students are more likely to be suspended or expelled (Skiba et al. 2002; Brooks, Schiraldi, and Zeidenberg 1999). There is also evidence that minority students experience discrimination in Canada (Alladin 1996; Cheng and Soudak 1994), which could in turn affect their school performance. Given recent research suggesting that the Quebec population is generally less accepting of immigrants than the populations of the other provinces of Canada, including Ontario (Andersen and Milligan 2009), it is possible that discrimination may be more prevalent in Quebec schools.

Martin Ruck and Scot Wortley (2002, 193) examined student perceptions of discriminatory implementation and administration of school discipline in Canadian high schools. Ruck and Wortley found that although immigrants believed that police were biased against their ethnic group and that students from their ethnic group were more likely than others to be disciplined in school, especially with regard to suspensions, immigrant students did not report differential treatment from teachers. Interestingly, perception of bias appeared to *increase* with length of stay in Canada. The authors suggest two possible mechanisms for this effect: (1) immigrants who have spent more time in Canada may be more cognizant of existing social inequalities and prejudices, and (2) recent immigrants might have experienced more-severe school disciplinary practices or discrimination in their country of origin, and as a result their Canadian experiences would be mild by comparison. It is possible that such differences in perceptions of fair discipline could transfer into differential effects on student performance.

As outlined in detail later, the educational systems in Ontario and Quebec are independent and quite different. It seems sensible to suggest that these differences could affect how discipline is applied. Although no research has yet addressed this question, it is possible that a greater gap in school performance between immigrant and nonimmigrant students results from differences in the disciplinary climate in the two provinces. Addressing this question is a main goal of our own analysis, which follows later.

### *The Canadian Educational System*

Education in Canada falls under provincial jurisdiction. There is no federal department of education or countrywide educational policy. The lack of federal governance of educational issues means that each province has a high degree of autonomy and authority to establish its own policy on how to handle disciplinary problems in schools. Provinces discuss common educational policy issues through the Council of Ministers of Education in Canada (CMEC), though ultimately the implementation of common strategies is left to the discretion of the province.[1] Nevertheless, Canada's educational systems are highly centralized at the provincial level. Each province has its own ministry of education, which establishes curricula, norms, assessment, and certification and provides the bulk of funding for public schools, though some provinces (e.g., Quebec) supplement provincial expenditures with local property taxes.

Beneath the provincial level are school boards, which are primarily responsible for ensuring that all students within their districts have access to educational services or policies dictated by the province. Schools, which provide these educational services to students, fall under the jurisdiction of school boards (see Lessard and Brassard 2009). Until recently provinces afforded a large degree of autonomy to school boards, schools, and teachers in implementing educational policies. However, greater involvement of provincial governments over the past decade or so has resulted in increasingly closer monitoring of school and teacher practices (Mawhinney 1995; Jull 2000).

Although provinces control the design of their educational systems, the structure of Canada's educational systems varies only minimally across the 10 provinces, with the exception of Quebec. Typically, Canadian students attend elementary school from kindergarten (ages 4 and 5) to grade 8 (usually age 13) and then attend secondary school from grades 9 to 12 (graduating around age 17). In the Quebec educational system, students attend elementary school only until grade 6 and then move to secondary school for grades 7 to 11. Students who wish to continue to postsecondary education enter the CEGEP (Collège d'enseignement général et professionnel) program after grade 11. Ontario students, on the other hand, continue to tertiary education immediately following grade 12.

One major provincial difference is in the provision of "separate" schools: publicly funded institutions with a religious orientation. In Ontario separate schools are now entirely associated with the Roman Catholic Church, because the majority of Protestant-based schools dissolved into the current public school system. Remnants of these religious beginnings in the public schools were evident even until the mid-1980s—the Lord's Prayer was still recited at the start of the school day. More recently, however, religion has been effectively removed from public school education in Ontario. On the other hand, separate schools continue to have a strong Catholic educational presence to this day.

Quebec had a similar system of publicly funded Catholic and Protestant school boards until 1998, when the separate Catholic and Protestant school boards were respectively replaced by English-language and French-language school boards that mirror the larger society (see Young and Bezeau 2003). At the time of reform in Quebec in 1998, there were 137 Catholic and 18 Protestant school boards that were replaced by 60 French-language and 9 English-language school boards (Smith, Foster, and Donahue 1999, 2). The distribution of school boards in Ontario is much more equal. According to the Ontario Ministry of Education (2009a), as of 2009 Ontario had 35 public school boards (31 English language and 4 French language) and 37 Catholic school boards (29 English language and 8 French language).

Finally, although the vast majority of schools in Canada are publicly funded, provincial differences are noteworthy in terms of the prevalence of private schooling. Although it has grown in recent years, the private educational sector is relatively small in Ontario. In 1999 only 4.3 percent of elementary and secondary students in Ontario were enrolled in private schools. In Quebec on the other hand 9.2 percent of elementary and secondary students attended private schools (Statistics Canada 2001). More recent estimates for Quebec suggest that about 17 percent of high school students attend private schools. It has also been estimated that nearly 30 percent of high school students in Montreal are enrolled in private institutions.[2] Although we have no evidence to support the idea, it seems sensible to suggest that the larger private sector in Quebec results in less provincewide standardization in how schooling is administered, even if there is relatively high standardization within the public school system.

### *Legal Context: The Charter of Rights and Freedoms and the Supreme Court*

To understand the limitations of administering school discipline in Canada, it is helpful to be aware of the legal context and in particular students' and educators' rights. Of course, this knowledge also helps facilitate cross-national comparisons of the differences in the nature and effects of school disciplinary climate. We start by noting that legal challenges to school policies and decisions are far less prevalent in Canada than they are in some other countries, especially the United States. Nevertheless, legal challenges have increased since the inception of the Charter of Rights and Freedoms in 1982 (Dennis 1996; Hartig and McDonald 1996; MacKay 2008). Although Canadian case law regarding students' rights and school discipline is well established, new challenges continually appear. Recent court challenges have fallen under six broad categories: (1) minority language education rights, (2) denominational rights, (3) freedom of religion, (4) freedom of expression of the teaching staff, (5) protection of students from unreasonable searches, and (6) students' equality rights with respect to educational services (LeBel 2006, 137). While court decisions with respect to human rights violations—especially regarding minority language and religion—have tended to side with inclusion, decisions regarding discipline have consistently sided with educational administrators (MacKay 2008; MacKay and Burt-Gerrans 2005; Keel 1998).

In general, school punishments and disciplinary procedures in Canada tend to reflect larger criminal justice practices in the wider Canadian society (Hirschfield 2008, 82). Nevertheless, students are afforded fewer rights within schools because of Supreme Court restrictions on the criminal code (section 43) that ensure deference to teachers and because parents can override what might otherwise be seen as violations to the Charter (MacKay 2008). Justice Louis LeBel (2006) states the approach of the Supreme Court regarding legal cases dealing with the educational system as follows:

> The Court recognizes the critical nature of the role played by teachers and various stakeholders from the educational community in forming students for their participation in Canadian society. Consequently, the Court adopted an approach that I would characterize as deferential to the expertise of members of the educational community. The Court does not claim to have absolute answers to the various problems within the educational community; it favours, as much as possible, respect of discretionary decisions made by school authorities. (138)

A typical example of how the courts tend to rule in favor of schools is shown in the Ontario case *Crown v. L. B.*, in which police found a loaded gun in a student's backpack on school property (MacKay 2008; see also Dickinson 2006). The student suspects were initially acquitted on the grounds that they were "psychologically detained" without being informed of their Charter right to legal counsel. Nevertheless, the decision was reversed by the Ontario Court of Appeal on the grounds that the safety of other students overruled the accused students' Charter rights. This ruling has resulted in an effective relaxation of the criteria required for carrying out police searches on school property (Dickinson 2006).

Another example of how the courts defer to school administrators and the perceived safety of the majority of students is the case of *M. v. Porter Creek Secondary School*, in which a student attempted to obtain a court injunction prohibiting the school from instituting a drug prevention program that included a drug detection dog on school premises. The student argued that she had a serious allergy to dogs and would need to withdraw from the school if the program went forward. The courts sided with the school on the grounds that the "public interest in pursuing an effective drug counselling program and a drug-free environment or an educational institution should prevail" (Singleton 2008, 387).

In summary, while court challenges to decisions made by educational administrators have increased significantly since the inception of the Charter of Rights and Freedoms in 1982, these challenges seem to have had little impact on administration of school discipline. Given that the courts tend to side with educators and school administrators in this regard, it seems unlikely that court challenges pose any real threat to administrators in terms of disciplinary policies. Of course, it is possible that the increased threat of legal action, even though the court usually sides with the school, could influence teacher behavior in Canada. That is, teachers may be less likely to administer discipline than in the past simply because they want to avoid the possible hassle of court action. To our knowledge, however, there is no evidence for us to be able to properly assess this question.

### *Administration of School Discipline: Developments in Policy since the Early 1990s*

Relative to the United States (see Chapter 9), school disciplinary policies and practices have historically received little attention in Canada. Nevertheless, both public concern over and media attention to school crimes rose sharply during the 1990s (Gabor 1995; Education Monitor 1998; Cloud 1999; Leschart 1999). A few rare shootings in large cities over the past decade apparently spurred rising concern over school discipline. Perhaps the most influential case occurred on April 28, 1999, when a 14-year-old boy at W. R. Myers High School in Taber, Alberta, opened fire with a .22-caliber rifle, killing one student and wounding another. As an isolated incident, this horrific event may have had only limited influence, but its impact was compounded by its taking place just one week after the Columbine High School massacre in the United States, which received considerable media attention in Canada. Reflecting public concern, school safety policies in all of Canada changed drastically following these events. For example, lockdown drills are now routinely performed once or twice a year in most Canadian public schools (Brown 2006).

Despite such isolated tragedies, and the media and public response to them, the limited research on the topic suggests that Canadian schools are very safe. For example, J. Frank and G. Lipps (1997) argue that 95 percent of Canadian elementary students had never had any dealings related to drugs, weapons, theft, or teacher assault. In other words, weapon violence occurs relatively infrequently and to a far less extent than it does in the United States (Gabor 1995; Walker 1994). Although police have become a greater presence in Canadian schools in recent decades (Ministry of Education and Training 1994), most school disciplinary concerns in Canada still involve bullying and disorderly behavior (Jull 2000; Gabor 1995). Trend data in youth crime at schools are not available, but crime statistics more generally suggest that youth crimes have actually declined since a peak in 1991. It is difficult to know whether this decline is real or a result of changes in ways to handle young offenders. For example, part of the most recent decline may be attributable to 2003's Youth Criminal Justice Act, which has led to significant efforts to handle minor offenses outside the formal justice system for fear of labeling nonviolent offenders as criminals. The act promotes use of cautions and warnings and other extrajudicial means rather than traditionally punitive solutions (Taylor-Butts and Bressan 2008).

A growing perception that schools were becoming less safe—whether true or not—led to widespread adoption of zero tolerance policies for Canadian schools in the 1990s. Inspired by U.S. policies on drugs and crime and with the goal of limiting significantly harmful behaviors in schools (National Center of Education Statistics 1998), these policies had stringent rules for how teachers and principals discipline students (Heineke and Drier 1998). An underpinning of zero tolerance policies is their attempt to create specific guidelines on how and when to administer school punishment, which remove teacher discretion (Hirschfield 2008). This trend is evident in the recent increase in standardized safe-school policies and other disciplinary procedures that many schools now post publicly on their websites. Some schools have formal, step-by-step disciplinary procedures for dealing with a wide range of misbehaviors, from name calling and ridiculing to possession of firearms and aggravated assault. Under zero tolerance policies, students committing serious crimes (e.g., drug or alcohol use, use of weapons) are supposed to face automatic expulsion or suspension.

Although zero tolerance is supposed to remove teacher discretion, a report to the Canadian Association of Principals suggests that there is "considerable variance" in the way principals interpret zero tolerance policies (Shannon and McCall 2009). Most important is the suggestion that principals not only have trouble defining what constitutes zero tolerance but tend to be unclear on whether there are predetermined consequences for specific disciplinary problems (see also Thompson 1994). Other authors suggest that much of how discipline is administered is still, in practice, determined by the principal of the school, whose ideas on discipline in turn are strongly influenced by the community (see Day et al. 1995; Gabor 1995). Unfortunately, reliable data on exactly how zero tolerance is applied in Canada—

that is, in terms of both consequences to misbehaviors and the number of sanctions given—are not available (Shannon and McCall 1999, 2009).

Consistent with the lack of data on how disciplinary policies are administered, it is unclear whether these policies have improved the educational experiences of Canadian youth or even reduced violence in schools. Still, some Canadians have questioned the implementation of zero tolerance disciplinary practices to combat school violence and bullying. Human rights commissions, in particular, have questioned the fairness of zero tolerance policies, calling for a review of the legal framework for applying school discipline in schools (see Ontario Human Rights Commission 2004).[3] Despite the dearth of empirical evidence, governments have heeded accounts of student perceptions of disproportionate implementation of zero tolerance policies, especially with regard to minorities (e.g., Ruck and Wortley 2002).

Most recently, some provinces have adopted new progressive disciplinary strategies in an attempt to improve school safety (Ontario Ministry of Education 2009b).[4] This new approach takes a holistic view that emphasizes positive school climates in which discipline is combined with opportunities for the penalized students to continue their education.[5] Under this new approach, principals are explicitly given discretion to choose consequences appropriate to students' needs and behavior, including suspensions but excluding expulsions, which can be given only by the school board. If a student is suspended, effort must be made to ensure that the student maintains his or her education. Depending on the length of suspension, students receive a homework package (1–5 days' suspension), an academic program developed by the school board (6–10 days), anger management or career counseling (11–20 days), or a combination of these. As one example, when suspended for five days for disruptive classroom behavior, a Toronto student was not sent home but instead required to attend school and continue with his work in a separate room while supervised by a teacher (see Brown 2008). Simply put, these new policies are geared toward understanding the social circumstances of troubled youth and establishing adequate supports to continue their education.

There has also been a widespread push to inform parents about changes in disciplinary policies (see Safe Schools Action Team 2005). For example, recent public opinion findings suggest that Ontarians seek a balance of power on educational issues shared among teachers, parents, and the provincial government (Zarifa and Davies 2007). This is exemplified in the action by Ontario's Ministry of Education to make yearly suspension and expulsion data for each school board publicly available starting in 2007. These data indicate that 112,829 students in Ontario were suspended in 2007 (5.4 percent of the total student population). Of those suspended, boys (7.9 percent of male students) were more than three times as likely to be suspended as girls (2.7 percent of female students), northern and rural boards were more likely than urban boards to have higher suspension rates, and 24,035 suspended students (21 percent of suspended students) were students in special education programs because of behavioral, mental, or physical disabilities (8 percent of all special education students). Taking a look at suspensions by school level, of all suspended students, 42 percent (3.4 percent of all elementary students) were elementary students and 58 percent were secondary students (9.2 percent of all secondary students) (Ontario Ministry of Education 2009c).

Other data on school dropout rates suggests that discipline may be handled differently in Quebec and Ontario. For example, Quebec has higher rates of high school dropouts, particularly among males (Bowlby and McMullen 2002, 25). More specifically, 16 percent of Quebec youth have not completed high school by age 20, compared to only 9.5 percent in Ontario (the Canadian national average is 12 percent). The differences are even more remarkable when broken down by gender. In Quebec 19.9 percent of males and 12.0 percent of females dropped out before finishing high school. In Ontario on the other hand only 7.8 percent of males and 11.2 percent of females drop out before graduating from high school.

## COMPARATIVE PROJECT

This chapter examines the causes and effects of three measures of disciplinary climates in Canada: (1) principal reports of disengagement, (2) teacher reports of classroom disruption, and (3) student reports of victimization. Our analysis seeks to address three major research questions of particular relevance to the Canadian situation: (1) Does disciplinary climate affect the academic performance and expectations of Canadian students? (2) Can differences in school disciplinary climate account for some of the provincial differences in school performance and expectations between Ontario and Quebec students? (3) Do differences in disciplinary climate account for some of the provincial differences in academic performance and expectations between immigrants and native-born students?

In line with this book's larger comparative project, we explore our research questions using Canadian data from the 2003 TIMSS. The TIMSS data provide information on fourth and eighth grade students and the schools they attended in Ontario and Quebec.[6] After removing missing data, our analytic sample consists of 3,589 students nested within 306 schools. A total of 1,553 of these students are from 155 schools in Ontario, and 2,036 students are from 151 schools in Quebec.

Following the mandate of the larger project, our analysis begins with the relationship between school disciplinary culture and other important school-level and community-level characteristics. We then proceed to multilevel models assessing influences on students' combined math and science test score and college expectations. Our main goal here, of course, is to assess the impact of school disciplinary climate net of individual-level social background variables and other important context variables.

## RESULTS

Table 1.1 displays descriptive statistics for student background characteristics, combined math and science test scores, college expectations, and the school and community context variables separately for students in Ontario and Quebec. A number of significant differences are worthy of note. Most importantly, school performance may differ across provinces, as average math and science (combined) test scores are higher in Quebec compared to Ontario. Although not shown in Table 1.1, our data also indicate that immigrants tend to perform relatively well in Ontario, where they have a mean combined math and science score of 1,064 compared to a mean score of 1,078 for native-born students. At the same time, the gap between immigrants (mean score of 1,048) and native-born students (mean score of 1,092) is far greater in Quebec.

Table 1.1 also suggests that school- and community-level characteristics may help explain differences in average provincial test scores, both overall and between immigrant and native-born students. One striking provincial difference pertains to the proportion of immigrant students. Reflecting overall immigrant compositions at the societal level, Ontario schools are less likely to have no immigrants (28.5 percent) relative to schools in

TABLE 1.1
*Descriptive statistics for individual respondents (students), Ontario and Quebec*

| | ONTARIO | | QUEBEC | |
|---|---|---|---|---|
| | *Mean* | *SE* | *Mean* | *SE* |
| STUDENT CHARACTERISTICS | | | | |
| Male | 0.471 | 0.499 | 0.503 | 0.5 |
| Age | 13.81 | 0.319 | 14.17 | 0.592 |
| Immigrant status | 0.142 | 0.348 | 0.057 | 0.233 |
| Highest parental education | 6.346 | 1.439 | 6.018 | 1.554 |
| Number of books in household | 3.504 | 1.221 | 3.16 | 1.263 |
| Household size | 4.445 | 1.258 | 4.346 | 1.19 |
| SCHOOL AND COMMUNITY CHARACTERISTICS | | | | |
| *School and community variables* | | | | |
| School size (log) | 5.942 | 0.547 | 6.648 | 0.707 |
| School highest grade level | 8.343 | 1.105 | 10.731 | 1.184 |
| Community size | 4.182 | 1.163 | 4.048 | 1.61 |
| *School-level student characteristics* | | | | |
| Male students | | | | |
| 46%–60% | 0.494 | 0.5 | 0.382 | 0.486 |
| >60% | 0.105 | 0.307 | 0.259 | 0.438 |
| Immigrant students | | | | |
| 1%–10% | 0.329 | 0.47 | 0.418 | 0.493 |
| >10% | 0.386 | 0.487 | 0.161 | 0.367 |
| Average parental education | 6.158 | 0.743 | 5.866 | 0.799 |
| Variation in parental education | 0.223 | 0.074 | 0.251 | 0.072 |
| *Disciplinary climate* | | | | |
| Principal reports: frequency of disciplinary disengagement | 2.555 | 0.831 | 3.078 | 1.224 |
| Teacher reports: frequency of classroom disruption | 3.127 | 0.806 | 3.327 | 0.737 |
| Student reports: victimization incidents | 0.844 | 0.969 | 0.674 | 0.885 |
| EDUCATIONAL ASPIRATION AND PERFORMANCE | | | | |
| College expectations | 0.757 | 0.428 | 0.662 | 0.473 |
| Math and science test score (combined) | 1,066.09 | 112.14 | 1,089.37 | 101.92 |
| N | 1,553 | | 2,036 | |

NOTE: SE = standard error.

Quebec (32.1 percent). Even more important to our research questions, there are some provincial differences in terms of school disciplinary climate. For example, compared to Quebec, Ontario has relatively fewer principal reports of disciplinary disengagement and teacher reports of classroom disruption. On the other hand, relative to Ontario students, Quebec students report slightly fewer incidents of victimization. To determine how disciplinary climate affects school performance and aspirations and whether or not differences in disciplinary climate can account for provincial differences in test scores, both overall and between immigrant and native-born students, our analyses turn to ordinary least squares regressions and multilevel models.

What effect do school- and community-level characteristics have on student disengagement, classroom disruption, and victimization in Canada? The ordinary least squares regression models in Table 1.2 show the effects of school and community characteristics on each of the three school disciplinary climate measures. The findings are mixed. That is, none of the predictors behaves in a consistent manner for all three measures. In fact, most predictors have no significant effect whatsoever, both in Ontario and in Quebec. Nevertheless, there are a few noteworthy relationships and differences between provinces. Principals from larger schools typically reported higher levels of student disengagement in both Ontario and Quebec. As mentioned in the introduction, student disengagement refers to the frequency of problem behavior among eighth graders (e.g., arriving late at school, unjustified absenteeism). Responses from principals were later averaged to create an index of disciplinary disengagement. No other factor has a statistically significant effect on disciplinary climate in Ontario, however. On the other hand, there are two further noteworthy relationships in the Quebec data only. First, principals of schools with high average levels of parental education tend to report significantly fewer incidences of disengagement. Second, immigrant composition has a very strong negative effect on disciplinary engagement in Quebec.

Perhaps most surprising is that none of the school and community predictors has a statistically significant effect on teacher reports of classroom disruption. This is the case for schools in both Ontario and Quebec. Still, there are several noteworthy predictors of student victimization. For Ontario schools, variation in parental education is positively related to victimization, though no other predictor has a statistically significant effect. For Quebec schools, only the proportion of males in the school seems to matter. In this regard, the more male students, the greater the number of victimization reports. We should note that although not statistically significant, the magnitude of the effect of male composition is similar for Ontario.

To assess the role of school disciplinary climate in student test performance, we fit several multilevel linear models to the TIMSS data to predict combined math and science scores. Initial models included only social

TABLE 1.2

*School-level regression models predicting school disciplinary climate, Ontario and Quebec*

| | PRINCIPAL REPORTS OF DISENGAGEMENT | | TEACHER REPORTS OF CLASSROOM DISRUPTION | | STUDENT REPORTS OF VICTIMIZATION | |
|---|---|---|---|---|---|---|
| | *Ontario* | *Quebec* | *Ontario* | *Quebec* | *Ontario* | *Quebec* |
| SCHOOL AND COMMUNITY CHARACTERISTICS | | | | | | |
| *School and community variables* | | | | | | |
| School size (log) | 0.268* | 0.579*** | 0.162 | 0.089 | 0.034 | –0.053 |
| | (0.130) | (0.116) | (0.129) | (0.086) | (0.056) | (0.028) |
| School highest grade level | –0.041 | –0.107 | 0.046 | 0.0189 | 0.048 | –0.0004 |
| | (0.062) | (0.073) | (0.062) | (0.054) | (0.027) | (0.018) |
| Community size | 0.076 | –0.068 | 0.089 | –0.072 | –0.001 | –0.017 |
| | (0.053) | (0.065) | (0.053) | (0.048) | (0.023) | (0.016) |
| *School-level student characteristics* | | | | | | |
| Average parental education | –0.031 | –0.604** | –0.301 | –0.236 | 0.119 | –0.027 |
| | (0.144) | (0.187) | (0.143) | (0.137) | (0.062) | (0.045) |
| Variation in parental education | 1.805 | –1.9 | –0.113 | –0.551 | 1.629** | –0.157 |
| | (1.229) | (1.977) | (1.217) | (1.454) | (0.525) | (0.480) |
| STUDENT BODY CHARACTERISTICS | | | | | | |
| *Male* | | | | | | |
| 46%–60% | –0.04 | 0.225 | 0.163 | 0.206 | 0.083 | 0.180*** |
| | (0.145) | (0.198) | (0.144) | (0.146) | (0.062) | (0.048) |
| >60% | 0.122 | –0.05 | 0.354 | 0.333 | 0.151 | 0.280*** |
| | (0.222) | (0.224) | (0.220) | (0.195) | (0.095) | (0.054) |
| *Immigrants* | | | | | | |
| 0%–10% | 0.183 | 0.462* | 0.017 | 0.209 | –0.049 | 0.018 |
| | (0.178) | (0.207) | (0.176) | (0.152) | (0.076) | (0.050) |
| >10% | 0.113 | 1.087*** | 0.279 | 0.333 | –0.085 | 0.045 |
| | (0.206) | (0.266) | (0.204) | (0.196) | (0.085) | (0.065) |
| Intercept | 0.654 | 4.251* | 3.081* | 4.162** | –0.837 | 1.130** |
| | (1.360) | (1.756) | (1.348) | (1.294) | (0.582) | (0.427) |
| $R^2$ | 0.106 | 0.306 | 0.118 | 0.096 | 0.098 | 0.208 |
| *N* | 155 | 151 | 155 | 151 | 155 | 151 |

NOTE: Standard errors are in parentheses.

* $p < .05$; ** $p < .01$; *** $p < .001$.

background characteristics, and subsequent models first added school and community characteristics and then several disciplinary climate measures. All of the models in Table 1.3 were estimated on the combined Ontario and Quebec data and included an interaction between province and immigrant status. In Model 1, we explore the effect of several social background characteristics on school performance. Consistent with well-established findings about the importance of parental education on school commitment (Jenkins 1995) and school achievement (Ho and Willms 1996; Knighton 2002; De Broucker and Lavallee 1998; Ryan and Adams 1999), we find a positive and statistically significant relationship between highest parental education and students' test scores. The results further suggest that cultural resources in the home, indicated by the number of books, also contribute to greater student performance and that students from larger households typically score significantly lower than those from smaller households.

Consistent with previous research, students in Quebec generally score better than students in Ontario. Even more important, the statistically significant interaction terms representing the effects of province and immigrant status corroborate other findings that the difference between immigrant students and Canadian-born students is quite small in Ontario but very large in Quebec (Bussiere, Knighton, and Pennock 2007). We return to a more detailed discussion of this relationship later, when we explore separate models for Ontario and Quebec.

School- and community-level characteristics may also contribute to differences in student performance. The results from Model 2 suggest that students tend to perform better in smaller communities and larger schools. There is also evidence that students who attend schools with a large proportion of immigrants tend to perform less well than students who attend schools with fewer immigrants. Moreover, average parental education has a positive effect, suggesting a social capital effect may be operating. This effect is not simply compositional—that is, it does not reflect the education of individual students' parents—because the effect of parental education at the individual level is included in the model. Finally, returning to the interaction between immigrant status and province, we see that the pattern observed in Model 1 persists, though slightly muted. In short, provincial differences in the community- and school-level variables account for a small amount of the relatively poor performance of Ontario students overall, but

TABLE 1.3

*Hierarchical linear models estimating the effects of student- and school-level characteristics on test score, Ontario and Quebec data combined (TIMSS 2003)*

| | *Model 1* | *Model 2* | *Model 3* | *Model 4* |
|---|---|---|---|---|
| STUDENT CHARACTERISTICS | | | | |
| Male | 26.586*** | 26.912*** | 27.991*** | 27.893*** |
| | (2.890) | (2.902) | (2.927) | (2.928) |
| Age | −14.342*** | −13.810*** | −13.738*** | −13.500*** |
| | (3.091) | (3.072) | (3.071) | (3.071) |
| Immigrant status | −25.480** | −24.345** | −24.386** | −24.107** |
| | (8.437) | (8.418) | (8.209) | (8.407) |
| Highest parental education | 4.621*** | 3.088** | 3.097** | 3.139** |
| | (1.069) | (1.083) | (1.082) | (1.083) |
| Number of books in household | 18.332*** | 17.711*** | 17.875*** | 17.857*** |
| | (1.281) | (1.278) | (1.278) | (1.277) |
| Household size | −4.040*** | −4.052*** | −4.056*** | −4.170*** |
| | (1.216) | (1.210) | (1.209) | (1.210) |
| PROVINCE | | | | |
| Ontario | −32.656*** | −24.259** | −26.809** | −92.862** |
| | (7.233) | (9.343) | (9.341) | (28.679) |
| Ontario* immigrant status | 26.185* | 25.507* | 25.655* | 25.049* |
| | (10.899) | (10.793) | (10.782) | (10.779) |
| SCHOOL AND COMMUNITY CHARACTERISTICS | | | | |
| *School and community variables* | | | | |
| School size (log) | | 24.298*** | 27.914*** | 27.593*** |
| | | (4.619) | (4.802) | (4.778) |
| School highest grade level | | −0.569 | −0.718 | −0.577 |
| | | (2.603) | (2.586) | (2.559) |
| Community size | | −5.827* | −5.676* | −6.436** |
| | | (2.313) | (2.286) | (2.290) |
| *School-level student characteristics* | | | | |
| Male students | | | | |
| 46%–60% | | −7.756 | −5.513 | −5.577 |
| | | (6.642) | (6.598) | (6.534) |
| >60% | | −2.395 | −1.378 | −2.009 |
| | | (8.561) | (8.480) | (8.396) |
| Immigrant students | | | | |
| 1%–10% | | −4.006 | −1.594 | −0.88 |
| | | (7.361) | (7.337) | (7.264) |
| >10% | | −23.613* | −17.577 | −17.711 |
| | | (9.251) | (9.392) | (9.334) |
| Average parental education | | 44.614*** | 40.189*** | 40.650*** |
| | | (6.571) | (6.634) | (6.634) |
| Variation in parental education | | −12.46 | −10.538 | −13.534 |
| | | (62.116) | (61.474) | (61.196) |
| *Disciplinary climate* | | | | |
| Principal reports: frequency of disciplinary disengagement | | | −5.984 | −4.484 |
| | | | (3.105) | (3.741) |

*(continued)*

TABLE 1.3 *(continued)*

| | *Model 1* | *Model 2* | *Model 3* | *Model 4* |
|---|---|---|---|---|
| Teacher reports: frequency of classroom disruption | | | −7.503* | −19.245*** |
| | | | (3.817) | (5.482) |
| Student reports: victimization incidents | | | −3.811* | −4.031 |
| | | | (1.558) | (2.131) |
| *Province (Ontario)* disciplinary climate* | | | | |
| Principal reports: disciplinary disengagement | | | | −2.175 |
| | | | | (6.127) |
| Teacher reports: classroom disruption | | | | 22.099** |
| | | | | (7.474) |
| Student reports: victimization incidents | | | | 0.552 |
| | | | | (3.094) |
| Intercept | 1,202.11*** | 829.77*** | 869.827*** | 906.478*** |
| | (5.576) | (76.550) | (77.178) | (78.602) |
| Pseudo $R^2$ | 0.470 | 0.476 | 0.476 | 0.476 |
| Proportion of variance between schools | 0.274 | 0.537 | 0.551 | 0.564 |
| *N* | 3,589 | 3,589 | 3,589 | 3,589 |

NOTE: Standard errors are in parentheses.
* $p < .05$; ** $p < .01$; *** $p < .001$.

they play no discernable role in the relatively poor performance of immigrant students in Quebec.

Model 3 further extends the analysis to include the influence of the three disciplinary climate measures—principal reports of disengagement infractions, teacher reports of classroom disruption, and student reports of victimization. The addition of these measures has only a minor impact on the other coefficients in the model, including those associated with the province and immigrant status effects. This suggests, then, that the lower scores of immigrants in Quebec cannot be accounted for by differences in the disciplinary climates in the schools. Nevertheless, two of the disciplinary measures have significant effects on school performance. For example, increases in teacher reports of classroom disruption and student reports of victimization are both associated with lower test scores on average. On the other hand, while the effect of principal reports of disengagement is in the expected negative direction, it is not statistically significant.

If we allow for differential effects of disciplinary measures on test scores by province, we uncover a somewhat different story. Most importantly, the results from Model 4 show statistically significant provincial differences in the effects of disciplinary climate on test scores. The several interaction terms associated with the province variable make the results from this model difficult to comprehend without further calculations, however. As a result, we now turn to separate analyses of the Ontario and Quebec data to further highlight these provincial differences.

Table 1.4 includes two separate models for both Quebec and Ontario. Model 5 includes all individual-level variables and contextual-level variables, and Model 6 extends this model by including all previous measures as well as the disciplinary measures. The findings are markedly different for the two provinces. After controlling for the other important context variables, school disciplinary climate has no apparent effect on test score performance in Ontario. The relative unimportance of these measures is further highlighted by the fact that their addition to the model results in very little change in any of the coefficients representing the effects of the other variables or in the proportion of the school differences in test score averages explained by the model. The story for Quebec is quite different, however. Teacher reports of classroom disruption are strongly related to school performance in Quebec. On average, test scores decrease by about 19 points (or approximately 1.9 percent) with every single increase in a teacher report of classroom disruption. None of the other disciplinary measures significantly affect test scores.

By estimating separate models for Ontario and Quebec, we can also more clearly see the provincial differences in the relative performance of immigrant students compared to native-born students. On average, immigrant students score approximately 22 points lower (about 2.2 percent) than native-born students in Quebec, while there is no difference in test scores between the two groups in Ontario. A comparison of Models 5 and 6 further suggests that disciplinary climate plays no role in the provincial differences in the relative performance of immigrant students. That is, immigrant students perform equally less well in Quebec even after considering variation in the disciplinary climate of the schools students attended.

In our final set of models, we explore the relationship between school disciplinary climate and students' college expectations. With a few exceptions, the models in Table 1.5 take the same general structure as those

TABLE 1.4

*Hierarchical linear models estimating the effects of student- and school-level characteristics on test score, for Ontario and Quebec data separately (TIMSS 2003)*

| | ONTARIO | | QUEBEC | |
|---|---|---|---|---|
| | *Model 5* | *Model 6* | *Model 5* | *Model 6* |
| STUDENT CHARACTERISTICS | | | | |
| Male | 24.210*** | 25.061*** | 31.404*** | 32.376*** |
| | (4.770) | (4.803) | (3.533) | (3.571) |
| Age | -12.138 | -11.683 | -14.702*** | -14.667*** |
| | (7.380) | (7.387) | (3.132) | (3.128) |
| Immigrant status | 0.067 | -0.261 | -22.365** | -22.103** |
| | (7.832) | (7.830) | (7.643) | (7.631) |
| Highest parental education | 7.275*** | 7.217*** | 0.101 | 0.274 |
| | (1.919) | (1.920) | (1.247) | (1.247) |
| Number of books in household | 26.857*** | 26.888*** | 11.467*** | 11.644*** |
| | (2.207) | (2.208) | (1.496) | (1.496) |
| Household size | -6.584** | -6.616** | -2.02 | -2.169 |
| | (2.072) | (2.074) | (1.423) | (1.421) |
| SCHOOL AND COMMUNITY CHARACTERISTICS | | | | |
| *School and community variables* | | | | |
| School size (log) | 15.963* | 18.491* | 22.801*** | 25.435*** |
| | (8.037) | (8.135) | (5.670) | (5.921) |
| School highest grade level | -5.109 | -5.414 | 2.719 | 3.016 |
| | (3.784) | (3.768) | (3.490) | (3.391) |
| Community size | -3.177 | -2.436 | -7.172* | -8.656** |
| | (3.237) | (3.269) | (3.117) | (3.027) |
| *School-level student characteristics* | | | | |
| Male students | | | | |
| 46%–60% | 2.425 | 2.313 | -21.573* | -17.103 |
| | (8.784) | (8.757) | (9.463) | (9.187) |
| >60% | 12.746 | 13.953 | -15.56 | -13.989 |
| | (13.960) | (13.924) | (10.694) | (10.300) |
| Immigrant students | | | | |
| 1%–10% | 11.759 | 13.442 | -16.344 | -11.23 |
| | (10.718) | (10.676) | (9.701) | (9.539) |
| >10% | 0.387 | 0.996 | -49.080*** | -40.015*** |
| | (12.588) | (12.559) | (12.959) | (13.239) |
| Average parental education | 32.190*** | 32.898*** | 48.430*** | 41.433*** |
| | (9.228) | (9.295) | (9.489) | (9.509) |
| Variation in parental education | -13.071 | 11.434 | -68.197 | -92.041 |
| | (77.654) | (77.872) | (100.286) | (97.057) |
| DISCIPLINARY CLIMATE | | | | |
| Principal reports: frequency of disciplinary disengagement | | -9.307 | | -2.068 |
| | | (5.070) | | (3.841) |
| Teacher reports: frequency of classroom disruption | | 0.54 | | -19.387*** |
| | | (5.186) | | (5.328) |

| | | | | |
|---|---|---|---|---|
| Student reports: victimization incidents | | –3.497 (2.508) | | –3.478 (1.925) |
| Intercept | 868.724*** (133.557) | 861.156*** (133.639) | 859.073*** (99.917) | |
| Pseudo $R^2$ | 0.414 | 0.414 | 0.533 | 0.533 |
| Proportion of school-level intercept variance explained | 0.558 | 0.569 | 0.575 | 0.614 |
| *N* | 1,553 | 1,553 | 2,036 | 2,036 |

NOTE: Standard errors are in parentheses.
* $p < .05$; ** $p < .01$; *** $p < .001$.

predicting test scores. First, guided by previous research showing an important positive relationship between educational expectations and academic abilities (Kaplan, Liu, and Kaplan 2001; Ainley, Foreman, and Sheret 1991; Marjoribanks 1987), we include the combined math and science test score as a control variable. Second, in contrast to the models predicting test score, preliminary analysis suggested that immigrant status and province do not interact in their effects on college expectations ($p$ = .174 for the $z$ test), so the related interaction terms are excluded from the model. Third, preliminary analysis also failed to show an interaction effect between province and any disciplinary climate measure (no individual measure's $z$ test had a $p$ value smaller than .144; the chi-square test for all three measures combined was 2.544, $p$ = .467), so terms related to such interactions are not included in any of the models. The first finding to report, then, is that college expectations in Quebec and Ontario are much more similar than combined math and science test score.

Many of the individual-level predictors on college expectations differ substantially from their effects on test scores (see Model 7 in Table 1.5). Although males tend to perform better on test scores than females, they are less likely to expect to finish college. Moreover, despite Ontario students performing less well on test scores, they tend to have higher expectations for college completion than Quebec students do. It is also interesting to note that immigrants performed less well on test scores (at least in Quebec) but have higher expectations than native-born students of finishing college. Finally, parental education and the number of books in the household have similar positive effects on both test scores and college expectations. Taken together, these findings suggest that the expectation of completing college

TABLE 1.5
*Multilevel logit models estimating the effects of student- and school-level characteristics on college expectations, Ontario and Quebec data combined (TIMSS 2003)*

| | *Model 7* | *Model 8* | *Model 9* |
|---|---|---|---|
| STUDENT CHARACTERISTICS | | | |
| Male | −0.748*** | −0.652*** | −0.652*** |
| | (0.091) | (0.093) | (0.094) |
| Age | −0.264** | −0.213* | −0.201* |
| | (0.088) | (0.088) | (0.088) |
| Immigrant status | 0.668*** | 0.387* | 0.393* |
| | (0.185) | (0.192) | (0.193) |
| Highest parental education | 0.477*** | 0.409*** | 0.411*** |
| | (0.032) | (0.033) | (0.033) |
| Number of books in household | 0.184*** | 0.162*** | 0.164*** |
| | (0.039) | (0.039) | (0.039) |
| Household size | 0.03 | 0.041 | 0.041 |
| | (0.037) | (0.037) | (0.037) |
| Math and science test score (combined) | 0.006*** | 0.006*** | 0.006*** |
| | (0.001) | (0.001) | (0.001) |
| PROVINCE: ONTARIO | 0.366** | 0.413* | 0.423* |
| | (0.114) | (0.170) | (0.173) |
| SCHOOL AND COMMUNITY CHARACTERISTICS | | | |
| *School and community variables* | | | |
| School size (log) | | −0.021 | −0.024 |
| | | (0.084) | (0.088) |
| School highest grade level | | 0.043 | 0.055 |
| | | (0.046) | (0.047) |
| Community size | | 0.159*** | 0.161*** |
| | | (0.041) | (0.041) |
| *School-level student characteristics* | | | |
| Male students | | | |
| 46%–60% | | −0.13 | −0.115 |
| | | (0.121) | (0.122) |
| >60% | | −0.343* | −0.333* |
| | | (0.154) | (0.154) |
| Immigrant students | | | |
| 1%–10% | | −0.233 | −0.232 |
| | | (0.127) | (0.128) |
| >10% | | −0.155 | −0.137 |
| | | (0.176) | (0.181) |
| Average parental education | | 0.456*** | 0.436*** |
| | | (0.122) | (0.124) |
| Variation in parental education | | 2.153 | 2.134 |
| | | (1.156) | (1.158) |
| *Disciplinary climate* | | | |
| Principal reports: frequency of disciplinary disengagement | | | 0.034 |
| | | | (0.055) |
| Teacher reports: frequency of classroom disruption | | | −0.138* |
| | | | (0.070) |

| | | | |
|---|---|---|---|
| Student reports: victimization incidents | | | 0.014 |
| | | | (0.048) |
| Intercept | −5.418*** | −9.123*** | −8.901*** |
| | (1.435) | (1.792) | (1.809) |
| Pseudo $R^2$ | 0.340 | 0.340 | 0.340 |
| Proportion of variance between schools | 0.795 | 0.795 | 0.795 |
| *N* | 3,589 | 3,589 | 3,589 |

NOTE: Standard errors are in parentheses.
* $p < .05$; ** $p < .01$; *** $p < .001$.

may have less to do with student performance and more to do with the social and cultural resources available in the home.

Several contextual variables also contribute in explaining differences in college expectations (see Model 8 in Table 1.5). For example, schools in larger communities, schools with proportionately fewer males, and schools with better-educated parents are all associated with higher college expectations. Including these predictors has little effect on most of the individual-level predictors, but it does affect those of most interest, namely, immigrant status and province. More specifically, the difference in expectations between immigrant students and native-born students is reduced by about 43 percent (0.387 versus 0.668), while the difference between Ontario and Quebec students increases by about 12.5 percent (0.423 versus 0.366). In other words, some of the differences between immigrant and nonimmigrant students and between Ontario and Quebec students have to do with the types of schools they attend.

The findings remain almost identical when including disciplinary climate measures (see Model 9 in Table 1.5). In other words, variations in disciplinary climate cannot account for the marked differences between immigrant and nonimmigrant students and between Ontario and Quebec students. Nevertheless, consistent with the findings with respect to test scores in Quebec, Model 9 still suggests that teacher reports of classroom disruption affect college expectations. With every increase in reported infractions, the odds of expecting to complete college decline by about 13 percent (odds ratio = $e^{-0.138}$ = 0.871). None of the other disciplinary measures has any notable effect on college expectations. Recall also that preliminary models tested for differential effects according to province, but none of the associated interaction terms was statistically significant. In other words, school disciplinary climate tends to affect students in very similar ways in Ontario and Quebec.

## CONCLUSION

We assessed the role of school disciplinary climate in student performance in Canada. We also explored how differences in school performance between students in the provinces of Ontario and Quebec and differences between immigrants and nonimmigrants within these provinces could be explained by school disciplinary climate. Taken together, our findings suggest that disciplinary climate does play a role in Canada, though much less so than in many other countries. Students in Ontario tend to score lower than students in Quebec, but this difference could not be accounted for by the disciplinary climate of the schools that students attended. Moreover, immigrants perform less well in Quebec than in Ontario, but this difference changes very little after controlling for disciplinary climate. In fact, the TIMSS data suggest that only one disciplinary climate measure—teachers' reports of classroom disruption—has a statistically significant effect on test scores, and this is only for students in Quebec. Teacher reports of classroom disruption is also the only disciplinary measure that appears to influence college expectations. This finding holds for both Ontario and Quebec.

Given that other research suggests that most disciplinary problems in Canadian schools are relatively minor (Frank and Lipps 1997)—that is, they seldom involve severe violence—it is perhaps not surprising that we failed to uncover a relationship between test scores and principal reports of disengagement or student reports of victimization. At the same time, it makes intuitive sense that frequent classroom disruptions hinder learning. Still, the differential effect of classroom disruptions on test scores by province is more difficult to explain.

Although our data do not enable us to conclusively determine the reasons for the provincial differences in the effect of classroom disruptions, we offer three possible explanations. First, it is possible that, compared to Quebec teachers, Ontario teachers may be more likely to be strict with disruptive students, thus limiting their influence on the other students in the class. This strictness could stem from closer adherence to zero tolerance policies that remove problem students from the classroom. Given the higher proportion of private schools in Quebec that are not under the jurisdiction of school boards, this is a realistic possibility. Second, the difference might also reflect the greater prevalence of Catholic schooling—which is known for its strictness—in Ontario. These are questions for future research, because the present data do not allow us to test these conjectures, and we are unaware of any other empirical evidence that could shed light on the issue.

The third possible explanation pertains to general cultural differences. In this regard, it is interesting to note that, despite disciplinary climate appearing to have a negative effect on academic performance only in Quebec, a recent survey commissioned by the Canadian Education Association suggests that Quebecers are more confident than Ontarians in their public school system (Dunleavy 2007). In Ontario only 36 percent reported "a great deal or quite a lot of confidence" in provincial public schools, whereas 61 percent report the same in Quebec. Moreover, only 13 percent in Ontario reported having a "great deal or quite a lot of confidence" in educational policy. In contrast, 29 percent of respondents in Quebec reported the same level of confidence. These findings suggest that attitudinal differences between the two provinces (see Andersen and Milligan 2009; Grabb and Curtis 2005) may also play a role in the differential effect of classroom disruptions.

Another limitation of this study is the absence of data from provinces other than Ontario and Quebec. Although it would be more desirable to explore all provinces in Canada, we focus on Ontario and Quebec because comparable data are not available for the other provinces. It is possible that the results for other provinces would differ. Nevertheless, the similarities in culture and schooling systems between Ontario and the provinces not included in our analysis are probably as great as the differences between Ontario and Quebec. We argue, then, that studying the contrast between Ontario and Quebec is sensible, and it is unlikely that we would have found a radically different story had we been able to explore other provinces.

Perhaps a more important limitation is the absence of possibly important variables in the TIMSS 2003 data. For example, we had no information on respondents' ethnicity or country of origin. Given that most new immigrants to Canada are visible minorities, it is possible that we observed an ethnicity effect rather than an effect of immigrant status. We are also missing some important information at the school level. For example, as we mentioned earlier, to better understand the provincial differences, we would further require information on the type of school that students attended. More specifically, we might expect differences in performance between the separate schools (i.e., Catholic) and public schools in Ontario. Similarly, there may be differences between private and publicly funded schools. More importantly, as suggested earlier, it is possible that the different school types have quite different disciplinary climates. These questions cannot be comprehensively addressed until new data become available.

## NOTES

1. Provincial responses to federal legislation also can vary, as is evident in the Young Offenders Act and the Multicultural Policy and Bill (see Ghosh 2004, 546).

2. There is some evidence that academic performance is much higher in private schools in Quebec. According to an article in the *National Post*, 86 of the top 100 schools in Quebec are private (see Cowley 2004).

3. These questions on effectiveness are consistent with research in the United States. For example, see *Opportunities Suspended: The Devastating Consequences of Zero Tolerance and School Discipline Policies*, a 2000 report by civil rights researchers at Harvard.

4. The Safe Schools Act was introduced in 2000 and implemented in 2001–2002 in Ontario. For further details, see http://www.resultsontario.gov.on.ca.

5. In Ontario these policies are laid out in Bill 212, the Education Amendment Act (Progressive Discipline and School Safety), which was passed in June 2007 and took effect on February 1, 2008. Bill 212 amends the safe-school provisions of Bill 81, implemented in 2000 (see http://www.etfo.ca/IssuesinEducation/SafeSchools/Pages/default.aspx).

6. Although it would be more desirable to explore all provinces in Canada, we focus only on Ontario and Quebec because TIMSS does not include comparable data for the other provinces.

## REFERENCES

Ainley, J., J. Foreman, and M. Sheret. 1991. "High School Factors That Influence Students to Remain in School. *Journal of Educational Research* 85:69–80.

Alladin, I. 1996. *Racism in Canadian Schools*. Toronto: Harcourt Brace.

Allen, Dawn. 2006. "Who's In and Who's Out? Language and the Integration of New Immigrant Youth in Quebec." *International Journal of Inclusive Education* 10 (2–3): 251–63.

Andersen, Robert, and Scott Milligan. 2009. "Inequality and Intolerance: Canada in Cross-national Perspective." Chap. 27 in *Social Inequality in Canada: Patterns, Problems, and Policies*, edited by Edward Grabb and Neil Guppy, 5th ed. Toronto: Prentice Hall.

Arum, Richard. 2003. *Judging School Discipline: The Crisis of Moral Authority.* Cambridge, MA: Harvard University Press.

Barton, Paul, Richard Coley, and Harold Wenglinsky. 1998. *Order in the Classroom.* Princeton, NJ: Educational Testing Service.

Bowlby, Jeffrey W., and Kathryn McMullen. 2002. *At a Crossroads: First Results for the 18- to 20-Year-Old Cohort of the Youth in Transition Survey.* Ottawa: Statistics Canada.

Boyd, Monica. 2002. "Educational Attainments of Immigrant Offspring: Success or Segmented Assimilation?" *International Migration Review* 36 (4): 1037–60.

Brooks, Kim, Vincent Schiraldi, and Jason Zeidenberg. 1999. *School House Hype: Two Years Later.* San Francisco, CA: Center on Juvenile and Criminal Justice.

Brown, Louise. 2006. "Lockdowns a New Way of Life at School Nowadays, They're as Common as a Fire Drill." *Toronto Star*, April 1.

———. 2008. "School Discipline Takes Kinder Turn: Provincially Mandated New-Look Suspensions That Stress Prevention Come into Effect Today." *Toronto Star*, February 1.

Bussiere, Patrick, Tamara Knighton, and Dianne Pennock. 2007. *Measuring Up: Canadian Results of the OECD PISA Study: The Performance of Canada's Youth in Science, Reading and Mathematics.* Ottawa: Human Resources and Social Development Canada, Council of Ministers of Education, Canada, and Statistics Canada.

Cheng. M., and A. Soudak. 1994. *Anti-Racism Education: A Literature Review.* Toronto: Toronto Board of Education, Research Services.

Chui, Tina, Kelly Tran, and Helene Maheux. 2007. *Immigration in Canada: A Portrait of the Foreign-Born Population, 2006 Census.* Ottawa: Statistics Canada. Cat. no. 97–557-XIE.

Cloud, J. 1999. "The Columbine Effect. Zero Tolerance Sounds like a Good Way to Treat Violence." *Time* (Canadian edition) 154 (23): 53–54.

Coleman, James, Ernest Campbell, Carol Hobson, James McPartland, Alexander Mood, Frederic Weinfeld, and Robert York. 1966. *Equality of Educational Opportunity.* Washington, DC: Government Printing Office.

Coleman, James, and Thomas Hoffer. 1987. *Public and Private Schools: The Impact of Communities.* New York: Basic Books.

Coleman, James S., Thomas Hoffer, and Sally Kilgore. 1982. *High School Achievement: Public, Catholic, and Private Schools Compared.* New York: Basic.

Cortes, Kalena E. 2006. "The Effects of Age at Arrival and Enclave Schools on the Academic Performance of Immigrant Children." *Economics of Education Review* 25:121–32.

Cowley, Peter. 2004. "Private Schools Are Leading the Way in Quebec." *National Post*, November 12, p. A15. Available at http://www.iedm.org/main/show_editorials_fr.php?editorials_id=94.

Day, D. M, C. A. Golench, J. MacDougall, and C. A. Beals-Gonzalez. 1995. *School-Based Violence Prevention in Canada: Results of a National Survey of Policies and Programs.* Ottawa, ON: Solicitor General of Canada.

De Broucker, Patrice, and Laval Lavallee. 1998. "Getting Ahead in Life: Does Your Parents' Education Count?" *Education Quarterly Review* 5 (1): 22–28.

Dennis, A. 1996. "Student Discipline and the Charter." *Canadian School Executive* 15 (8): 13.

Dickinson, Greg M. 2006. "Court of Appeal Upholds Exclusion of Evidence Obtained in Dog Sniff Search of Backpack." *Education Law Journal* 16 (2): 245–51.

DiPrete, Thomas A., Chandra Muller, and Nora Cate Shaeffer. 1981. *Discipline and Order in American High Schools.* Washington, DC: National Center for Educational Statistics.

Dunleavy, Jodene. 2007. *Public Education in Canada: Facts, Trends, Attitudes.* Toronto: Canadian Education Association.

Education Monitor. 1998. "Most Canadians See Increased Violence, Lax Discipline as Top School Problems." *Education Monitor* 2 (3): 14.

Frank, J., and G. Lipps. 1997. "The Social Context of School for Young Children." *Canadian Social Trends* 47 (Winter): 22–26.

Gabor, T. 1995. *School Violence and the Zero Tolerance Alternative: Some Principles and Policy Prescriptions.* Solicitor General Canada. Cat. no. JS 42-67/1995.

Ghosh, Ratna. 2004. "Public Education and Multicultural Policy in Canada: The Special Case of Quebec." *International Review of Education* 50 (5–6): 543–66.

Gluszynski, Tomasz, and Urvashi Dhawan-Biswal. 2008. *Reading Skills of Young Immigrants in Canada: The Effects of Duration of Residency, Home Language Exposure and Schools.* Gatineau, Quebec: Human Resources and Social Development Canada.

Grabb, Edward, and James Curtis. 2005. *Regions Apart: The Four Societies of Canada and the United States.* Toronto: Oxford University Press.

Hartig, A. J., and K. McDonald. 1996. "Implications of the Charter for School Discipline." *Canadian School Executive* 15 (7): 3–6.

Heineke, W. F., and H. S. Drier. 1998. "Research for Better Classroom Practice and Policy." *Educational Forum* 62:273–80.

Hirschfield, Paul J. 2008. "Preparing for Prison? The Criminalization of School Discipline in the USA." *Theoretical Criminology* 12 (1): 79–101.

Ho, Esther, and Doug Willms. 1996. "Effects of Parental Involvement on Eighth-Grade Achievement." *Sociology of Education* 69:126–41.

Jenkins, Patricia H. 1995. "School Delinquency and School Commitment." *Sociology of Education* 68 (July): 221–39.

Jull, Stephen. 2000. "Youth Violence, Schools, and the Management Question: A Discussion of Zero Tolerance and Equity in Public Schooling." *Canadian Journal of Educational Administration and Policy*, no. 17.

Kaplan, Diane S., Xiaoru Liu, and Howard B. Kaplan. 2001. "Influence of Parents' Self-Feelings and Expectations on Children's Academic Performance." *Journal of Educational Research* 94 (6): 360–70.

Keel, R. 1998. *Student Rights and Responsibilities: Attendance and Discipline.* Toronto: Emond Montgomery.

Knighton, Tamara. 2002. "Post Secondary Participation: The Effects of Parents' Education and Household Income." *Education Quarterly Review* 8 (3): 25–31.

LeBel, L. 2006. "Supreme Court of Canada Case Law Regarding Fundamental Rights in Education." *Education Law Journal* 16 (2): 137–81.

Lee, Valerie E., and Anthony S. Bryk. 1989. "A Multilevel Model of the Social Distribution of High School Achievement." *Sociology of Education* 62 (3): 172–92.

Leschart, M. 1999. "Schools Are Overwhelmed by Discipline Problems." *Canadian Press Newswire*, April 26.

Lessard, Claude, and Andre Brassard. 2009. "Education Governance in Canada, 1990–2003: Trends and Significance." In *Canadian Perspectives on the Sociology of Education*, edited by Cynthia Levine-Rasky, 255–74. Don Mills, Ontario: Oxford University Press.

MacKay, W. 2008. "Safe and Inclusive Schooling—Expensive Quality Education—Priceless. For Everything Else There Are Lawyers." *Education Law Journal*, 18(1): 21–55.

MacKay, W., and J. Burt-Gerrans. 2005. "Student Freedom of Expression: Violent Content and the Safe School Balance." *McGill Journal of Education* 40:423.

Marjoribanks, K. 1987. "Ability and Attitude Correlates of Academic Achievement: Family-Group Differences." *Journal of Educational Psychology* 79:171–78.

Mawhinney, H. E. 1995. "Towards an Archeology of Policy That Challenges Conventional Framing of the Problem of Violence in Schools." *Canadian Journal of Educational Administration and Policy*, no. 2 (August 2). Available at http://umanitoba.ca/publications/cjeap/articles/mawhinney.html.

McAndrew, Marie. 2003. "Immigration and Diversity: Some Policy Issues Confronting the Quebec School System." *Policy Options*, October, 59–62.

McMurtry, Roy, and Alvin Curling. 2008. *The Review of the Roots of Youth Violence.* Toronto: Queen's Printer for Ontario.

Ministry of Education and Training. 1994. *Violence-Free Schools Policy.* Toronto: Ministry of Education and Training.

Myers, David E., Ann M. Milne, Keith Baker, and Alan Ginsburg. 1987. "Student Discipline and High School Performance," *Sociology of Education* 60:18–33.

National Center of Education Statistics. 1998. *Appendix A. School Practices and Policies Related to Safety and Discipline: Indicators of School Crime and Safety.* Washington, DC: U.S. Department of Education. Available at http://nces.ed.gov/pubs98/safety/appendixA.asp.

Ontario Human Rights Commission. 2004. "Disproportionate Impact of 'Zero Tolerance' Discipline." http://www.ohrc.on.ca/en/resources/submissions/SubmSafeSch/pdf.

Ontario Ministry of Education. 2009a. "Education Facts: Schools and School Boards." http://www.edu.gov.on.ca/eng/educationFacts.html.

———. 2009b. "Progressive Discipline: A New Approach to Help Make Schools Safer." http://www.edu.gov.on.ca/eng/safeschools/discipline.html.

———. 2009c. "Suspension and Expulsion Facts, 2006–07." http://www.edu.gov.on.ca/eng/safeschools/facts0607.html.

Ruck, Martin D., and Scot Wortley. 2002. "Racial and Ethnic Minority High School Students' Perceptions of School Disciplinary Practices: A Look at Some Canadian Findings." *Journal of Youth and Adolescence* 31 (3): 185–95.

Ryan, B. A., and G. R. Adams. 1999. "How Do Families Affect Children's Success in School?" *Education Quarterly Review* 6 (1): 30–43.

Safe Schools Action Team. 2005. *Safer Schools . . . Safer Communities*. Ontario: Ministry of Education.

Shannon M., and D. McCall. 1999. *Safe, Secure, Healthy Schools: An Inventory of Resources and Research*. Ottawa, ON: Canadian Association of Principals.

———. 2009. "Zero Tolerance Policies in Context: A Preliminary Investigation to Identify Actions to Improve School Discipline and School Safety." Report prepared for the Canadian Association of Principals. http://www.schoolfile.com/safehealthyschools/whatsnew/capzerotolerance.htm.

Singleton, A. 2008. "Court Refuses Injunction against School's Drug Detection Program." *Education Law Journal* 17 (3): 385–88.

Skiba, Russell J., Robert S. Michael, Abra Carroll Nardo, and Reece L. Peterson. 2002. "The Color of Discipline: Sources of Racial and Gender Disproportionality in School Punishment." *Urban Review* 34 (4): 317–42.

Smith, William J., William F. Foster, and Helen M. Donahue. 1999. *The Contemporary Education Scene in Quebec: A Handbook for Policy Makers, Administrators and Educators*. Montreal: Office of Research on Educational Policy, McGill University.

Statistics Canada. 2001. "Trends in the Use of Private Education, 1987/88 to 1998/99." *The Daily*, July 4. http://www.statcan.ca/Daily/English/010704/d010704b.htm.

———. 2008a. *2006 Census of Population*. Cat. no. 97-557-XCB2006013. Ottawa: Statistics Canada.

———. 2008b. *2006 Census of Population*. Cat. no. 97-557-XCB2006019. Ottawa: Statistics Canada.

Stewart, Eric A. 2003. "School, Social Bonds, School Climate, and School Misbehavior: A Multilevel Analysis." *Justice Quarterly* 20 (3): 575–604.

Taylor-Butts, Andrea, and Angela Bressan. 2008. *Youth Crime in Canada, 2006*. Ottawa: Statistics Canada. Cat. no. 85-002-XIE.

Thompson, L. 1994. *One Incident Is Too Many: Policy Guidelines for Safe Schools*. Regina: Saskatchewan School Trustees Association.

Walker, S. G. (1994). *Weapons Use in Canadian Schools.* Solicitor General Canada. Cat. no. JS4-1/1994-5.

Young, David, and Lawrence Bezeau. 2003. "Moving from Denominational to Linguistic Education in Quebec." *Canadian Journal of Educational Administration and Policy*, no. 24 (February 28). Available at http://umanitoba.ca/publications/cjeap/articles/youngbezeau.html.

Zarifa, David, and Scott Davies. 2007. "Balance of Powers: Public Opinion on Control in Education." *Canadian Journal of Sociology* 32 (2): 259–78.

CHAPTER TWO

# School Discipline in Chile

*Florencia Torche and Alejandra Mizala*

Educational enrollment expanded dramatically in Chile in the last decades. While primary education was already universal in the mid-1980s, secondary enrollment increased from 78 percent in 1987 to 91 percent in 2006. Postsecondary enrollment grew even more impressively: from 27 percent to 40 percent in the same period (Mideplan, 1990, 2006b). Despite these gains, Chileans perceive education to be one of the most important problems facing the country (Centro de Estudios Publicos [CEP] 2004, 2006, 2008), and in 2006 secondary school students launched large demonstrations demanding better-quality education (Gutiérrez and Caviedes 2006). In particular, the public and students alike are concerned about the low quality of Chilean education and high inequalities in educational achievement.

Chilean primary and secondary students rank low in international achievement tests. Almost 40 percent of Chilean adolescents perform lower than at what is considered basic literacy, and a dismal 2 percent surpass the international threshold of top performance (Hanushek and Woessman 2007). The relative performance of Chilean students has improved only modestly over the last three decades (Hsieh and Urquiola 2006), despite substantial increase in educational expenditures, particularly for teachers' salaries (Vegas 2007).

Inequality in achievement is also a major problem, as test scores are strongly correlated with students' economic resources. Chile and South Africa have the widest achievement gap between students in the lower and upper socioeconomic strata among the countries included in the Trends in International Mathematics and Science Study (TIMSS; Akiba, LeTendre, and Scribner 2007). These sharp educational disparities are striking given that since the 1990s the Chilean government has implemented aggressive compensatory policies targeting schools serving the most deprived students (Garcia-Huidobro 2000).

The Chilean K–12 system comprises three sectors: public schools, private-voucher schools, and private-paid institutions. Private-paid institutions charge high tuition and serve the Chilean elite. Private-voucher schools tend to serve middle-class and upper-middle-class students, and public schools mostly serve lower-class and lower-middle-class students. Not surprisingly, given the high correlation between socioeconomic status and educational achievement, substantial differences in performance exist across sectors.

While much research exists on the individual correlates of achievement and on the relative performance of public and voucher schools (McEwan 2001; Mizala and Romaguera 2001; Sapelli and Vial 2002, 2005; Anand et al. 2009; Lara et al. 2011), surprisingly little is known about school-level factors that may contribute to the low quality of education and the high inequality of educational achievement in Chile (Mizala and Torche 2012). The educational literature has shown that school organizational characteristics, cultural norms and values, and peer composition may play a substantial role in educational achievement (Alexander et al. 1979; Rumberger and Palardy 2004, 2005). For example, research indicates that Catholic schools have higher mean educational outcomes than public schools and more equitable distribution of achievement within schools (Coleman et al. 1982; Coleman and Hoffer 1987). The "Catholic advantage" is accounted for by aspects of the normative environment and academic organization, such as a better disciplinary climate and less student tracking (Lee and Bryk 1989; Lee et al. 1998). This body of research is not without criticism (Alexander and Pallas 1985; Willms 1985), but it highlights dimensions of school climate—norms, practices, and regulations—as important determinants of the level and distribution of educational achievement.

This chapter examines the influence of one such school-level factor, disciplinary climate, on student achievement. Previous research suggests that discipline may substantially affect educational achievement (Coleman and Hoffer 1987; Arum 2003; Ma and Willms 2004; Le Blanc et al. 2008). Multiple mechanisms may account for this influence. Continual disruption of classroom activity may prevent optimal teaching, students who are regularly victimized may have difficulty focusing on lessons, and unsafe environments may redirect teachers' energy from teaching to ensuring basic security.

School discipline as a determinant of achievement is a new concern in Chile, triggered in the early 2000s by media reports such as "Children Are Taking Guns," "Chaotic Students," and "Violence among ABC1 Students" (referring to students in private-paid institutions).[1] As a response to growing awareness, the Chilean Ministry of Education launched a school coexistence (*convivencia escolar*) policy in 2003. This policy establishes, for the first time in the country, explicit rules about school sanctions, educators' interactions with parents and students, and conflict resolution strategies.

To date, however, there is no research on the association between school disciplinary climate and educational quality and inequality in Chile, a question that this chapter addresses. We start by describing the Chilean demographic legal and organizational context of school discipline, and we present descriptive evidence about the main disciplinary issues in Chilean schools. After introducing the research questions we ask and the data and methods we use, we offer our analysis and findings.

## THE CONTEXT OF SCHOOL DISCIPLINE

### *Population Heterogeneity*

Chile is a middle-income country that has experienced substantial economic growth in the last two decades. Economic expansion has reduced the proportion experiencing poverty from 38.6 percent in 1990 to 13.7 percent in 2006 (Mideplan 2006a). Economic growth has not, however, been accompanied by a decline in economic inequality. With a Gini coefficient of .57 and 47 percent of total income going to the top income decile in 2003, Chile is currently one of the most economically unequal nations in the world (De Ferranti et al. 2004). The inequality is largely driven by the income concentration in the wealthiest decile (Torche 2005b). Economic inequality is visible and prevalent in Chilean society, and it is coupled with geographic segregation and marked cultural differences across socioeconomic strata (Rodriguez and Arriagada 2004).

While other countries have diverse sources of differentiation that compete with economic advantage as the basis for group identity—for example, race/ethnicity, language, religion, or region—Chile is highly homogeneous in these respects. Spanish is universally spoken, and the population is only

4.6 percent indigenous, with less than 0.01 percent of African and Asian descent and only 0.75 percent foreign born (Torche 2009). Regional cleavages are absent, and 85 percent of the population identify themselves as Christian—82 percent of them as Catholics. Economic growth and globalization, however, are slowly inducing social and cultural heterogeneity. For example, Chile has recently attracted immigration from neighboring Latin American countries such as Argentina, Peru, and Ecuador. In particular, Peruvian migration increased by 400 percent between 1992 and 2002, bringing with it cultural and ethnic variation (Stefoni 2007). Despite these incipient trends, Chilean society remains highly homogeneous and socioeconomic status stands as the main source of social differentiation.

### *Organizational Structure of the Educational System*

The Chilean K–12 educational system comprises 12 years of compulsory education—8 years of primary and 4 years of secondary school. There is no academic-ability grouping at any level. Tracking starts at the secondary level, when students choose between vocational and academic high schools. Students can, however, switch tracks at any time, and there are no track-related restrictions in accessing postsecondary education.

The Chilean educational system underwent a major transformation in 1981. In a context of a market-oriented transformation, a universal voucher system was implemented. This transformation gave rise to a three-tier K–12 system of public (municipal), private-voucher, and private-paid schools. In the new voucher system, all public and private schools receive a per-student government subsidy provided they do not charge tuition and all families are allowed to use their voucher in the school of their choice (Mizala and Romaguera 2000; Cox and Lemaitre 1999). In contrast to U.S. voucher systems, in which the subsidy is given directly to the family, in the Chilean design funds are allocated directly to the school selected by the family, a system known as "funds follow the student" (Mizala and Romaguera 2000).

After the 1981 reform, many new private schools willing to take vouchers were created and a substantial migration from the public sector to this new type of school ensued. By 2003 private-voucher schools accounted for 40.5 percent of primary enrollment, public school enrollment had dropped to 53.1 percent, and private-paid schools accounted for the remaining 6.3 percent of enrollment. Private-paid schools were conspicuously unaffected by this transformation. Their fees were on average five times the per-student voucher, and they did not enter the competitive educational market created by the voucher reform, instead continuing to serve the Chilean elite.

Students who migrated from the public sector to the private-voucher one were mostly of higher socioeconomic status than those who remained in public schools, suggesting that socioeconomic sorting followed the voucher transformation (Torche 2005a; Hsie and Urquiola 2006). As shown in Table 2.1, median monthly household income (in U.S. dollars) is $300 among families attending public schools, $410 in private-voucher institutions, and $2,216 in private-paid schools. The educational gradient across sectors is also pronounced, with the median years of parental education reaching 8 in public, 10 in private-voucher, and 16 in private-paid schools.

Institutional design characteristics of the Chilean voucher system contribute to the socioeconomic stratification between public and private-voucher schools. First, until 2008 the voucher payment was flat,

TABLE 2.1
*Socioeconomic composition and standardized test scores by school sector, 2002–2004*

| | SCHOOL SECTOR | | | |
|---|---|---|---|---|
| | *Public* | *Private voucher* | *Private paid* | *All schools* |
| SOCIOECONOMIC STATUS | | | | |
| Median parental education[a] | 8 | 10 | 16 | 8 |
| Median household income[b] | 300.3 | 409.9 | 2,215.5 | 336.9 |
| TEST SCORES[c] | | | | |
| *4th graders (2002)* | | | | |
| Spanish | 239 | 259 | 300 | 251 |
| Math | 235 | 254 | 298 | 247 |
| *8th graders (2004)* | | | | |
| Spanish | 240 | 259 | 296 | 251 |
| Math | 241 | 260 | 305 | 253 |
| *10th graders (2003)* | | | | |
| Spanish | 241 | 257 | 301 | 253 |
| Math | 230 | 250 | 317 | 246 |

SOURCE: SIMCE (Sistema de Medición de la Calidad de la Educación, or System of Educational Quality Measurement), Chilean Ministry of Education, CASEN Survey 2003.

[a] Years of completed schooling, calculated as the highest of mother's and father's (or guardian's) schooling.

[b] Monthly household income measured in 2003 dollars.

[c] On the SIMCE standardized test given to all students in the indicated grade.

independent of student socioeconomic characteristics. This provided incentives for schools to select higher-resource students, who are cheaper to educate.[2] As the literature on school finance shows, educating children from low-income families entails higher costs related to compensation for household-deficient resources and higher cost of attracting teachers (Downes and Pogue 1994; Duncombe and Yinger 2000; Reschovsky and Imazeki 2001). Second, private-voucher schools can establish their own admission and expulsion policies, whereas public schools have to accept all applicants unless they are oversubscribed; thus, they effectively constitute suppliers of last resort. Third, public and private-voucher schools differ in ability to raise additional funds. A 1993 reform allowed private-voucher schools to charge parents add-on fees, which supplement the government voucher, under a withdrawal schedule that reduces the subsidy as parental fees increase (Vial 1998). This system—known as shared financing (*financiamiento compartido*)—expanded rapidly: 80 percent of private-voucher schools charged add-on fees by 1998 (Valenzuela, Bellei, and de los Ríos 2010). As a result of these voucher characteristics, private schools have the incentive and the ability to cream skim students.

Since 1990 the Chilean government has devoted substantial resources to improving the quality and equity of educational outcomes and has implemented targeted programs focused on the poorest, lowest-performing schools (Garcia-Huidobro 2000). The main principles of the voucher system—the unconstrained ability to choose and the competition between schools—have, however, remained intact for the last three decades.

Socioeconomic disparities across school sectors are closely related to differences in educational achievement. To illustrate this, we use scores from the SIMCE (Sistema de Medición de la Calidad de la Educación, or System of Educational Quality Measurement), a standardized test administered by the Ministry of Education to all Chilean students of a particular grade. The SIMCE test has a mean of 250 and a standard deviation of 50 by design. Table 2.1 presents scores from the Spanish and math SIMCE tests by school sector for 4th graders (2002), 8th graders (2004), and 10th graders (2003). Differences across school sectors are substantial. Private-voucher-school students score about 0.4 standard deviation higher than public school students in both Spanish and math. The performance gap between public and private-paid schools is even wider, reaching more than 1 standard deviation.

A widely researched question is whether the achievement gap across school sectors is entirely driven by the socioeconomic characteristics of the students they recruit or whether there are performance differences across sectors. Most studies find that students attending voucher schools have higher test scores than those attending public schools when taking into account individual attributes (Mizala and Romaguera 2001; Sapelli and Vial 2002, 2005; Anand et al. 2009). However, some studies find no consistent difference between public and nonreligious private-voucher schools but a higher effectiveness of Catholic private-voucher institutions (McEwan 2001). Furthermore, recent research finds virtually no achievement differences between public and private-voucher schools once students' previous test scores are accounted for (Lara et al. 2011). To date, however, no research exists on school-level characteristics—in particular, disciplinary climate—that can account for differences in achievement across sectors.

### *Legal Context and Administration of School Discipline*

Until the 1990s, school discipline was not considered a legal matter in Chile. Although several legal documents—the Chilean Constitution, the Universal Declaration of Children's Rights, the Convention for Children's Rights, and the Organic Constitutional Education Law of 1990—regulate students' rights, disciplinary matters were largely considered autonomous school issues. However, since the late 1990s the Chilean government has moved to explicitly establish educational rights and duties, with the objective of preventing arbitrariness and ensuring due process in the exercise of discipline. These steps have emerged as an attempt to expand democratization in the educational domain after national democracy was reestablished in 1990.

Two initiatives are central: in 2002 the Ministry of Education created a Citizen's Department (*Oficina de Atención Ciudadana*) with the task of informing families and students about their rights and addressing complaints and questions about school procedures. In 2003 the Ministry of Education launched the school coexistence policy (*política de convivencia escolar*). This policy formally established—for the first time in Chile—the rights and duties of school administrators, teachers, parents, and students, and it set guidelines for implementing discipline. Schools were required by law to have explicit bylaws regulating the exercise of discipline and establishing minimum norms. The policy also required the bylaws to correspond with

Chilean law, particularly with respect to ensuring equality and nondiscrimination. This regulation targeted prevalent unlawful school practices, such as expelling students without the right to appeal if they were pregnant, had HIV/AIDS, or had committed disciplinary violations. Schools were also required to clearly describe punishable behaviors, establish sanctions proportional to the offense, and inform the school community about their bylaws.

This policy attempted to reduce arbitrary school disciplinary decisions and to ensure due process, which included the ability of students to be heard, warned before being expelled, and given opportunity to appeal. The expansion of students' legal protection has been accompanied by the emergence of the use of courts to address disciplinary issues that cannot be resolved at the school level, via injunction suits. Although the number of cases brought to justice is small—about two dozen between 2000 and 2010—they are growing. Most of these injunction suits are related to what are seen as arbitrary and excessive disciplinary actions for insulting teachers, repeated misbehavior, or fighting with classmates, for example.

Chilean courts usually side with the student if the measure threatens the child's right to receive an education or fails due process—for example, if the student is expelled from school in the middle of the academic year or if the punishment was not clearly stated in the school bylaws. Otherwise, courts uphold the right of school administrators to impose and enforce discipline. Two court cases are illustrative. In a 1998 case, a Santiago appellate court ruled that schools did not have the right to regulate students' personal appearance (in particular, long hair and earrings in the case of male students and brightly colored hair dye in the case of female students) because these were personal matters. However the Supreme Court overruled the verdict, leaving Chilean schools free to enforce not only curricular and pedagogical standards but also standards pertaining to behavior and personal appearance. In a 2004 case in Concepción, the local court ruled that a school was not allowed to expel a student in the middle of the academic year for fighting with a classmate outside school even if the sanction was in the school bylaws, because this would threaten the student's right to receive an education. However, the court explicitly allowed the school not to renew the student's enrollment at the end of the academic year.

Chilean law gives schools substantial autonomy to design and impose disciplinary regulations. Schools regularly use demerits, parent-teacher interviews, and detention and occasionally use suspension and expulsion as disciplinary measures. Policing strategies such as security guards, metal detectors, and drug-sniffing dogs are, however, unheard of. Corporal punishment is banned by law, although anecdotal evidence suggests that it is practiced by a small proportion of educators, especially in rural and isolated areas. An important component of discipline in Chile is the regulation of personal appearance. Uniforms are universally used, and their legitimacy emerges from a rhetoric of equality, intended to reduce visible socioeconomic differences. The use of uniforms is strictly enforced, as are rules about hairstyle, makeup, body art, and other aspects of personal appearance. These rules enable easily identification and monitoring of students, reducing disciplinary infractions such as skipping class.

### *Main Disciplinary Issues in Chilean Schools: Descriptive Analysis*

Recent Chilean history is marked by political violence. An authoritarian military regime in power between 1973 and 1989 consistently used repression to subdue the political opposition (Schneider 1995). Civil society responded with grassroots protests and persistent street violence. Democracy was reestablished in 1990, and political violence declined sharply, but demonstrations escalating into violence are not uncommon, particularly those involving youth (Hempel 2007).

Despite Chile's recent history of political conflict, other types of violence occur infrequently by international standards. Chile has the lowest rate of violence in Latin America, and substantially lower than in the United States (Briceño Leon et al. 2008). Chile also has low rates of domestic and public violence in the Latin American context (Morrison and Biehl 1999; Londono and Guerrero 1999). Physical violence in schools also appears to be moderate. An international comparative study based on the 2005 Global School-Based Health Survey (GSHS) of the World Health Organization (WHO 2009) indicates that 41 percent of Chilean adolescents have been involved in a physical fight over the past 12 months (Rudatsikira, Muula, and Siziya 2008). This places Chile at the lower end compared with European and North American countries, whose numbers range from 37 percent in Finland to 69 percent in the Czech Republic (Pickett et al. 2005).[3]

The GSHS also indicates that nonaggressive infractions, such as skipping class, are low in Chile and parental supervision of adolescents is relatively high. Furthermore, obedience and conformity to rules are highly valued, and they are regarded as important attributes to cultivate in children.

In 1999–2000, the World Values survey asked respondents what characteristics were most important to teach children. Some 55 percent of Chileans included "obedience" among the five most important characteristics, the 15th-highest percentage among the 82 countries included in the survey and much higher than any other nation included in this book.[4]

These comparative figures depict Chile as a country where obedience is valued and taught and where school disciplinary issues are not pronounced. There is, however, one dimension of school discipline that appears to be particularly troublesome in Chile—student victimization and bullying. According to the 2005 GSHS, 43 percent of Chilean 13–15-year-olds report having been bullied in the past month, the highest figure among Latin American countries included in the study (WHO 2009; Fleming and Jacobsen 2009). The most common types of bullying reported are being teased about appearance and being made fun of through sexual jokes, comments, or gestures.

Not surprisingly, bullying has received substantial attention by Chilean scholars. Researchers suggest that group rather than individual bullying predominates in Chile, with the typical bullying incident involving a group of students attacking vulnerable children (Madriaza 2006). Several factors may account for the high prevalence of school bullying and aggression in Chile. Bullying appears to be more common in countries with higher levels of inequality, although the factors driving this relationship are unclear (Due et al. 2009). Rather than expressing hierarchical differences, the function of bullying may be to establish equality in a highly hierarchical context. In fact, demeaning jokes and name-calling appear to be widespread in Chilean society, and the country seems to have a culture of name-calling (Castillo-Feliu 2000). Other scholars argue that school violence in Chile reflects a need for protection and belonging in the growing individualism and indifference brought by rapid economic modernization (UNDP 1998; Flores 2008; Madriaza 2006; Aron and Milicic 1999; Aron 2000). Yet another viewpoint suggests that school aggression is a response to a historically authoritarian and rigid educational culture (Llana and Escudero 2003).

While some international comparative studies find a negative correlation between student socioeconomic status (SES) and bullying victimization (Due et al. 2009), bullying appears to be prevalent across all social classes and school sectors, although its motivations appear to vary by SES (Zeron 2006). Researchers speculate that among affluent students violence is a strategy to escape social conventions, while in the lower classes violence may relate to conditions of deprivation and neighborhood and family violence, and it may be used as a strategy to establish rights, impose ideas, and demand respect (Madriaza 2006).

In what follows, we use the first National Survey of School Violence (NSSV) in Chile, a nationally representative survey conducted by the Ministry of Education in 2005,[5] to examine bullying and aggression in Chilean schools. Figure 2.1 displays the prevalence of different types of aggressive behavior according to students and teachers. Several interesting findings emerge. First, students consistently report higher levels of aggressive behavior in schools than teachers do—suggesting that the latter may be unaware of the level of violence in their school. Second, results are highly consistent with the literature, with the most prevalent type of aggressive behavior being insults and demeaning jokes. Third, both physical (pushing, kicking, spitting) and psychological (demeaning jokes, gossip, discrimination) aggressive behaviors are highly prevalent in Chilean schools.

To examine the relationship between socioeconomic stratification and school aggression, we created a school-level SES index by combining the averages of mother's education, father's education, and family income with a measure of the school socioeconomic vulnerability provided by the

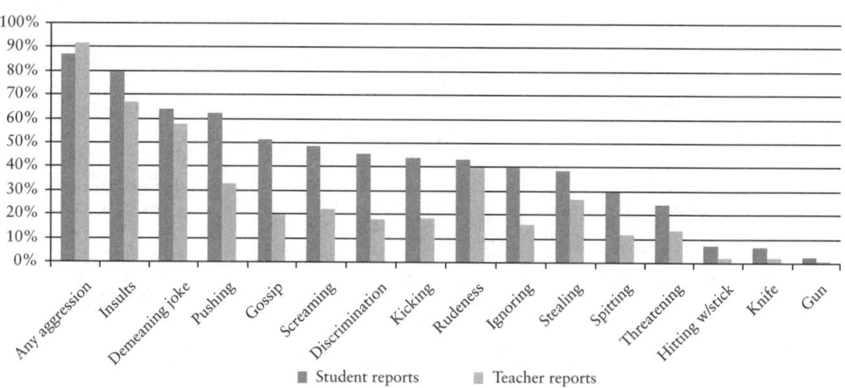


*Figure 2.1.* Prevalence of different types of aggression among Chilean students in 2005

SOURCE: 2005 National Survey of School Violence, Ministry of Education, Chile.

NOTE: Prevalence is based on students' and teachers' answers to the question "During 2005, which types of aggressions have taken place among students in this school?"

Ministry of Education. We then collapsed the SES index into three categories: lower 40 percent, middle 30 percent, and upper 30 percent. Figure 2.2 displays type of aggression by school SES. In upper-class schools 80 percent of students report aggressive behavior in their classmates; the percentage rises to 87 percent in middle-class schools and 91 percent in lower-class schools. A similar gradient exists across school sectors, with the reported prevalence of aggressive behavior being 77 percent in private-paid schools, 84 percent in private-voucher schools, and 92 percent in public schools (Figure 2.3). Given the very high level of inequality in Chilean society, we interpret the socioeconomic and school-type gradient in school violence as relatively weak. As shown by Figures 2.2 and 2.3 psychological aggressive behavior, such as demeaning jokes or ignoring, are more common among high-SES and elite private-paid schools, while spontaneous aggression, usually involving a direct physical component such as kicking or spitting, is more common in less advantaged and public schools. This finding resonates with approaches highlighting different types of socialization and cultural capital across social classes (e.g., Bourdieu 1984; Lareau 2003).

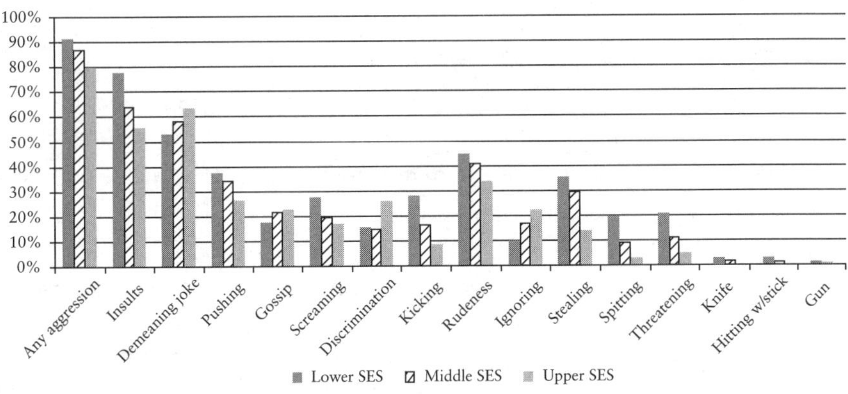


*Figure 2.2.* Prevalence of different types of aggression among Chilean students by school socioeconomic status (SES) in 2005

SOURCE: 2005 National Survey of School Violence, Ministry of Education, Chile.

NOTE: Prevalence is based on students' answers to the question "During 2005, which types of aggressions have taken place among students in this school?" School SES is based on a composite index of mother's education, father's education, household income, and school economic vulnerability and apportioned into three categories: upper (30%), middle (30%), and lower (40%).

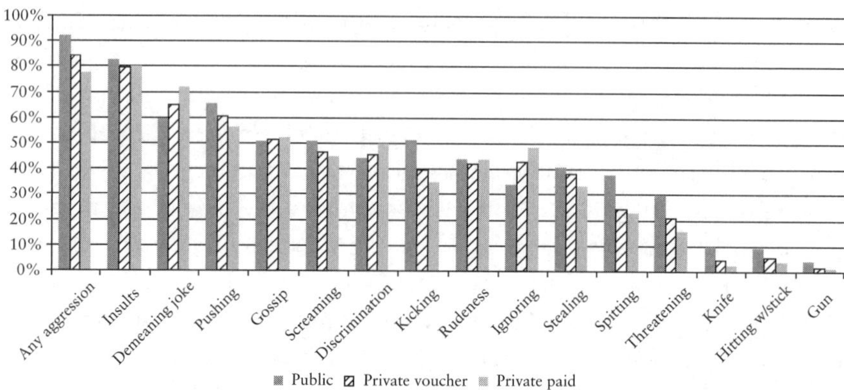


*Figure 2.3.* Prevalence of different types of aggression among Chilean students by school sector in 2005

SOURCE: 2005 National Survey of School Violence, Ministry of Education, Chile.

NOTE: Prevalence is based on students' answers to the question "During 2005, which types of aggressions have taken place among students in this school?"

## RESEARCH QUESTIONS, DATA, AND METHODS

The descriptive information in the previous section suggests that schools' disciplinary problems are not acute in Chile, with the notable exception of bullying and aggressive behavior among students, which appear to be widespread across socioeconomic strata. With this preliminary evidence, we now move to the core of the analysis. First, what are the school-level correlates of school disciplinary climate—including school socioeconomic and demographic characteristics? Second, is the school disciplinary climate related to student achievement once individual-level and school-level socioeconomic characteristics are accounted for, and do differences in disciplinary climate between public, private-voucher, and private-paid schools contribute to the achievement gap across school sectors? Third, does the relationship between school discipline and student achievement vary across school sectors?

To answer these questions, we use TIMSS data. The TIMSS is a survey of fourth and eighth graders conducted by the International Association for the Evaluation of Educational Achievement (IEA) in 1995, 1999, 2003, and 2007. TIMSS gives all students in sampled schools a math and science standardized test and accompanies it with student, teacher (from math and science classes), and school principal questionnaires. We use the 2003 version of the survey, which included 49 countries and four benchmark participant regions (two in Canada, one in the United States, and one in Spain). We restrict the analysis to eighth graders; as the last grade of primary school in Chile, it is the only group available. Surveyed students were, on average, 14.2 years old. School enrollment is nearly universal for this age group (97.7 percent of Chilean 14-year-olds attended school in 2003), ruling out potential sampling selectivity.

The sampling design consists of a two-stage stratified cluster design. The first stage samples schools, and the second stage selects intact classrooms from the targeted grade in the sampled schools. Stratification included region of the country and school sector (public, private-voucher, and private-paid institutions). The sample consists of 195 schools and 6,377 students. Weights adjust for the sampling design.

### *Variables*

In addition to the TIMSS variables used by all countries in this project (see introduction for a detailed description), we include two additional measures relevant to Chile. The first is an indicator for urban schools. The second is the school sector, distinguishing public, private-voucher, and elite, private-paid schools. These variables were constructed using information about the schools included in the TIMSS dataset, provided by the Chilean Ministry of Education. Information about school sector allows us to examine the central question for this analysis: the differences in disciplinary climate across school sectors, when taking into account school demographic and socioeconomic characteristics.

### *Methods*

We first examine the school-level determinants of disciplinary climate using linear regression models. We then examine the association between individual-level and school-level characteristics and student test scores using a two-level hierarchical linear model (HLM). The first-level units are students (within-school model), and each student's outcome is represented as a function of a set of individual characteristics. In the second level (school-level model) the regression coefficients in the first-level model are treated as outcome variables hypothesized to depend on school characteristics. The HLM methodology explicitly recognizes the clustering of students within schools and allows simultaneous consideration of the association between school factors and average school achievement and the relationships between students' characteristics and achievement within schools. Furthermore, this methodology captures variation across schools in the relationships between individual characteristics and outcomes (Raudenbush and Bryk 1992; Rumberger and Palardy 2004). Cases for which one or more variables were missing were deleted from the analysis. Results from models using mean imputation and dummy indicators for missing values are substantively identical to those reported here.

## ANALYSIS: SCHOOL-LEVEL DETERMINANTS OF DISCIPLINE AND THE ASSOCIATION BETWEEN DISCIPLINE AND STUDENTS' TEST SCORES

Table 2.2 presents descriptive statistics for the entire sample and by school sector. Differences across school sectors are pronounced. Average parental education increases across sectors; levels are lowest in public schools, private-voucher schools have higher levels, and private-paid schools have the highest. The proportion of immigrant students is highest in public schools and lowest in private-paid ones.[6]

Not surprisingly, a pattern across school sectors similar to parental education emerges for test scores. Public schools score 0.58 standard deviation lower than private-voucher schools in aggregate math-science test score; the difference between public and private-paid schools is a massive 1.74 standard deviations (note that the test score gaps across school sectors are much more pronounced in math than in science). The differences in disciplinary climates across sectors are less pronounced than achievement gaps, with the exception of student victimization.

### *Determinants of School-Level Disciplinary Climate*

We now examine the determinants of school-level disciplinary climate, including demographic and socioeconomic characteristics of schools and school sector. The models for each school disciplinary indicator are presented in Table 2.3. Several interesting findings emerge. First, the association between the socioeconomic status of the school and the disciplinary climate is very weak in Chile. The coefficient for average parental education is insignificant for all indicators of discipline except student victimization,

TABLE 2.2

*Descriptive statistics, TIMSS 2003, Chilean eighth graders*

| | PUBLIC | | PRIVATE VOUCHER | | PRIVATE PAID | | ALL SCHOOLS | |
|---|---|---|---|---|---|---|---|---|
| | *Mean* | *SD* | *Mean* | *SD* | *Mean* | *SD* | *Mean* | *SD* |
| STUDENT-LEVEL VARIABLES | | | | | | | | |
| Male | 0.517 | 0.500 | 0.544 | 0.498 | 0.454 | 0.498 | 0.520 | 0.500 |
| Age | 14.299 | 0.772 | 14.191 | 0.626 | 14.151 | 0.405 | 14.247 | 0.699 |
| Parental education | 3.513 | 1.265 | 4.406 | 1.650 | 6.764 | 1.222 | 4.112 | 1.684 |
| Household size | 5.122 | 1.539 | 4.919 | 1.425 | 4.992 | 1.453 | 5.039 | 1.495 |
| Number of books in household | 2.028 | 0.960 | 2.539 | 1.004 | 3.380 | 1.032 | 2.331 | 1.064 |
| Victimization index | 1.201 | 1.006 | 1.048 | 0.943 | 0.711 | 0.863 | 1.103 | 0.982 |
| Immigration status | 0.051 | 0.220 | 0.039 | 0.195 | 0.035 | 0.185 | 0.046 | 0.209 |
| SCHOOL-LEVEL VARIABLES | | | | | | | | |
| School size (log) | 6.454 | 0.661 | 6.664 | 0.712 | 6.666 | 0.620 | 6.548 | 0.684 |
| School highest grade level | 8.471 | 1.256 | 10.313 | 1.924 | 11.838 | 0.735 | 9.430 | 1.885 |
| Community size | 3.517 | 1.648 | 4.598 | 1.334 | 5.218 | 0.971 | 4.058 | 1.615 |
| Urban | 0.841 | 0.365 | 0.951 | 0.215 | 1.000 | 0.000 | 0.894 | 0.307 |
| *Male students* | | | | | | | | |
| 0–45% (reference) | 0.312 | 0.463 | 0.285 | 0.451 | 0.374 | 0.484 | 0.308 | 0.462 |
| 46%–60% | 0.496 | 0.500 | 0.405 | 0.491 | 0.382 | 0.486 | 0.454 | 0.498 |
| >60% | 0.192 | 0.394 | 0.310 | 0.463 | 0.244 | 0.430 | 0.238 | 0.426 |
| *Immigrant students* | | | | | | | | |
| 0 (reference) | 0.259 | 0.438 | 0.436 | 0.496 | 0.455 | 0.498 | 0.339 | 0.473 |
| 1–10% | 0.593 | 0.491 | 0.451 | 0.498 | 0.502 | 0.500 | 0.535 | 0.499 |
| >10% | 0.148 | 0.356 | 0.113 | 0.317 | 0.044 | 0.204 | 0.127 | 0.332 |
| Average parental education | 3.512 | 0.529 | 4.420 | 1.005 | 6.770 | 0.476 | 4.130 | 1.189 |
| Variation in parental education | 0.329 | 0.067 | 0.302 | 0.057 | 0.165 | 0.061 | 0.304 | 0.078 |
| Student disengagement | 2.796 | 0.958 | 2.546 | 0.820 | 2.429 | 0.821 | 2.674 | 0.910 |
| Classroom disruption | 3.725 | 0.847 | 3.326 | 0.840 | 3.492 | 0.665 | 3.563 | 0.850 |
| Victimization index | 1.202 | 0.332 | 1.048 | 0.273 | 0.711 | 0.382 | 1.103 | 0.349 |
| Math and science scores | 746.836 | 120.255 | 831.470 | 134.698 | 999.963 | 116.405 | 799.731 | 145.836 |
| Math scores | 357.119 | 62.866 | 404.973 | 72.065 | 498.649 | 64.424 | 386.880 | 78.504 |
| Science scores | 389.717 | 69.543 | 426.497 | 74.056 | 501.314 | 65.500 | 412.851 | 78.076 |
| *N* (unweighted) | 2,685 | | 1,624 | | 1,088 | | 5,397 | |

NOTE: SD = standard deviation.

TABLE 2.3

*School-level determinants of school discipline indicators, Chile 2003*

| | *Student disengagement* | | *Classroom disruption* | | *Student victimization* | |
|---|---|---|---|---|---|---|
| School size (log) | −0.117 | (0.123) | 0.041 | (0.119) | −0.031 | (0.042) |
| School highest grade level | 0.037 | (0.047) | −0.006 | (0.045) | 0.041* | (0.016) |
| Community size | 0.014 | (0.049) | 0.007 | (0.047) | 0.045** | (0.017) |
| Urban | 0.727** | (0.224) | 0.590** | (0.216) | 0.243** | (0.077) |
| Immigrant students: 0 (reference) | | | | | | |
| Immigrant students: 1%–10% | 0.392** | (0.142) | −0.165 | (0.137) | 0.062 | (0.049) |
| Immigrant students: >10% | 0.320 | (0.202) | −0.286 | (0.195) | 0.070 | (0.069) |
| Average parental education | −0.081 | (0.094) | 0.088 | (0.091) | −0.092** | (0.032) |
| Variation in parental education | 0.276 | (1.015) | −1.185 | (0.979) | 0.369 | (0.348) |
| Male students: <46% (reference) | | | | | | |
| Male students: 46%–60% | 0.391* | (0.160) | 0.147 | (0.155) | 0.217*** | (0.055) |
| Male students: >60% | 0.323† | (0.180) | 0.126 | (0.174) | 0.360*** | (0.062) |
| Public school (reference) | | | | | | |
| Private-voucher school | −0.290† | (0.166) | −0.516** | (0.160) | −0.175** | (0.057) |
| Private-paid school | −0.321 | (0.338) | −0.925** | (0.326) | −0.352** | (0.116) |
| Constant | 2.227* | (0.939) | 3.072*** | (0.906) | 0.663* | (0.322) |
| *N* | 181 | | 181 | | 181 | |
| $R^2$ | 0.105 | | 0.117 | | 0.355 | |

NOTE: Standard errors are in parentheses.

† $p < .10$; * $p < .05$; ** $p < .01$; *** $p < .001$.

while the coefficient for variation of parental education is insignificant for all discipline measures. Furthermore, schools with higher proportions of immigrant students do not have more disciplinary problems, with the partial exception of student disengagement. The weak socioeconomic stratification of disciplinary problems is surprising given the high level of inequality in Chile. It suggests that schools serving higher-SES students are not better at enforcing discipline or, alternatively, that reporting of disciplinary problems by principals and teachers varies by school SES, such that personnel in affluent schools are more aware of disciplinary issues or have higher expectations for student behavior.

Second, school disciplinary climate is correlated with the type of community in which the school is located. Urban schools are more likely to experience student disengagement, classroom disruptions, and student victimization. Given that about 90 percent of Chilean students attend urban schools, this finding likely highlights disciplinary advantages in the small percentage of rural Chilean schools—probably due to different socialization styles and stronger social control in rural areas—rather than inner city disciplinary problems. Furthermore, schools in larger communities are more likely than those in small cities to experience victimization incidents.

Third, interesting differences across school sectors emerge. When controlling for school-level characteristics, private schools are associated with better disciplinary climates than public institutions. This finding suggests that school-level normative or organizational features of private schools may contribute to a better disciplinary climate. While all public schools are secular by law, 35 percent of private schools are religious, mostly Catholic, institutions (Elacqua 2006). We examined and rejected the hypothesis that the disciplinary advantage of private-voucher schools is because of the numbers that are religious (ancillary analysis not shown, available from the authors upon request). Alternatively, the disciplinary advantage of private schools may be due to the more advantageous demographic and socioeconomic characteristics of their student bodies, not fully controlled for in this analysis. In an ancillary analysis, we control for additional indicators of school SES, including the number of books owned by families and the proportion of students who are economically deprived, based on principal assessments. The disciplinary advantage of private-paid and private-voucher schools is virtually unaffected by the addition of these indicators, suggesting that the private-paid school advantage is not due to the economic and demographic characteristics of the student body.

Finally, student victimization has a clearly gendered pattern. Consistent with findings in most of the countries included in this study and with previous research in Chile, victimization increases as the proportion of male students increases, and it is the highest in all-male schools.

### *Determinants of Student Test Score*

An important reason to study school discipline is that it may be related to students' educational achievement. We now examine the association between school disciplinary climate and student math-science test score. The analysis addresses our second question—is there an association between school discipline and student achievement once individual-level and school-level variables are accounted for? Three models are estimated. The first model includes only individual-level variables—student sex, age, immigration status, parental education, number of books in the household, household size, and student-level victimization—and school-sector-indicator variables. Model 2 adds all school-level covariates with the exception of school disciplinary indicators, and Model 3 incorporates measures of school disciplinary climate. Comparison between Models 1 and 2 helps us examine whether the achievement gap across school sectors is accounted for by school-level characteristics. Comparison between Models 2 and 3 serves two purposes. First, it explores whether the association between school-level economic and demographic factors and student achievement is mediated by school disciplinary climate. Second, it assesses whether achievement differences across school sectors are accounted for by school disciplinary climate.

Results are presented in Table 2.4. Model 1 shows that the association between each student-level characteristic and student achievement is substantial and has the expected sign. Males perform better than females on the math and science test (the reverse is true for Spanish; see Mizala and Torche 2012). Older students (more likely to have been held back) perform worse; those whose parents have higher educational attainment, more books at home, and who live in smaller households have higher test scores. Immigrant students perform substantially worse, with an average gap of almost half a standard deviation. The only exception to the pattern of significant associations is student victimization. Students who report

*Student- and school-level determinants of student test score, 2003*

| | Model 1 | | Model 2 | | Model 3 | |
|---|---|---|---|---|---|---|
| Male | 40.849*** | (2.780) | 41.212*** | (2.788) | 41.235*** | (2.788) |
| Student age | −37.630*** | (1.994) | −36.892*** | (1.991) | −36.740*** | (1.992) |
| Student immigrant status | −70.321*** | (6.377) | −69.638*** | (6.384) | −69.750*** | (6.385) |
| Parental education | 14.411*** | (1.075) | 13.195*** | (1.082) | 13.208*** | (1.082) |
| Number of books in household | 18.724*** | (1.456) | 18.130*** | (1.454) | 18.076*** | (1.453) |
| Household size | −3.534*** | (0.893) | −3.456*** | (0.892) | −3.435*** | (0.892) |
| Student victimization | −0.910 | (1.387) | −0.944 | (1.385) | -0.702 | (1.393) |
| Public school (reference) | | | | | | |
| Private-voucher school | 51.788*** | (9.909) | 10.508 | (10.158) | 3.480 | (10.334) |
| Private-paid school | 176.107*** | (15.185) | 44.174* | (20.85) | 35.986+ | (20.784) |
| School size (log) | | | 12.765 | (7.015) | 12.688 | (6.854) |
| School highest grade level | | | 0.716 | (2.714) | 1.689 | (2.666) |
| Community size | | | −0.892 | (2.951) | 0.381 | (2.919) |
| Urban | | | 18.099 | (14.347) | 27.756* | (14.317) |
| Male students: <46% (reference) | | | | | | |
| Male students: 46-60% | | | −8.265 | (9.016) | −1.925 | (9.075) |
| Male students: >60% | | | 3.16 | (10.339) | 9.854 | (10.744) |
| Immigrant students: 0 (reference) | | | | | | |
| Immigrant students: 0–10% | | | −15.259+ | (8.252) | −11.846 | (8.221) |
| Immigrant students: >10% | | | −33.315** | (12.029) | −29.245* | (11.852) |
| Average parental education | | | 34.916*** | (5.715) | 32.538*** | (5.695) |
| Variation of parental education | | | −67.849 | (64.015) | −61.546 | (62.617) |
| Student disengagement | | | | | −9.962* | (4.403) |
| Classroom disruption | | | | | −4.913 | (4.784) |
| Victimization | | | | | −13.442 | (12.895) |
| Constant | 1,200.256*** | (29.936) | 1,013.644*** | (63.069) | 1,051.865*** | (62.871) |
| *Variance components* | | | | | | |
| Between-school | 3,403.04*** | | 2,065.93*** | | 1,931.73*** | |
| Within-school | 8,664.87*** | | 8,661.23*** | | 8,661.49*** | |
| Intraclass correlation | .282 | | .193 | | .182 | |
| *N* | 5,397 | | 5,397 | | 5,397 | |
| Pseudo $R^2$ | .0194 | | .0207 | | .0208 | |
| Bayesian information criterion | 64,829.171 | | 64,831.381 | | 64,841.831 | |

NOTE: Standard errors are in parentheses.
† $p < .10$; * $p < .05$; ** $p < .01$; *** $p < .001$.

having had something stolen, been hit or threatened, or been made fun of during the last year do not perform worse on average.

After controlling for student characteristics, the achievement gap between public and private-voucher schools declines to 52 points and the gap between public and private-paid schools is 176 points. This corresponds to 0.35 and 1.2 standard deviations, respectively, compared to gaps of 0.58 and 1.74 standard deviations before accounting for individual-level characteristics (see Table 2.2). Even if reduced, a substantial achievement gap persists across sectors after accounting for observed student attributes.

Model 2 adds school-level characteristics to Model 1. The only significant school-level predictors of test score are school SES measures—average parental education and the proportion of students who are immigrants. This contrasts sharply with the weak socioeconomic stratification of school disciplinary problems. Accounting for the school's socioeconomic composition substantially reduces the achievement gaps across school sectors. The difference between public and private-voucher schools is now insignificant, and the gap between public and private-paid institutions drops from 1.2 to 0.3 standard deviations. The avenues for the influence of school SES are likely multiple. Average parental education may be an indicator of unobserved characteristics of families (such as more motivated or ambitious families searching for higher-SES peers for their children) or beneficial peer effects. The findings suggest that the achievement gaps across school sectors may be affected by both factors.

Model 3 addresses the two main questions in this analysis: Does school disciplinary climate affect student achievement? Does it mediate the influence of school-level demographic and socioeconomic factors? The analysis indicates a weak relationship between disciplinary climate and student performance. Only student disengagement has a significant negative association with achievement. Interestingly, the high levels of student victimization that characterize Chilean society do not appear to affect students' learning process. Furthermore, the coefficients associated with school SES remain virtually unchanged after school disciplinary climate is accounted for, and the additional amount of between-school variance explained by the model when accounting for disciplinary climate is small (the variance explained increases by only 3.3 percent). The most significant change in the association between variables included in Model 2 and student achievement is the reduction of the private-paid school advantage, suggesting that part of the value added by private-paid schools emerges from their more advantageous disciplinary climates.

This finding introduces the last question of our analysis: Does the association between school disciplinary climate and student achievement vary across school sectors? Table 2.5 presents separate models for public, private-voucher, and private-paid schools. Before moving to the core of the analysis, it is worth noting the substantial differences in the socioeconomic composition of private-paid schools vis-à-vis the other two sectors, including the absence of private-paid schools in rural areas.

Interestingly, the association between average parental education and student test score varies across sectors. It is stronger in private-voucher schools than in public ones, and it is substantially stronger in the private-paid sector. In other words, the socioeconomic distribution of test scores across schools is more egalitarian in the public sector, probably because of the compensatory government policies targeting the most vulnerable schools. In contrast, in the private-paid sector the advantages families bring to schools appear to directly translate into achievement differences.

Moving to our main question, the association between school disciplinary climate and achievement varies across sectors. The previous analysis showed a weak association between student disengagement and test score. Analysis by sector shows that this is driven by a strong association in the private-voucher sector (a 1-standard-deviation increase in student disengagement is associated with a 0.17-standard-deviation decline in test score). This substantial effect is probably driven by the heterogeneity in the SES composition of student bodies, educational missions, and normative environments across private-voucher schools, which may induce widely different responses to shaping student behavior and controlling misbehavior.

It is noteworthy that the overall association between discipline and achievement appears to be weaker in public schools than in private ones. Several factors may account for this. It is possible that the detrimental influence of disciplinary issues emerges only after more basic infrastructural, pedagogical, and administrative school needs are satisfied. This threshold effect—analogous to the effect of school resources on achievement found in international comparative research (Baker, Goesling, and LeTendre 2002)—may explain why disciplinary climate matters so little in the more deprived public schools and so much in the more affluent private ones.

TABLE 2.5

*Student- and school-level determinants of student test score by school sector, 2003*

| | *Public school* | | *Private voucher* | | *Private paid* | |
|---|---|---|---|---|---|---|
| Male | 40.351*** | (−3.652) | 42.832*** | (−4.808) | 40.162*** | (10.054) |
| Student age | −37.243*** | (−2.488) | −36.423*** | (−3.538) | −30.490** | (10.975) |
| Student immigrant status | −74.676*** | (−8.1) | −68.309*** | (−11.694) | −17.961 | (23.504) |
| Parental education | 13.960*** | (−1.574) | 11.798*** | (−1.62) | 15.070*** | (3.616) |
| Number of books in household | 19.889*** | (−2.04) | 15.390*** | (−2.361) | 17.909*** | (4.171) |
| Household size | −4.332*** | (−1.178) | −1.763 | (−1.523) | −4.643 | (3.127) |
| Student victimization | −0.411 | (1.851) | −1.807 | (2.296) | 0.944 | (5.481) |
| School size (log) | 15.870 | (10.425) | −9.354 | (11.418) | 41.653** | (14.248) |
| School highest grade level | 1.171 | (3.688) | 2.943 | (4.156) | 6.525 | (11.761) |
| Community size | −2.899 | (3.446) | 17.052** | (5.574) | −10.947 | (10.633) |
| Urban | 29.043† | (16.917) | −1.534 | (34.480) | | |
| Male students: <46% (reference) | | | | | | |
| Male students: 46%–60% | −10.324 | (10.284) | −8.129 | (17.389) | 1.930 | (25.273) |
| Male students: >60% | −0.425 | (13.371) | −3.807 | (20.957) | 1.265 | (29.468) |
| Immigrant students: 0 (reference) | | | | | | |
| Immigrant students: 0–10% | −18.051† | (10.846) | −26.647† | (14.857) | 16.953 | (22.214) |
| Immigrant students: >10% | −25.240† | (14.192) | −76.969* | (32.559) | −6.716 | (42.378) |
| Average parental education | 20.968* | (10.254) | 33.088*** | (8.048) | 108.458* | (47.490) |
| Variation in parental education | −20.292 | (65.644) | −64.872 | (153.880) | 576.422 | (370.073) |
| Student disengagement | −0.071 | (5.212) | −28.073*** | (8.281) | −4.991 | (12.403) |
| Classroom disruption | −1.636 | (5.827) | −3.080 | (7.977) | −25.352 | (14.597) |
| Victimization | −26.871† | (14.289) | 32.240 | (26.667) | −50.250† | (28.256) |
| Constant | 1,064.588*** | (79.249) | 1,147.416*** | (114.119) | 280.561 | (377.292) |
| *Variance components* | | | | | | |
| Between-school | 1,333.49 | | 1,760.89 | | 897.18 | |
| Within-school | 9,081.33 | | 8,064.76 | | 8,140.19 | |
| Intraclass correlation | .128 | | .179 | | .099 | |
| *N* | 2,685 | | 1,624 | | 1,088 | |
| Pseudo $R^2$ | .0202 | | .0190 | | .0154 | |
| Bayesian information criterion | 36,312.219 | | 22,635.776 | | 6,118.297 | |

NOTE: Standard errors are in parentheses.

† $p < .10$; * $p < .05$; ** $p < .01$; *** $p < .001$.

Alternatively, school administrators, teachers, and students may have less accurate information about disciplinary problems in public schools, inducing attenuation bias due to measurement error.

## CONCLUSION

We return now to the three main questions guiding this analysis: (1) What are school-level determinants of disciplinary climate in Chilean schools? (2) Is discipline related to student educational achievement, and does it explain the substantial test score gap between public, private-voucher, and private-paid schools? (3) Does the relationship between school disciplinary climate and student performance vary across school sectors?

Beginning with the first question, our results suggest a weak association between school socioeconomic composition and disciplinary climate in Chile. Despite high levels of inequality in the country, more affluent schools do not appear to impose more discipline on their pupils. An alternative explanation for the weak socioeconomic stratification of school discipline may have to do with different expectations about student behavior depending on the socioeconomic composition of the school. In particular, teachers and principals in schools with more resources may have higher disciplinary standards and report infractions accordingly. However, the weak socioeconomic gradient that emerges for student reports of victimization casts doubt on this hypothesis.

In contrast with the weak stratification of disciplinary climates, there is a substantial association between school location and discipline, such that rural schools and those in small communities have fewer disciplinary problems. We speculate that different types of socialization and levels of community control account for these differences.

We find also that private schools are associated with more positive disciplinary climates than public ones. Specifically, classroom disruption and student victimization is less frequent in private schools—after taking into account the schools' socioeconomic and demographic factors. This finding suggests that private schools may be more capable of promoting and enforcing orderly behavior. Before reaching a conclusive answer, however, controls for unobserved selectivity of pupils attending private schools should be incorporated into future work, to account for private schools' ability to screen, select, and expel students much more easily than public schools and for the Chilean voucher system providing a strong incentive to cream skim the best students.

Our second question addresses the potential influence of school discipline on student performance. The findings indicate that this association is moderate. There is a negative association with student disengagement—frequency of students' arriving late, being absent, and skipping classes, based on principals' reports—but no influence of classroom disruption and student victimization on test score. Not surprisingly then, school disciplinary climates do not substantially contribute to the achievement gap between public, private-voucher, and private-paid schools. In fact, our analysis shows that the SES composition of schools alone largely explains the achievement gap across school sectors.

Interesting differences emerge across sectors, however. The overall association between student disengagement and achievement is driven by a strong relationship in private-voucher schools. The relationship between school disciplinary climate and student performance is weakest in the public sector. We speculate that this is due to a threshold effect similar to what has been suggested for the influence of school resources on achievement: discipline may matter only after more basic pedagogical, economic, and administrative needs have been fulfilled, as could be the case in more affluent private schools.

As in any analysis based on subjective reports, we see our findings as an initial step in the examination of correlates and outcomes of school discipline in Chile. Even if the descriptive results from the TIMSS dataset are consistent with other national and international surveys, thus providing reassurance about their validity, studies using administrative reports of disciplinary climates would be an important addition. Furthermore, we have restricted our measurement of educational achievement to test scores. While we acknowledge that this is an important outcome, particularly in terms of individual economic returns (Hanushek and Woessman 2007), the formative role of schools arguably transcends the cultivation of skills measured by test scores and includes the teaching of values such as tolerance and respect and the shaping of responsible citizens. Our analysis provides a motivation to look at the association between school discipline and other dimensions of the benefits of education.

## NOTES

1. "Children Are Taking Guns" appeared in *El Mercurio* March 26, 2000; "Chaotic Students" appeared in *La Nación* October 1, 2004; and "Violence among ABC1 Students" was investigative journalism broadcast on Chilevisión in August 2004.

2. Since 2008 the voucher also includes a means-tested voucher (*subvención preferencial*) for low-income students.

3. Percentages of adolescents who have been involved in a physical fight in other countries in this project and the GSHS are Canada 48 percent, United States 48 percent, Italy 57 percent, Israel 61 percent, and Russia 65 percent (Pickett et al. 2005).

4. The proportions for other nations included in this volume are as follows: Russia 34 percent United States 32 percent, Canada 30 percent, Italy 28 percent, Netherlands 26 percent, Israel 16 percent, South Korea 13 percent, and Japan 4 percent.

5. The study surveyed 14,761 students and 3,670 teachers from 7th to 12th grades.

6. Immigrant students' country of origin is also different across school sectors; in public schools immigrant students are mostly working-class Peruvians, but in private-paid institutions they are usually the children of foreign college-educated professionals temporarily relocated to Chile.

## REFERENCES

Akiba, M., G. K. LeTendre, and J. P. Scribner. 2007. "Teacher Quality, Opportunity Gap, and National Achievement in 46 Countries." *Educational Researcher* 36 (7): 369–87.

Alexander, K., J. Fennessey, E. McDill, and R. D'Amico. 1979. "School SES Influences—Composition or Context? *Sociology of Education* 52 (4): 222–37.

Alexander, K., and A. Pallas. 1985. "School Sector and Cognitive Performance: When Is a Little a Little?" *Sociology of Education* 58 (2): 115–28.

Anand, P., A. Mizala, and A. Repetto. 2009. "Using School Scholarships to Estimate the Effect of Private Education on the Academic Achievement of Low-Income Students in Chile." *Economics of Education Review* 28, no. 3 (June): 370–81.

Aron, A. 2000. "An Education Program for Non-violent Behavior." *Psykhe* 9 (2).

Aron, A., and N. Milicic. 1999. *School Climate and Personal Development.* Santiago: Andres Bello.

Arum, R. 2003. *Judging School Discipline.* Cambridge, MA: Harvard University Press.

Baker, D., B. Goesling, and G. LeTendre. 2002. "Socioeconomic Status, School Quality and National Economic Development: A Cross-National Analysis of the 'Heyneman-Loxley Effect' on Mathematics and Science Achievement." *Comparative Education Review* 46 (3): 291–312.

Bourdieu, P. 1984. *Distinction: A Social Critique of the Judgment of Taste.* London: Routledge.

Briceño Leon, R., A. Villaveces, and A. Concha-Eastman. 2008. "Understanding the Uneven Distribution of the Incidence of Homicide in Latin America." *International Journal of Epidemiology* 37 (4): 751–57.

Castillo-Feliu, G. 2000. *Culture and Customs of Chile.* Westport, CT: Greenwood Press.

CEP. 2004, 2006, 2008. *Public Opinion National Survey.* Machine readable dataset. Santiago: CEP.

Coleman, J., and T. Hoffer. 1987. *Public and Private High Schools: The Impact of Communities*, New York: Basic Books.

Cox, C., and M. Lemaitre. 1999. "Market and State Principles of Reform in Chilean Education: Policies and Results." Chap. 4 in *Chile: Recent Policy Lessons and Emerging Challenges*, edited by G. Perry and D. Leipzinger. Washington, DC: World Bank.

De Ferranti, D., G. Perry, F. Ferreira, and M. Walton. 2004. *Inequality in Latin America. Breaking with History?* Washington, DC: World Bank.

Downes, T., and T. Pogue. 1994. "Adjusting School Aid Formulas for the Higher Cost of Educating Disadvantaged Children." *National Tax Journal* 47 (1): 89–110.

Due, P., J. Merlo, Y. Harel-Fisch, M. Damsgaard, B. Holstein, J. Hetland, C. Currie, S. N. Gabhainn, M. Gaspar de Matos, and J. Lynch. 2009. "Socioeconomic Inequality in the Exposure to Bullying during Adolescence: A Comparative, Cross-Sectional, Multilevel Study in 35 countries." *American Journal of Public Health* 99 (5): 907–14.

Duncombe, W., and J. Yinger. 2000. "Financing Higher Student Performance Standards: The Case of New York State." *Economics of Education Review* 19:363–86.

Elacqua, G. 2006. "Public, Catholic, and For-Profit School Enrollment Practices in Response to Vouchers: Evidence from Chile." Research paper 125, National Center for the Study of Privatization in Education, Teachers College, Columbia University.

Fleming, L, and K. Jacobsen. 2009. "Bullying and Symptoms of Depression in Chilean Middle School Students." *Journal of School Health* 79 (3): 130–37.

Flores, L. 2008. "Keys to Improve Learning Using 'School Coexistence' Strategies to Improve Educational Quality." Final report FONIDE Project. Santiago: Ministry of Education.

Garcia-Huidobro, E. 2000. "Educational Policies and Equity in Chile." Chap. 7 in *Unequal Schools, Unequal Chances*, edited by F. Reimers. Cambridge, MA: Harvard University Press.

Gutiérrez, T., and C. Caviedes. 2006. *Revolución Pinguina: La Primera Gran Movilización del Siglo XXI en Chile* [The Penguin Revolution: The First Large Mobilization in the 21st Century in Chile]. Santiago: Ayun.

Hanushek, E., and L. Woessman. 2007. "The Role of Education Quality in Economic Growth." Policy Research Working Paper 4122. Washington, DC: World Bank.

Hempel, K. 2007. "Youth Activism in Chile—Why Do Chilean Youth Choose Open Street Protests as Their Common Method of Political Expression?" Working Document. Baltimore, MD: School of Advanced International Studies, Johns Hopkins University.

Hsieh, C., and M. Urquiola. 2006. "The Effect of Generalized School Choice on Achievement and Stratification: Evidence from Chile's School Voucher Program." *Journal of Public Economics* 90:1477–503.

Lara, B., A. Mizala, and A. Repetto. 2011. "The Effectiveness of Private Voucher Education: Evidence from Structural School Switches." *Educational Evaluation and Policy Analysis* 33 (2): 119–37.

Lareau, A. 2003. *Unequal Childhoods: Class, Race, and Family Life*. Berkeley: University of California Press.

Le Blanc, L., R. Swisher, F. Vitaro, and R. Tremblay. 2008. "High School Social Climate and Antisocial Behavior: A 10 Year Longitudinal and Multilevel Study." *Journal of Research on Adolescence* 18 (3): 395–419.

Lee, V., and A. Bryk. 1989. "A Multilevel Model of the Social Distribution of High School Achievement." *Sociology of Education* 62 (3): 172–92.

Lee, V., T. Chow-Hoy, D. Burkam, D. Geverdt, and B. Smerdon. 1998. "Sector Differences in High School Course Taking: A Private School or Catholic School Effect?" *Sociology of Education* 71:314–35.

Llana, M., and E. Escudero. 2003. *Students and Teachers: Implications of Misunderstanding*. Mimeo. Santiago: University of Chile.

Londono, J., and R. Guerrero. 1999. "Violence in Latin America: Epidemiology and Costs." Working document R375. Washington, DC: Inter-American Development Bank.

Ma, X., and J. D. Willms. 2004. "School Disciplinary Climate: Characteristics and Effects on Eighth Grade Achievement." *Alberta Journal of Educational Research* 50:169–89.

Madriaza, P. 2006. "Sentido social de la violencia escolar transformaciones culturales en el discurso marginal de los que están sujetos de la violencia." Master's thesis. University of Chile, Santiago.

McEwan, P. 2001. "The Effectiveness of Public, Catholic, and Non-Religious Private Schools in Chile's Voucher System." *Economics of Education* 9 (2): 103–28.

Mideplan. 1990. *Social Characterization Survey*. Santiago: Ministry of Planning.
———. 2006a. "Situacion de la Pobreza en Chile (Poverty Situation in Chile)." Working paper no. 1. Santiago: Ministry of Planning.
———. 2006b. *Social Characterization Survey*. Santiago: Ministry of Planning.
Ministry of Education and Universidad Alberto Hurtado. 2005. *National Survey of School Violence*. Santiago: Ministry of Education.
Mizala, A., and P. Romaguera. 2000. "School Performance and Choice: The Chilean Experience." *Journal of Human Resources* 35 (2): 392–417.
———. 2001. "Factores explicativos de los resultados escolares en la educación secundaria en Chile." *El Trimestre Económico* 68 (4): 515–49.
Mizala, A., and F. Torche. 2012. "Bringing the Schools Back In: The Stratification of Educational Achievement in the Chilean Voucher System." *International Journal of Educational Development* 32 (1): 132–44.
Morrison A., and L. Biehl. 1999. *The Cost of Silence: Domestic Violence in the Americas*. Washington, DC: Inter-American Development Bank.
Pickett, W., W. Craig, Y. Harel, J. Cunningham, K. Simpson, M. Molcho, J. Mazur, S. Dostaler, M. Overpeck, and C. Currie. 2005. "Cross-National Study of Fighting and Weapon Carrying as Determinants of Adolescent Injury." *Pediatrics* 116:855–63.
Raudenbush, S., and A. Bryk 1992. *Hierarchical Linear Models: Applications and Data Analysis*. Thousand Oaks, CA: Sage.
Reschovsky, A., and J. Imazeki. 2001. "Achieving Educational Adequacy through School Finance Reform." *Journal of Education Finance* 26:373–96.
Rodriguez, J., and C. Arriagada. 2004. "Residential Segregation in the Latin American City." *Eure* 29 (89): 5–24.
Rudatsikira, E., A. Muula, and S. Siziya. 2008. "Prevalence and Correlates of Physical Fighting among School-Going Adolescents in Santiago, Chile." *Revista Brasileira de Psiquiatria* 30 (3): 197–202.
Rumberger, R., and G. Palardy. 2004. "Multilevel Models for School Effectiveness Research." In *Handbook of Quantitative Methodology for the Social Sciences*, edited by D. Kaplan, 235–58. Thousand Oaks, CA: Sage.
———. 2005. "Does Segregation Still Matter? The Impact of Student Composition on Academic Achievement in High School." *Teachers College Record* 107 (9): 1999–2045.
Sapelli, C., and B. Vial. 2002. "The Performance of Private and Public Schools in the Chilean Voucher System." *Cuadernos de Economía* 39 (118): 423–54.
———. 2005. "Private vs Public Voucher Schools in Chile: New Evidence on Efficiency and Peer Effects." Working paper no. 289. Santiago: Department of Economics, Catholic University of Chile.
Schneider, C. 1995. *Shantytown Protests in Pinochet's Chile*. Philadelphia, PA: Temple University Press.
Stefoni, C. 2007. "Migration in the Chilean-Peruvian Agenda." In *Our Neighbors*, edited by M. Artaza and P. Milet, 551–64. Santiago: Ril.

Torche, F. 2005a. "Privatization Reform and Inequality of Educational Opportunity: The Case of Chile." *Sociology of Education* 78:316–43.

———. 2005b. "Unequal but Fluid Social Mobility in Chile in Comparative Perspective." *American Sociological Review* 70 (3): 422–50.

———. 2009. "Social Status and Cultural Consumption: The Chilean Case in Comparative Perspective." In *Social Status, Lifestyle and Cultural Consumption*, edited by T. W. Chan and J. Goldthorpe, 109–38. New York: Cambridge University Press.

UNDP. 1998. *The Paradoxes of Modernization. Human Development Report, Chile.* Santiago: UNDP.

Valenzuela, J. P., C. Bellei, and D. de los Rios. 2010. "Segregacion escolar en Chile." In *Cambios en la gobernanza del sistema educativo chileno,* edited by S. Martinic and G. Elacqua. Santiago: UNESCO and Pontificia Universidad Catolica de Chile.

Vegas, E. 2007. "Teacher Labor Markets in Developing Countries." *Future of Children* 17 (1): 219–32.

Vial, V. 1998. "Shared Financing of Education." *Cuadernos de Economia* 35 (106): 325–42.

WHO. 2009. *Global School-Based Health Survey (GSHS).* Geneva, Switzerland: WHO.

Willms, J. D. 1985. "Catholic-School Effects on Academic Achievement: New Evidence from the High School and Beyond Follow-Up Study." *Sociology of Education* 58 (2): 98–114.

World Values Survey. 2009. *World Values Survey 1981–2008*, official aggregate v. 20090901. Madrid: ASEP/JDS. Available at http://www.wvsevsdb.com/wvs/WVSData.jsp.

Zeron, A. M. 2006. "The Meaning of School Violence in Chile. An Interpretative Study." Master's thesis. Department of Education, Catholic University of Chile.

CHAPTER THREE

# School Discipline and Achievement in Israel

*Yossi Shavit and Carmel Blank*
*with the assistance of Idit Fast*

Israel is often said to be an unruly society. Formed through immigration and colonization, Israeli society is ethnically heterogeneous and conflict ridden. Although a welfare state, Israeli income inequality is higher than most European countries' and is similar to that reported for less developed countries. Many residents of the state, whether Jewish or Arab, religious or secular, subscribe to an oppositional culture that is contemptuous of authority and discipline and that celebrates defiance and cutting corners.

In addition to the macrosocial and cultural factors that affect civil obedience, specific characteristics of the school system in Israel are also conducive to lack of discipline among students. Classes are typically very large (except in religious schools, which generally benefit from more funding than nonreligious schools), teachers' salaries are low, and they often complain that it is difficult for them to maintain an effective and orderly learning environment. In most schools children call teachers by their first name and the class is a noisy place, where students volunteer answers by not hand raising but spontaneous outburst. In addition, the disciplinary sanctions that teachers can legally employ are limited. Ironically, Israel's progressive legislation is more concerned with students' rights to avoid disciplinary sanctions than it is with students' and teachers' rights to an orderly learning environment, although recently this attitude has been changing.

We first review discipline in Israeli culture and previous studies on school violence and discipline. This is followed by a more in-depth discussion on ethnoreligious diversity and conflict in Israel, background information on the Israeli school system, and a review of the institutional and legal context of school discipline in Israeli schools. We then summarize our main research questions, describe the dataset, and present the findings of our analysis. We conclude with a summary of the results and a methodological note.

## DISCIPLINE IN ISRAELI CULTURE

Sociological studies on Israeli and Jewish culture portray it as anything but conducive to discipline. A prominent feature of the society is the *sabra* culture, a native Jewish-Israeli youth culture that emerged in Palestine before and since the establishment of the Israeli state (Almog 1997, 2004). The term *sabra* refers to cactus fruit and is the nickname for the Israeli-born Jew who, like the fruit, is prickly on the outside and sweet on the inside. Stereotypically, the *sabra* is "young, naughty and rebellious" (Almog 1997, 18), independent, defiant, and daring. In reaction to what they consider to be the bogus civility of Diaspora Jews, the *sabra* adopt *Dugri* speech, a unique form of Hebrew that is direct, simple, and does not mince words (Katriel 1986). With no niceties or politenesses, *Dugri* speech is often taken by outsiders to be rude.

An important derivative of the *sabra* culture is the *smokh* (literally, "Trust me! Don't worry!") attitude pervasive in Israeli society (Kamir 1999). O. Kamir claims that this attitude was necessary in the state's early days, when formal institutions were still undeveloped and people resorted to improvised solutions to daily problems. The *smokh* attitude has little respect for procedure and discipline and is conducive to negligence, haste, and a haphazard way of doing things.

S. Smooha (cited in Mendel 2007) and A. Kfir (1997) trace the roots of Israeli disrespect for authority and lack of discipline to the Diaspora Jewish existence. Diaspora Jews were often surrounded by a hostile environment and developed a sense of alienation from the host country's laws and customs. Diaspora Jewish culture, both in Europe and the Arab world, relied on favors and dubious business deals designed to circumvent formal procedure (Kfir 1997), and Jewish immigrants brought these attitudes and practices to Israel.

These cultural attitudes toward discipline are reflected in a study of 52 countries that found that Israelis hold the lowest regard for authority (Hofstede 1994). In the 2000 World Values Survey, parents were asked to assess the importance of 11 skills and traits that children can acquire at home. Of Israeli parents, 84 percent thought that "tolerance and respect for others" were very important and 80 percent thought "good manners" were very important. But only 19 percent thought that "obedience" was a very important quality. The study also revealed striking differences in opinion between Arabs and Jews: while only 15 percent of Jews ranked obedience as very important, 65 percent of Arabs did so. This is consistent with previous research finding that Arab parents (Dwairy 1998) and teachers (Abu Sa'ad and Hendrix 1993) are more authoritarian on average than Jewish parents.

## DISCIPLINARY PRACTICES IN SCHOOLS

Israeli schools have never been strict. O. Almog (2004) describes Israeli education in its early years as informal and more liberal than in most European countries. Lack of uniforms, calling teachers by their first names, and noisy classrooms were prevalent then, as today.

Until recently, schools were free to set their own policy on discipline. Some have graded students for their behavior, while in others teachers were allowed to subtract points from students' final grade for unsatisfactory behavior in class. In 2007 the Ministry of Education issued directives requesting schools to grade students for their behavior in each subject, alongside their grade on performance (Ministry of Education 2007). In addition, the *bagrut* (matriculation) diploma includes a grade for behavior (although it is not included in the grade point average used when applying to colleges and universities). In addition, the ministry issued clear guidelines for schools to track and grade students' attendance. It is not clear whether, or to what extent, these directives are followed by schools. There seems to be a wide discrepancy between the directives and actual practice in schools (Forman 1994; Yakobson 1995).

Except for these directives, we were unable to find documentation, either academic or official, of the actual practice of disciplinary enforcement in schools. The Students Rights Law, enacted in 2000, sets limitations on student expulsion and transfer to other schools, and we can only assume that these practices are now rare. Corporal punishment is forbidden, as is excluding students from school activities such as trips (Students Rights Law 2000). Teachers can still warn students, rebuke them, and summon parents, and as any parent knows, these practices are common and quite effective.

Y. Katz and K. Yablon (2001) studied public opinion regarding the school system and found that 77 percent of the public are dissatisfied with the level of discipline in schools: 80 percent believe that the Israeli school system is inept at handling violence and alcohol and drug problems. Teacher surveys show that school discipline and violence are very high among their concerns (Smith and Pniel 2003), and 64 percent claim they are ill equipped to handle discipline and violence problems and wanted more authority.

Interestingly, in recent years the disciplinary practices in schools changed in both directions. On the one hand, the Students Rights Law imposed limitations on the use of punishment, while on the other hand, many schools now insist on more rigid dress and behavioral codes than before. In 2006 about 80 percent of schools request students to rise when the teacher enters the class, and about 70 percent request uniforms or some other form of standard dress code (Trabelsi-Hadad, 2006). Some schools even practice morning formation, including physical exercise and raising the national flag. However, in this study, we analyze data collected in 2003, before these practices were introduced.

## ISRAELI STUDIES OF SCHOOL VIOLENCE AND DISCIPLINE

School violence has received considerable attention by scholars in Israel, but other aspects of school discipline have received less attention. Research indicates that during the late 1990s and early 2000s a relatively large number of students were affected by school violence and that there has been no significant decline over time (Harel et al. 2002; Benbenishty et al., 2006a). R. Benbenishty, M. Khoury-Kassabri, and R. A. Astor (2006a) report that nearly 80 percent of students in grades 4 to 11 have been exposed to recent verbal or indirect social violence (such as gossip), nearly 60 percent have been exposed to moderate physical violence, and 20 percent have been exposed to severe physical violence. R. A. Astor and colleagues (2006) find that nearly 16 percent of elementary school students skipped school at least once in the past month because they feared victimization by other students.

Subgroup analyses indicate that rates of victimization are higher for certain groups of students. Arabs are more vulnerable than Jews to most forms of violence, especially severe physical violence, with Arabs being almost twice as likely to suffer victimization as Jews (28 percent of Arabs versus 16 percent of Jews; Benbenishty, Khoury-Kassabri, and Astor 2006a, 2006b). Analyses of change over time reveal some decline in the rates of violence among Jews between the 1990s and the 2000s, but among Arabs rates are stable and possibly even increase (Harel, Molcho, and Tillinger 2003; Benbenishty, Khoury-Kassabri, and Astor 2006b). Like Arabs, students from lower- to middle-class backgrounds are more likely to suffer from school violence than those from more privileged social backgrounds (Khoury-Kassabri 2002; Khoury-Kassabri, Astor, and Benbenishty 2009). Further, all studies indicate that girls are less likely to be victimized than boys (Benbenishty, Khoury-Kassabri, and Astor 2006; Harel, Molcho, and Tillinger 2003; Harel et al. 2002, Laufer and Harel 2003).

In addition to student-level characteristics, several school-level variables have been associated with school violence. For example, school violence is more prevalent in primary schools than in middle and upper secondary schools (e.g., Benbenishty, Khoury-Kassabri, and Astor 2006a; Harel et al. 2002). Furthermore, the level of violence is inversely related to the socioeconomic composition of the school's student body (e.g., Khoury-Kassabri et al. 2009; Khoury-Kassabri et al. 2005), while violence and disruption are inversely related to the school's proportion of female students (Lavy and Schlosser 2007). Larger schools are associated with more violence (Khoury-Kassabri et al. 2009), but levels of violence are lower in schools with clear policies on violence (Khoury-Kassabri et al. 2005; Harel, Molcho, and Tillinger 2003). Finally, there is somewhat more violence in Arab schools than in Jewish schools, largely due to socioeconomic composition (Khoury-Kassabri, Benbenishty, and Astor 2005), and there are small differences between religious and nonreligious Jewish schools (Benbenishty, Khoury-Kassabri, and Astor 2006a, 2006b; Khoury-Kassabri 2002).

Several studies compare Israeli school violence to violence in other countries. For example, R. Benbenishty and R. A. Astor (2005) compared Israel to California and found higher levels of violence in the former. Further, as part of an international study funded largely by the World Health Organization, Y. Harel and his associates (2002) studied health behavior in school-age children and collected information on victimization. Of the 28 countries included in the project, Israel ranked 8th in percentage of students who had been victimized in the preceding year and 11th in percentage of students who had bullied or harassed other students. With respect to victimization and violence, Israel ranked higher than Canada or the United States but was on par with Russia (Harel et al. 2002, 184–91).

In comparison to the extensive research on school violence in Israel, data on other aspects of school discipline are scant. In one of the few studies to include disciplinary climate measures, Harel and colleagues (2003) found that almost half middle school students were absent from school at least once in the previous year and that 25 percent of students were absent for more than three days. They also found that Jewish students are absent twice as often as Arab students. Aside from this study, we were unable to find research on school discipline using representative data that provided information on the prevalence of other forms of school disciplinary infractions. Thus, our study is pioneering in this regard.

## CONTEXT

### *Population Heterogeneity: Social Diversity, Inequality, and Conflict*

The main axis of social diversity, inequality, and conflict lies between Israel's Jewish and Arab communities. Israel's population is about 7.3 million people, excluding the inhabitants of the occupied West Bank and the Golan Heights. About 75 percent of the population identify themselves as Jews (whether ethnically, nationally, or religiously), and about 20 percent are Palestinian Arabs comprising Sunni Muslims (80 percent of Arabs), Christians (10 percent), and Druze (10 percent). Arabs and Jews have been engaged in a bitter, often violent, political conflict for decades. The State of Israel is founded on hegemonic Zionist ideology, which views it as a Jewish nation-state based on the memory of the ancient Jewish civilization that existed in the region during the first and second millennia BC. It was also founded as a haven for Jews who have been persecuted by anti-Semitism, which has been prevalent worldwide and peaked in the Shoah (the genocide by Nazi Germany of approximately six million Jews during World War II). Israel was formally recognized by the United Nations in 1947 but barely withstood a massive military onslaught by several Arab armies. From the Arab perspective, Zionism is viewed as an occupying colonial movement that has sought to drive out the indigenous Palestinian population and gain control of Palestinian land for the establishment of a racist and exclusionary Jewish society (Smooha 2002; Ghanem 1998).

Caught in the broader Israeli-Arab conflict, Palestinians are viewed by many Israeli Jews as a hostile minority and are exposed to overt discrimination both collectively and individually. Collective discrimination is most pronounced in the allocation of public resources and the provision of social services to citizens living in Arab communities (e.g., Swirski and Yecheskel 1999). Individually, Arabs are overtly discriminated against in the competition for lucrative jobs in Jewish-owned firms and businesses and for jobs in the civil service (Semyonov and Cohen 1990; Shavit 1990; Lewin-Epstein and Semyonov 1994; Kraus and Yonay 2000). Israel's Palestinian Arabs would appear to fit S. Fordham and J. U. Ogbu's (1986) definition of a nonvoluntary minority group (Eisikovits 1997), and as such one might expect Arab students to resist the state, to have little regard for the law and authority of the state, and to behave in an oppositional manner in schools.

In addition to Arab-Jewish inequalities, there are striking inequalities between ethnic groups within the Jewish population, most notably between *Ashkenazim* and *Mizrahim*. When the State of Israel was proclaimed, the majority of its Jewish population was of European origin (*Ashkenazim*). Historically, European Jewry was relatively well educated and middle class. With the creation of the state, many immigrants arrived—including Jewish refugees and Holocaust survivors from Europe and Jews from Middle Eastern countries (Sikron 1957; Goldscheider 2002). Immigrants from Arabic-speaking Middle Eastern countries were referred to as *Mizrahim* (literally, "eastern"). Their average educational level was lower than that of *Ashkenazim*, especially among women, and they were viewed by *Ashkenazim* as undeveloped and less modern (Swirsky 1990). Many *Mizrahi* immigrants were forced to settle in the undeveloped periphery of the country, where the provision of education and other social services was poorer than in urban centers. As a consequence of both the initial educational differences between the two groups and discrimination, large inequalities developed between the two ethnic blocs.

Economic inequality in Israel is quite high compared with Western democracies. In 2006 the Gini coefficient for pretax economic income in Israel was 0.38 (Adva Center 2007), higher than most economically developed democracies (Wikipedia 2009).[1] It should be noted, however, that the Israeli welfare state, through progressive taxation and various transfer payments, is quite effective in reducing inequality in net income (Endeweld, Fruman, and Gottlieb 2008).

Finally, there is the cleavage between more recent immigrants and those longer in the country. Since 1989 alone, about one million immigrants have come from the former Soviet Union (FSU). Immigrants from the FSU are likely to be educated, and many of them hold professional, semiprofessional, or technical occupations. Their children do well in school, with grades similar to those of native Jewish students (Kristen et al., n.d.). However, S. Chachashvili-Bolotin (2007) reports that immigrant students from FSU families are more likely than natives to drop out of school and suggests this may be due to the difficulties that some immigrant students encounter in adapting to the new and often denigrating local culture. Following this logic, we hypothesize that disciplinary infractions and violence will be more prevalent in schools attended by large proportions of immigrants.

*Organizational Structure: The Israeli School System*

The Israeli educational system reflects the divisions of the different populations we have described. Arabs and Jews are highly segregated in the school system, as in Israeli society at large. Most Arab students attend Arabic schools (Al-Haj 1995), and virtually all Jews attend Hebrew schools. Very few students, especially in Jaffa and other ethnically mixed towns, attend ethnically mixed schools. The Hebrew school system consists of three main sectors: nonreligious public schools that are made up of about 55 percent Jewish students, religious public schools that are made up of about 20 percent Jewish students, and ultra-orthodox independent schools. Both religious and ultra-orthodox schools are largely funded by the state but enjoy a great deal of cultural and administrative autonomy.[2] Unlike ultra-orthodox schools, all religious public schools are supervised by the state and comply with the core curricular requirements of the Ministry of Education, although they place special emphasis on religious studies. In both forms of religious education, girls and boys attend separate schools. In fact, only religious schools separate boys and girls.

Most Arabs attend public schools (there are no public religious Arab schools), but a sizable minority of Arab students, both Christian and Muslim, attend private parochial Christian schools founded by various Christian denominations, which are generally regarded as better quality than the public schools.

At age 12, after a year in preschool and six years in primary school, most Israeli children enter middle schools, where they spend grades 7, 8, and 9. Middle school is followed by upper secondary school in grades 10 through 12. Students in secondary school can choose between the academic track, which prepares them for academic studies, and the vocational track, which combines academic and vocational training. Vocational tracks are usually attended by scholastically weaker students who have not done well in middle school. Both tracks prepare students for the matriculation examinations leading to the *bagrut* diploma required for higher education; however, matriculation rates to higher education are much higher for students in the academic track (Ayalon and Shavit 2004). Overall, 50 percent of the birth cohort obtains a *bagrut*.

Israeli education is severely underfunded. When standardized per student and purchasing power parity (PPP) the Israeli expenditure for education is low. In 2008 the Israeli annual expenditure per student was $6,885, compared to the OECD mean of $8,831. The corresponding figures for expenditures on primary education are $5,314 versus $7,153 and $6,429 versus $8,972 at the secondary level (OECD 2011).

Underfunding has two important implications: classes are large and teachers are underpaid. At the primary level, the average class size in Israel for public, religious, and ultra-orthodox schools is 27.4 students, compared with the OECD average of 21.4; at the lower secondary level, the average is 32.2, compared with 23.7.[3] In addition, there are marked inequalities in class size between the secular public schools (30.2) and the religious schools (25.1) and between Arab (31.2) and Jewish public schools (27.4; Vergan 2007). The OECD (2011) computes the ratio of teacher salary after 15 years of experience to gross domestic product per capita. The OECD mean ratio varies between 1.15 and 1.25 at the primary and secondary school levels. In Israel it is much lower, between 0.96 and 0.98.[4]

### *The Legal Context and Public Discourse on School Discipline*

In this section, we review discussions of school discipline and school violence in the following important arenas: the debates of the Knesset (the Israeli parliament) Committee for Education, Culture and Sports; the Students Rights Law; the blue-ribbon commission on school violence, the Vilnayi Commission; and the directives of the director general of the Ministry of Education that formulate the concrete policies of the ministry. We conclude the section with a discussion of the public discourse on school discipline in the media.

When the Knesset is in session, the Committee for Education, Culture and Sports assembles several times a week. Participating are Knesset members; educational professionals, many from the Ministry of Education; and parent representatives. If needed, professionals from other fields are invited, such as police officers, psychologists, and social workers. We searched the protocols of the committee for the last 10 years (1998–2008)[5] for the terms "school discipline" (*mishma-at* in Hebrew) and "violence" (*alimut* in Hebrew). We found six sessions in which school discipline was discussed. Of these, only two sessions focused on school discipline (and violence) and the other four dealt with the Students Rights Law, which we discuss later. School violence, on the other hand, was a more prominent issue discussed in 20 meetings of the committee.[6]

Two committee protocols dealt with Israeli students' low test scores in the 2000 Program for International Student Assessment (PISA) and focused on the relevance of school discipline to student achievement (protocol 96, November 19, 2003; protocol 152, December 28, 2004). Committee members agreed that how Israel handles school violence and discipline is a serious problem and that school violence is likely related to the poor PISA test results. In most of the protocols that we examined, there was also agreement among committee members that the main reason for these problems is lack of teacher authority in Israel: "The teacher doesn't have any authority. . . . There are no deterring means in schools, [and] teachers are afraid to confront students on the most ordinary things" (Shilgy, protocol 47, November 19, 2003). It seems that teachers are caught in a bind between the students, parents, headmasters, and students' rights and do not receive institutional support when attempting to deal with undisciplined or violent students (e.g., protocol 96, November 19, 2003; protocol 90, March 27, 2000; protocol 210, December 11, 2000).

The lack of respect for teachers, and for authority in general, was also lamented: "We live in a time in which there is tolerance for smashing all the values . . . even ones we used to respect" (Karni, protocol 152, January 18, 2004). An important part of the discussions in the committee centered on whether responsibility for these problems should be placed with parents, who do not educate their children well; the Ministry of Education, which does not provide clear directives to teachers; or the schools, which focus too much of their energy on reaching achievement standards and not enough on values. The discussions ended with a call to the Ministry of Education to state clearer policies concerning school discipline (Shilgy, protocol 152, January 18, 2004; Orlev, protocol 3, July 26, 1999; protocol 90, March 27, 2000; protocol 391, January 9, 2002). While the committee did initiate some legislation to address the subject of school violence, no concrete legislative steps were taken on the matter of school discipline.

By contrast, and ironically, Knesset was more effective in legislating the Students Rights Law, which severely curtails the practice of expulsion as a disciplinary sanction in schools. Passed in 2000 and amended in 2004, the law aimed to "establish principles defending student's rights in the spirit of human dignity and the principles of the UN Children's Rights Convention" (Students Rights Law 2000, par. 1). The law as it now reads begins with the 2004 amendment, which states that all students and their parents must be informed about students' rights and the ministry's guidelines concerning the need for mutual respect, discipline, and prevention of violence in school (Students Rights Law, amendment, 2004). The amendment, "On the Dignity of Education Workers," was introduced as an attempt to appease the teachers' representatives, who claimed that the bulk of the law severely curtails teachers' authority (protocol 73, February 14, 2000). The amendment was adopted despite the opposition of parent organizations, who argued that "if the teacher can't handle the student and educate him, then maybe he shouldn't be a teacher" (Arjuany, protocol 339, November 30, 2004). Most committee members agreed with the teachers' perspective that the law does little to help them enforce discipline.

The law prohibits corporal punishment and exclusion of students from school activities such as class trips. The most important section in the law concerns procedures for expelling students or transferring them to another school. In both cases the student and the parents have the right to a hearing before a regional committee consisting of representatives of the school district and representatives of student and parent organizations. Parents have the right to appeal the committee's ruling, and the school cannot expel a student until after the hearing and appeal. Thus, the law makes it very difficult to expel or transfer students from school.[7] The law was passed despite considerable opposition from teachers and some parents who were concerned that schools were losing control of discipline and students were becoming unmanageable. In the summer of 2009, the Ministry of Education introduced an amendment to the law that essentially overturned the previous version. It allowed schools to quickly expel severely disruptive and violent students and hold the hearing and the appeal at a later date (Aharonovich 2009).

Much of the public discussion on school violence in Israel was generated by the Vilnayi Commission, which was appointed by the minister of Education in the late 1990s. The Vilnayi Commission was chartered to study the determinants of violence among students and to formulate policy recommendations. The commission sought input from academic scholars in the field (e.g., R. Benbenishty and Y. Harel) and adopted their ecological perspective on school violence. This perspective asserts that the prevalence of violence in schools is affected by student, family, school, and community factors. As a result, policies aimed at reducing violence among students call for cooperation between agents at these various levels to be effective. More importantly, the commission called on the ministry and school administrators to formulate clear guidelines on acceptable disciplinary sanctions that could be employed to curtail disciplinary infractions and school violence.

As is common in Israeli public administration, the commission's recommendations were not fully implemented, but a few were included in several of the Ministry of Education director general's communiqués (Ministry of Education, December 1, 2000, November 1, 2007). The communiqués called on school principals to engage parents, teachers, and students in the formulation of clear school policies regarding discipline and violence. It also listed the sanctions that schools and teachers are permitted to use when dealing with unruly and violent students.[8] One of the more concrete instructions issued by the director general was to include discipline scores on student report cards (November 1, 2007), but it is not clear how far, or if at all, these directives are enforced by schools.

Reading the protocols of the Vilnayi Commission, one is struck by the familiar tension between the will to curb violence and disciplinary infractions on the one hand and the desire to safeguard student rights and dignity on the other. Historically, legislation, directives, and public discourse tend to emphasize individual rights and provide teachers with very few effective sanctions with which to enforce discipline in schools. However, an amendment to the Students Rights Law may tilt the balance toward more effective disciplinary measures. In August 2009 Ministry of Education communiqués introduced new, presumably stricter, rules to handle violent or undisciplined students. The ministry requires schools to create rules about school norms, including appearance and classroom behavior. The process for handling disciplinary infractions follows the familiar steps of talking to students, warning them, informing parents, and so on, and it also allows a few days' suspension in severe cases of class disruption or repeated misbehavior by a student (Ministry of Education, August, 2009, section 3.2.5). This is the first attempt to establish clear rules for schools regarding school discipline and a clear acknowledgment of the importance of positive disciplinary climates. As a member in the team assigned to change the law said, "We have debated a lot around the issue of individual rights versus team rights. . . . A child coming to school should be free to learn and not be occupied by being afraid of violent students" (Aharonovich, September 18, 2009).

An emphasis on student rights over an orderly and safe learning environment also emerges from our study of media discussions on school discipline. We scanned 10 years of back issues of Israel's two main daily newspapers, *Ha'aretz* and *Yediot Aharonot*, and searched them for articles in which "discipline" or "violence" occurred with "school" or "education" and analyzed all resulting articles. We found only 16 articles on school discipline and 26 articles on school violence.[9] Of the 16 articles on discipline, none appeared on the first page and all but one appeared after page 7, suggesting that school discipline is not a top priority for newspaper editors. On the other hand, a majority of the articles (10) were longer than half a page, indicating that editors believed the topic had some public interest. Of the articles on discipline, 7 discussed student absences from school, 3 discussed uniforms in schools, and 2 focused on the Ministry of Education's decision to grade students for behavior. Considering the broad media coverage of Israel's poor performance in the PISA and Trends in International Mathematics and Science Study (TIMSS), one would have expected to see considerable attention given to behavioral infractions that may disrupt learning and lower student achievement, such as tardiness, talking out of turn, or using cell phones in class. Instead, we found that the main concern was students' individual rights, including opposition to the uniform requirement.

Another goal of our media analysis was to examine who the articles blamed for disciplinary problems in schools. About half the articles suggested that school staff was responsible for student behavior and should enforce discipline. Two articles held the Ministry of Education responsible for not providing teachers with the necessary tools to enforce discipline. Only two articles held students responsible for their behavior, and two articles blamed parents for their children's misbehavior.

The press reflects public opinion, in which almost 80 percent are dissatisfied with the level of discipline in schools (Katz and Yablon 2001). The same proportion, 80 percent, believe that the Israeli school system is inept at handling violence and alcohol and drug problems. Teacher surveys show that 64 percent of teachers claim they are ill equipped to handle discipline and violence problems and want more authority to deal with these (Smith and Pniel 2003).

## ANALYSIS

### *Research Questions*

Our study is the first to use representative data on school discipline in Israel. Using the Israeli TIMSS 2003 dataset we study the determinants of disciplinary infractions and victimization in Israeli schools. We also study the effect of disciplinary climate in schools and classrooms on student achievement in math and science, their educational expectations, and their victimization in schools.

### *Data*

The Israeli TIMSS 2003 dataset includes information for approximately 4,300 eighth grade students in 146 schools. The schools were sampled in three strata: Arab schools (38 schools), nonreligious Jewish schools (69 schools), and religious Jewish schools (39 schools). In each school, questionnaires and tests were administered to a science and a math class. In addition, data were obtained from about 390 math and science teachers and from the principals of the sampled schools (Martin, Mullis, and Chrostowski 2004). We analyze the data according to the methodological guidelines of the comparative project discussed in the introduction.

### *Findings*

In Table 3.1 we present Israeli descriptive statistics of the variables included in the study and compare their distributions to those of the other countries in this project. We compare the statistics for nonreligious Jewish public schools, religious Jewish public schools, and Arab schools. Comparing the total means for Israel to the means of the other countries in this comparative project reveals a striking result: Israeli students benefit from higher-than-average levels of parental education and more books in their homes.

Table 3.1
*Descriptive statistics*

| | Israel—All | | Nonreligious Jewish Schools | | Religious Jewish Schools | | Arab Schools | | All Project Countries | |
|---|---|---|---|---|---|---|---|---|---|---|
| | *Mean* | *SD* | *Mean* | *SD* | *Mean* | *SD* | *Mean* | *SD* | *Mean* | *SD* |
| STUDENT BACKGROUND | | | | | | | | | | |
| Male | 0.481 | 0.016 | 0.501 | 0.500 | 0.422 | 0.494 | 0.470 | 0.499 | 0.470 | 0.499 |
| Age | 14.032 | 0.455 | 14.073 | 0.454 | 13.981 | 0.465 | 13.963 | 0.439 | 13.963 | 0.439 |
| Immigrant status | 0.138 | 0.345 | 0.167 | 0.373 | 0.101 | 0.302 | 0.090 | 0.286 | 0.090 | 0.286 |
| Highest parental education | 5.706 | 1.937 | 6.128 | 1.766 | 5.991 | 1.946 | 4.637 | 1.880 | 5.302 | 0.029 |
| Number of books in household | 3.367 | 1.168 | 6.428 | 1.131 | 3.813 | 1.125 | 3.334 | 1.217 | 3.114 | 0.016 |
| Household size | 5.328 | 1.446 | 4.787 | 1.176 | 5.988 | 1.379 | 6.289 | 1.448 | 4.552 | 0.014 |
| College plans | 0.712 | 0.450 | 0.740 | 0.437 | 0.738 | 0.438 | 0.640 | 0.481 | 0.654 | 0.007 |
| SCHOOL AND COMMUNITY CHARACTERISTICS | | | | | | | | | | |
| School size (log) | 6.381 | 0.585 | 6.428 | 0.621 | 6.015 | 0.577 | 6.513 | 0.337 | 6.478 | 0.018 |
| School highest grade level | 9.864 | 1.480 | 9.661 | 1.424 | 10.813 | 1.527 | 9.791 | 1.371 | 9.450 | 0.041 |
| Community size | 3.346 | 1.330 | 3.654 | 1.263 | 3.631 | 1.415 | 2.401 | 0.931 | 3.916 | 0.042 |
| Male students | | | | | | | | | | |
| 46%–60% | 0.428 | 0.495 | 0.491 | 0.500 | 0.000 | 0.000 | 0.561 | 0.497 | 0.480 | 0.013 |
| >60% | 0.151 | 0.358 | 0.130 | 0.336 | 0.412 | 0.493 | 0.028 | 0.164 | 0.181 | 0.011 |
| Immigrant students | | | | | | | | | | |
| 1%–10% | 0.307 | 0.461 | 0.250 | 0.433 | 0.333 | 0.472 | 0.432 | 0.496 | 0.398 | 0.013 |
| >10% | 0.546 | 0.498 | 0.667 | 0.471 | 0.434 | 0.496 | 0.318 | 0.466 | 0.238 | 0.012 |
| Average parental education | 5.721 | 1.004 | 6.104 | 0.760 | 5.938 | 0.988 | 4.618 | 0.702 | 5.344 | 0.028 |
| Variation in parental education | 0.306 | 0.105 | 0.271 | 0.074 | 0.300 | 0.109 | 0.396 | 0.117 | 0.281 | 0.002 |

| | | | | | | | | | | |
|---|---|---|---|---|---|---|---|---|---|---|
| DISCIPLINARY CLIMATE | | | | | | | | | | |
| Principal reports: disciplinary disengagement | 2.847 | 0.913 | 3.038 | 0.893 | 2.898 | 0.888 | 2.319 | 0.760 | 2.756 | 0.028 |
| Teacher reports: classroom disruption | 3.609 | 0.669 | 3.697 | 0.657 | 3.436 | 0.785 | 3.501 | 0.564 | 3.312 | 0.021 |
| Student reports | | | | | | | | | | |
| Victimization, student level | 0.708 | 0.926 | 0.721 | 0.929 | 0.566 | 0.873 | 0.774 | 0.945 | 0.648 | 0.010 |
| Victimization, school level | 0.711 | 0.296 | 0.722 | 0.246 | 0.573 | 0.457 | 0.778 | 0.235 | 0.648 | 0.010 |
| COGNITIVE PERFORMANCE: MATH AND SCIENCE TEST SCORE | 983.848 | 151.425 | 998.197 | 153.529 | 1,012.204 | 140.399 | 928.835 | 139.474 | 1,028.096 | 3.252 |
| *N* | 4,318 | | 2,069 | | 1,093 | | 1,156 | | 50,381 | |

NOTE: SD = standard deviation.

Research has shown repeatedly (e.g., De Graaf, De Graaf, and Kraaykamp 2000) that these two variables are among the most important determinants of student achievement.

Therefore, we would have expected the achievement of Israeli students in math and science to be relatively high. However, as seen in the table, their test scores are 45 points lower than the test scores of students in the nine countries. This finding is consistent with results reported by other analyses of TIMSS and PISA, which have shown that Israeli mean scores rank below those of the most economically advanced countries but above most developing ones (e.g., Yogev, Livneh, and Feniger 2009).

Consistent with our review on discipline in Israeli society, Table 3.1 shows that Israeli students are less disciplined on average and are more likely to be victimized than the average student in the other eight countries. Our subsequent multivariate analyses examine the hypothesis that these low test scores are due to lack of school discipline. Our subgroup comparisons of the three sectors within the Israeli school system also reveal important differences: Arab parents are the least educated group in the sample, and they have fewer books in their homes but more people in their households. Religious families fall between nonreligious and Arab families with respect to parental education, books at home, and family size.

As one would expect, a large proportion of Israeli students are immigrants (14 percent compared with 9 percent in the nine-country sample) and more than half (55 percent) attend schools with student bodies that are more than 10% immigrant. Surprisingly, however, 9 percent of the Arab students in the sample were classified as immigrants and 31 percent attend schools in which more than 10 percent of students are immigrants. This seems peculiar because the common assumption is that Palestinians are an indigenous minority rather than an immigrant population. This finding may be because of the emigration of Palestinian families from the West Bank and Gaza into Israel proper. If one of the parents is an Israeli citizen, the children would report that at least one of their parents was born abroad (in Palestine), thus classifying them as immigrants. The finding may also be a result of measurement error (children are not always aware of their parent's birthplace) or to political semantics, whereby some Palestinian residents of Israel refer to it as Palestine, leading their answers to be coded as though they were born elsewhere.

Contrary to our hypothesis that Arab students may exhibit oppositional behavior in schools, Arab principals report lower levels of disciplinary disengagement than principals in the two Jewish sectors. However, Arab students report more victimization by other students (recall that virtually all Arab students attend all-Arab schools). Finally, and consistent with their lower socioeconomic background, the mean scholastic achievement of Arab students is lower than that of students in both religious and nonreligious Jewish schools.

The math and science scores of students attending religious Jewish schools are higher than the test scores of students in the other two sectors. This result coincides with research conducted by J. S. Coleman and his associates (Coleman, Hoffer, and Kilgore 1982; Coleman and Hoffer 1987), who argue that religious communities are more cohesive than secular ones and that teachers and principals in religious schools feel a strong commitment to serve their communities. In cohesive communities, there is also a high degree of mutual social control, and students attending religious schools are less likely to misbehave. This would suggest that the higher achievement of students in religious schools is in part because of the stricter disciplinary climate in their classrooms. However, contrary to this social capital hypothesis, we do not find large differences between religious and nonreligious Jewish schools in principal and teacher reports of discipline problems. Instead, only victimization is lower in religious schools.

In Table 3.2 we present Pearson correlations among the three measures of school discipline and between each of these variables and student test scores in math and science. Two results are noteworthy. First, although the correlations among the three indicators of discipline are significant, their magnitudes are very small. This suggests a Rashomon effect: the subjectivity of perception of the principals, teachers, and students of school discipline differ quite a bit. R. Benbenishty and R. A. Astor (2005) conducted several large surveys of students, teachers, and principals on school violence and victimization and also find medium to low correlations between the levels of school violence they each reported. In an unreported analysis, we factor analyzed the component questionnaire items that comprise the three indicators of school discipline and find that they tend to form factors that represent the respondent—principal, teacher, or student—rather than specific types of infractions (e.g., classroom disruption or violence among students). Evidently, as suggested by Benbenishty and Astor (2005), students,

TABLE 3.2
*Correlations of disciplinary and cognitive performance*

| | *Frequency of disciplinary disengagement* | *Frequency of classroom disruption* | *School-level student victimization index* |
|---|---|---|---|
| DISCIPLINARY CLIMATE | | | |
| Teacher reports: frequency of classroom disruption | 0.315*** | | |
| Student reports: victimization incidents, school level | 0.173*** | 0.277*** | |
| COGNITIVE PERFORMANCE: MATH AND SCIENCE TEST SCORE | −0.089*** | −0.200*** | −0.147*** |

NOTE: *** $p < .001$.

teachers, and principals experience school somewhat differently. Alternatively, the low correlations may suggest that the reliability of our measures of discipline is quite low. Table 3.2 also indicates that there is a negative, albeit weak, correlation between measures of school discipline and student test scores. In the multivariate analysis that follows we test whether these correlations withstand statistical controls or are spurious.

Turning now to Table 3.3, we present ordinary least squares regressions for the three indicators of discipline at the school level. The results suggest that there are fewer discipline problems in schools attended by students whose parents are well educated. The gender composition of the student body also affects discipline, such that having more male students in a school leads to more classroom disruption and victimization. Victimization is also more prevalent in schools attended by larger numbers of immigrants. Intriguingly, *ceteris paribus*, the school climate in Arab schools is more disciplined than in Jewish schools. Although the descriptive analysis indicates higher victimization rates in Arab schools, in the multivariate analysis victimization in these schools appears no higher than in the other sectors. This result is in line with the argument (Khoury-Kassabri, Benbenishty, and Astor 2005) that the greater violence experienced in Arab schools is due to their lower mean socioeconomic composition.

As Table 3.1 demonstrates, none of the students in religious Jewish schools attend mixed-sex schools. In addition, there is a strong relationship between school sector and the proportion of male students in the school.

TABLE 3.3

*Regression models estimating the effects of student- and school-level characteristics on disciplinary disengagement, classroom disruption, and school-level victimization*

| | *Frequency of disciplinary disengagement* | *Frequency of classroom disruption* | *School-level victimization* |
|---|---|---|---|
| SCHOOL AND COMMUNITY CHARACTERISTICS | | | |
| *School and community variables* | | | |
| School size (log) | 0.288* | −0.058 | −0.034 |
| | (0.144) | (0.112) | (0.059) |
| School highest grade level | −0.027 | 0.023 | 0.024 |
| | (0.056) | (0.043) | (0.020) |
| Community size | 0.057 | −0.056 | −0.014 |
| | (0.058) | (0.045) | (0.020) |
| *School-level student characteristics* | | | |
| Average parental education | −0.319* | −0.358** | −0.095 |
| | (0.155) | (0.120) | (0.054) |
| Variation in parental education | −0.848 | −1.752† | −0.134 |
| | (1.303) | (1.005) | (0.454) |
| STUDENT BODY CHARACTERISTICS | | | |
| *Male* | | | |
| 46%–60% | 0.212 | 0.370** | 0.205** |
| | (0.183) | (0.141) | (0.063) |
| >60% | 0.158 | 0.351* | 0.363*** |
| | (0.197) | (0.153) | (0.069) |
| *Immigrants* | | | |
| 0–10% | 0.199 | 0.068 | 0.152* |
| | (0.206) | (0.160) | (0.072) |
| >10% | 0.026 | 0.290 | 0.192** |
| | (0.196) | (0.153) | (0.069) |
| SCHOOL SECTOR | | | |
| Religious Jewish schools | −0.047 | −0.182 | −0.125 |
| | (0.202) | (0.155) | (0.069) |
| Arab schools | −1.217*** | −0.568** | −0.020 |
| | (0.244) | (0.189) | (0.084) |
| Intercept | 3.357* | 6.299*** | 1.018 |
| | (1.554) | (1.203) | (0.545) |
| $R^2$ | 0.190 | 0.145 | 0.331 |
| *N* | 140 | 145 | 146 |

NOTE: Standard errors are in parentheses. Missing covariates (with the exception of gender variables) are mean substituted; dummy variables flagging missing covariates are included in the analyses but not shown. Analyses are adjusted using weights provided by TIMSS.

† $p \geq .10$; * $p < .05$; ** $p < .01$; *** $p < .001$.

Religious Jewish schools are fully segregated by sex (except for one school in the sample). Arab schools have a mixed composition, but only one Arab school in the sample has more than 60 percent male students. Therefore, only 2.8 percent of Arab students attend schools in which 61 percent or more of the student body is male. Only the nonreligious Jewish schools have the full variation of gender composition. Therefore, the effects of gender composition of schools and school sector may be largely confounded, and it is possible that the positive effect of the proportion that is male is an effect of religious all-male schools. We explored this possibility by estimating school-level regressions of the three discipline variables within each of the three sectors. The results for the nonreligious schools are essentially similar to those in Table 3.3: positive and significant effects of 46–60 percent males and of more than 60 percent males on classroom disruption and on victimization, and insignificant effects on disciplinary disengagement. In the Arab schools, the effect of sex composition was positive and significant only for classroom disruption. Finally, among religious schools, victimization is much higher in all-male schools than in all-female schools, but no other significant effects of sex compositions on discipline were found. We conclude that school disciplinary disengagement, classroom disruption, and student victimization increase as the number of male students in the student body increases.

We run supplementary analyses that exclude sex composition from the three models and find that, compared to nonreligious Jewish schools, there are significantly lower disciplinary disengagement and classroom disruption in Arab schools, refuting the oppositional culture hypothesis stated earlier. We find lower classroom disruption and victimization also in religious schools. The results provide some, albeit weak, support for the hypothesis that religious schools are more cohesive and disciplined.

In Table 3.4 we present the results of hierarchical linear models of student test scores. The first model includes only student-level variables. Similar to other countries, boys score higher than girls on the math and science test. Younger students do better than older ones; presumably some of the older students are academically weaker and were held back a grade. Parental education and the number of books at home are positively associated with test scores, and immigrants score lower than natives.[10]

Model 2 in Table 3.4 adds several school-level predictors of student test scores to Model 1. The results indicate that the socioeconomic composition

TABLE 3.4

*Hierarchical linear models estimating the effects of student- and school-level characteristics on test score, college plans, and student victimization*

| | TEST SCORE | | | COLLEGE PLANS | STUDENT VICTIMIZATION |
|---|---|---|---|---|---|
| | *Model 1* | *Model 2* | *Model 3* | *Model 4* | *Model 5* |
| STUDENT BACKGROUND | | | | | |
| Male | 22.912*** | 23.200*** | 26.595*** | -0.200* | 0.348*** |
| | (4.011) | (3.996) | (4.058) | (0.104) | (0.030) |
| Age | -16.968*** | -17.179*** | -17.736*** | -0.059 | -0.082* |
| | (4.213) | (4.214) | (4.210) | (0.101) | (0.033) |
| Immigrant status | -23.554*** | -23.093*** | 21.739** | 0.020 | 0.192*** |
| | (5.734) | (5.746) | (5.749) | (0.140) | (0.044) |
| Highest parental education | 13.176*** | 12.057*** | 12.126*** | 0.307*** | 0.012 |
| | (1.253) | (1.264) | (1.262) | (0.033) | (0.010) |
| Number of books in household | 14.927*** | 14.570*** | 14.711*** | 0.098* | 0.016 |
| | (1.769) | (1.772) | (1.769) | (0.040) | (0.014) |
| Household size | -0.780 | -0.184 | -0.224 | -0.001 | -0.012 |
| | (1.493) | (1.506) | (1.504) | (0.038) | (0.012) |
| Math and science test score (combined) | | | | 0.006*** | |
| | | | | (0.000) | |
| SCHOOL AND COMMUNITY CHARACTERISTICS | | | | | |
| *School and community variables* | | | | | |
| School size (log) | | 14.820 | 10.983 | 0.007 | -0.114** |
| | | (11.127) | (11.205) | (0.129) | (0.043) |
| School highest grade level | | -6.351 | -5.443 | 0.043 | 0.029 |
| | | (4.561) | (4.436) | (0.047) | (0.018) |
| Community size | | 3.857 | 1.545 | -0.001 | 0.015 |
| | | (4.746) | (4.561) | (0.060) | (0.018) |
| *School-level student characteristics* | | | | | |
| Immigrants | | | | | |
| 1%–10% | | -5.027 | -1.336 | 0.091 | 0.064 |
| | | (16.838) | (16.133) | (0.179) | (0.065) |

*(continued)*

Table 3.4 *(continued)*

| | TEST SCORE | | | COLLEGE PLANS | STUDENT VICTIMIZATION |
|---|---|---|---|---|---|
| | *Model 1* | *Model 2* | *Model 3* | *Model 4* | *Model 5* |
| >10% | | −8.239 | 0.295 | 0.099 | 0.124† |
| | | (16.683) | (16.360) | (0.204) | (0.066) |
| Average parental education | | 64.747*** | 51.670*** | 0.132 | −0.070 |
| | | (12.339) | (12.202) | (0.106) | (0.049) |
| Variation in parental education | | 203.320† | 142.400 | 1.340 | −0.342 |
| | | (105.690) | (101.860) | (1.054) | (0.410) |
| Religious Jewish schools | | 18.509 | 7.810 | −0.148 | −0.124† |
| | | (15.846) | (15.615) | (0.179) | (0.064) |
| Arab schools | | 11.322 | −11.078 | 0.060 | 0.115 |
| | | (18.815) | (19.801) | (0.202) | (0.079) |
| *Disciplinary climate* | | | | | |
| Principal reports: frequency of disciplinary disengagement | | | −11.612 | 0.001 | 0.069* |
| | | | (6.948) | (0.070) | (0.027) |
| Teacher reports: frequency of classroom disruption | | | −21.953* | 0.044 | 0.064 |
| | | | (8.858) | (0.103) | (0.035) |
| Student reports | | | | | |
| Victimization incidents, school level | | | −11.640 | 0.400 | |
| | | | (18.999) | (0.220) | |
| Victimization incidents, student level | | | −7.910*** | −0.028 | |
| | | | (2.091) | (0.057) | |
| Intercept | 1107.070*** | 640.290*** | 890.780*** | −7.967*** | 2.095** |
| | (60.717) | (137.950) | (147.110) | (2.090) | (0.705) |
| Pseudo $R^2$ | 0.011 | 0.014 | 0.015 | 0.008 | 0.011 |
| Proportion of variance between schools | 0.300 | 0.221 | 0.203 | | 0.038 |
| *N* | 3,942 | 3,942 | 3,942 | 3,942 | 3,942 |

NOTE: Standard errors are in parentheses. Missing covariates (with the exception of gender variables) are mean substituted; dummy variables flagging missing covariates are included in the analyses but not shown. Analyses are adjusted using weights provided by TIMSS.

† $p < .10$; * $p < .05$; ** $p < .01$; *** $p < .001$.

of the school, as measured by mean parental education, positively predicts student achievement. Socioeconomic diversity in the school (measured by the coefficient of variation of parental education in the school) is also positively related to student test score. This latter result, however, should be treated with caution as it is inconsistent with findings reported for other countries in our project, some of which find negative effects of within-school socioeconomic diversity on student achievement.

Model 3 in Table 3.4 adds measures of the school disciplinary climate to Model 2. The coefficients suggest that all of the indicators of discipline are negatively related to student test score. The effect of teacher reports of classroom disruption and student-level victimization are statistically significant, while principal reports of student disciplinary disengagement and school-level victimization (while controlling for student-level victimization) are not. Controlling for discipline increases the net effect of being a male student on test scores, from 23.2 to 26.6, suggesting that were it not for boys' tendency to misbehave, their advantage over girls would be somewhat greater than its observed effect. Finally, controlling for discipline reduces the net advantages associated with high socioeconomic status (as indicated by parents' mean education) and of attending religious or Arab schools.

Are the negative effects of school discipline large enough to account for the relatively low test scores of Israeli students? The answer depends on our choice of the hypothetical alternative to the present situation. If Israeli students were perfectly disciplined, the national mean test score would have increased by about 140 points. Clearly, however, this is not a reasonable hypothetical alternative. What about a scenario in which school discipline in Israel approximates the international averages? In that case, the Israeli mean test score would have increased by only about 12 points (recall that the Israeli mean test score falls below the international mean by about 41 points). In short, lack of discipline may explain only a small part of Israel's relatively low test scores.

Before turning to the other outcomes, the bottom of Table 3.4 presents variance components and percentage of variance within and between schools by the three hierarchical linear models of test scores. The intercept model suggests that before adding covariates to the models, most of the variance in student test scores lies within (63 percent), rather than between schools (34 percent). This means that for all their socioeconomic and other differences, schools account for only a third of overall inequality in test scores. The lion's share of inequality is due to student and family characteristics rather than the schools students attend.

However, once we include student- and school-level covariates in our models, they explain a large proportion of the variance between schools in test scores, most of which can be attributed to the differences in student body composition. Specifically, student characteristics account for 30 percent of the between-school variance, and adding the school-level variables explains an additional 23 percent. (Note that of the school-level variables added in Model 2 the most significant effect is that of mean parental education.) Our model is much less effective in explaining within-school between-student inequality in test scores because it does not include important student characteristics that affect learning such as aptitude and motivation. Most importantly, from the standpoint of this project, although school discipline contributes substantially (5 percent) to explaining between-school variance, it does not add explanatory power at the student level.

As a next step in the analysis, Model 4 in Table 3.4 is a nonlinear hierarchical (logit) model for students' college expectations. We find positive effects of student test score, parental education, and number of books at home. As in most other countries, boys in Israel are marginally less likely than girls to expect a college education. School discipline does not affect college plans, except for a marginally positive effect of school-level victimization.

Finally, we study the determinants of student victimization (Model 5 in Table 3.4). As would be expected (Benbenishty, Khoury-Kassabri, and Astor 2006a, 2006b; Harel et al. 2002), boys are more likely to be victimized than girls. In addition, older students are less likely to be victimized than younger ones, presumably because they are physically stronger. Immigrants are more likely to be victimized, and victimization is more prevalent in schools attended by immigrants. Victimization is less prevalent in larger and religious Jewish schools (compared to nonreligious Jewish schools) and is more prevalent in schools in which principals report higher levels of disciplinary disengagement.

## CONCLUSION

Israeli society at large and its school system in particular have all the ingredients that have been found to erode school discipline. Israel is an ethnically stratified immigrant society that is deeply divided and conflict ridden. The state has been engaged for many decades in violent conflict with the Arab world both outside and within its borders. Economic and educational inequalities are higher in Israel than in most other economically developed societies. Its dominant Jewish culture celebrates informality, contempt of authority, and defiance. Israeli classes are usually large, teachers are poorly paid, and most of them feel ill equipped to handle undisciplined and violent students. While Israeli legislators share teachers' concern about school discipline and violence, actual legislation and policy directives tend to safeguard and promote students' civil rights and to impose strict limitations on the sanctions that teachers and principals can employ in their attempts to enforce discipline in schools.

It is little wonder, then, that school discipline in Israel is low in comparison to the other countries that are represented in this project. This finding is consistent with results from the 2002 PISA, which show that student absenteeism is more frequent in Israel than in any of the other 41 countries that participated in the PISA and that it scores well below the international average on other measures of discipline (Kramarski and Mevarech 2004).[11] Israeli students also have substantially lower test scores than the other countries in this project, despite benefiting from higher-than-average levels of parental education, more books in the household (a proxy for reading behavior, which has been shown repeatedly to enhance learning), and higher educational expectations. Thus, we explored the possibility that the underachievement of Israeli students is due to their relatively low levels of school discipline.

Our results suggest that the Israeli disciplinary climate has significant, if modest, associations with student outcomes, particularly test scores, and accounts for about a fourth of the gap in test scores between Israel and the nine-country mean. Specifically, we found significant negative effects of principal reports of student disciplinary disengagement, teacher reports of classroom disruption, and student victimization on student test scores. To better understand how these relationships apply to subgroups in Israel, we explored these effects among the three main sectors of the Israeli school system: nonreligious Jewish schools, religious Jewish schools, and Arab schools. Our descriptive results reveal expected socioeconomic and academic achievement disadvantages for Arab students, relative to Jews, and advantages for students attending religious schools, compared to those attending nonreligious schools (Feniger 2009). In our multivariate analysis, we find the expected positive effects of individual and school socioeconomic composition on student test score but no significant differences between religious, Arab, and nonreligious schools. This finding refutes the hypotheses that (1) school climate is more disciplined in religious schools than in secular ones and (2) this contributes to the achievement of their students (Coleman, Hoffer, and Kilgore 1982; Coleman and Hoffer 1987).

Our results also speak to the literature on oppositional culture. Oppositional culture theory (Fordham and Ogbu 1986) views Arab citizens of Israel as nonvoluntary minorities (Eisikovits 1997) and predicts that they would resist Zionism and its school system.[12] The results refute this prediction and show that Arab students are more disciplined than Jewish students, a finding that may be attributable to authoritarian educational norms employed by Arab teachers (Abu Sa'ad and Hendrix 1993). Further, while there seems to be more victimization in Arab schools, it is statistically accounted for by differences between sectors in the socioeconomic composition of schools.

In sum, Israeli politicians and the public at large are very concerned about the mediocre test scores of Israeli students in international comparative studies, attributing this failure to the lack of discipline in Israeli schools. Our study shows that although school discipline does affect student achievement, the effect is not large and accounts for only a small proportion of the variation in test scores among students. The bulk of the variation, both between Israeli students as a whole and between schools, is due not to discipline but rather to the socioeconomic composition of the student body. Namely, inequality between students in their social origins is responsible for a large share of the explained differences among them in test scores. This result is consistent with those reported by most studies of educational stratification in economically developed societies (e.g., Shavit and Blossfeld 1993) and is highly robust. Its implications for social policy are clear: educational inequality of opportunity cannot be substantially reduced unless social inequalities are themselves reduced. Reforms targeted at enhancing school discipline are important in their own right, but even if effective, they are not likely to boost achievement by much. We should not lose sight of the fact that these inequalities are largely reflections of the class structure of our society.

NOTES

1. However, the Gini coefficient for Israel is about average compared with other countries in this comparative study. The coefficients for the other eight countries are Canada, 0.32; Chile, 0.55; Italy, 0.33; Japan, 0.38; Korea, 0.35; Netherlands, 0.31; Russia, 0.41; United States, 0.45.

2. There are numerous shades of orthodoxy in Judaism (Sharot 1990). For the purpose of this paper we distinguish three main categories: ultra-orthodox (*Haredim*), orthodox, and nonreligious Jews. The *Haredi* communities, about 15 percent of the population, do not fully respect the sovereignty of the Jewish state's secular institutions and believe strongly that *Halacha* (Jewish religious law) is the only legitimate law and the sole basis of moral and political authority for Jews. *Haredi* students attend separate schools, which although largely funded by the state, do not adhere to state-sanctioned curricula. Although it would have been very interesting to compare *Haredi* school discipline with other communities', this group is not represented in our data because *Haredim* do not usually participate in social surveys.

3. The mean class sizes at the primary level for the other countries participating in this project are Chile, 30.8; Italy, 18.4; Japan, 28.3; Korea, 31.6; Netherlands, 22.4; Russia, 15.5; United States, 23.1 (data are not available for Canada). The rank order of the countries' mean class sizes at the lower secondary level is similar to those at the primary level.

4. In this study's other eight countries the ratios for primary school teachers are Chile, 1.11; Italy, 1.01; Japan, 1.54; Korea, 2.29; Netherlands, 1.15; United States, 0.97 (data are not available for Canada and Russia).

5. Committee for Education, Culture and Sports, http://www.knesset.gov.il/protocols/heb/protocol_search.aspx (1998–2008).

6. http://www.knesset.gov.il/protocols/heb/protocol_search.aspx [in Hebrew].

7. In addition, the law prohibits discrimination in schools on ethnic or socioeconomic grounds. Incidentally, there is no mention of discrimination on the grounds of gender, national identity (Arab versus Jewish), or religious affiliation. We suspect that such mention would not have received support from religious and nationalist Jewish Knesset members.

8. For example, the teacher must explain the punishment to the student, the punishment must be proportionate to the infraction in its substance and severity, and it should be limited in time. Students must be given a chance to explain themselves to the teacher or the principal, preferably before the punishment is executed. These instructions are followed by a detailed list of sanctions that teachers can employ.

9. Regarding school violence, we focused only on articles that discussed violence on school property or on the way to or from school. Our analysis does not include incidents that occurred among students during nonschool hours.

10. It is unfortunate that TIMSS does not provide information on immigrants' country of origin, as the negative effect of being an immigrant varies considerably between groups. In Israel there are large differences in the achievement of students who immigrated from Russia and the western republics of the FSU and those who arrived from the FSU's southern republics or from Ethiopia (Chachashvili-Bolotin 2007). As Hauser (2009) notes, the immigration handicap in educational achievement is related to the cultural difference between the country of origin and destination.

11. However, other comparative studies (Harel et al. 1998, 2002) place Israel at about the middle of the international hierarchy of the discipline scale.

12. Although virtually all Arab students attend all-Arab schools, these schools are supervised by the central Ministry of Education, which appoints teachers and sets the curriculum. Therefore, it is not unreasonable to expect some Arab students to view the school system as a whole as an agency of the Zionist state.

## REFERENCES

Abu Sa'ad, I., and V. L. Hendrix. 1993. "Pupil Control Ideology in a Multicultural Society: Arab and Jewish Teachers in Israeli Elementary Schools." *Comparative Education Review* 37 (1): 21–30.

Adva Center. 2007. "Gini Index." Retrieved February 17, 2009 from http://www.adva.org/UserFiles/File/Gini%202007.pdf [in Hebrew].

Aharonovich, E. 2009. "'Striking' Amendment." *Ha'aretz Supplement*, September 18, 45–50 [in Hebrew].

Al-Haj, M. 1995. *Education, Empowerment, and Control: The Case of the Arabs in Israel.* Albany: State University of New York Press.

Almog, O. 1997. *The Sabra—A Portrait.* Tel Aviv: Am Oved [in Hebrew].

———. 2004. *Farewell to "Srulik": Changing Values among the Israeli Elite.* Haifa: Haifa University Press and Zmora Beitan [in Hebrew].

Astor, R. A., R. Benbenishty, A. D. Vinokur, and A. Zeira. 2006. "Arab and Jewish Elementary School Students' Perceptions of Fear and School Violence: Understanding the Influence of School Context." *British Journal of Educational Psychology* 76 (1): 91–118.

Ayalon, H., and Y. Shavit. 2004. "Educational Reforms and Inequalities in Israel: The MMI Hypothesis Revisited." *Sociology of Education* 77 (2): 103–20.

Benbenishty, R., and R. A. Astor. 2005. *School Violence in Context: Culture, Neighborhood, Family, School and Gender.* New York: Oxford University Press.

Benbenishty, R., M. Khoury-Kassabri, and R. A. Astor. 2006a. "A National Study of School Violence in Israel." *Mifgash* 23:15–44 [in Hebrew].

———. 2006b. *Violence in the Education System.* Jerusalem: Hebrew University in Jerusalem, School of Social Work [in Hebrew].

Chachashvili-Bolotin, S. 2007. "The Effects of the Immigration on Educational Attainments of Immigrants and Native Israelis." PhD diss., Tel Aviv University [in Hebrew].

*Coleman*, J. S., and T. *Hoffer. 1987. Public and Private High Schools: The Impact of Communities.* New York: Basic Books.

Coleman, J. S., T. Hoffer, and S. Kilgore. 1982. *Public and Private Schools.* Washington, DC: National Center for Education Statistics.

De Graaf, N. D., P. M. De Graaf, and G. Kraaykamp. 2000. "Parental Cultural Capital and Educational Attainment in the Netherlands: A Refinement of the Cultural Capital Perspective." *Sociology of Education* 73 (2): 92–111.

Dwairy, M. A. 1998. *Cross-Cultural Counseling: The Arab-Palestinian Case.* New York: Haworth.

Eisikovits, R. A. 1997. "The Educational Experience and Performance of Immigrant and Minority Students in Israel," *Anthropology and Education Quarterly* 28 (3): 394–410.

Endeweld, M., A. Fruman, and D. Gottlieb. 2008. *Poverty and Social Gaps in 2007, Annual Report.* Jerusalem: National Insurance Institute, Research and Planning Administration [in Hebrew]. Retrieved May 9, 2009, from http://www.btl.gov.il/SiteCollectionDocuments/btl/Publications/DochHaOni/oni2007.pdf.

Feniger, Y. 2009. "Educational Opportunities in Israel's State Religious Education: Learning Climate, Student Achievement and Educational Inequality." PhD diss., Tel Aviv University [in Hebrew].

Fordham, S., and J. U. Ogbu. 1986. Black Students' School Success: Coping with the "Burden of 'Acting White.'" *Urban Review* 18:176–206.

Ghanem, A. 1998. "State and Minority in Israel: The Case of Ethnic State and the Predicament of its Minority." *Ethnic and Racial Studies* 21 (3): 428–48.

Goldscheider, C. 2002. *Israel's Changing Society: Population, Ethnicity, and Development.* Boulder, CO: Westview Press.

Harel, Y., S. Ellenbogen-Frankovitz, M. Molcho, Kh. Abu-Asbah, and J. Habib. 2002. *Youth in Israel: Social Well-Being, Health and Risk Behaviours from an International Perspective: Summary of Findings from the Second Study* (1998). Jerusalem: The Center for Children and Youth JDC—Brookdale Institute [in Hebrew].

Harel, Y., M. Molcho, and E. Tillinger. 2003. *Youth in Israel: Health, Mental and Social Welfare and Risk Behavior Pattern: A Summary of the 3rd National Research (2002) and Analyze of Trends between the Years 1994–2002.* Ramat Gan: International Research Program on Youth Health and Wellbeing, Department of Sociology and Anthropology, Bar Ilan University [in Hebrew].

Hauser, R. M. 2009. "On Quality and Equity in the Performance of Students and Schools." Presented at the Yale Meeting of RC28, Yale University, New Haven, CT, August 3–6.

Hofstede, G. 1994. *Culture and Organizations.* New York: McGraw-Hill.

Kamir, O. 1999. "Country which Improvises its Disasters—About the 'Smokh' in Israeli Culture and Trial." *Democratic Culture* 1. Ramat Gan: Bar Ilan University [in Hebrew].

Katriel, T. 1986. *Talking Straight: Dugri Speech in Israeli Culture.* Cambridge: Cambridge University Press.

Katz, Y., and K. Yablon. 2001. *Israeli Public Opinion on the Education System towards 2001–2002 (Tash'sab) School Year.* Ramat Gan: Communal Research and Education Institute, School of Education, Bar-Ilan University [in Hebrew].

Kfir, A. 1997. *Organization and Management—Design and Change.* Tel Aviv: Tcherikover [in Hebrew].

Khoury-Kassabri, M. 2002. "The Correlation between School Ecological Characteristics and its Students Victimization Level." PhD diss., Hebrew University in Jerusalem [in Hebrew].

Khoury-Kassabri, M., R. A. Astor, and R. Benbenishty. 2009. "Middle Eastern Adolescents' Perpetration of School Violence against Peers and Teachers: A Cross-Cultural and Ecological Analysis." *Journal of Interpersonal Violence* 24 (1): 159–82.

Khoury-Kassabri, M., R. Benbenishty, and R. A. Astor. 2005. "The Effects of School Climate, Socioeconomics, and Cultural Factors on Student Victimization in Israel." *Social Work Research* 29 (3): 165–80.

Kramarski, B., and Z. R. Mevarech. 2004. "Reading, Mathematic and Science Scores in PISA 2002, Summary Report." Israel, Ministry of Education. Retrieved May 8, 2009, from http://cms.education.gov.il/EducationCMS/Units/Scientist/Mehkar/Mechkarim [in Hebrew].

Kraus, V., and Y. Yonay. 2000. "The Power and Limits of Ethnonationalism: Palestinians and Eastern Jews in Israel, 1974–1991." *British Journal of Sociology* 51 (3): 525–51.

Kristen, C., Y. Shavit, S. Chachashvili-Bolotin, and T. Roth. "Competencies and Achievements among Immigrant and Native Students in Israel and Germany." Unpublished manuscript.

Laufer, A., and Y. Harel. 2003. "The Correlation between School Perception and Students Involvement in Bulling." *Megamot* 42 (3): 437–59 [in Hebrew].

Lavy, V., and A. Schlosser. 2007. "Mechanisms and Impacts of Gender Peer Effects at School." NBER Working Paper no. 13292, National Bureau of Economic Research.

Lewin-Epstein, N., and Moshe Semyonov. 1994. "Sheltered Labor Markets, Public Sector Employment, and Socio-Economic Returns to Education of Arabs in Israel." *American Journal of Sociology* 100 (3): 622–51.

Martin, M. D., I. V. S. Mullis, and S. J. Chrostowski. 2004. *TIMSS-2003 Technical Report.* Chestnut Hill, MA: Boston College.

Mendel, R. 2007. "The Support in Cops—A Tradition of Disobeying the Law." November 22. Retrieved January 2, 2009, from http://www.ynet.co.il/articles/1,7340,L-3474636,00.html [in Hebrew].

Ministry of Education. 2000. Directive of CEO, Tash'sag/4 (a), "Creating Safe Environment and Reducing Educational Institutions Violence." December 1. Retrieved April 3, 2008, from http://cms.education.gov.il/EducationCMS/applications/mankal/arc/sa4ck2_1_3.htm [in Hebrew].

———. 2007. Directive of CEO, Tasha'ch/3 (a), November 1. Retrieved April 3, 2008, from http://cms.education.gov.il/EducationCMS/Applications/Mankal/EtsMedorim/6/6-6/HoraotKeva/K-2008-3a-6-6-1.htm [in Hebrew].

———. 2009. Directive of CEO, Tasha/1 (a), "Promoting Safe Environment and Dealing with Educational Institutions Violence." August. Retrieved October 29, 2009, from http://cms.education.gov.il/EducationCMS/Applications/Mankal/EtsMedorim/2/2-1/HoraotKeva/K-2010-1a-2-1-12.htm [in Hebrew].

OECD. 2011. *Education at a Glance 2011: OECD Indicators.* Retrieved September 23, 2011, from http://www.oecd.org/dataoecd/61/2/48631582.pdf.

Semyonov, M., and Y. Cohen. 1990. "Ethnic Discrimination and the Income of Majority Group Workers." *American Sociological Review* 55 (1): 107–14.

Sharot, S. 1990. "Israel: Sociological Analyses of Religion in the Jewish State." *Sociological Analysis* 51 (special issue): 63–76.

Shavit, Y. 1990. "Segregation, Tracking and the Educational Attainment of Minorities: Arabs and Oriental Jews in Israel." *American Sociological Review* 55 (1): 115–26.

Shavit, Y., and H. P. Blossfeld, eds. 1993. *Persistent Inequalities: A Comparative study of educational attainment in thirteen countries.* Boulder, CO: Westview Press.

Sikron, M. 1957. *Immigration to Israel from 1948 to 1953: Statistical Supplement.* Jerusalem: Falk Institute [in Hebrew].

Smith, R., and O. Pniel. 2003. "Public Opinion Survey among Teachers in Israel," *Panim* 24: 22–88. http://itu.cet.ac.il/Inner.aspx?nItemID=802 [in Hebrew].

Smooha, S. 2002. *Survey of Arab Voters and the Arab Public in the Election to the 16th Knesset.* Research Report Submitted to Israel Democracy Institute and the Jewish-Arab Center. Retrieved October 3, 2008, from http://soc.haifa.ac.il/~s.smooha/download/Survey ArabVoter2002.pdf [in Hebrew].

Students Rights Law. 2000. Hatash'sa, State of Israel law section 42, 401. Retrieved March 15, 2008, from http://cms.education.gov.il/EducationCMS/Units/Zchuyot/ChukimVeamanot/Chukim/ch_zchyt_talmid.htm [in Hebrew].

———. 2004. Amendment. Hatash'sah, State of Israel law section 44. Retrieved March 15, 2008, from http://cms.education.gov.il/EducationCMS/Units/Zchuyot/ChukimVeamanot/Chukim/Tikun_Chok_Zchuyot_Talmid2004.htm [in Hebrew].

Swirsky, S. 1990. *Education in Israel: Schooling for Inequality.* Tel Aviv: Breirot [in Hebrew].

Swirsky, S., and Y. Yecheskel. 1999. "How the 2000 Israel State Budget Affects Arab Citizens." Tel Aviv: Adva Center.

Trabelsi-Hadad, Tamar. 2006. "Stand Up, Stand Up, Children." *Yediot-Aharonot*, October 31, p. 12.

Vergan, Y. 2007. *Class Size in the Israeli Education System*. Report Submitted to the Knesset Education, Culture and Sport Committee. Jerusalem: Knesset Research and Information Center. http://www.knesset.gov.il/mmm/data/pdf/m01903.pdf [in Hebrew].

Wikipedia. 2009. "List of Countries by Income Equality." Retrieved March 17, 2008, from http://en.wikipedia.org/wiki/List_of_countries_by_income_equality.

World Values Survey. 2000. *World Values Survey 2000*, official data file v. 20090914. Madrid: ASEP/JDS. Available at http://www.wvsevsdb.com/wvs/WVSData.jsp.

Yakobson, Yehuda. 1995. "Struggles over Discipline and Control in a High-School: An Anthropological Perspective." PhD diss. Tel Aviv University [in Hebrew].

Yogev, A., I. Livneh, and Y. Feniger. 2009. "Singapore Instead of Karkur? International Comparisons of Student's Achievement and the Globalization of Educational Targets." *Megamot* 46 (3): 337–55 [in Hebrew].

CHAPTER FOUR

# School Discipline, Performance, and Presence of Immigrants in Italian Schools

*Paolo Barbieri and Stefani Scherer*

School discipline has become an issue of international public debate. A comparative study on learning and teaching environments conducted by the Organization for Economic Cooperation and Development (OECD 2009) marks a new interest in school discipline. The study finds that Italian schools (according to their principals' assessment) have discipline problems less problematic than the average of participating countries, with the exception of classroom disturbance. Accordingly, Italians have mostly not participated in the public debate.[1]

The perception of no serious problem by Italian society is one thing; the objective situation is another. In fact, discipline in Italian schools, or rather the lack of it, is a moderate-level problem. In 2003, according to Trends in International Mathematics and Science Study (TIMSS) data, 60 percent of principals of middle schools, or lower secondary schools—*scuole medie*, which are mandatory for all pupils between ages 12 and 14, or sixth to eighth grades—reported that their schools had considerable problems with classroom disruption, 25 percent declared that they had problems with student intimidation by other students, over 25 percent faced frequent problems of students coming late to school, and 10 percent had more than occasional student absenteeism. Survey results indicate that between 2003 and 2007 all these forms of misbehavior increased, with absenteeism and late arrival at school nearly doubling (TIMSS data). More serious disciplinary infractions, however, are considerably rarer: only 6 percent of middle school principals declared that they had problems with vandalism, and only 2 percent of schools reported episodes that resulted in teacher injuries. This helps explain why school discipline is perceived by the Italian public as not particularly deserving of attention. Also, disciplinary climate does not seem worthy of attention amid the heated debate on educational reforms and especially cuts in spending on education.

There is, however, an exception: in Italy mass media coverage of school discipline has linked it with social (in)security, microcrime, and increased presence of immigrants in schools. The linkage is a result of manipulation of the issues by politicians and public opinion makers. Immigrant students have been presented as a threat to security in Italian schools—as immigrants in general were presented as a threat to the security of Italian society—and certain problems present in schools have been explicitly related to their presence and much less so to inherent features of the educational system.

There are probably two main, interrelated, reasons for the prevalence of this issue in the current Italian political and public policy debate. The first concerns the recent but very rapid growth of the immigrant student population in the public educational system. It has undoubtedly been unsettling for middle-class Italian families to see immigrants as classmates for their children, rather than as cheap labor in industry or in labor-intensive services. The combination of sudden increase in immigrants in schools and in concentration of immigrants (and immigrant pupils) in specific areas or towns disturbs native families, who conjecture that the increase menaces their children and hampers their accumulation of human capital.

The second reason relates to politics. In the past decade Italy has experienced frequent changes of government. Safety issues have been used by both political coalitions to attract middle-class middle-aged and elderly voters—notwithstanding lack of evidence supporting the immigration-crime link (Bianchi et al. 2008; Bell, Machin, and Fasani 2010).[2] The public has thus come to believe that young immigrants, deviant behavior, and disciplinary problems in Italian schools are linked.

Academic research has also largely neglected the topic of school discipline in Italy. Apart from a general survey of teachers on the disciplinary climate at their school (Salerni 2005), which confirmed its importance for learning but also showed that the majority of teachers believe that sanctions are not of instructional value, social science has not contributed much to the topic. While there is a growing body of literature focusing on immigrants in schools, their presence has not been related to school discipline by research; neither the effect of immigrants in Italian schools, nor their lack of integration and its possible connections with poor school discipline and deviant behavior, nor the nexus between learning and performance has been investigated. We seek to remedy this shortcoming in this chapter. Specifically, we investigate the association of social background with school disciplinary climate and the relationship between school disciplinary climate and student achievement. We extend the scope of the comparative project by asking the following supplementary questions: What is the current disciplinary situation in Italian schools, and how is it affected by the presence of immigrant students? Who is most affected by undisciplined behavior and microcrime in schools; that is, who are the victims? What consequences does the presence of immigrant students have on cognitive performance, and what is the role of the school's disciplinary climate? Is there evidence that immigrant status constitutes a new cleavage in contemporary Italian society, this time within the educational system?

In what follows we first briefly describe the institutional characteristics of the Italian school system, provide an overview on the current situation of students with immigration backgrounds,[3] document their recent increase and regional distribution, and comment on associations among youth microcrime, security, and immigrants.

We present evidence based on TIMSS data from 2003. So that regional disparities can be better assessed, these national data are integrated with information from a local survey on schools in Trentino, an Italian province with a high quality of life, traditionally good performance on standardized tests, and a large share of immigrants. Methodologically, we analyze both school-level and individual-level data by drawing on multilevel and fixed-effect regression models.

## BACKGROUND

### *The Italian Educational System*

As confirmed by the OECD (2010), Italy generally falls short of international educational standards. Italy is at the lower end of developed countries in investment in education and training, spending 4.5 percent of gross domestic product on education, compared with an OECD-country mean of 6.2 percent (OECD 2010). This figure does not take account of cuts in 2008 and in 2010 to deal with the financial crisis and Italy's severe public debt. And although in recent years younger cohorts have been rapidly catching up with European standards, participation in upper secondary and higher education is still low. Even among younger cohorts (ages 24–34), only 17 percent have a tertiary degree, and percentages are much lower for older cohorts. At the same time, more than 10 percent of 15–19-year-olds have what was once called "NEET," that is, youth neither in employment nor in education or training. These findings are accompanied by a well-documented regional diversity: participation rates in education beyond compulsory schooling, which in Italy ends at age 16, are particularly low in the south of the country, while the north is in line with the rest of Europe. These regional diversities are confirmed not only for participation in education but also for student performance, as indicated by Program for International Student Assessment (PISA) data (OECD 2007; Bratti, Checchi, and Filippin 2003). Regional differences prevail even though the Italian educational system is set up to be highly standardized and almost entirely public. The differences are possibly due to the different amounts of resources allocated to the educational system in different regions.

The Italian educational system was born in the second half of the 19th century in parallel with the nation-state building known as the Italian Risorgimento. The Casati Law (1859) sought to create a public, nationwide, generalist educational system that would supersede the country's traditional fragmented, Catholic, and elitist system. The new public system was based on four years of elementary schooling, the first two mandatory. Education was conceived of as a means to foster national unification, besides its labor-market-oriented function. As was not unusual in Italy, the Casati Law—although ambitious and progressive in its intent—was implemented in such a way that its declared goals were not achieved, and it was only in 1911 that elementary school financing became the responsibility of the state. One consequence of the delay in implementing the reforms was a very high illiteracy rate, which was around 80 percent in 1861 (the year of Italian unification) and stayed in double digits beyond World War II. Illiteracy was strongly stratified by gender and region: even into 1961, 10 percent of the female population could not write and read fluently. Moreover, the Italian ruling class's lack of interest in educating the lower classes (Barbagli 1974), combined with a chronic shortage of funding,[4] became the basis for what is still today notoriously high social inequality in access to education. The modern educational system was introduced by the Fascist regime with the so-called *riforma Gentile*, legislation that—together with the strict standardization and centralization of the entire educational system—prolonged compulsory education until age 14. School attendance thus consisted of five years of elementary school and an additional three or four years of lower secondary school, subsequently unified. But whereas basic schooling up to the lower secondary level was extended, access to higher education, especially to universities, was markedly restricted. Moreover, it replicated a clear class structure: basic education for the working class; secondary, technical education for the middle class; and classical studies, which gave entry to tertiary education, restricted to the upper class. Access to higher education is still today markedly stratified by social background, although access has increased considerably for the lower class.

Access to tertiary education was facilitated by a reform law in 1962 that mainly concerned lower secondary schools but also gave rise to the *licealization* (Schizzerotto and Barone 2006) of upper secondary schools—or their transformation to *licei*, which prolonged most of the upper secondary tracks to five years to prepare for university—with the exception of some vocational schools.[5] In 2003 the compulsory schooling age was raised to 16; the number of *licei* was increased by converting the secondary, five-year technical schools into *licei*; and the vocational schools were—at least on paper—made more similar to *licei*. Years since have been characterized by numerous reforms and counterreforms, often unimplemented, that have brought great uncertainty to all levels of the Italian educational system and jeopardized the quality of the educational process.

Today, Italy has an educational system in which, after eight years of comprehensive schooling (five years at elementary school and three years at middle school, *scuola media*), pupils choose among five-year tracks, some academic tracks leading to university and others vocationally oriented and intended to train students for labor-market entry (Brauns, Steinmann, and Scherer 2003). Some of the vocational tracks are of shorter duration, two to three years, but since 1969, others are five-year tracks and enable entry to tertiary education. At the tertiary level, usually a first university degree is awarded after three years and a second degree after a further two years, possibly followed by three years of doctoral studies. The school system is almost entirely public, with a very small number of private, mostly Catholic, schools, whose graduates achieve less than those of public schools (Bertola, Checchi, and Oppedisano 2007).[6] The school system is still centralized and highly standardized,[7] at least formally, with standardized curricula and state examinations; access to tertiary education is relatively open and tracking occurs relatively late. Notwithstanding these features, participation in higher education is still low and access is limited by social class. Regional disparities are well documented. International studies on student performance show that elementary schooling, as documented by Progress in International Reading Literacy Study (PIRLS) data (Mullis et al. 2007; Checchi 2004), works reasonably well, providing fourth grade pupils with cognitive capacities above the European standard.[8] By contrast, students attending middle school (TIMSS data on eighth grade students)[9] or the first year of upper secondary school (PISA data on 15-year-old students) lag those in other OECD countries, and Italy ranks lowest in reading, writing, and mathematical and scientific capacities. Regional differences are also prevalent with regard to performance, with the well-known north-south divide replicated in school performances.

This school system must today cope with increasing numbers of students with immigration backgrounds. With chronic underfunding and complete absence of clear educational policies, the possible consequences are nonintegration of immigrants and further deterioration of student performance.

### *Legal Background and Disciplinary Measures*

We briefly present the legal situation regarding school discipline. In Italy, education is a matter that mainly concerns families and the school system. In the school system teachers and school councils (which represent teachers, students, and parents) are the principal actors for discipline and other kinds of activities. Italian legislation (Decreto del President della Repubblica [DPR] 235, 2007) explicitly promulgates an educational alliance among schools, students, and families to promote maturation and responsibility in pupils. Neither formal means of legal and social control (e.g., police, private guards, or security checks) nor informal ones (e.g., uniforms) are present in Italian schools, and even the "uniform," a sort of smock (*il grembiule*), at elementary schools was abandoned almost everywhere some 20 years ago.

This principle of shared responsibility between families and schools and teachers is also codified by Italian civil legislation (article 2048), which states that both parents and teachers are legally responsible for any act by a minor pupil constantly under their joint responsibility. Parents are subject to *culpa in educando*, which means that they must demonstrate if necessary that they have educated their children in "proper and licit" behavior, reflecting parents' legal responsibility for their children's behavior. At the same time, teachers are subject to *culpa in vigilando*—that is, they must supervise minors when they are at school or engaged in school-organized activities (sports or trips). This principle has been recently confirmed by the highest Italian court.[10]

Pupils usually respect standard rules of behavior, including prohibitions such as not smoking at school and not leaving school premises during free periods. Within the classroom, discipline is typically maintained by teachers, and their authority is generally recognized and not questioned by families. The teacher's authority covers everyday school life and more serious disciplinary issues. In the case of severe misbehavior, teachers are supported by the school councils (at both the class and school levels), which usually decide whether to suspend students or transfer them to an alternative school—although these are extremely rare events. Schools deal with problem students by first involving the student's family and—in extreme cases, which means when the family fails—then referring the student to social services.[11]

This reflects the Italian belief that education is a social right and the school's function is primarily educative and constructive, not merely punitive. Moreover, by law disciplinary sanctions must not enter into evaluation of performance (article 4, par. 3, DPR 249, 1998). Only in extreme cases can a poor grade in overall behavior (*voto di condotta*) mean failure (*bocciatura*). Corporal punishment is prohibited and would be prosecuted under the law as any other form of violence. Overall, regulations are much more concerned with the rights of students than with teachers' ability to discipline misbehavior.

School discipline and school enforcement is not a matter of courts and lawyers but of political interventions and policy measures, collectively claimed and defended. The 1960s' tradition of participatory forms of school governance, or shop-floor democracy, gave rise to a collective approach to school issues that in some way persists in Italian schools.[12] Public schools, a public good, are not viewed as a private issue: as a consequence, private recourse to courts to sue teachers and administrators for disciplinary acts is very unusual. If students believe that their rights have been infringed by a teacher or a principal, they may resort to the *organo di garanzia*, a regulatory authority of students, parents, and teachers, within the school (first level) and subsequently one at regional level.

### *Immigration and Italian Schools*

In the last century, Italy experienced large-scale emigration, which gradually slowed and came almost to a halt by the 1960s and 1970s, when internal south–north migrations replaced flows to the European Union. Migration within the country, mainly from the poorer south to the richer north, remains a substantive social reality. The presence of immigrants from places outside the European Union in Italy is a relatively recent, but rapidly growing, phenomenon. As of 2009 the foreign-resident population in Italy amounted to about 6.5 percent of the total population, or 3.9 million persons, including new entrants and foreigners born within the country. The latter—given the comparatively high fertility rate of immigrants[13] (2.4 children compared with 1.28 for natives)—accounted for a rapidly increasing proportion of foreigners compared with other countries, such as Germany, France, or Great Britain (ISTAT 2006, 2008; Ministero dell'Interno 2007). The largest number of immigrants come from Albania, Morocco, China, the former Eastern Europe and Soviet Union countries (e.g., Romania, Ukraine, and Moldavia), and countries in the Far East (India, the Philippines). Immigrants are concentrated in the richest regions of northern Italy, such as Emilia-Romagna (8.6 percent of residents), Lombardy (8.5 percent), and Veneto (8.4 percent),[14] with especially high numbers in some areas. Many immigrants are undocumented: according to conservative estimates, there were 540,000 in 2005 and 760,000 in 2007 (Ministero dell'Interno 2007).

This increase in immigration has created new challenges, especially for the educational system, which plays a key role in the socialization and integration of second-generation migrants. The proportion of immigrant students grew very rapidly, to 6.4 percent in 2007.[15] Italy, together with a few other European Union countries, explicitly permits school enrollment for the children of undocumented immigrants (Eurydice 2009).

Students with immigration backgrounds are unevenly distributed across the country and among different school types. Southern regions have very low rates (around 1 percent) of immigrant students. In some regions in the north, up to 12 percent of students are non-Italians,[16] and in some areas, non-Italian students are the majority and at risk of ghettoization, with its well-documented barriers to integration and acculturation and its negative selection. Italian families, sometimes justifiably (Brunello and Rocco 2011), fear that a high concentration of immigrant pupils in schools will lower the quality of education and tend to avoid these schools. The government intervened and instituted a 30 percent maximum of immigrant students in each class. The proportion of immigrant pupils is highest in primary schools (7.7 percent), lower in upper-secondary ones (4.3 percent), and even lower in universities (2.6 percent) (ISTAT 2008). Distribution is also unequal over the different tracks, with students with immigration backgrounds clearly overrepresented in vocational tracks and underrepresented in the traditional academic tracks leading to university.[17] These concentrations seem to result from two main factors. The first is a purely demographic one: immigrants' children are on average young. The second has to do with the previously mentioned social selectivity of the Italian educational system.

Peculiarities are also documented with regard to school careers and performance. Immigrant students are more likely older than their Italian classmates: 52 percent of students with immigration backgrounds in lower secondary school are older than the average age but less than 7 percent of natives are. Repeating a school year because of poor performance is more common among immigrant pupils: 6.4 percent compared with 2.7 percent of natives attending middle school (ISTAT 2008). The reason for this may be inadequate language skills or prevalence of lower social classes among immigrants. In light of all these circumstances, immigrant students receive less education and more frequently drop out, both factors subsequently leading to greater disadvantages in the labor market. Failure at school, dropping out, and non-integration into society are strong risk factors for the deviant behavior that public opinion often attributes to young migrants.

### *Delinquency and Immigration—A Necessary Link?*

Despite a downward trend in crimes (Ministero dell'Interno 2007), Italians feel increasingly insecure: 35 percent of families felt threatened by crime in 2006–2007. In the northwestern regions with strong concentrations of immigrants, the number was 38.4 percent. Some of this perceived insecurity may be because of the rapid aging of Italian society, but it is clearly fed by the media and political parties in search of votes. The perceived threat is strongly linked to immigrants, especially young migrants (minors or very young adults) concentrated in big cities. Large cities in 2001 had a high concentration of persons charged with offenses (ISTAT 2003), and they also have a high concentration of immigrant youth. Around 31 percent of persons under age 18 charged with offenses (*denunciati*)[18] were concentrated in five large cities.[19]

In short, adolescents with immigration backgrounds are often regarded as delinquents and a menace to security. The higher incidence of crime in areas with large concentrations of immigrants and their overrepresentation among those charged with offenses (who should be kept distinct from those convicted) supports this view. Because schools concentrate young people, and increasingly immigrants, many Italians equate young immigrants with violence, deviant behavior, and victimization of other, possibly native, students. In the following we analyze two specific aspects of this question: first, whether there is a correlation between concentration of immigrants in schools and the school disciplinary climate and, specifically, incidence of student victimization and microcrime, and second, the consequences for academic performance.

## RESULTS

We use the Italian TIMSS data from 2003 in our investigation. TIMSS samples students in the eighth grade—that is, in their last year of compulsory middle school—and therefore before the stratification of the school system into different tracks begins.[20] Table 4.1 provides descriptive statistics on all variables from the TIMSS dataset used in the analysis. Analyses are weighted.

We first give a detailed description of school discipline and its correlates in Italy and then turn to the consequences in terms of cognitive performance—namely, test scores in math and science.[21] We use a combined index of both scores because we are interested in an overall measure, not in specific disciplines. It should be noted, however, that the science and math scores are very highly correlated. To profit fully from the information available, we combine school-level analysis and individual-student-level analysis in a multilevel approach (Rabe-Hersketh and Skrondal 2005).

School disciplinary measures are available at different levels of aggregation. First, TIMSS provides school-level information based mainly

TABLE 4.1
*Description of variables (TIMSS 2003)*

| | *Mean* | *SE* |
|---|---|---|
| STUDENT CHARACTERISTICS | | |
| Male | 0.503 | 0.009 |
| Age | 13.893 | 0.012 |
| Immigrant status | 0.046 | 0.004 |
| Highest parental education | 4.385 | 0.065 |
| Number of books in household | 2.985 | 0.038 |
| Household size | 4.281 | 0.025 |
| SCHOOL AND COMMUNITY CHARACTERISTICS | | |
| *School and community variables* | | |
| School size (log) | 6.424 | 0.023 |
| School highest grade level | 8.064 | 0.045 |
| Community size | 3.246 | 0.117 |
| *School-level student characteristics* | | |
| Male students | | |
| 46%–60% | 0.483 | 0.039 |
| >60% | 0.180 | 0.029 |
| Immigrant students | | |
| 1%–10% | 0.404 | 0.039 |
| >10% | 0.164 | 0.028 |
| Average parental education | 4.388 | 0.064 |
| Variation in parental education | 0.340 | 0.005 |
| *Disciplinary climate* | | |
| Principal reports: frequency of disciplinary disengagement | 2.095 | 0.053 |
| Teacher reports: frequency of classroom disruption | 3.496 | 0.071 |
| Student reports | | |
| Victimization incidents, student level | 0.602 | 0.021 |
| Victimization incidents, school level | 0.603 | 0.021 |
| COGNITIVE PERFORMANCE | | |
| Math and science test score (combined) | 974.490 | 6.657 |
| Math test score | 483.599 | 3.400 |
| Science test score | 490.891 | 3.365 |
| *N* | 4,278 | |

NOTE: SE = standard error.

on assessments by principals. We construct a single index measuring[22] disciplinary disengagement at school according to assessments by principals. Items include coming late to school, skipping class, and being absent from school. All items investigate the frequency of these events, with response categories ranging from never to very often (every day). This is complemented by a measure of student classroom disruption based on math and science teachers' assessments, both of which enter the index. In cases in which more than one class was interviewed per school, the average is calculated to obtain a school-level measure. On the individual, that is, student, level, school discipline is assessed from the student victimization index: a single measure of students' having something stolen, being hurt, or being teased. To have an equivalent measure at the school level, student measures are aggregated.

Other school-level data were available, including concentration of immigrant students at school. We categorize schools into those without immigrants, those with up to 10 percent, and those with more than 10 percent. We define immigrants as only first-generation immigrants, that is, students born outside the country. The results, however, remain largely the same for a wider definition of all students with immigration backgrounds. Moreover, school-level parental education and its heterogeneity prove important, both theoretically and empirically. Finally, school size is taken into consideration where appropriate. All models control for community size. Student-level analysis controls for individual and family characteristics such as gender, social and cultural background (measured as parental education and number of books in the household), and number of persons in the household.[23]

We supplement TIMSS data with data from Trentino, a province with high incomes and high cognitive performance as revealed by PISA data. The data were collected to study the integration of immigrants in Trentino schools, so that classes with at least three immigrant students were sampled (Cvajner 2008). Besides shedding more light on possible regional differences, these data had the advantage of being collected in the ninth grade, after tracking, which allowed comparisons. The student victimization index could be constructed identically to TIMSS, enabling straightforward comparison.

## SCHOOL DISCIPLINE

If the presence of immigrants, as the public debate seems to assume, causes disciplinary problems, one would expect disciplinary behavior differences between schools according to immigrant student concentration. We therefore investigate school-level data. We compare associations between the three disciplinary measures (that is, disciplinary disengagement, overall student victimization, and classroom disruption) at the school level among schools with different concentrations of immigrants (Table 4.2).[24] We find that, after taking into account other school characteristics, teachers com-

TABLE 4.2
*Regression models predicting disciplinary disengagement*

| | *Disciplinary disengagement* | *Classroom disruption* | *School victimization* |
|---|---|---|---|
| SCHOOL AND COMMUNITY CHARACTERISTICS | | | |
| *School and community variables* | | | |
| School size (log) | -0.029 | 0.151 | -0.106 |
| | (0.152) | (0.212) | (0.062) |
| School highest grade level | 0.219** | 0.006 | 0.026 |
| | (0.070) | (0.097) | (0.028) |
| Community size | 0.035 | -0.022 | 0.014 |
| | (0.039) | (0.054) | (0.016) |
| *School-level student characteristics* | | | |
| Average parental education | -0.157* | -0.181 | -0.019 |
| | (0.067) | (0.093) | (0.027) |
| Variation in parental education | -0.143 | -0.479 | -0.112 |
| | (0.839) | (1.165) | (0.342) |
| STUDENT BODY CHARACTERISTICS | | | |
| *Male* | | | |
| 46%–60% | 0.018 | 0.487** | 0.168*** |
| | (0.113) | (0.157) | (0.046) |
| >60% | 0.061 | 0.097 | 0.106 |
| | (0.146) | (0.203) | (0.060) |
| *Immigrants* | | | |
| 1%–10% | 0.021 | 0.200 | 0.054 |
| | (0.115) | (0.160) | (0.047) |
| >10% | -0.082 | 0.789*** | 0.171** |
| | (0.135) | (0.190) | (0.055) |
| Intercept | 1.087 | 3.014 | 1.029* |
| | (1.132) | (1.571) | (0.461) |
| $R^2$ | 0.270 | 0.185 | 0.171 |
| N | 171 | 170 | 171 |

NOTE: Standard errors are in parentheses. Missing covariates (with the exception of gender variables) are mean substituted; dummy variables flagging missing covariates are included in the analyses but not shown. Analyses are adjusted using weights provided by TIMSS.

* $p < .05$; ** $p < .01$; *** $p < .001$.

plain about disciplinary disengagement less in schools with students from higher social backgrounds (measured by parents' education). More interestingly, the analysis reveals that in schools with high immigrant concentrations classroom disruption appears much higher and victimization is slightly more common. Both indicators are more common in mixed-sex schools, which cover the large majority of Italian schools. Hence the high presence of immigrants is associated with more disturbances in classes. We see later whether this has negative consequences on learning and performance.

At the student level, two discipline-related measures are available: individual responses with regard to student victimization, and subjective safety at school. Because the assessment of safety at school by individual students almost identically reflects the results based on the victimization index (those with higher values of student victimization also felt less safe at school), we restrict results to student victimizations, which have the advantage of being easier to interpret, given that they are objective measures of actual behavior (Table 4.3).

The risk of being victimized is not equally distributed among students but depends on both student and school characteristics. Immigrants, after taking into account control variables, generally suffer higher levels of victimization: that is, they are more often teased, hurt, or have property stolen. In supplementary analysis we find that the association between immigrant status and victimization is moderated by language use. Speaking Italian at home very slightly reduces the likelihood of being victimized and immigration status loses importance, showing that victimization is most likely related to integration in the new home country, including speaking the language. No differences are found between genders, among different ages, or among students with different social backgrounds (i.e., parental education).

As regards school-level characteristics, multilevel models show that victimization is not significantly more common in schools with high concentrations of immigrants (more than 10 percent). The same does not hold, however, for mixed-sex schools: compared with female-dominated schools, these have higher probabilities of victimization. Thus a male-dominated school comes with higher relative risk of victimization than one with many immigrants. School or community size does not matter. Interestingly, disruption during classes and disciplinary disengagement at the school level is not correlated with an individual's risk of victimization. Overall, school-level characteristics add little to the statistical explanation and variance across schools is limited, probably because student victimization is very much an individual-level phenomenon.

However, the pertinent question here is whether presence of immigrants increases student victimization or microcrime, given that the index includes "having things stolen." Our models do not reveal a higher risk to students in general of being victimized in schools with large numbers of immigrants. However, immigrants themselves are at greater risk of being victimized. These results say nothing about the aggressors, so a possible

TABLE 4.3
*Hierarchical linear models estimating the effects of student- and school-level characteristics on student reports of victimization*

| | *Model 1* | *Model 2* | *Model 3* |
|---|---|---|---|
| STUDENT BACKGROUND | | | |
| Male | −0.016 | −0.024 | −0.025 |
| | (0.026) | (0.026) | (0.026) |
| Age | −0.054 | −0.055 | −0.055 |
| | (0.030) | (0.030) | (0.030) |
| Immigrant status | 0.246*** | 0.235*** | 0.235*** |
| | (0.065) | (0.066) | (0.066) |
| Highest parental education | 0.006 | 0.010 | 0.010 |
| | (0.009) | (0.009) | (0.009) |
| Number of books in household | 0.012 | 0.014 | 0.014 |
| | (0.011) | (0.011) | (0.011) |
| Household size | 0.004 | 0.003 | 0.003 |
| | (0.012) | (0.012) | (0.012) |
| SCHOOL AND COMMUNITY CHARACTERISTICS | | | |
| *School and community variables* | | | |
| School size (log) | | −0.124 | −0.123 |
| | | (0.072) | (0.072) |
| School highest grade level | | 0.022 | 0.022 |
| | | (0.037) | (0.037) |
| Community size | | 0.016 | 0.016 |
| | | (0.015) | (0.015) |
| *School-level student characteristics* | | | |
| Male students | | | |
| 46%–60% | | 0.169*** | 0.159*** |
| | | (0.046) | (0.047) |
| >60% | | 0.125* | 0.122* |
| | | (0.059) | (0.060) |
| Immigrant students | | | |
| 1%–10% | | 0.059 | 0.054 |
| | | (0.046) | (0.046) |
| >10% | | 0.091 | 0.080 |
| | | (0.059) | (0.061) |
| Average parental education | | −0.061* | −0.057* |
| | | (0.027) | (0.028) |
| Variation in parental education | | 0.182 | 0.191 |
| | | (0.345) | (0.347) |
| *Disciplinary climate* | | | |
| Principal reports: frequency of disciplinary disengagement | | | −0.001 |
| | | | (0.032) |
| Teacher reports: frequency of classroom disruption | | | 0.020 |
| | | | (0.023) |
| Intercept | 1.258** | 1.896** | 1.823** |
| | (0.427) | (0.698) | (0.706) |
| Pseudo $R^2$ | −0.001 | −0.003 | −0.004 |
| Proportion of variance across schools | 0.061 | 0.053 | 0.054 |
| N | 4,236 | 4,236 | 4,236 |

NOTE: Standard errors are in parentheses. Missing covariates (with the exception of gender and disciplinary climate measures) are mean substituted; dummy variables flagging missing covariates are included in the analyses but not shown. Analyses are adjusted using weights provided by TIMSS.

* $p < .05$; ** $p < .01$; *** $p < .001$.

interpretation is that immigrants victimize other immigrants. This would still match public perception. There are, however, reasons to doubt this interpretation. First, in supplementary analysis we examine a cross-level interaction between student immigration status (specifically, first-generation immigrants) and immigrant concentration at the school level. This analysis reveals that victimization of immigrants is much lower in schools with high immigrant concentrations—in fact, in these schools immigrants have victimization levels identical to those of Italians. Second, the results on language use suggest that immigrants more integrated (into the native student population) would be less victimized. Taken together, these findings suggest that immigrants are victims of natives, rather than the source of violence.

Although the models include all possible relevant information, we cannot control for all distorting heterogeneity, especially when unobserved. Fixed-effect multilevel models are of some help because they eliminate bias from unobserved heterogeneity at school level. The models fully confirm our victimization interpretation, underlining that nonobserved differences among schools are not responsible for the higher victimization of immigrants.

Repeating the analysis on the Trentino provincial data, we obtain basically the same results, thus suggesting a pattern. In addition, the provincial data make it possible to stratify the results by different school tracks at the upper secondary level. These results should be treated with some caution because the number of sampled schools is low. Victimization is particularly common in technical schools, which usually are of five-year duration and give access to university, but considerably lower in *licei*, which are the traditional academic track leading to university, and at the vocational schools, which prepare pupils for skilled manual occupations. Immigrant concentration does not matter.

The Trentino provincial data also make it possible to investigate the disciplinary measures, such as reprimand by the teacher, employed by teachers and schools (see Table 4.4). Reprimand is most common, with about 80 percent of students reporting that they had been reprimanded at least once; being made to stand in a corner is an experience shared by about 15 percent of students; and parents being called to school concerns 5 percent of students but is much more common among students with immigration backgrounds. However, the reasons for immigrant parents being

TABLE 4.4

*Disciplinary consequences in Trentino*

| | REPROVED BY TEACHER | | | SENT TO CORNER | | | PARENTS CALLED | | | VISITED PRINCIPAL'S OFFICE | | | TEMPORARILY SUSPENDED | | |
|---|---|---|---|---|---|---|---|---|---|---|---|---|---|---|---|
| | *Mean* | *95%* | *CI* | *Mean* | *95%* | *CI* | *Mean* | *95%* | *CI* | *Mean* | *95%* | *CI* | *Mean* | *95%* | *CI* |
| Native | 0.83 | 0.81 | 0.85 | 0.14 | 0.12 | 0.16 | 0.04 | 0.03 | 0.05 | 0.06 | 0.05 | 0.07 | 0.02 | 0.01 | 0.02 |
| Immigrant, first generation | 0.65 | 0.58 | 0.71 | 0.16 | 0.11 | 0.21 | 0.10 | 0.06 | 0.15 | 0.09 | 0.05 | 0.13 | 0.03 | 0.01 | 0.06 |
| Immigrant, second generation | 0.84 | 0.78 | 0.89 | 0.19 | 0.13 | 0.25 | 0.09 | 0.05 | 0.14 | 0.09 | 0.04 | 0.13 | 0.04 | 0.01 | 0.07 |
| All | 0.81 | 0.79 | 0.83 | 0.15 | 0.13 | 0.17 | 0.05 | 0.04 | 0.07 | 0.07 | 0.06 | 0.08 | 0.02 | 0.01 | 0.03 |

LOGISTIC REGRESSION: VISITED PRINCIPAL'S OFFICE

| | *Coefficient* | *SE* | $p > z$ |
|---|---|---|---|
| Male student | 0.85 | 0.22 | 0.00 |
| Immigrant, first generation | 0.07 | 0.36 | 0.84 |
| Immigrant, second generation | 0.36 | 0.31 | 0.25 |
| School mark | –0.49 | 0.12 | 0.00 |
| Level of education, mother | 0.19 | 0.10 | 0.06 |
| Language skills (1–4) | 0.50 | 0.26 | 0.06 |
| Student victimization index | 0.50 | 0.15 | 0.00 |
| *Liceo* | 0.98 | 0.41 | 0.02 |
| Vocational school (*istituto tecnico*) | 0.65 | 0.41 | 0.11 |
| Intercept | –5.73 | 1.08 | 0.00 |

NOTE: Trento school data, 2008.

Coding of all variables is never = 0; at least once = 1. CI = confidence interval; SE = standard error.

called to school are not necessarily related to their child's misbehavior. For instance, parents are usually informed by the school of poor student performance, which may explain the differences between natives and immigrants, who usually perform worse, as we shall see in the next section. These conferences are initiated by the teacher and do not involve school-level authority. It should be borne in mind that there is huge variety among teachers in use of these measures.

More serious disciplinary infractions usually involve the school's principal, to whom students are sent and who usually informs them of possible additional disciplinary measures. Less than 10 percent of students reported this experience. Much more severe is temporary suspension from school, which must be approved by the school council, with an accordingly much lower incidence: about 2 percent of students. Overall, we find no substantial differences between native students and those with immigration backgrounds in the frequency of these disciplinary measures, apart from teachers calling the parents of immigrant children more frequently, while natives are more often reprimanded by their teachers. From a multivariate perspective, we examine being sent to the principal as the most significant event. Our analysis shows that this is much more frequent for male students, students with lower grades, those lacking language skills, and those with a high victimization index. *Licei* seem to apply severe disciplinary measures more often. Immigration status, as in the bivariate correlation, is not of importance here. Overall, Table 4.4 shows that students less integrated both culturally (inadequate language skills) and socially (more victimized by their schoolmates) have higher risks of being sent to the principal.

## PERFORMANCE

Aside from disciplinary questions, it is often argued that academic performance at school could suffer from the presence of immigrants (Brunello and Rocco 2011). A very simple mechanism may be responsible for this: students with immigration backgrounds, especially first-generation immigrants, usually are not fluent in the host country's language. This may cause them problems in understanding and following lessons and also lower the overall performance of the class, because the teacher must reduce the amount of classwork and the speed of teaching, so as not to create a gap between native and immigrant pupils.

We therefore ask whether concentration of immigrants is associated with an overall lower level of student cognitive performance and, especially, what the consequences are for native, nonimmigrant, students. We also investigate the role of overall disciplinary climate and student victimization in shaping individual performance. All the analyses are based on a combined math and science score used to assess overall student performance.

On comparing Italy with other countries, it must be acknowledged that student performance in the secondary system is far from optimal. As confirmed by PISA and TIMSS data for various years, Italian adolescent students are chronically located below the international average (Checchi 2004; Barone 2006). The 2006 PISA data on student performance shows a mean score for Italian students considerably below the overall international mean of 500, both in science, with a score of 475, and in math, with only 462. By comparison, Finnish 15-year-old students perform best, with mean scores of 563 in science and 548 in math, and French students are at the mean for both subjects.[25] Surprisingly, this occurs despite Italy ranking among the top-performing countries in regard to elementary school students, as PIRLS data show for language and literacy performance, thereby confirming Checchi's findings (2004). The problem thus seems to lie with lower secondary school (*scuole medie*), although better assessment of this point requires comparison with upper secondary school data, provided by TIMSS Advanced 2008 data.[26]

As shown in Table 4.5, the majority of variance in cognitive performance occurs at the individual level, but a considerable share, over 30 percent, of the overall variance is due to school-level variance, highlighting the importance of school context for learning.

Consequently, school composition plays an important role. First, parental education is important. This effect operates mainly, though not exclusively, through a student's (cultural, economic, and social) resources. Heterogeneity of parental education at the school level is of no relevance. And interestingly, performance does not vary systematically with immigrant concentration at schools. Finally, performance is lower in larger communities.

Turning to individual-level variables, multivariate analyses confirm gender differences in math and science performance. It is well documented that boys usually perform better in math and science and girls have better reading and writing skills. The importance of social background for

TABLE 4.5

*Hierarchical linear models estimating the effects of student- and school-level characteristics on test score*

| | *Model 1* | *Model 2* | *Model 3* |
|---|---|---|---|
| STUDENT BACKGROUND | | | |
| Male | 27.337*** | 27.601*** | 27.387*** |
| | (3.271) | (3.276) | (3.264) |
| Age | −34.857*** | −34.562*** | −35.267*** |
| | (3.836) | (3.836) | (3.824) |
| Immigrant status | −29.581*** | −29.104*** | −26.592*** |
| | (8.246) | (8.261) | (8.245) |
| Highest parental education | 8.612*** | 8.092*** | 8.204*** |
| | (1.116) | (1.124) | (1.120) |
| Number of books in household | 22.526*** | 22.338*** | 22.460*** |
| | (1.359) | (1.360) | (1.355) |
| Household size | −4.614** | −4.538** | −4.469** |
| | (1.547) | (1.547) | (1.541) |
| SCHOOL AND COMMUNITY CHARACTERISTICS | | | |
| *School and community variables* | | | |
| School size (log) | | 15.355 | 8.424 |
| | | (20.038) | (19.481) |
| School highest grade level | | −21.731* | −14.487 |
| | | (10.248) | (10.070) |
| Community size | | −11.472** | −9.283* |
| | | (4.131) | (4.016) |
| *School-level student characteristics* | | | |
| Male students | | | |
| 46%–60% | | −9.432 | 1.128 |
| | | (12.660) | (13.020) |
| >60% | | −17.777 | −11.573 |
| | | (16.264) | (15.890) |
| Immigrant students | | | |
| 1%–10% | | −4.730 | 0.063 |
| | | (12.714) | (12.434) |
| >10% | | −18.727 | −12.409 |
| | | (16.254) | (16.147) |
| Average parental education | | 32.693*** | 25.984*** |
| | | (7.382) | (7.329) |
| Variation in parental education | | −119.130 | −100.340 |
| | | (95.258) | (91.915) |
| *Disciplinary climate* | | | |
| Principal reports: frequency of disciplinary disengagement | | | −27.199** |
| | | | (8.557) |
| Teacher reports: frequency of classroom disruption | | | −4.944 |
| | | | (6.282) |
| Student reports | | | |
| Victimization incidents, school level | | | −30.236 |
| | | | (21.923) |
| Victimization incidents, student level | | | −10.828*** |
| | | | (1.965) |

| | | | |
|---|---|---|---|
| Intercept | 1,361.010*** | 1,385.090*** | 1,485.630*** |
| | (54.790) | (163.260) | (161.400) |
| Pseudo $R^2$ | 0.014 | 0.016 | 0.017 |
| Proportion of variance across schools | 0.336 | 0.304 | 0.288 |
| *N* | 4,236 | 4,236 | 4,236 |

NOTE: Standard errors are in parentheses. Missing covariates (with the exception of gender and disciplinary climate measures) are mean substituted; dummy variables flagging missing covariates are included in the analyses but not shown. Analyses are adjusted using weights provided by TIMSS.

* $p < .05$; ** $p < .01$; *** $p < .001$.

performance and educational achievement is extensively documented, and possible mechanisms have been widely discussed (see Ballarino and Schadee 2006, 2008). Notwithstanding "parental social background" being a term involving different concepts for various mechanisms of intergenerational transmission of resources, the number of books in the home, taken as an indicator of cultural resources, has a strong positive effect on cognitive performance. Age has a significantly negative effect: being older than the usual eighth grade age of 14 years is most often the result of repeating a grade because of low performance. Obviously, repeating a year is not helpful in achieving even median performance later. This negative effect is lower for immigrants (first generation), though the differences with natives are not statistically significant (result of interaction not reported). Finally, performance decreases with increasing household size.

As expected, the lower performance of immigrants clearly emerges from the data.[27] In supplementary analysis, an interaction emerges for immigration status and school immigrant concentration: first-generation immigrants perform considerably worse when they attend schools with high concentrations of immigrant pupils than when they attend schools with low concentrations. This may indicate the importance of educational policies targeted to integration of young immigrant pupils in nonsegregated schools. Such policies will help immigrants' school performance and their integration into the host society.[28]

As for disciplinary climate and performance, results are not straightforward. The frequency of classroom disruption does not matter for student performance, significantly, neither does victimization incidence at the school level. However, a principal report of more incidences of disciplinary disengagement in the school is associated with lower average student performance, that is, in schools where disengagement is more frequent, performance is worse. Hence, school disciplinary climate affects cognitive performance and the teaching success of schools.

The greater the student victimization, the worse the cognitive performance—equally for Italians and immigrants (we do not report detailed interactions). Whether victimization is of intellectually weaker students or victimization has consequences on performance is unknown. Further, we found no indication that school-level disciplinary climate has different consequences for different students, especially natives and immigrants (we do not report details).

## CONCLUSION

We have examined school discipline and its consequences for student performance. We have shown that a lack of discipline at school may hinder student learning and thus cognitive performance. In particular, we find that the students being victimized have significantly lower cognitive performance. Though school-level characteristics—such as amount of disciplinary disengagement or its socioeconomic composition—have a role in student cognitive performance or victimization risk, these turn out to be mainly individual-level phenomena that must be explained at the micro-level. Thus, social composition of the school adds little to the explanation, which instead resides in the social interaction among pupils, families, and teachers. This is an interesting result that highlights the family's role as the prime locus for teaching basic behavior and teachers' role in promoting school discipline and student performance.

Despite Italian television linking school bullying, violence, and lack of discipline with immigrants, evidence of significant disciplinary problems in Italian schools is scant, as is the effect of school disciplinary climate on cognitive performance. A lack of school discipline can therefore hardly be responsible for Italy's overall low performance on test scores in secondary schools. It is more likely due to structural problems (such as lack of funds, inadequacy of school buildings and infrastructure, and shortage or high turnover of teaching staff). The real problems of the Italian educational system—its structural backwardness and lack of resources and investment in teacher training—have much more to do with classic patterns of social inequality and class privileges than with a serious lack of discipline per se.

NOTES

1. Searching a year's issues of a major journal (*Sole 24 ore*) for "discipline" and "school" did not return a single relevant match.

2. Letizia Moratti, former mayor of Milan, repeatedly equated undocumented immigrant status with criminal behavior.

3. In this chapter "immigrants" or "persons with immigration backgrounds" refers to persons born outside the country and their children born in Italy; that is, immigrants are both first- and second-generation migrants. In the Italian legal context second-generation immigrants are also "foreigners"—a term less commonly used—because they remain non-Italian nationals. Naturalizations are very low.

4. In the 19th century per capita educational spending was higher on secondary and tertiary schools than it was on elementary schools (notwithstanding the tremendously high illiteracy rate).

5. These developments almost canceled out both the strictly vocational nature of the technical secondary schools and the selective function of the "maturity" examination at the end of the five years of secondary education.

6. Bertola, Checchi, and Oppedisano (2007) find that educational and labor-market outcomes are more favorable for students who attended public schools than for those who attended private schools.

7. This high standardization was partly weakened in the mid-1970s, when fragmentation of the educational system increased. But problems remained, whether inequalities of educational opportunities or quality of the educational process or mismatch between education and labor market.

8. This favorable position is threatened by reforms implemented in 2009, mainly because of welfare cuts for budgetary reasons. The formula of three teachers for two classes, which was introduced in 1990 and provided good teaching quality and good assistance for problematic children, is to be abandoned, and Italian elementary schools will resume the classic formula of one teacher per class. At the time of this writing, 80,000–90,000 elementary teachers will be made redundant. Many Italian teachers are hired on a temporary contract basis. The result will be loss of younger and better-prepared teachers, usually hired on precarious work agreements, to protect the older ones (most of whom are not even university graduates).

9. Usually perceived as particularly problematic is the three-year middle school (ages 11 to 14), because it does not allow differentiation according to ability.

10. Cassazione, Sez 3, September 21, 2000, n. 12501; November 26, 1998, n. 11984.

11. Pronounced differences in discipline, of course, do exist among regions and among schools. The most difficult students are often those attending low-grade schools in southern regions or suburbs.

12. The reaction to Minister of Education Gelmini's reform, which—for mere budgetary reasons—cut the jobs of tens of thousands of temporary teachers in

elementary schools, is an example of this collective approach to education, which in principle is still regarded as a public good.

13. In northern Italy, new births from immigrant parents amount to 20 percent of total births.

14. In central Italy, only Umbria has a comparable number of immigrants.

15. Despite this rapid growth, the total number of immigrant students in the educational system is still quite low compared with other EU countries with longstanding immigration: Switzerland, 23.6 percent; Germany, 10 percent; Netherlands, 13 percent; UK, 15 percent; Spain, 5.7 percent; Portugal, 5.5 percent; France, 5 percent.

16. Emilia-Romagna has 12 percent non-Italian students; Umbria, 11.4 percent; Lombardy, 10.3 percent; Veneto, 10.2 percent; and Marche, 9.9 percent.

17. Of course, it is difficult to assess whether tracks are chosen as a consequence of career choices of immigrant students and their families or is instead imposed. However, after controlling for individual capabilities (votes), our analysis shows that the odds of an immigrant student entering *liceo* are significantly lower than those of a native.

18. Being charged with an offense does not necessarily mean being more violent or being more criminal in intent and behavior. Our data on youth crime, in fact, may be biased by various factors: differences in police efficiency between northern and southern Italy or politically driven local policies on microcriminality.

19. In 2001, 41,542 teenagers (under 18) were charged with 51,097 offenses. About 4 teenagers out of every 1,000 were prosecuted. Among these 4, at least 1 had committed the offense in one of the five largest cities in Italy (Milan, Turin, Rome, Naples, Palermo).

20. For a detailed description of the Italian data in the TIMSS survey see http://archivio.invalsi.it/ricerche-internazionali/iea-timss/ (in Italian).

21. The analyses presented here strictly follow the comparative framework of this book. We invite the interested reader to refer to the working paper (http://events.unitn.it/en/famine/pubblications) for more analyses relevant to the Italian context.

22. For the sake of interpretability, we abstained from using the available subjective measures of overall climate, overall safety, or severity of specific problems at school.

23. Regional diversity, including education, is a well-documented characteristic of Italy (Reyneri 2002; Bratti, Checchi, and Filippin 2003; Schizzerotto and Barone 2006). Analyses therefore should always control for region, distinguishing north, center, and south. Regional differences, however, can hardly be responsible for divergences. Therefore, to investigate the reasons for these differences, we initially included two indices of educational resource availability, knowing distribution is unequal: structural shortage of instruction space and buildings, and functional shortage of teaching materials and budget. These indices were confirmed by factor analysis. We found that structural and functional shortages

were much more common in southern schools and that there were no statistically significant differences between northern and central schools, as expected.

24. More disciplinary disengagement occurred in the south and in schools with more severe functional shortages, as expected.

25. See http://www.pisa.oecd.org/dataoecd/15/13/39725224.pdf and http://pirls.bc.edu.

26. In a supplementary analysis, very much in line with the results of previous research on the topic (Bratti et al. 2003), we found strong regional differences with a clear north–south gradient. At the same time, and closely correlated with the regional disparities, a shortage of functional and structural resources is associated with considerably lower student performance.

27. No significant differences were found for regional performance of immigrants (we do not report details). Immigrant disadvantage was considerably reduced, but not completely explainable, when controlling for social background variables and whether Italian was spoken at home, which was the only measure available to substitute for language skills. Speaking Italian at home increases performance. This became even more evident when the analysis was restricted to students with immigration backgrounds, as one might argue was necessary, because Italians are all assumed to speak Italian at home (although this is not always the case, given the widespread use of dialects).

28. Performance gains for native pupils (through better learning conditions) attending schools with low immigrant concentration are very small.

## REFERENCES

Ballarino, Gabriele, and Hans M. A. Schadee. 2006. "Espansione dell'istruzione e diseguaglianza delle opportunità educative nell'Italia contemporanea." *Polis*, no. 2 (August): 207–32.

———. 2008. "La disuguaglianza delle opportunità educative in Italia, 1930–1980: Tendenze e cause." *Polis*, December, no 3: 373–402.

Barbagli, Marzio. 1974. *Disoccupazione intellettuale e sistema scolastico in Italia*. Bologna: Il Mulino.

Barone, C. 2006. "Cultural Capital, Ambition and the Explanation of Inequalities in Learning Outcomes: A Comparative Analysis." *Sociology* 40 (6): 1039–58.

Bell, Brian, Stephen Machin, and Francesco Fasani. 2010. "Crime and Immigration: Evidence from Large Immigrant Waves." London: Centre for Research and Analysis of Migration. http://www.econ.ucl.ac.uk/cream/pages/CDP/CDP_12_10.pdf.

Bertola, Giuseppe, Daniele Checchi, and Veruska Oppedisano. 2007. "Private School Quality in Italy." IZA [Institute for the Study of Labor] Discussion Paper no. 3222. Bonn, Germany: IZA. http://ftp.iza.org/dp3222.pdf.

Bianchi, M., P. Buonanno, and P. Pinotti. 2008. "Do Immigrants Cause Crime?" Paris School of Economics Working Paper no. 2008-05.

Bratti, Massimiliano, Daniele Checchi, and Antonio Filippin. 2003. "Territorial Differences in Italian Students' Mathematical Competencies: Evidence from PISA 2003." IZA Discussion Paper no. 2603. http://ftp.iza.org/dp2603.pdf.

Brauns, Hildegard, Susanne Steinmann, and Stefani Scherer. 2003. "The CASMIN Educational Classification in International Comparative Research." In *Advances in Cross-National Comparison. A European Working-Book for Demographic and Socio-Economic Variables*, edited by Jürgen H. P. Hoffmeyer-Zlotnik and Christof Wolf, 196–221. New York: Kluwer Academic/Plenum.

Brunello, Giorgio, and Lorenzo Rocco. 2011. The Effect of Immigration on the School Performance of Natives: Cross Country Evidence Using PISA Test Scores. IZA Discussion Paper no. 5479.

Checchi, Daniele. 2004. Da dove vengono le competenze scolastiche? L'indagine PISA 2000 in Italia. http://checchi.economia.unimi.it/pdf/un24.pdf.

Cvajner, Martina. 2008. "Immigrati nelle scuole del Trentino." Unpublished paper. Università di Trento.

Eurydice. 2009. *Integrating Immigrant Children into Schools in Europe*. Brussels: Eurydice. http://eacea.ec.europa.eu/education/eurydice/documents/thematic_reports/101EN.pdf.

ISTAT. 2003. *La criminalità minorile nei grandi centri urbani, anno 2001*. Rome: ISTAT.

———. 2006. *Rapporto Annuale*. Rome: ISTAT.

———. 2008. *Rapporto Annuale*. Rome: ISTAT.

Ministero dell'Interno. 2007. Primo Rapporto sugli Immigrati in Italia. Rome. Retrieved November 22, 2009, from http://www1.interno.it/mininterno/export/sites/default/it/assets/files/15/0673_Rapporto_immigrazione_BARBAGLI.pdf.

Mullis, Ina, V. S. Michael, O. Martin, Ann M. Kennedy, and Pierre Foy. 2007. IEA's Progress in International Reading Literacy Study in Primary School in 40 Countries. Chestnut Hill, MA: IMSS and PIRLS International Study Center, Boston College.

OECD. 2007. *PISA 2006 Science Competencies for Tomorrow's World*. Paris: OECD.

———. 2009. *Creating Effecting Teaching and Learning Environments: First Results from TALIS*. Paris: OECD.

———. 2010. *Education at a Glance*. Paris: OECD.

Rabe-Hersketh, Sophia, and Anders Skrondal. 2005. *Multilevel and Longitudinal Modeling Using Stata*. College Station, TX: Stata Press.

Reyneri, Emilio. 2002. *Sociologia del mercato del lavoro*, 2nd ed. Bologna: Il Mulino.

Salerni, Anna. 2005. *La disciplina a scuola*. Rome: Carocci.

Schizzerotto, Antonio, and Carlo Barone. 2006. *Sociologie dell'Istruzione*. Bologna: Il Mulino.

CHAPTER FIVE

# School Discipline and Academic Achievement in Japan

*Hiroshi Ishida and Satoshi Miwa*

Youth crime and delinquency attract considerable attention in the media all over the world. One of the most shocking instances involving juvenile crime in Japan was probably the 1997 killings of several elementary school students by a middle school student in Kobe. A boy attacked elementary school girls with a hammer in February and March during the daytime at school and on the street. In May 1997 he killed a schoolboy living nearby who was a friend of his younger brother. After the killing, he chopped off the victim's head and left it in a garbage bag at the school entrance. The crime attracted media attention because of its extreme cruelty and gruesomeness and the boy's motives: killing to experience murder. There was provocative media coverage about the incident, including controversial identification of the delinquent boy in weekly magazines, despite his being only 14 years old and protected by the Juvenile Law. The incident also had large social impacts. Hotlines for children were established, and there were discussions about amending the Juvenile Law to include more severe punishment, including lowering the age limit for prosecution, monitoring and restricting media coverage, and protecting the rights of victims and juvenile delinquents.

Whenever there is sensational media coverage about juvenile delinquency, the public tends to assume that juvenile crime and delinquency are on the rise and becoming more malignant. Official statistics on juvenile crime in Japan, however, do not support such an assumption (Ayukawa 2001). Figure 5.1 shows trends of juvenile delinquent arrests and the rate by 100,000 young people ages 10 to 19. The number and rate of arrests peaked in the early 1980s, followed by a steady decrease. Although juvenile crimes increased in the late 1990s, since 2003 the rate has continued to decline. Figure 5.2

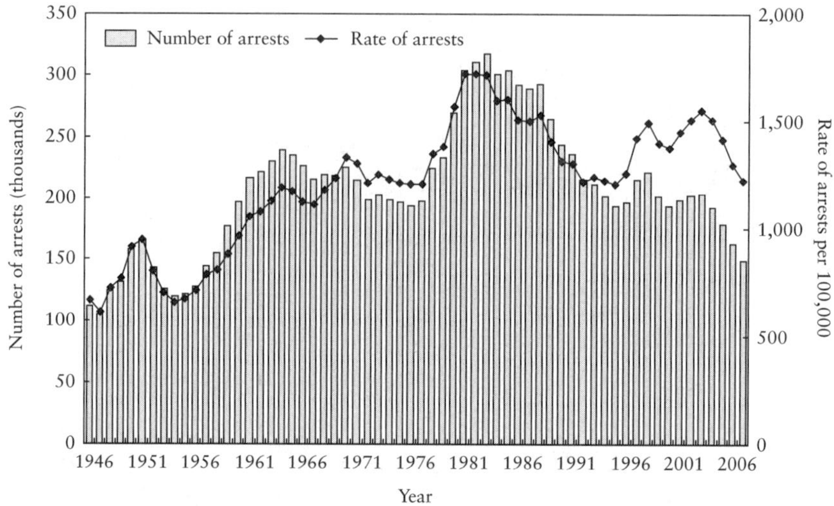


*Figure 5.1.* The number of juvenile arrests and the rate of juvenile arrests per 100,000

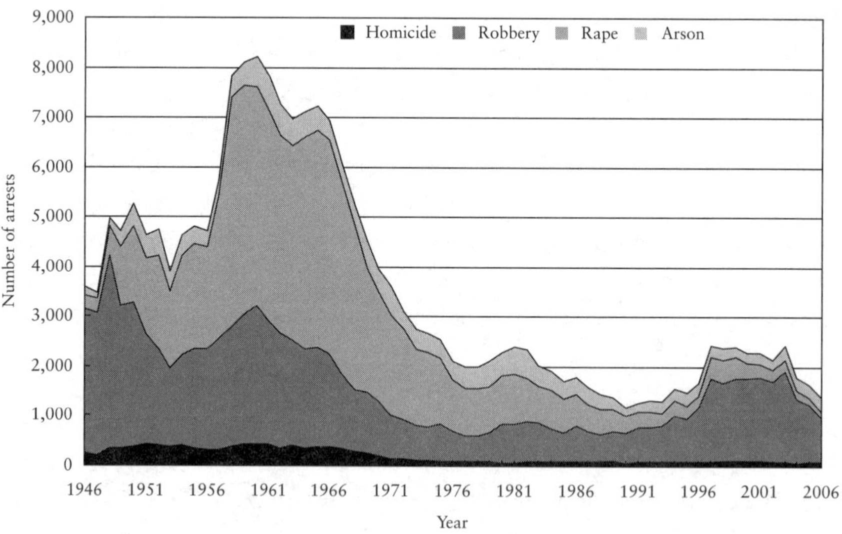


*Figure 5.2.* Trend of brutal crimes committed by juveniles

shows a similar pattern for trends of juvenile arrests for brutal crimes (homicide, robbery, rape, and arson). Despite a slight increase in the late 1990s (attributable mainly to a jump in robberies from 1996 to 1997), the number of brutal crimes has been on the decline since the early 1960s. The slight increase in these crimes observed in the late 1990s corresponds with public recognition of the rise of heinous crimes, and some attribute the increase to more stringent enforcement by juvenile police at the time (Kuzuno 2003). However, taken as a whole, crimes committed by juveniles have been on the decline and therefore public perception about juvenile delinquency does not always reflect reality.

## DELINQUENCY IN JAPAN

In Japan in recent years, reporting of any serious juvenile delinquency is almost always associated with school education. It is now common to assume that the school environment acts as a causal factor in student misbehavior, especially for misbehavior at school. However, historically, juvenile delinquency and school climate have not been associated. As highlighted in Figure 5.2, immediately following the end of World War II and up until the early 1960s, there were many more incidents of delinquencies and serious crimes committed by youth. However, most offenses were committed by youth who were already out of school (age 15 or older for middle school graduates and 18 to 19 for high school graduates). In the late 1950s, the high school attendance rate was about 50 percent, and going to school was considered a privilege because school was protected from the real world. Many young people who were not able to continue their schooling moved from rural areas to urban settings that were still in turmoil following the defeat in the war, leading some of them to break the law (Matsumoto 1984). Lack of education and poor socioeconomic conditions were thought to be the two major factors in explaining juvenile delinquency.

During the high economic growth of the 1960s and 1970s, the high school attendance rate jumped, reaching 90 percent in 1974, and many young people remained in school for most of their teenage years. The extension of school-leaving age changed the relationship between delinquency and school. As the high school attendance rate increased, ranking and stratification among high schools became more and more pronounced. The competition intensified among middle school students for entry into high school and among high school students for entry into university. In this context, the pressure to achieve and the conflict between those who advanced to high-ranking schools and those who did not were singled out as the leading causes of misbehavior among youth. Thus, the causal factor responsible for delinquency was no longer the lack of education but the excessive competition for further education (Ito 1999).

In the late 1970s and early 1980s, school violence plagued many middle and high schools in Japan (Ito 2007d). The media reported violence against teachers and the destruction of school facilities, and delinquency and student life at school were closely connected in people's minds. There was a widespread belief that the education and guidance offered by teachers at school were not adequate, causing delinquency among students. Thus, schools and teachers were considered responsible for the misbehavior (Hirota 2001). Violence within schools began to subside by the late 1980s, following the stricter enforcement of school rules by teachers. Regulations and new rules regarding students' lives both inside and outside school were strictly enforced, especially in middle school. These rules were comprehensive and totalitarian because they covered student behavior not only at school but also outside school. For example, while historically most middle schools required school uniforms, new rules often require students to wear them after school and on weekends to more easily identify them if they stay out late on the street or go places where minors are prohibited. Although some rules were reexamined and found excessive in the 1990s, the enforcement of basic rules and regulations by and large continues to the present day (Noda 2000).

Beginning in the 1990s, school misbehavior began to take on a different form. Until the 1980s, delinquency was often targeted at teachers and school facilities, and it generally took the form of physical violence. In the 1990s, however, disciplinary problems began manifesting in the form of noncompliance (Ito 2007b). Some students stopped paying attention to teachers and began walking around the classroom or going outside to play on school grounds. Because the student-teacher ratio is high in Japanese schools (often 30–40 students are supervised by one teacher),[1] it was not possible for teachers to maintain the usual classroom activities if a few students were breaking the rules. The situation was called classroom breakdown, and to remedy it additional staff was necessary to chase students who did not sit still or who ran away to the playground.

In addition to classroom breakdown, bullying of students by other students became a widespread phenomenon in the 1990s (Matsunaga and

Okura 1999).[2] Bullying can be physical violence, such as hitting and pushing, but can also be more subtle, such as not allowing a student to join a group, hiding belongings, or spreading rumors. Although bullying is not defined by law as delinquent behavior except in those cases that involve physical violence, it is widely recognized as a problem at school by teachers and the Japanese Ministry of Education.[3] The ministry has compiled statistics on bullying since 1985. In 2007 there were 48,896 cases of bullying reported in elementary schools, or in 39 percent of elementary schools; 43,505 cases in middle schools, or 64 percent; and 8,385 cases in high schools, or 51 percent (Ministry of Education 2008c).

Another type of misbehavior reported in schools involves absenteeism (Hosaka 2000; Ito 2007a, 2007c). "Absenteeism" generally refers to the nonattendance of a student who is expected to be at school; in Japan it is so prevalent that there is a special category of absenteeism called school refusal, defined as absence from school for more than 30 days per year (Okano and Tsuchiya 1999). According to the School Basic Survey of the Ministry of Education (2008b), over 100,000, or about 3 percent, middle school students were absent from school for more than 30 days per year and about 24,000, or less than 1 percent, elementary school students were. In addition, there are students who come to school but cannot take part in the regular school program and spend most of their time at the school's nurse's office, known as attendance at the nurse's office. It is estimated that 6.6 per 1,000 students in elementary and middle schools are classified as in attendance at the nurse's office in a given year (Akiba 2007). The proportion of students who refuse to attend ordinary school programs has been increasing gradually since the late 1990s. This has been attributed to increased numbers of students who cannot establish personal relationships with others and parents' increased tolerance for absenteeism.

Although bullying, classroom breakdown, and absenteeism have been receiving more attention recently, this does not mean that the traditional form of delinquent behavior has disappeared from schools. On the contrary, there have been persistent reports of violent school incidents in the 1990s and 2000s. According to a survey by the Ministry of Education in 2007, violent behavior at school was reported by 6 percent of elementary schools, 37 percent of middle schools, and 54 percent of high schools. The behavior included physical violence against teachers, fellow students, and other individuals and destruction of school facilities. In total, 5,000 violent incidents were reported in elementary schools, 37,000 incidents in middle schools, and 11,000 incidents in high schools, compared to 100,000 incidents of bullying in all schools from elementary to high school. Therefore, the proportion of students involved in violent incidents is still very low, less than 1 percent of all students, even in middle schools, where the incidents are most frequent (Ministry of Education 2008c).

When we examine the disciplinary actions taken against students who committed violent acts (physical violence against teachers or students and vandalism), there is a clear difference between elementary and middle school level and high school level. Among delinquent students in elementary and middle schools, less than 5 percent were expelled, suspended, or reprimanded, whereas over 80 percent of delinquent students in high school experienced these punishments (Ministry of Education 2008c). Japanese elementary and middle schools are extremely cautious in giving formal punishment to students, because they are considered immature and could be disadvantaged in later life if labeled delinquent.

Delinquent behavior at school is related to educational outcome of the students. Compared with schools with less frequent incidents, schools that report more frequent incidents of violent behavior are more likely to enforce stricter rules and to have low-achieving students. Classroom breakdown affects achievement of other students, and students from disadvantaged backgrounds are more likely to be affected by breakdowns because they have less access to after-school private tutoring. Absenteeism (or school refusal) similarly affects student performance, especially for those who cannot afford to supplement education after school (Hida 1999; Ito 2007c).

In contemporary Japan, juvenile delinquency and misbehavior are closely related to school environment and discipline. Delinquent behavior is more frequently reported within school than outside school. Therefore, the organizational context of schools and the administration of rules and discipline in the school setting are important factors in understanding juvenile misbehaviors. In the next section, we describe characteristics of school environment, school organization, and administration of school discipline in Japan.

## JAPANESE SCHOOLS AND SCHOOL DISCIPLINE

### *Population Heterogeneity*

Population heterogeneity at the societal level may have a large impact on school pedagogical environment. Racial and ethnic heterogeneity may create great challenges for students and teachers as they attempt to share goals, norms, and cultures. However, at both the societal and school levels, Japanese society is characterized by a low degree of population heterogeneity. Slightly over two million registered foreigners reside in Japan, or 1.7 percent of the total Japanese population of about 128 million people in 2008. The largest subgroups are Chinese (607,000) and Koreans (593,000), each constituting 28 percent of all foreigners (Ministry of Justice 2008). Many of these "foreigners" are second- and third-generation Koreans and Chinese who were born in Japan and attend Japanese schools. These young Koreans and Chinese face the difficult challenge of being a minority while growing up in Japan, but most of them are integrated into the Japanese school system (Okano and Tsuchiya 1999; Lie 2001, 2008). There are also groups of recent immigrants, especially those who are descendants of Japanese living in Latin America. Brazilians and Peruvians of Japanese ancestry come to Japan under special immigration laws that allow them to work in Japan (Takenaka 2003; Tsuda 2003). As a result, Brazilians (317,000) constitute 15 percent of all foreigners and Peruvians (60,000) 3 percent. Immigrants from the Philippines (203,000) account for 9 percent of foreigners (Ministry of Justice 2008).

The children of recent immigrants do seem to suffer at school, particularly in mastering the Japanese language (Kojima 2007). About 25,000 foreign students in over 5,000 elementary, middle, and high schools require special assistance in Japanese language. However, this is only 0.2 percent of the student body (Ministry of Education 2008d). The Japanese 2003 Trends in International Mathematics and Science Study (TIMSS) data used in this study also show that 1.2 percent of eighth graders were born outside Japan, and 60 percent of them arrived in Japan before age five. Japanese society at large and schools in particular are not characterized by a high degree of population heterogeneity. Racial and ethnic differentiation is not clearly manifested in Japanese schools.

### *Organizational Structure*

Japanese elementary and secondary education is highly centralized under the control of the national government. Compulsory education consists of six years of elementary school and three years of lower secondary education, with uniformity and equality being the schools' governing principles (Cummings 1980; Ishida 1998). Most students in compulsory education attend local schools near their residence. Virtually all elementary school students and over 90 percent of lower secondary school students are enrolled in local public schools.[4] School facilities, personnel, and curricula are highly standardized. The school curriculum set forth by the national government specifies the course of study, and the textbooks are approved by a governmental committee. Teachers are required to cover all of the material contained in the course of study (Ministry of Education 2008a). Japanese students throughout the entire country therefore learn the same material at approximately the same time and pace.

Students receive instruction in all subjects except music, science lab, and physical education in their homeroom and remain in the same classroom and with the same classmates for the entire school year. Homeroom teachers are responsible for not only classroom management but also student well-being, known as lifestyle guidance (*seikatsu shido*). Homeroom teachers try to detect problems at an early stage by closely monitoring students' behavior. For example, some teachers ask students to keep individual diaries, and review them regularly. There are also annual visits to students' homes, and parents are invited to classroom observation days, which are held once a semester (Fukuzawa 1994; LeTendre 1994; Shimizu 1992).

Japanese elementary and secondary education practices assume that all students have the ability and willingness to learn well and master the school curriculum. Progression from grade to grade is automatic as long as students attend classes. Students do not repeat a grade nor do they skip ahead, so each grade is virtually age homogeneous. There is no curriculum tracking or ability grouping in compulsory education. The emphasis on equality and the avoidance of repeating or skipping a grade strongly discourage schoolteachers from invoking any kind of punishment that results in retaining a student in a grade (Mimizuka 1999).

While equality and homogeneity are emphasized in compulsory education, this does not necessarily mean that there are few differences in academic achievement among students. On the contrary, schools inevitably produce high achievers and low achievers. Many students attend a variety of after-school private education courses for tutorial or remedial purposes and for entrance examination preparation. Toward the end of lower secondary education, students must prepare for the high school entrance examination. Entrance into high school marks the completion of compulsory education, although over 95 percent of students enroll in the noncompulsory upper secondary education. School districts are composed of several high schools with differing academic quality, and students are sorted into one of these schools, which are ranked hierarchically (Rohlen 1983). School grades and the results of the entrance examination determine high school placement. It is not difficult to imagine that ninth graders are under pressure to perform well, and indeed, statistics show that delinquent behavior peaks at around age 14 (Ministry of Education 2008c; Okabe 2007).

### *Legal Background*

The rights of children are guaranteed by the Japanese Constitution, enacted in 1946, the Education Basic Law (*Kyoiku Kihonho*) of 1947, and the UN Convention on the Rights of the Child, ratified in 1994. Children have the right to be educated and protected by parents, and they should be free from violence. The School Education Law (*Gakko Kyoikuho*) enacted in 1947 states that principals and school teachers are prohibited from using corporal punishment. Despite corporal punishment not being legal, the media has reported its use and, in extreme cases, lawsuits have occurred.

According to the Japanese General Social Surveys of 2000 and 2001, 55 percent of respondents agreed that "corporal punishment by teachers is sometimes necessary," 25 percent neither agreed nor disagreed, and only 19 percent disagreed with the statement. When the same respondents were asked about their attitude toward corporal punishment by parents, 60 percent agreed with the statement, 23 percent neither agreed nor disagreed, and the remaining 17 percent disagreed.[5] Legal challenges to corporal punishment by teachers are still rare in contemporary Japan, and the Japanese public seems to have a tolerant attitude toward corporal punishment both at school and at home.

### *Administration of Discipline at School*

Entrance into middle school marks the beginning of a more serious and rigid academic school life that is different from the caring and nurturing environment of an elementary school. For the first time, public school students are required to wear uniforms and other aspects of personal appearance and daily activities are also regulated. For example, bags, shoes, and accessories that students carry and wear every day to school are strictly regulated. There are even rules for hairstyle, type of trousers worn by boys, length of skirts worn by girls, and type and color of socks. Regular inspections examining whether the students follow these rules are conducted in some schools. It is well known that teachers have authority to enforce these rules, not only as respected professionals but also because homeroom teachers must fill out a student report when the students apply to high schools. Since the student report is evaluated by high schools at the time of application, the students do not want to hurt their chances of acceptance by engaging in deviant behaviors (Noda 2000).

Students complain about the extensive regulations, but there is little resistance because most accept the serious nature of the transition from elementary to middle school and believe that the rules are necessary for order in school. According to a survey conducted by the Japanese national government (Management and Coordination Agency 1993), 60 percent of middle school students agree that school regulations deprive them of their freedom and another 60 percent agree that some rules have no reason. Rules regarding hairstyle and clothing are the least popular, with over 60 percent of students responding that the rules about hairstyle should be abolished or relaxed and about half responding that dress codes should be abolished or relaxed. Nonetheless, students generally follow these rules. About 60 percent of middle school students respond that they always follow the hairstyle rule, 25 percent say they "sometimes do not follow the rule," and only 10 percent report that they do "not follow the rule," with the remaining 5 percent saying that "no rule regarding hairstyle existed at school." Dress code compliance is even higher. Furthermore, in response to the statement that those who do not follow the rules should receive severe sanctions, over 50 percent of students agreed, less than 20 percent disagreed, and the remaining 30 percent had no opinion.

The same survey asked parents of middle school students about their acceptance of detailed regulations in eight areas: hairstyle, uniform, personal belongings that can be brought to school, proper etiquette, rules regarding coming to school and going home, classroom attitude, clothes worn outside school, and out-of-school activities. The regulations in all eight areas were satisfactory to over 60 percent of parents. The rules regarding hairstyle were too strict for 20 percent of parents, and 10 percent responded that dress code rules were too strict. Two-thirds of the parents believed that school regulations help prevent juvenile delinquency. In short, the extensive regulations governing middle school students inside and outside school are generally accepted by the students and their parents.

The combination of student compliance and support from parents, principals, and teachers for these regulations minimizes disciplinary problems at school. By closely monitoring the changes in students' attitudes and behavior at school, homeroom teachers are able to detect early signs of delinquency or bullying and intervene in the students' lives. When schools do experience delinquent behavior, they are concerned with preventing the behavior and rehabilitating students. As previously described, formal punishment for delinquent behavior by elementary and middle school students is not prevalent (Ministry of Education 2008c). During this compulsory stage of education, principals and teachers avoid reporting any delinquency on official records because it may have negative consequences for the future of students.

## RESEARCH QUESTIONS

This study contributes to the larger project's focus on cross-national school discipline by examining the relationship between school characteristics, individual background and achievement, and school disciplinary climate in Japan. Specifically, the study focuses on the following five research questions. The first explores variation among schools in the prevalence of student misbehavior and asks what the determinants of school-level disciplinary climate are. The second question addresses the variation in individual achievement and examines the impact of disciplinary climate, school-level characteristics, and individual background factors on student test scores. The third question involves college expectations and attempts to identify whether school disciplinary climate is associated with the expectation of finishing college. The fourth question focuses on student victimization and its correlates. The last question asks about the consequences of school disciplinary climate and delinquency on later life stages by examining whether achievement in high school and participation in higher education are associated with student misbehavior and school environment in middle schools.

## DATA

Data for this study were drawn from the Japanese 2003 TIMSS, which includes surveys of teachers, principals, and about 4,800 eighth grade students in 146 Japanese schools (National Institute for Educational Policy Research 2005). As for supplementary analysis, we use the Japanese Life Course Panel Survey, which is composed of a youth panel of those aged 20 to 34 in 2007 and a middle-aged panel of those who were 35 to 40 in 2007. Our analysis combines the two surveys.[6] Survey questions regarding delinquent behavior committed by the respondents in middle school and the subjective school environment were used to analyze the impact of delinquency on high school type, achievement in high school, and attendance in higher education.

## ANALYSIS

Table 5.1 presents descriptive statistics for the Japanese TIMSS sample as a whole and by gender. First, regarding student characteristics, we note several unique patterns in the Japanese sample, compared with those of other nations. Japan has by far the lowest proportion of students with immigrant status. College expectations are relatively low in Japan, a phenomenon that stems partly from gender differences in educational attitudes. Male students expect to go to college at a rate of 62 percent, which is significantly higher than the rate for female students (48.9 percent). Female students aspire to go to both four-year universities and two-year junior colleges; the two-year colleges are predominantly attended by women. Because of the gender gap in college aspirations, the overall college expectations percentage is attenuated.

Second, with regard to school and community characteristics, it is clear that Japanese schools are the smallest compared to all other countries: the logged school size is 6.14, which is equivalent to about five hundred students per school. This average is in line with the organization of Japanese middle schools, in which most are composed of three grade levels (seventh, eighth, and ninth grades) averaging 3.5 homeroom classes per grade. Similarly, the mean for the school's highest grade level reflects the fact that there were only two possible answers to this question: 9 or 12. Most schools (95 percent) are public middle schools that stop at the ninth grade. The remaining schools are predominantly private schools that have both middle and high schools and end at the 12th grade. Given this distribution of possible answers, we should be cautious in interpreting any effects of this variable on our outcome measures. Finally, unlike many other nations, Japanese middle schools are predominantly mixed-sex institutions, and about 80 percent of schools have an almost equal male to female ratio (46–60 percent male). This percentage is by far the highest among the nations in this volume.

Japanese schools are much less heterogeneous with respect to parental education, ethnic background, and gender composition than schools in other nations. Japanese schools have the lowest proportion of immigrant students among the nations studied in this project. As previously described, the number of immigrants living in Japan is lower than many industrial nations. Similarly, variation in parental education is the lowest in Japan compared to all other nations except Russia.

With regard to cognitive performance, Japanese students outperform those in all other nations. The math and science test scores for Japanese

Table 5.1
*Descriptive statistics*

| | All students | | Male students | | Female students | | All project countries | |
|---|---|---|---|---|---|---|---|---|
| | *Mean* | *SE* | *Mean* | *SE* | *Mean* | *SE* | *Mean* | *SE* |
| STUDENT CHARACTERISTICS | | | | | | | | |
| *Background variables* | | | | | | | | |
| Male | 0.470 | 0.015 | | | | | 0.502 | 0.005 |
| Age | 14.400 | 0.006 | 14.398 | 0.007 | 14.402 | 0.009 | 14.193 | 0.008 |
| Immigrant status | 0.009 | 0.002 | 0.009 | 0.003 | 0.008 | 0.002 | 0.072 | 0.003 |
| Highest parental education | 5.585 | 0.059 | 5.589 | 0.068 | 5.581 | 0.077 | 5.302 | 0.029 |
| Number of books in household | 3.085 | 0.038 | 3.136 | 0.046 | 3.040 | 0.048 | 3.114 | 0.016 |
| Household size | 4.765 | 0.042 | 4.758 | 0.048 | 4.771 | 0.050 | 4.552 | 0.014 |
| *Educational attitudes: college expectations* | 0.552 | 0.019 | 0.624 | 0.022 | 0.489 | 0.026 | 0.654 | 0.007 |
| SCHOOL AND COMMUNITY CHARACTERISTICS | | | | | | | | |
| *School and community variables* | | | | | | | | |
| School size (log) | 6.140 | 0.049 | 6.122 | 0.053 | 6.157 | 0.052 | 6.478 | 0.018 |
| School highest grade level | 9.226 | 0.090 | 9.185 | 0.100 | 9.263 | 0.124 | 9.450 | 0.041 |
| Community size | 4.551 | 0.114 | 4.488 | 0.127 | 4.606 | 0.114 | 3.916 | 0.042 |
| *School-level student characteristics* | | | | | | | | |
| Male students | | | | | | | | |
| 46%–60% | 0.781 | 0.039 | 0.808 | 0.040 | 0.757 | 0.046 | 0.480 | 0.013 |
| >60% | 0.054 | 0.021 | 0.076 | 0.034 | 0.034 | 0.014 | 0.181 | 0.011 |
| Immigrant students | | | | | | | | |
| 1%–10% | 0.311 | 0.042 | 0.298 | 0.044 | 0.323 | 0.047 | 0.398 | 0.013 |
| >10% | 0.006 | 0.006 | 0.007 | 0.007 | 0.004 | 0.004 | 0.238 | 0.012 |
| Average parental education | 5.543 | 0.058 | 5.522 | 0.060 | 5.561 | 0.073 | 5.344 | 0.028 |
| Variation in parental education | 0.247 | 0.004 | 0.248 | 0.005 | 0.246 | 0.006 | 0.281 | 0.002 |

*(continued)*

TABLE 5.1 *(continued)*

| | ALL STUDENTS | | MALE STUDENTS | | FEMALE STUDENTS | | ALL PROJECT COUNTRIES | |
|---|---|---|---|---|---|---|---|---|
| | *Mean* | *SE* | *Mean* | *SE* | *Mean* | *SE* | *Mean* | *SE* |
| *Disciplinary climate* | | | | | | | | |
| Principal reports | | | | | | | | |
| Frequency of disciplinary disengagement | 2.992 | 0.094 | 2.939 | 0.101 | 3.039 | 0.096 | 2.756 | 0.028 |
| Frequency of serious disciplinary infractions | 1.667 | 0.046 | 1.649 | 0.051 | 1.684 | 0.045 | | |
| Teacher reports: frequency of classroom disruption | 2.530 | 0.048 | 2.522 | 0.048 | 2.536 | 0.052 | 3.312 | 0.021 |
| Student reports | | | | | | | | |
| Victimization incidents, student level | 0.550 | 0.023 | 0.728 | 0.036 | 0.393 | 0.024 | 0.648 | 0.010 |
| Victimization incidents, school level | 0.548 | 0.020 | 0.562 | 0.026 | 0.536 | 0.019 | 0.648 | 0.010 |
| COGNITIVE PERFORMANCE | | | | | | | | |
| Math and science test score (combined) | 1,141.592 | 6.916 | 1,151.547 | 8.335 | 1,132.779 | 9.334 | 1,028.096 | 3.252 |
| Math test score | 580.464 | 4.151 | 583.930 | 5.047 | 577.395 | 5.602 | 513.783 | 1.812 |
| Science test score | 561.129 | 2.889 | 567.618 | 3.442 | 555.384 | 3.882 | 514.314 | 1.479 |
| *N* | 2,738 | | 1,286 | | 1,452 | | 50,381 | |

NOTE: SE = standard error. Standard errors are adjusted for clustering of students within schools.

students are higher than those of any other nation in the entire TIMSS study, except South Korea. Results from another cross-national survey, the 2003 Program for International Student Assessment (PISA), rank Japanese 15-year-olds sixth-highest in math literacy and second-highest in science literacy in the world (National Institute for Educational Policy Research 2004). It is also worth noting that when the Japanese middle school students in the TIMSS study were asked to evaluate their math and science performance, they scored lowest on their perceived math and science ability compared to the other nations in the TIMSS project (these results are not shown in the tables). This suggests that Japanese students' modest self-evaluation causes them to underestimate how well they perform in reality.

When we shift our attention to disciplinary climate, Japan again stands out compared to the other countries in this project. Although the frequency of principal-reported disciplinary disengagement (arriving late at school, absenteeism, and skipping classes) is not particularly low in Japan, the frequency of more serious disciplinary infractions is. We created a measure that captured the frequency of cheating, profanity, vandalism, theft, and intimidation and injury to other students. Japan has the lowest number of these serious disciplinary infractions compared to the other countries in this project (we do not show the results). Likewise, the frequency of classroom disruption reported by teachers is much lower in Japan than in other nations. These descriptive results suggest that Japanese schools are relatively free of serious disciplinary problems.

While frequencies of disciplinary disengagement and student victimization are comparable to other countries, intriguing patterns emerge when these categories are disaggregated. Turning first to the measures that constitute the disciplinary disengagement measure, we see that Table 5.2 shows the score for absenteeism as higher in Japan than in other nations, while the means for the other two components are similar to those of all countries. The frequency distribution of absenteeism (we do not show results) shows that 57 percent of Japanese principals report at least one student not showing up at school every day. Thus, it is the large number of principals reporting high absenteeism that is responsible for the relatively high levels of disciplinary disengagement in Japan. As previously discussed, it is very common in Japan for students to miss school because they cannot adjust to the school environment or because they become the target of bullying. Schools are generally tolerant of this absenteeism and allow these students who stay at home to remain registered at the school because middle schools are part of compulsory education. Since these nonattending students are counted as part of the student body, rather than as students who have left school, they push up the rate of absenteeism in Japan.

Table 5.2 also reports the means of the responses to three questions about student victimization. Few Japanese students experienced the most serious of the three (having something stolen), and the average is much smaller than other nations'. Means for the other two components of student victimization (being hit and being made fun of), on the other hand, are comparable to the means for all nations. However, wording for the question about being hit included the examples "such as being pushed, hit, and kicked" (National Institute for Educational Policy Research 2005, 230). It is possible that the

TABLE 5.2
*Distribution of disciplinary climate items*

| | JAPAN | | ALL PROJECT COUNTRIES | |
|---|---|---|---|---|
| | *Mean* | *SD* | *Mean* | *SD* |
| PRINCIPAL REPORTS | | | | |
| *Frequency of disciplinary disengagement* | | | | |
| Arrive late at school | 3.344 | 1.452 | 3.290 | 1.340 |
| Absenteeism | 3.900 | 1.406 | 2.780 | 1.260 |
| Skipping class | 1.969 | 1.152 | 2.200 | 1.070 |
| *Frequency of serious disciplinary infractions* | | | | |
| Cheating | 1.403 | 0.507 | 2.080 | 0.830 |
| Profanity | 1.617 | 0.799 | 2.480 | 1.230 |
| Vandalism | 1.843 | 0.798 | 1.890 | 0.810 |
| Theft | 1.586 | 0.582 | 1.870 | 0.710 |
| Intimidation of other students | 1.866 | 0.791 | 2.480 | 1.070 |
| Injury to other students | 1.806 | 0.674 | 1.850 | 0.660 |
| TEACHER REPORTS | | | | |
| Disruptive students (reported by math teacher) | 2.642 | 0.751 | 3.300 | 0.970 |
| Disruptive students (reported by science teacher) | 2.531 | 0.649 | 3.370 | 0.930 |
| STUDENT REPORTS | | | | |
| Victimization incidents | | | | |
| Something of mine was stolen | 0.074 | 0.262 | 0.210 | 0.410 |
| Hit or hurt by other student | 0.196 | 0.397 | 0.170 | 0.380 |
| Made fun of or called names | 0.291 | 0.454 | 0.280 | 0.450 |
| *N* | 3,705 | | 48,275 | |

NOTE: SD = standard deviation.

inclusion of "being pushed" as an example yielded responses that include minor quarrels. Finally, disaggregation of the serious disciplinary infraction measure and teacher reports on classroom disruption indicates that these issues occur much less frequently in Japan than in other countries. Taken together, the results of Table 5.2 suggest that most Japanese students do not commit or experience serious delinquent behaviors.

Table 5.3 moves away from our descriptive results and examines the first research question on the relationship between school-level characteristics and four disciplinary climate measures. In general, none of the school-level characteristics have a consistent or particularly strong effect on disciplinary measures. However, school size significantly predicts principal reports of both disciplinary disengagement and serious infractions, and larger community size predicts increased serious disciplinary infractions. Because Japanese schools tend to have a high student-teacher ratio, surveillance and control of students may increase in difficulty as school and community size increase. The table indicates that none of the school-level characteristics are significant predictors of teacher reports of classroom disruption. As noted in the descriptive results, frequency of classroom disruption is lowest in Japan compared to the other nations in this project, and disruption does not appear to be a function of school-level characteristics.

Student victimization on the other hand is significantly associated with the school's highest grade level, variation in parental education, and proportion of males in the school. Because the measure for highest grade level has only two values (9 and 12) and higher values predict more victimization, the results indicate that victimization is higher in private schools that combine middle and high school grades than in public middle schools, which stop at the 9th grade. When high schools are combined with middle schools, it is possible that middle school students become targets of victimization by high school students. In addition to highest grade level, schools with more variation in parental education have higher levels of victimization. Finally, similar to other nations, the gender composition of the school significantly predicts victimization, with female-dominated schools showing a lower propensity for victimization.[7]

For our second research question, the first three models in Table 5.4 present the relationship between student- and school-level predictors and test scores. The first model includes individual-level characteristics and school-level characteristics, the second adds variables measuring school-level

TABLE 5.3
*Regression models estimating the effects of school-level characteristics on disciplinary climate*

| | *Principal report: disciplinary disengagement* | *Principal report: serious disciplinary infractions* | *Teacher report: classroom disruption* | *School level: victimization* |
|---|---|---|---|---|
| SCHOOL AND COMMUNITY CHARACTERISTICS | | | | |
| *School and community variables* | | | | |
| School size (log) | 0.847*** | 0.233*** | 0.031 | −0.013 |
| | (0.133) | (0.061) | (0.076) | (0.029) |
| School highest grade level | −0.078 | −0.022 | −0.084 | 0.090** |
| | (0.136) | (0.062) | (0.079) | (0.030) |
| Community size | 0.008 | 0.082* | 0.059 | −0.002 |
| | (0.071) | (0.032) | (0.041) | (0.016) |
| *School-level student characteristics* | | | | |
| Average parental education | −0.190 | −0.066 | 0.034 | 0.087 |
| | (0.237) | (0.108) | (0.136) | (0.053) |
| Variation in parental education | 5.408 | 1.898 | −0.521 | 1.542* |
| | (2.828) | (1.287) | (1.630) | (0.626) |
| STUDENT BODY CHARACTERISTICS | | | | |
| *Male* | | | | |
| 46%–60% | 0.362 | 0.022 | 0.118 | 0.154** |
| | (0.223) | (0.102) | (0.133) | (0.049) |
| >60% | 0.182 | −0.096 | −0.059 | 0.192* |
| | (0.340) | (0.155) | (0.208) | (0.075) |
| *Immigrants* | | | | |
| 1%–10% | 0.106 | −0.054 | −0.038 | −0.035 |
| | (0.189) | (0.086) | (0.110) | (0.042) |
| >10% | 0.958 | 0.359 | 0.376 | −0.174 |
| | (0.962) | (0.438) | (0.550) | (0.213) |
| Intercept | −2.155 | −0.051 | 2.685* | −1.168** |
| | (1.858) | (0.846) | (1.071) | (0.412) |
| $R^2$ | 0.420 | 0.345 | 0.089 | 0.180 |
| N | 140 | 140 | 135 | 140 |

NOTE: Standard errors are in parentheses. Missing covariates are listwise deleted. Analyses are adjusted using weights provided by TIMSS.

* $p < .05$; ** $p < .01$; *** $p < .001$.

disciplinary climate, and the third adds serious disciplinary infractions. Several findings stand out in the test score analysis in Table 5.4. First, individual student characteristics have a substantial influence on student achievement scores.[8] Male students perform better than female students, and immigrant students have lower average test scores than nonimmigrant students.

TABLE 5.4

*Regression models estimating the effects of student- and school-level characteristics on test score, expectation of finishing college, and individual reports of victimization*

| | HIERARCHICAL LINEAR MODELS ESTIMATING EFFECTS ON TEST SCORE | | | LOGISTIC REGRESSION MODELS ESTIMATING EFFECTS ON FINISHING COLLEGE | | | HIERARCHICAL LINEAR MODELS ESTIMATING EFFECTS ON INDIVIDUAL STUDENT REPORTS OF VICTIMIZATION | | |
|---|---|---|---|---|---|---|---|---|---|
| | *Model 1* | *Model 2* | *Model 3* | *Model 1* | *Model 2* | *Model 3* | *Model 1* | *Model 2* | *Model 3* |
| STUDENT BACKGROUND | | | | | | | | | |
| Male | 10.569** | 13.233** | 13.262** | 0.660*** | 0.665*** | 0.673*** | 0.318*** | 0.318*** | 0.318*** |
| | (3.997) | (4.067) | (4.066) | (0.098) | (0.102) | (0.103) | (0.027) | (0.027) | (0.027) |
| Age | 20.020** | 19.519** | 19.446** | 0.112 | 0.112 | 0.104 | –0.073 | –0.074 | –0.074 |
| | (6.519) | (6.505) | (6.505) | (0.165) | (0.165) | (0.164) | (0.045) | (0.045) | (0.045) |
| Immigrant status | –66.369** | –65.753** | –65.910** | 0.184 | 0.192 | 0.169 | 0.009 | 0.006 | 0.005 |
| | (20.504) | (20.462) | (20.461) | (0.604) | (0.605) | (0.598) | (0.141) | (0.141) | (0.141) |
| Highest parental education | 18.195*** | 18.341*** | 18.322*** | 0.393*** | 0.393*** | 0.395*** | 0.014 | 0.014 | 0.014 |
| | (1.496) | (1.494) | (1.494) | (0.037) | (0.038) | (0.038) | (0.010) | (0.010) | (0.010) |
| Number of books in household | 23.983*** | 24.149*** | 24.227*** | 0.141*** | 0.142*** | 0.150*** | 0.030** | 0.031** | 0.031** |
| | (1.664) | (1.660) | (1.662) | (0.039) | (0.040) | (0.040) | (0.011) | (0.011) | (0.011) |
| Household size | –0.805 | –1.040 | –1.058 | –0.069 | –0.070 | –0.075 | –0.020 | –0.019 | –0.019 |
| | (1.719) | (1.712) | (1.712) | (0.041) | (0.041) | (0.040) | (0.012) | (0.012) | (0.012) |
| Math and science test score (combined) | | | | 0.008*** | 0.008*** | 0.008*** | | | |
| | | | | (0.000) | (0.000) | (0.000) | | | |
| SCHOOL AND COMMUNITY CHARACTERISTICS | | | | | | | | | |
| *School and community variables* | | | | | | | | | |
| School size (log) | –9.544 | –5.129 | –4.258 | 0.244 | 0.232 | 0.269* | –0.018 | –0.013 | –0.008 |
| | (6.067) | (6.131) | (6.167) | (0.124) | (0.132) | (0.131) | (0.038) | (0.040) | (0.040) |
| School highest grade level | 31.137*** | 31.581*** | 32.152*** | 0.191 | 0.192 | 0.217 | 0.090* | 0.095** | 0.098** |
| | (5.725) | (5.610) | (5.616) | (0.119) | (0.122) | (0.124) | (0.036) | (0.035) | (0.035) |

*(continued)*

TABLE 5.4 *(continued)*

| | HIERARCHICAL LINEAR MODELS ESTIMATING EFFECTS ON TEST SCORE | | | LOGISTIC REGRESSION MODELS ESTIMATING EFFECTS ON FINISHING COLLEGE | | | HIERARCHICAL LINEAR MODELS ESTIMATING EFFECTS ON INDIVIDUAL STUDENT REPORTS OF VICTIMIZATION | | |
|---|---|---|---|---|---|---|---|---|---|
| | *Model 1* | *Model 2* | *Model 3* | *Model 1* | *Model 2* | *Model 3* | *Model 1* | *Model 2* | *Model 3* |
| Community size | 3.022 | 3.820 | 4.487 | 0.012 | 0.011 | 0.042 | 0.019 | 0.019 | 0.023 |
| | (2.762) | (2.651) | (2.719) | (0.048) | (0.050) | (0.051) | (0.018) | (0.017) | (0.018) |
| *School-level student characteristics* | | | | | | | | | |
| Male | | | | | | | | | |
| 46%–60% | –0.086 | 5.382 | 5.017 | –0.208 | –0.214 | –0.228 | 0.140** | 0.136** | 0.134** |
| | (8.054) | (8.060) | (8.040) | (0.165) | (0.167) | (0.168) | (0.051) | (0.050) | (0.050) |
| >60% | 1.641 | 7.678 | 6.510 | 0.035 | 0.022 | –0.032 | 0.135 | 0.136 | 0.129 |
| | (15.045) | (14.640) | (14.635) | (0.354) | (0.351) | (0.327) | (0.095) | (0.094) | (0.094) |
| Immigrant | | | | | | | | | |
| 1%–10% | –5.403 | –6.139 | –7.120 | 0.216 | 0.216 | 0.171 | 0.006 | 0.007 | 0.001 |
| | (6.329) | (6.030) | (6.082) | (0.129) | (0.130) | (0.129) | (0.040) | (0.039) | (0.040) |
| >10% | –24.389 | –19.109 | –19.439 | 0.670*** | 0.666*** | 0.645*** | –0.185 | –0.206 | –0.207 |
| | (36.362) | (35.037) | (34.937) | (0.138) | (0.152) | (0.149) | (0.233) | (0.230) | (0.229) |
| Average parental education | 5.426 | 6.684 | 6.068 | 0.349* | 0.354* | 0.329 | 0.011 | 0.000 | –0.004 |
| | (8.673) | (8.318) | (8.312) | (0.168) | (0.169) | (0.169) | (0.055) | (0.054) | (0.054) |
| Variation in parental education | –517.459*** | –466.443*** | –452.674*** | –1.257 | –1.347 | –0.526 | 0.970 | 0.974 | 1.046 |
| | (113.451) | (110.299) | (110.711) | (2.124) | (2.208) | (2.163) | (0.718) | (0.708) | (0.711) |
| *Disciplinary climate* | | | | | | | | | |
| Principal reports | | | | | | | | | |
| Frequency of disciplinary disengagement | | –5.540 | –3.756 | | 0.019 | 0.110 | | –0.014 | –0.005 |
| | | (3.033) | (3.473) | | (0.061) | (0.075) | | (0.020) | (0.023) |

| | | | | | | | | | |
|---|---|---|---|---|---|---|---|---|---|
| Frequency of serious disciplinary infractions | | −8.051 | | | −0.402** | | | −0.044 |
| | | (7.725) | | | (0.147) | | | (0.050) |
| Teacher reports: frequency of classroom disruption | −10.012 | −7.638 | | −0.022 | 0.099 | | 0.082* | 0.095* |
| | (5.389) | (5.834) | | (0.107) | (0.109) | | (0.035) | (0.037) |
| Student reports | | | | | | | | | |
| Victimization incidents, school level | | −7.486 | −7.995 | | −0.015 | −0.015 | | | |
| | | (14.520) | (14.479) | | (0.071) | (0.072) | | | |
| Victimization incidents, student level | | −8.768*** | −8.792*** | | 0.009 | 0.002 | | | |
| | | (2.549) | (2.549) | | (0.279) | (0.277) | | | |
| Intercept | 527.048*** | 525.015*** | 515.393*** | −17.682*** | −17.619*** | −18.050*** | 0.149 | −0.012 | −0.062 |
| | (125.562) | (124.555) | (124.709) | (2.960) | (3.072) | (3.093) | (0.834) | (0.831) | (0.832) |
| Pseudo $R^2$ | 0.014 | 0.015 | 0.015 | 0.280 | 0.280 | 0.283 | 0.021 | 0.022 | 0.022 |
| Proportion of variance between schools | 0.041 | 0.034 | 0.034 | NA | NA | NA | 0.029 | 0.027 | 0.026 |
| $N$ | 3,349 | 3,349 | 3,349 | 2,738 | 2,738 | 2,738 | 3,349 | 3,349 | 3,349 |

NOTE: Standard errors are in parentheses. NA = not applicable.

* $p < .05$; ** $p < .01$; *** $p < .001$.

Students with better-educated parents and more books in the household have higher test scores. Thus, having a more advantaged social background tends to increase student performance. Second, only a limited number of school-level characteristics significantly affect student achievement. Students in schools with larger variation in parental education score lower, and those in schools with high school students (coefficient for the school's highest grade level) score higher. This finding implies that students in private schools that include both middle school and high school students have substantially higher test scores than students in public middle schools. Last, turning to the school disciplinary climate measures, the results indicate that only the student-level victimization measure significantly predicts test scores, with more victimization predicting lower test scores. The effects of other variables do not change with the introduction of school disciplinary climate variables, suggesting that they do not mediate the effects of other predictors.

The next three models in Table 5.4 address our third question, about the relationship between student- and school-level characteristics and the expectation of completing a four-year degree. Generally, the results are similar to those with respect to test score. Male students are more likely than female students to expect to finish college. This finding is in line with the fact that many women who go to college attend two-year institutions. Also with results similar to the test score analysis, students whose parents have more education and have more books in the house are more likely to expect finishing college, and student test score is a powerful predictor of college expectations. With regard to school-level characteristics, students in schools with higher average parental education are more likely to expect to finish college and students in schools with a very high proportion of immigrant students are less likely to expect to finish college. It is also worth noting that although the proportion of immigrant students is not associated with test scores, it is related to college expectations, suggesting that perceptions are more sensitive to school environment than actual performance. Finally, looking at disciplinary climate variables, increased frequency of serious disciplinary infractions is negatively associated with college expectations. It is possible that both of the significant school-level predictors, the proportion of immigrant students and frequency of serious disciplinary infractions, are indicators of the quality of life in the neighborhood surrounding the middle school.

The final three models in Table 5.4 examine the relationship between student- and school-level characteristics and the student victimization index, our fourth research question. Among the student-level predictors, there is a substantial gender difference in victimization experiences: male students are much more likely than female students to report victimization. Students with more books in their home report higher levels of victimization. These students may be more reserved and more likely to become the target of ridicule than students with fewer books in their home. Similarly to the school-level student victimization measure, students who attend private six-year schools (as proxied by the highest-grade-level measure) are more likely to experience victimization than those in public middle schools. Among the school-level characteristics, students in schools with equal gender composition are more likely to report victimization compared to students in schools with different gender compositions. In addition, increased frequency of classroom disruption positively predicts the likelihood of victimization. Classroom disruption may be a sign of breakdown of teacher authority, which deters incidents of victimization.

## LONG-LASTING IMPACTS OF SCHOOL DISCIPLINARY CLIMATE AND DELINQUENCY

Finally, we address our last research question about the consequences of school disciplinary climate and delinquency at later stages of the life course. Using the Japanese Life Course Panel Survey (JLPS), we examine whether student misbehavior and school environment in middle school predicts high school achievement and the probability of entering higher education. Table 5.5 reports the results of logistic regression analyses with three dependent variables: (1) high school type (academic high schools versus vocational and other types), (2) high school grades (very good and good versus other grades), and (3) entrance in higher education. Similar to the TIMSS analysis, these dependent variables are regressed onto a series of student- and school-level characteristics, including disciplinary climate. In particular, the JLPS asked respondents whether their middle schools had a disruptive school environment, whether they experienced delinquency (skipped classes, smoked at school, or hit teachers), and whether they were the target of bullying at school.[9]

With over 95 percent of middle school students advancing to high school, most Japanese students are sorted into high schools that are ranked hierarchically (academic schools are ranked higher than vocational schools) within each district. As the results of Table 5.5 indicate, in addition to middle school grades, the odds of going to an academic high school are strongly associated with social background. Students from more advantaged class backgrounds (that is, the professional and managerial class, or

TABLE 5.5

*Logistic regression models estimating the effects of school discipline and social background on high school type, high school grade, and attendance in higher education*

| | *Model 1: high school type* | *Model 2: high school grade* | *Model 3: attendance in higher education* |
|---|---|---|---|
| STUDENT BACKGROUND | | | |
| Male | −0.082 | −0.090 | 0.133 |
| | (0.091) | (0.078) | (0.085) |
| Father's class (no father = no occupation) | | | |
| Professional-managerial (I+II) | 0.849** | −0.163 | 0.163 |
| | (0.261) | (0.253) | (0.272) |
| Routine nonmanual (III) | 0.624* | −0.378 | −0.118 |
| | (0.295) | (0.279) | (0.298) |
| Self-employed (IVab/IVc/VIIb) | 0.389 | −0.283 | −0.538* |
| | (0.260) | (0.256) | (0.273) |
| Skilled manual (V/VI) | 0.259 | −0.326 | −0.427 |
| | (0.267) | (0.265) | (0.281) |
| Unskilled manual (VIIa) | 0.143 | −0.292 | −0.421 |
| | (0.280) | (0.278) | (0.294) |
| Father's education | 0.668** | −0.025 | 1.098** |
| | (0.117) | (0.089) | (0.102) |
| MIDDLE SCHOOL ACHIEVEMENT: GRADE | 0.482** | 0.360** | 0.809** |
| | (0.041) | (0.037) | (0.042) |
| DISCIPLINARY CLIMATE | | | |
| Disruptive school environment | −0.016 | 0.041 | 0.076 |
| | (0.101) | (0.088) | (0.096) |
| Delinquent experience | −0.331** | −0.199* | −0.519** |
| | (0.106) | (0.103) | (0.107) |
| Victimization experience | −0.085 | 0.032 | 0.006 |
| | (0.107) | (0.094) | (0.102) |
| Intercept | −0.406** | −1.754** | −2.310** |
| | (0.141) | (0.253) | (0.272) |
| −2 log likelihood | 3,101.760 | 3,872.489 | 3,436.573 |
| Cox & Snell $R^2$ | 0.106 | 0.043 | 0.251 |
| *N* | 3,139 | 3,017 | 3,164 |

NOTE: Standard errors are in parentheses. Missing covariates are listwise deleted.

* $p < .05$; ** $p < .01$.

Erikson-Goldthorpe-Portocarero class I+II; Erikson and Goldthorpe 1992) and those whose fathers attended higher education are more likely to attend academic high schools. Disruptive school environment and victimization experience do not affect where students go to high school, but having experienced delinquent behavior in middle school negatively affects the odds of attending an academic high school. Because middle school reports affect the type of high school students attend, those who engaged in delinquent behaviors and received negative reports had lower chances of attending high-ranking schools.

The second model presents the relationship between student- and school-level covariates and high school grades. As would be expected, the most significant predictor of high school grades is middle school grades. However, in addition, delinquent experiences in middle school negatively predict high school grades. The third model presents the relationship between student- and school-level characteristics and the probability of attending higher education. Students whose father attended higher education and who had higher middle school grades are more likely to attend higher education. In addition, experiencing delinquency in middle schools lowers the chances of attending institutions of higher education. Taken together, one of the most consistent findings across models is that delinquency experiences in middle school appear to have long-lasting effects on later life outcomes.

## CONCLUSION

Japanese society stands out in a number of respects in this cross-national project. To begin with, Japanese schools are characterized by a low prevalence of delinquent behavior. Serious disciplinary infractions and classroom disruption have the lowest frequencies among all the nations in this volume. Japanese schools are also much less heterogeneous with respect to student and school characteristics: very few Japanese schools report that they have a large proportion of economically disadvantaged students, a large variation in parental education, or a sizable immigrant population. Further, because most middle schools are local public schools, which are mixed sex, the male-female ratio is virtually one in most schools.

We asked five research questions in this study. With respect to the first question about school-level variations in disciplinary climate, we found a weak association with school-level characteristics. None of the school-level characteristics consistently affected all aspects of disciplinary climate. School size was the most salient predictor among the factors we considered, although it affected only principal reports of disciplinary disengagement and of serious infractions. Given that Japanese society has a low level of delinquency to begin with and variations among schools with respect to educational, ethnic, and gender compositions are small, these factors are probably responsible for the weak association between the prevalence of delinquency and school-level characteristics. In other words, Japanese schools generally have a low level of delinquency, and the variations among schools in student misbehavior are not easily explained by school differentiation in parental education, ethnicity, and gender.

School-level victimization is more responsive to school-level characteristics than principal reports of disciplinary disengagement and serious infractions. It is associated with the school's highest grade level, variation in parental education, and gender composition. Private schools that have both middle and high schools show higher levels of victimization than public middle schools because middle school students may be victimized by high school students in the same school. Schools with more variation in parental background show greater chances of their students being victimized, and female-dominated schools tend to have lower propensity for victimization because male students are more likely to be victimized than female students.

When we shifted our attention to individual achievements, we found that student test score (our second question) is not associated with many of the school-level characteristics. Furthermore, features of school-level disciplinary climate (frequency of disciplinary disengagement, frequency of serious infractions, frequency of classroom disruption, and victimization incidents) do not have a significant relationship to student performance. Japanese students tend to have relatively high average test scores, compared to those in most other nations, and the differences in test scores are not associated with obvious school-level characteristics, including disciplinary environment.

With respect to individual expectations of college completion (our third question), students in schools with higher average parental education are more likely to have an expectation of attending college. Students in schools with a very high proportion of immigrant students and those in schools with serious disciplinary infractions are less likely to have an expectation of attending college. In short, visible features of school environment such as the proportion of immigrant students and the occurrence of serious disciplinary infractions appear to affect students' perception of future trajectories.

When we examined students' experience of victimization (our fourth question), we found that it is largely independent of school-level characteristics. Exceptions are gender composition and highest grade level. Students in gender-equal schools are more likely to experience victimization than those in male- or female-dominated schools, and students in six-year private schools are more prone to victimization than those in three-year public schools. The only school disciplinary climate variable associated with victimization is the teacher report of classroom disruption. Classroom disruption is related to higher incidents of victimization, probably because classroom disruption indicates breakdown of teacher authority, which deters incidents of victimization.

Our supplementary analysis examined the long-term effect of school disciplinary climate on life chances following middle school graduation, our fifth question. The experience of delinquency in middle school affects the type of high school attended after middle school, high school grades, and eventually the chances of attending institutions of higher education. However, the disciplinary environment of the school or the experience of victimization does not seem to affect later individual achievement.

In summary, the school disciplinary climate in Japan is distinctive because of the infrequency of disciplinary problems and their weak association with student outcomes and school-level characteristics. Despite the comparatively low prevalence of delinquency in Japanese schools, Japanese school teachers and the Ministry of Education alike are concerned about delinquency at school and wish to enforce stricter rules. Japanese educators might have to find the right balance between prevention of delinquent behavior and strict control of students' lives both inside and outside schools. School disciplinary climate does not seem to affect the future life chances of students after leaving middle school, as far as high school type, high school grade, and college attendance are concerned. However, experiences of delinquency in middle school show lasting influence on students' life chances after leaving middle school. Because delinquency in middle school is still rare in Japan, those who did commit the rare event are probably disadvantaged in the later life course. Given the relative homogeneity among middle schools and the low prevalence of delinquency, school climate is probably much more homogeneous in Japan than in other nations, thereby having a limited long-term influence on students' subsequent lives.

## APPENDIX

*Regression models predicting school disciplinary climate*

| | PRINCIPAL REPORT: DISCIPLINARY DISENGAGEMENT | | | PRINCIPAL REPORT: | | |
|---|---|---|---|---|---|---|
| | *Arrive late at school* | *Absentee-ism* | *Skipping class* | *Cheating* | *Profanity* | *Vandalism* |
| SCHOOL AND COMMUNITY CHARACTERISTICS | | | | | | |
| *School and community variables* | | | | | | |
| School size (log) | 0.818*** | 1.317*** | 0.408** | 0.142* | 0.328*** | 0.164 |
| | (0.189) | (0.188) | (0.129) | (0.064) | (0.093) | (0.092) |
| School highest grade level | 0.194 | −0.327 | −0.109 | −0.013 | −0.094 | −0.002 |
| | (0.194) | (0.193) | (0.132) | (0.065) | (0.096) | (0.094) |
| Community size | 0.090 | −0.125 | 0.068 | 0.047 | 0.013 | 0.167*** |
| | (0.101) | (0.101) | (0.069) | (0.034) | (0.050) | (0.049) |
| *School-level student characteristics* | | | | | | |
| Average parental education | −0.154 | −0.350 | −0.064 | 0.057 | −0.061 | −0.173 |
| | (0.337) | (0.336) | (0.229) | (0.113) | (0.166) | (0.163) |
| Variation in parental education | 8.534* | 4.532 | 3.070 | 1.169 | 0.716 | 1.292 |
| | (4.023) | (4.002) | (2.736) | (1.344) | (1.981) | (1.946) |
| STUDENT BODY CHARACTERISTICS | | | | | | |
| *Male* | | | | | | |
| 46%–60% | 0.320 | 0.680* | 0.103 | 0.077 | −0.023 | 0.092 |
| | (0.317) | (0.316) | (0.216) | (0.106) | (0.156) | (0.154) |
| >60% | −0.064 | 0.554 | 0.072 | 0.081 | −0.020 | −0.178 |
| | (0.484) | (0.481) | (0.329) | (0.161) | (0.238) | (0.234) |
| *Immigrants* | | | | | | |
| 0–10% | −0.031 | 0.331 | −0.003 | 0.009 | −0.032 | 0.038 |
| | (0.269) | (0.268) | (0.183) | (0.090) | (0.132) | (0.130) |
| >10% | 1.389 | 1.384 | 0.065 | 0.539 | 0.457 | 0.921 |
| | (1.368) | (1.361) | (0.931) | (0.456) | (0.674) | (0.662) |
| Intercept | −5.413* | −0.492 | −0.524 | −0.271 | 0.540 | 0.636 |
| | (2.643) | (2.630) | (1.798) | (0.882) | (1.302) | (1.279) |
| $R^2$ | 0.314 | 0.418 | 0.196 | 0.187 | 0.174 | 0.261 |
| *N* | 140 | 139 | 140 | 140 | 140 | 140 |

NOTE: Standard errors are in parentheses. Missing covariates (with the exception of gender variables) are mean substituted; dummy variables flagging missing covariates are included in the analyses but not shown.
* $p < .05$; ** $p < .01$; *** $p < .001$.

| SERIOUS INFRACTIONS | | | SCHOOL LEVEL: VICTIMIZATION | | |
|---|---|---|---|---|---|
| *Theft* | *Intimidation of students* | *Injury to students* | *Something of mine was stolen* | *Hit or hurt by other student* | *Made fun of or called names* |
| 0.232** | 0.237* | 0.295*** | -0.008 | -0.007 | 0.001 |
| (0.070) | (0.094) | (0.078) | (0.009) | (0.014) | (0.014) |
| 0.133 | -0.066 | -0.091 | 0.051*** | 0.015 | 0.024 |
| (0.071) | (0.096) | (0.080) | (0.009) | (0.015) | (0.015) |
| 0.036 | 0.141** | 0.085* | 0.003 | 0.002 | -0.006 |
| (0.037) | (0.050) | (0.042) | (0.005) | (0.008) | (0.008) |
| 0.071 | -0.260 | -0.032 | 0.019 | 0.007 | 0.062* |
| (0.124) | (0.167) | (0.139) | (0.016) | (0.026) | (0.025) |
| 4.646** | 0.977 | 2.568 | 0.847*** | 0.057 | 0.640* |
| (1.477) | (1.995) | (1.654) | (0.192) | (0.307) | (0.302) |
| 0.226 | -0.078 | -0.163 | 0.023 | 0.080** | 0.051* |
| (0.117) | (0.157) | (0.130) | (0.015) | (0.024) | (0.024) |
| 0.060 | -0.294 | -0.224 | 0.092*** | 0.092* | 0.010 |
| (0.178) | (0.240) | (0.199) | (0.023) | (0.037) | (0.036) |
| -0.156 | -0.084 | -0.102 | 0.010 | -0.019 | -0.026 |
| (0.099) | (0.133) | (0.110) | (0.013) | (0.020) | (0.020) |
| 0.183 | -0.019 | 0.072 | 0.052 | -0.113 | -0.113 |
| (0.503) | (0.679) | (0.563) | (0.065) | (0.104) | (0.103) |
| -2.920** | 1.618 | 0.097 | -0.709*** | -0.018 | -0.443* |
| (0.971) | (1.311) | (1.087) | (0.126) | (0.201) | (0.198) |
| 0.302 | 0.240 | 0.331 | 0.357 | 0.109 | 0.144 |
| 140 | 140 | 140 | 140 | 140 | 140 |

NOTES

An earlier version of the chapter was presented at the meeting of the Comparative School Discipline Project in Milano, Italy, June 25–26, 2009. The authors are grateful to the participants of the meeting for helpful comments, to Richard Arum and Melissa Velez for assistance in computing, and to David Slater and Matt Wickens for editorial assistance. This research was supported by a Grant-in-Aid for Scientific Research (S) of the Japan Society for the Promotion of Science (grant numbers 18103003 and 22223005).

1. The maximum teacher-student ratio is 40 students per teacher. If there are more than 40 students in one class, the class must be divided into two.

2. Although there are no statistics on bullying before 1985, incidents of bullying did seem to increase during the 1990s on the basis of Ministry of Education reports (2008c).

3. The official name of the Japanese Ministry of Education is the Ministry of Education, Culture, Sports, Science, and Technology. However, for brevity, it will be called the Ministry of Education throughout the paper.

4. The proportion of elementary school students who attend private school is less than 1 percent.

5. The Japanese General Social Surveys (JGSS) are designed and carried out by the Institute of Regional Studies at Osaka University of Commerce in collaboration with the Institute of Social Science at the University of Tokyo under the direction of Ichiro Tanioka, Michio Nitta, Hiroki Sato, and Noriko Iwai, with Project Manager Minae Osawa. The project is financially assisted by a Gakujutsu Frontier Grant from the Japanese Ministry of Education, Culture, Sports, Science, and Technology for the 1999–2003 academic years, and the datasets are compiled and distributed by the SSJ Data Archive of the Information Center for Social Science Research on Japan, located at the Institute of Social Science, University of Tokyo.

6. For details of the survey, see Ishida, Miwa, and Oshima 2008 and Ishida, Miwa, and Murakami 2009.

7. The appendix to this chapter reports the results of the school-level models using the components of each of the disciplinary climate indices. With the exception of school and community size, the school-level characteristics generally do not significantly predict the individual measures. Large schools probably have more problems controlling and monitoring student behavior because of the size of the student body. In addition, urban environments, as proxied by larger community sizes, may be conducive to delinquent behaviors against school property and other students. It is also worth noting that the frequency of arriving late at school and experiencing theft are significantly predicted by increased variation in parental education. Finally, similar to Table 5.3, the data in the appendix indicate that school-level victimization is associated with the gender composition of the school: having more males in a school is associated with more theft, and schools with more equal gender distributions have a higher proportion of students being pushed, hit, kicked, and made fun of.

8. Age has a significant positive effect on test scores. However, because Japanese schools seldom allow students to skip or repeat grades, each grade is age homogeneous, and the difference in age reflects the difference in birth month. Therefore, we should not derive substantive conclusions from the age coefficient.

9. The disruptive school environment pertains to school environment, and delinquency and victimization pertain to individual experience. In addition to school discipline variables, the models include gender (male dummy variable), father's class (Erikson-Goldthorpe-Portocarero six-category class), father's education (dummy variable for attendance in higher education), and grades in middle school (five-point scale). See Erikson and Goldthorpe (1992) for details of the class category.

## REFERENCES

Akiba, Masaki. 2007. "Hokenshitsu no Kozo, Kino, Imi [Structure, function and meaning of school nurse office]." In *Gakko Rinsho Shakaigaku* [The clinical sociology of schools], edited by Akira Sakai, 83–95. Tokyo: Hoso Daigaku Kyoiku Shinkokai.

Ayukawa, Jun. 2001. *Shonen Hanzai* [Crimes committed by minors]. Tokyo: Heibonsha.

Cummings, William. 1980. *Education and Equality in Japan.* Princeton, NJ: Princeton University Press.

Erikson, Robert, and John H. Goldthorpe. 1992. *The Constant Flux: A Study of Class Mobility in Industrial Nations.* Oxford: Clarendon Press.

Fukuzawa, Rebecca. 1994. "The Path to Adulthood According to Japanese Middle Schools." *Journal of Japanese Studies* 20:61–86.

Hida, Daijiro. 1999. "Koko Itsudatsu Tosei no Naiyo, Hoho oyobi Paradaimu no Henyo [Changes in content, methods, and paradigm of deviant control in high schools]." *Hanzai Shakaigaku Kenkyu* [Japanese Journal of Sociological Criminology] 24:43–59.

Hirota, Teruyuki. 2001. *Kyoiku Gensetsu no Rekishi Shakaigaku* [Historical sociology of educational discourse]. Nagoya: Nagoya University Press.

Hosaka, Toru. 2000. *Gakko wo Kessekisuru Kodomotachi* [Children who do not come to school]. Tokyo: University of Tokyo Press.

Ishida, Hiroshi. 1998. "Educational Credentials and Labour-Market Entry Outcomes in Japan." In *From School to Work: A Comparative Study of Educational Qualifications and Occupational Destinations*, edited by Yossi Shavit and Walter Muller, 287–309. Oxford: Clarendon Press.

Ishida, Hiroshi, Satoshi Miwa, and Akane Murakami. 2009. "Hatarakikata to Raifusutairu no Henka ni Kansuru Zenkoku Chosa 2008 ni miru Gendai Nihonjin no Raifusutairu to Ishiki [Lifestyles and attitudes among contemporary Japanese people as seen in the Japanese Life Course Panel Survey 2008]." *Chuo Chosaho* [Central research report] 616:1–7.

Ishida, Hiroshi, Satoshi Miwa, and Masao Oshima. 2008. "Tokyo Daigaku Shakai Kagaku Kenkyusho no Paneru Chosa ni Tsuite: Hatarakikata to Raifusutairu no Henka ni Kansuru Zenkoku Chosa 2007 no Kekka Kara [Panel Survey of the Institute of Social Science, University of Tokyo: Japanese Life Course Panel Survey 2007]." *Chuo Chosaho* [Central research report] 604:1–7.

Ito, Shigeki. 1999. "Aratana Gakko Paradaimu wa Itsudatsu wo Kaiketu Dekiruka" [Can a new paradigm of school solve delinquency?]. *Hanzai Shakaigaku Kenkyu* [Japanese Journal of Sociological Criminology] 24:26–42.

———. 2007a. "Futoko wo Domiruka [How to understand absenteeism]." In *Gakko Rinsho Shakaigaku* [The clinical sociology of schools], edited by Akira Sakai, 38–51. Tokyo: Hoso Daigaku Kyoiku Shinkokai.

———. 2007b. "Gakko Chitsujyo no Yuragi [Changes in school order]." In *Gakko Rinsho Shakaigaku* [The clinical sociology of schools], edited by Akira Sakai, 24–37. Tokyo: Hoso Daigaku Kyoiku Shinkokai.

———, ed. 2007c. *Ijime Futoko* [Bullying and absenteeism]. Tokyo: Nihon Tosho Senta.

———. 2007d. "Shonen Hiko to Gakko [Juvenile delinquency and schools]." In *Gakko Rinsho Shakaigaku* [The clinical sociology of schools], edited by Akira Sakai, 187–201. Tokyo: Hoso Daigaku Kyoiku Shinkokai.

Kojima, Akira. 2007. "Newcomer to Gakko Kyoiku [Newcomers and school education]." In *Gakko Rinsho Shakaigaku* [The clinical sociology of schools], edited by Akira Sakai, 140–54. Tokyo: Hoso Daigaku Kyoiku Shinkokai.

Kuzuno, Hiroyuki. 2003. *Shonen Shiho no Saikochiku* [Reconstructing juvenile justice]. Tokyo: Nihon Hyoronsha.

LeTendre, Gerald. 1994. "Guiding Them On: Teaching, Hierarchy, and Social Organization in Japanese Middle Schools." *Journal of Japanese Studies* 20:37–59.

Lie, John. 2001. *Multiethnic Japan*. Cambridge, MA: Harvard University Press.

———. 2008. *Zainichi* [Koreans in Japan]. Berkeley: University of California Press.

Management and Coordination Agency [Somucho]. 1993. *Seishonen no Kihan Ishiki Keisei Yoin nikansuru Kenkyu Chosa* [Survey on factors that contribute to forming norms among youth]. Tokyo: Management and Coordination Agency.

Matsumoto, Yoshio. 1984. *Zusetsu Hiko Mondai no Shakaigaku* [Illustration: Sociology of juvenile problems]. Tokyo: Koseikan.

Matsunaga, Yoshiaki, and Yuji Okura. 1999. "Ijime Gensho to Gakko Seido no Kozo [Bullying phenomenon and school structure]." *Hanzai Shakaigaku Kenkyu* [Japanese Journal of Sociological Criminology] 24:113–28.

Mimizuka, Hiroaki. 1999. "Gakko Paradaimu no Henyo to Seishonen no Itsudatsu [The new paradigm of schooling in Japan and adolescent deviant behavior]." *Hanzai Shakaigaku Kenkyu* [Japanese Journal of Sociological Criminology] 24:4–25.

Ministry of Education, Culture, Sports, Science, and Technology. 2008a. *Chugakko Gakushu Sidoyoryo Kaisetsu* [Guidance to the course of study for middle schools]. Tokyo: Ministry of Education, Culture, Sports, Science, and Technology.

———. 2008b. *Gakko Kihon Chosa Hokokusho: Shoto Chuto Kyoiku Kikan* [The school basic survey: Primary and secondary institutions]. Tokyo: Ministry of Education, Culture, Sports, Science, and Technology.

———. 2008c. *Heisei 19 Nendo Jido Seito no Mondai Kodo nado Seito Sidojyo no Shomondai nikansuru Chosa* [2007 Survey on problem behaviors associated with guidance of pupils and students]. Tokyo: Ministry of Education, Culture, Sports, Science, and Technology.

———. 2008d. *Nihongo Shido ga Hitsuyona Gaikokujin Jido Seito no Ukeire Jyokyo nado nikansuru Chosa Heisei 19 Nendo* [Survey on pupils and students who require assistance in Japanese, 2007]. Tokyo: Ministry of Education, Culture, Sports, Science, and Technology.

Ministry of Justice. 2008. *Shitsunyukoku Kanri Heisei 20 Nendo* [Immigration control 2008]. Tokyo: Immigration Bureau, Ministry of Justice.

National Institute for Educational Policy Research, ed. 2004. *Ikiru Tameno Chisiki to Gino: OECD Seito no Gakushu Totatsudo Chosa PISA* [Knowledge and skills for life: OECD student PISA results]. Tokyo: Gyosei.

———. 2005. *TIMSS 2003 Sansu Sugaku Kyoiku no Kokusai Hikaku* [TIMSS 2003 international comparison of mathematics education]. Tokyo: Gyosei.

Noda, Yoko. 2000. *Gakkoka Shakai niokeru Kachi Ishiki to Itsudatsu Gensho* [Value orientation and deviant behavior in schooling society]. Tokyo: Gakubunsha.

Okabe, Takeshi. 2007. "Hiko Hassei no Jyudanteki Patan [The longitudinal pattern of offending among Japanese boys]." *Hanzai Shakaigaku Kenkyu* [Japanese Journal of Sociological Criminology] 32:45–59.

Okano, Kaori, and Motonori Tsuchiya. 1999. *Education in Contemporary Japan*. New York: Cambridge University Press.

Rohlen, Thomas P. 1983. *Japan's High Schools*. Berkeley: University of California Press.

Shimizu, Kokichi. 1992. "*Shido*: Education and Selection in a Japanese Middle School." *Comparative Education* 28:109–29.

Takenaka, Ayumi. 2003. "Paradoxes of Ethnicity-Based Immigration: Peruvian and Japanese-Peruvian Migrants in Japan." In *Global Japan: The Experience of Japan's New Immigrants and Overseas Communities*, edited by R. Goodman, C. Peach, A. Takenaka, and P. White, 222–35. London: Routledge Curzon.

Tsuda, Takayuki. 2003. *Strangers in the Ethnic Homeland: Japanese Brazilian Return Migration in Transnational Perspective*. New York: Columbia University Press.

CHAPTER SIX

# School Disciplinary Climate, Behavioral Problems, and Academic Achievement in the Netherlands

*Herman G. van de Werfhorst, Machteld Bergstra, and René Veenstra*

Within the last few years, the discussion on school order and safety in the Netherlands has evolved from a matter to be dealt with by schools internally into a heated public debate that gained momentum after the 2004 murder of a secondary school deputy director by a student. This incident marked the first killing of a school official committed by a student in the country. It was followed by the killing of a secondary school student by another student in 2008 and the killing of a primary school pupil by an adult intruder who entered the school during school hours that same year.

This increase in school violence has resulted in responses from educators and the government alike. According to a survey (by the largest union of educators, the *Algemene Onderwijsbond*) administered to educators on school safety in 2003 and again in 2007, awareness and stringency of security measures at schools increased in this period. Similarly, the Dutch government has responded to school disciplinary issues by implementing a compulsory yearly registration of incidents. However, despite the increased visibility of school disciplinary issues in recent years and the severe nature of the incidents that sparked the public debate, it is important to keep in mind that the discussion on school disciplinary climates revolves mainly around more mundane issues of classroom disorder and student disrespect of teachers.

The shift in the discussion of disciplinary issues into the public sphere can also be attributed to a redistribution of power from educators to parents and students as a result of changes in school management. Educational institutions are increasingly subject to marketlike competition, as are many other services previously included in the public sector. Legal appeals by newspapers caused the government to make publicly available since the late 1990s annual rankings of schools (Karsten et al. 2010).

Increased marketization fostered a demand-oriented stance of parents toward their children's education. More and more, Dutch families view schools as organizations that cater to their demands as "customers." If the customers (parents or children) are not satisfied by the service delivered by the school (e.g., a child is expelled), they are increasingly prone to express their dissatisfaction to the school board or even eventually bring the case to court.

For example, a well-known legal case concerned the underachievement of a pupil, whose mother attributed this to low-quality teaching in the Montessori primary school her son attended. The mother, Karina Schaapman, went to court and demanded compensation for the financial burden of private tutoring, a case she won and wrote a book about (Schaapman 2000). Since Schaapman's success, parents' lawsuits against schools have grown steadily. Though still rare, increased litigation has placed educators in a difficult position, hindering teachers' and principals' ability to execute the disciplinary measures that help ensure a favorable teaching environment.

Given the emerging school disciplinary climate in the Netherlands, this chapter explores the correlates of school disciplinary problems. First, we review school safety and disciplinary issues in the Netherlands. Next, we discuss the disciplinary context in the Netherlands, including Dutch population, educational system, legal context, and administration of school discipline. In particular, our discussion of the educational system traces how schools' historic roots may help account for levels of disciplinary problems. Following this, our empirical analysis draws on two different data sources to explore the determinants of school disciplinary climates and the predictive power of individual-level disciplinary problems on student academic achievement.

## DISCIPLINARY PROBLEMS IN THE NETHERLANDS AND CONSEQUENCES FOR STUDENT ACHIEVEMENT

Whereas a number of recent violent incidents might have led to a perceived lack of safety and order within schools, it is useful to describe the disciplinary climate in more absolute terms. Records of periodic secondary school visits that the Inspectorate of Education made between January 2006 and

April 2009 show that 85 percent of schools were rated as having sufficient safety and 9.5 percent as having very high safety. Only 5.5 percent of schools were rated as having insufficient safety. None of these schools were found to neglect school safety altogether.

Increasingly, society calls on schools to provide solutions for societal problems such as ethnic segregation, racism, alcohol abuse, and obesity. Can schools be responsible for such a wide range of topics and the upbringing of children in general without reducing performance of their primary task, the transfer of knowledge and skills? Students dropping out of school and incidents of aggressive behavior between students or of students toward teachers might be a sign that schools indeed are overburdened. According to IRISvo (2008), a national registration system for incidents occurring at secondary schools, of the total number of 8,255 incidents registered among participating schools in 2007–2008, fights (20 percent), theft (19 percent), and threats (11 percent) constituted the most incidents. In contrast, drug use, possession of weapons, and sexual intimidation were rare events (1 percent each). These latter types of events are, however, likely to be underreported and are thus probably underrepresented in the IRIS registration.

It is relevant to know whether the disciplinary context in schools and individual disciplinary problems of students have an effect on academic achievement. Although disciplinary problems of schools and pupils are a concern in their own right, they are arguably of even greater concern if they negatively affect school performance. We explore this relationship in this chapter.

## DISCIPLINARY CONTEXT IN THE NETHERLANDS

### *Population Heterogeneity*

The Dutch population has always been heterogeneous with regard to religion. Originally the country consisted of a large minority of Roman Catholics, mostly but not exclusively in the southern provinces, and a majority of Protestants. Since the beginning of the Dutch Republic in the 17th century, none of the religious denominations have claimed political power. Secularization has increased tremendously since the mid-20th century, and now only a minority consider themselves a member of a religious denomination.

Since the 1960s many immigrants have come to the Netherlands. The largest groups of immigrants come from Suriname and the Netherlands

Antilles (Suriname was a Dutch colony until 1975, and the Antilles are still part of the Kingdom of the Netherlands) and from Turkey and Morocco (the latter two groups as "guest workers"). More recent immigrant groups consist of refugees from Iran, Iraq, Somalia, and former Yugoslavia. Official population statistics show that in 2009 around 80 percent of residents in the Netherlands were of Dutch descent. Moroccan, Surinamese or Antillean, and Turkish immigrant groups each constitute between 2 and 3 percent of the population (first and second generations together), and other non-Western migrant groups total close to 4 percent. Around 9 percent of the population consists of Western immigrants or their children.

Children of non-Western immigrants do substantially worse in school than students of Dutch origin. On the national standardized school test at the end of primary school, children of Turkish and Moroccan descent score around 0.6 standard deviation below the national average (Van de Werfhorst and Van Tubergen 2007). However, ethnic inequality is mostly explained by socioeconomic background; children of immigrants are strongly overrepresented in lower social classes, which explains their educational disadvantage in terms of achievement and the level attained (Van de Werfhorst and Van Tubergen 2007).

Ethnic segregation in schools is rather high in the Netherlands. In school year 2006–2007 almost 40 percent of primary schools in the two largest cities had more than 80 percent of children with a non-Western immigrant background (Social and Cultural Planning [SCP] Office 2009). Segregation in Dutch primary schools in large cities is larger than in American inner cities (Ladd, Fiske, and Ruijs 2009). In secondary schools segregation is lower than in primary schools, but Dutch secondary schools are still more ethnically segregated than schools in many other Western societies (Karsten 2010). Plausibly, ethnic segregation in schools is perpetuated by the Dutch tradition of free school choice (Karsten et al. 2006; see also later discussion).

### *Organizational Structure of the Educational System*

Core elements in the Dutch educational system may account for the disciplinary problems experienced in the Netherlands today. Specifically, the guarantee of state funding for public and private schools alike, the high level of nationwide standardization of educational organization and examinations, and the strong differentiation of students via early tracking in the secondary school system are all hallmarks of the Dutch school system. Whereas a high level of standardization across schools might lessen disciplinary problems, early tracking and stratification across schools fosters segregation across ethnic and socioeconomic lines. Large variations in school composition, in turn, can be expected to lead to large variations in disciplinary problems across schools.

The Dutch government provides funds for public and private schools under Article 23 of the Dutch Constitution. The Article came into effect in 1917, after demand for separate socialization of children from different religions (Hofman and Hofman 2001). Parents from different religious denominations wished to exert control over the curriculum covered by their children's schools and demanded the same state funding for private religious schools as that received by public schools. Article 23 fostered the growth of the private school sector and exemplified the "pillarized" society that characterized the Netherlands until the 1960s. During this time the country was highly segregated along religious lines or other convictions, to the point that people led their lives strictly within one section of society, isolating themselves in their schools, trade unions, sports clubs, shops, and, of course, political parties. As a result, unlike other European countries with similar educational systems, a single religious denomination (e.g., Catholic or Protestant) does not dominate the private school system in the Netherlands, which instead includes schools of various denominations and religions, as well as secular schools based on a nonreligious ideology (Dronkers 1995).

Today, children are no longer expected to attend a school simply congruent with their parents' religious beliefs. Instead, well-educated parents demand the very best education for their children and look for an education that meets the specific needs of their child. Further, over the past decades, a strong secularization of Dutch society, combined with the influx of significant numbers of immigrants, has led to a "mismatch between the denomination of schools and their actual population" (Janssens and Leeuw 2001, 43). The ambiguity of a great number of private denominational schools within a highly secular society is referred to by Hofman and Hofman (2001, 147) as the "Dutch paradox."

State funding under Article 23 is not unconditional. To qualify for government support, schools have to adhere to certain characteristics defined by the state. As a result, public and private schools in the Netherlands are subject to strong regulation by the government, and private schools have moved into a "quasi-governmental" sphere (Janssens and Leeuw 2001). Teacher education is controlled by the Ministry of Education, Culture, and Sciences; budgets for schools and universities are nationally determined, as are tuition fees; and salaries of teachers and lecturers follow standardized pay scales. School quality is controlled by the Inspectorate of Education, which monitors school quality.

A major component of the government's educational regulation is the nationally standardized examination administered at the conclusion of primary school (known as the CITO test, for Centraal Instituut voor Toetsontwikkeling, or Central Institute for Test Development), by around 85 percent of all schools on a voluntary basis. The CITO test is highly important in determining the track that students can enter in secondary school. Together with a student's teacher recommendations, this test largely determines which secondary school track a student is admitted to at age 12: prevocational school (or VMBO, four years, preparing for upper secondary vocational school), intermediate general education (HAVO, five years, preparing for tertiary vocational college), or university preparatory (VWO, six years, preparing for university). Many schools offer one or two bridge years, in which usually two, but sometimes all three, programs are combined.

Numerous studies (see, e.g., Crul and Schneider 2009; Crul and Vermeulen 2003) have addressed the effects of tracking on the ethnic and socioeconomic composition of schools and suggest that differentiated educational systems are likely to increase racial/ethnic and class-based educational inequalities (Brunello and Checchi 2007; Entorf and Lauk 2008; Van de Werfhorst and Mijs, 2010). In the Dutch context, the result of early tracking is that students of low socioeconomic status and students of immigrant background are overrepresented at the prevocational track, and students from more advantaged backgrounds are largely in the university preparatory track. However, research also indicates that the social class effect on track placement is lower in schools that use CITO relative to schools that do not (Luyten and Bosker 2004). Despite this, we expect the difference in school composition resulting from a differentiated educational system to influence the distribution of disciplinary problems across tracks, with lower tracks experiencing more disciplinary problems. The variation in school discipline across tracks may, however, be tempered by the standardized nature of the Dutch educational system (reflected in centralized monitoring of every school's performance by the Inspectorate of Education).

### *Legal Context and Administration of School Discipline*

The formalization of school discipline is strongly linked to the question of who bears responsibility for administering discipline within the school context. Given that in Dutch law only two disciplinary measures are regulated, expulsion and suspension, school discipline is generally not seen as a legal issue in the Netherlands. The law does not prescribe guidelines for appropriate reasons for suspension. However, students may not be suspended for more than one week, and suspensions exceeding one day must be reported to the Inspectorate of Education. In the case of permanent expulsion, the law is slightly stricter: for students younger than 17, the school board must find a new school that is willing to accept the student, the inspectorate must agree to the expulsion, and poor academic achievement may never be the reason for expulsion.

Students have a say in the way school discipline is managed within their own schools. Since 1992 all schools are legally required to draw up a student statute that includes the rights and duties of students. This statute must be approved by student representatives and a committee of parents, teachers, and principals. The national secondary-school student union LAKS (Landelijk Aktie Komitee Studenten, or National Action Committee for Students) provides guidelines for student statutes and informs students of their legal rights.

How schools handle disciplinary problems, both minor and serious, differs between schools and depends on the content of the student statutes drawn up for the individual schools. Disciplinary sanctions often used for minor infractions, such as disturbing class, include a warning, temporary removal from class, contacting the parents, or assigning students to community service (*taakstraf*). More serious infractions incur harsher measures, such as suspension and, in very rare cases, expulsion.

## COMPARATIVE PROJECT

This chapter explores the predictors of school disciplinary problems and the impact of school disciplinary climates on student performance. We perform analyses on two datasets, Trends in International Mathematics and

Science Study (TIMSS) and Tracking Adolescents' Individual Lives Survey (TRAILS). The TIMSS analysis follows the format of the larger comparative project. In particular, we focus on the incidence of school disciplinary problems as encountered by principals, teachers, and students and on the impact of social origin and school disciplinary climate on educational achievement.

The TRAILS analysis brings in microlevel information on disciplinary and behavioral problems of parents and children and can be seen as an important supplement to the TIMSS analysis on educational performance. This analysis helps us see whether school-level characteristics still matter for educational performance after taking individual and parental misbehavior into account.

## ANALYSES

### *TIMSS Data*

TIMSS is a survey of eighth grade students conducted in 2003. Following a two-stage sample design, we first randomly draw a sample of schools, and then randomly sample one or more classes. TIMSS includes surveys of students, teachers, and school principals. For the Netherlands, 130 schools participated, of which 90 percent answered the questions on disciplinary measures. Our analysis includes around 2,000 students.

Given the importance of the tracking system in the Dutch context, to the standard variables used in all the chapters we add dummy variables indicating the school track (prevocational, general, or university preparatory) students were following at the time of the survey and the tracks offered by schools. Some schools in the sample offer the prevocational track only, others offer the general and university preparatory tracks, and still others offer all three tracks. Although the standard TIMSS survey does not include questions regarding school tracks, because of its significance in the Dutch context we identify school track by using the Dutch-specific TIMSS data, not the international TIMSS dataset. It should be emphasized that "tracks" in the Dutch context refer to separate school types with a fully differentiated curriculum and examination.

### *Descriptive Statistics*

Reflecting previous findings, the descriptive statistics in Table 6.1 indicate that Dutch students have very high average math and science test scores and

TABLE 6.1
*Descriptive statistics, TIMSS*

| | *Mean* | *SE* |
|---|---|---|
| STUDENT CHARACTERISTICS | | |
| Male | 0.508 | 0.500 |
| Age | 14.248 | 0.517 |
| Immigrant status | 0.069 | 0.254 |
| Highest parental education | 5.500 | 1.684 |
| Number of books in household | 3.258 | 1.238 |
| Household size | 4.532 | 1.127 |
| SCHOOL AND COMMUNITY CHARACTERISTICS | | |
| *School and community variables* | | |
| School size (log) | 6.790 | 0.600 |
| School highest grade level | 11.140 | 1.110 |
| Community size | 3.764 | 1.007 |
| *School-level student characteristics* | | |
| Male students | | |
| 46%–60% | 0.393 | 0.488 |
| >60% | 0.204 | 0.403 |
| Immigrant students | | |
| 1%–10% | 0.376 | 0.484 |
| >10% | 0.284 | 0.451 |
| Average parental education | 5.409 | 0.826 |
| Variation in parental education | 0.278 | 0.082 |
| DISCIPLINARY CLIMATE | | |
| Principal reports: frequency of disciplinary disengagement | 3.327 | 1.036 |
| Teacher reports: frequency of classroom disruption | 2.777 | 0.531 |
| Student reports | | |
| Victimization incidents, student level | 0.468 | 0.262 |
| Victimization incidents, school level | 0.466 | 0.762 |
| COGNITIVE PERFORMANCE | | |
| Math and science test score (combined) | 1,080.674 | 120.151 |
| Math score | 541.069 | 66.876 |
| Science score | 539.604 | 58.585 |

NOTE: SE = standard error.

low levels of variability (Micklewright and Schnepf 2007). For instance, the mean math and science score in the Netherlands is sixth highest of the participating countries, with an average score of 1,080 (math and science scores combined). Across the whole TIMSS, only east Asian countries and Flemish Belgium had higher math scores than the Netherlands (Mullis et al. 2004). The dispersion is also known to be among the lowest in all countries (Mullis et al. 2004; Micklewright and Schnepf 2007). The latter is especially remarkable, given that the Dutch educational system begins tracking students at age 12. It has been argued that the relatively high achievement of students in the lower parts of the distribution is caused by national standardized school examinations (Van de Werfhorst and Mijs 2010).

### *Determinants of Disciplinary Climate*

Table 6.2 presents the results of school-level ordinary least squares models regressing disciplinary problems reported by principals, teachers, and students on school-level characteristics. The results suggest that very few school-level characteristics have a significant effect on any of the disciplinary climate variables. Important exceptions are, however, the effects of the types of tracks offered: prevocational (VMBO), general (HAVO), and university preparatory (VWO). Schools that offer only the general and university preparatory tracks are less likely to encounter classroom disruption or student victimization than schools that offer only prevocational training. Schools that offer all three tracks also have fewer disciplinary problems than schools with only a prevocational track. This suggests that students in schools that offer more academically oriented tracks enjoy a school climate with fewer disciplinary problems.

In addition to the significant effects of tracks, schools with higher average parental education face less disciplinary disengagement than schools with less educated parents. Interestingly, the variation in parental education does not significantly affect disciplinary problems, a result that is incongruent with James Coleman and Thomas Hoffer's (1987) thesis that homogeneity in school networks leads to higher performance and lower levels of deviant behavior (see Dijkstra, Veenstra, and Peschar 2004 for the Netherlands). With regard to school composition in terms of gender, schools that are more than 60 percent male experience more classroom disruption (and although only marginally significant, student victimization). Finally, schools with higher percentages of immigrant students have higher rates of student victimization. This is an important finding given that ethnic segregation in education is comparatively high in the Netherlands. We control this effect for the track composition of schools.

### *Effects on School Performance*

Table 6.3 presents multilevel models predicting school performance at the student level. The first model is a standard educational stratification model.

TABLE 6.2

*Regression models estimating the effects of school-level variables on disciplinary climate*

| | *Disciplinary disengagement* | *Classroom disruption* | *Student victimization* |
|---|---|---|---|
| SCHOOL AND COMMUNITY CHARACTERISTICS | | | |
| *School and community variables* | | | |
| School size (log) | 0.241 | –0.053 | –0.103 |
| | (0.212) | (0.112) | (0.057) |
| School highest grade level | –0.103 | 0.025 | 0.030 |
| | (0.155) | (0.082) | (0.042) |
| School tracks offered: general and university prep (HAVO/VWO) | –0.676 | –0.422* | –0.305** |
| | (0.398) | (0.212) | (0.107) |
| School tracks offered: prevocational, general, and university prep (VMBO/HAVO/VWO) | –0.508* | –0.314* | –0.186* |
| | (0.269) | (0.141) | (0.072) |
| Community size | 0.062 | 0.092 | 0.021 |
| | (0.099) | (0.052) | (0.026) |
| *School-level student characteristics* | | | |
| Average parental education | –0.314* | –0.010 | 0.033 |
| | (0.150) | (0.079) | (0.040) |
| Variation in parental education | 0.930 | –0.695 | –0.455 |
| | (1.034) | (0.545) | (0.278) |
| STUDENT BODY CHARACTERISTICS | | | |
| *Male* | | | |
| 46%–60% | 0.008 | 0.157 | 0.054 |
| | (0.219) | (0.114) | (0.058) |
| >60% | –0.108 | 0.296* | 0.130 |
| | (0.250) | (0.132) | (0.067) |
| *Immigrants* | | | |
| 1%–10% | –0.168 | 0.046 | 0.139* |
| | (0.228) | (0.120) | (0.061) |
| >10% | 0.126 | 0.181 | 0.123* |
| | (0.230) | (0.121) | (0.062) |
| Intercept | 4.353** | 2.795*** | 0.699 |
| | (1.338) | (0.695) | (0.355) |
| $R^2$ | 0.291 | 0.235 | 0.280 |
| *N* | 116 | 117 | 118 |

NOTE: Standard errors are in parentheses.

* $p < .05$; ** $p < .01$; *** $p < .001$.

TABLE 6.3

*Hierarchical linear models estimating the effects of student- and school-level characteristics on test score*

| | *Model 1* | *Model 2* | *Model 3* |
|---|---|---|---|
| STUDENT BACKGROUND | | | |
| Male | 32.531*** | 32.994*** | 32.621*** |
| | (2.478) | (2.532) | (2.582) |
| Age | -6.539* | -5.280* | -5.067 |
| | (2.592) | (2.667) | (2.694) |
| Immigrant status | -39.891*** | -38.889*** | -38.822*** |
| | (5.161) | (5.267) | (5.363) |
| Highest parental education | 0.994 | 0.498 | 0.481 |
| | (0.832) | (0.851) | (0.866) |
| Number of books in household | 5.553*** | 5.719*** | 5.829*** |
| | (1.157) | (1.173) | (1.195) |
| Household size | -1.443 | -1.864 | -2.404* |
| | (1.145) | (1.158) | (1.180) |
| School track: general (HAVO) | 66.616*** | 51.388*** | 50.424*** |
| | (6.769) | (6.941) | (7.013) |
| School track: university prep (VWO) | 106.121*** | 86.007*** | 84.357*** |
| | (7.979) | (8.469) | (8.513) |
| SCHOOL AND COMMUNITY CHARACTERISTICS | | | |
| School size (log) | | -9.287 | -9.824 |
| | | (10.886) | (10.691) |
| School highest grade level | | 12.403 | 10.445 |
| | | (6.780) | (6.742) |
| Community size | | -16.187*** | -13.705** |
| | | (5.035) | (5.023) |
| Male | | | |
| 46%–60% | | -5.312 | -1.755 |
| | | (11.054) | (10.761) |
| >60% | | -14.631 | 2.805 |
| | | (13.379) | (13.800) |
| Immigrants | | | |
| 1%–10% | | 9.876 | 16.734 |
| | | (11.510) | (11.337) |
| >10% | | -17.439 | -10.092 |
| | | (12.713) | (12.455) |
| Average parental education | | 40.528*** | 39.163*** |
| | | (7.537) | (7.669) |
| Variation in parental education | | -125.699* | -127.561* |
| | | (58.565) | (58.422) |
| DISCIPLINARY CLIMATE | | | |
| Principal reports: frequency of disciplinary disengagement | | | -0.358 |
| | | | (5.091) |
| Teacher reports: frequency of classroom disruption | | | -16.686 |
| | | | (9.335) |
| Student reports | | | |
| Victimization incidents, student level | | | -54.085** |
| | | | (18.824) |

*(continued)*

TABLE 6.3 *(continued)*

| | *Model 1* | *Model 2* | *Model 3* |
|---|---|---|---|
| Victimization incidents, school level | | | 4.097* |
| | | | (1.760) |
| Intercept | 1,091.417*** | 900.341*** | 987.190*** |
| | (38.546) | (76.427) | (85.480) |
| Pseudo $R^2$ | 0.287 | 0.338 | 0.358 |
| Proportion of variance between schools | 0.614 | 0.466 | 0.443 |
| *N* | 2,113 | 1,972 | 1,915 |

NOTE: Standard errors are in parentheses. Proportion of variance for intercept model is 0.783.
* $p < .05$; ** $p < .01$; *** $p < .001$.

The number of books in the household, a measure for a family's socioeconomic status, positively affects academic performance. Remarkably, parental education does not have a significant direct influence after taking into account number of books in the household (see De Graaf, De Graaf, and Kraaykamp 2000; Schütz, Ursprung, and Wössmann 2008 for similar findings). Importantly, though unsurprisingly, there is strong variation in performance between school tracks. Students in the general (HAVO) and academic (VWO) tracks have better test results than students in the prevocational track (VMBO).

Model 2 adds school-level compositional characteristics to Model 1. As would be expected, students score lower in schools that have a higher proportion of students with less educated parents, net of controls for school track differences and family background characteristics. Interestingly, the results also indicate that students in schools with more variation in parental education (more heterogeneous schools) have worse test scores, supporting Coleman and Hoffer's (1987) thesis that school homogeneity is associated with higher achievement. A school's highest grade level has a positive relationship with performance, net of individual track. This means that students at schools that offer an academic track do better than those at schools that do not offer higher-level tracks. This effect of school organization is highly important, as it indicates that academic performance is higher in schools that offer higher-level tracks, even for those not in the highest track themselves. To be clear, the Dutch context is such that even in mixed-track schools the curriculum is completely separate between tracks, meaning that this finding does not result from effects within the classroom. Finally, adding the school-level characteristics in Model 2 reduces the positive effects of being in general or university preparatory tracks, compared to the prevocational track: the coefficient for the general track decreases by 23 percent, the university preparatory track by 19 percent. Coefficients for the other student-level variables, however, remain about the same in Model 2.

Model 3 adds the central variables of this study to Model 2, those measuring the school disciplinary climate. The results suggest that student reports of the frequency of victimization incidents at both the student and school level predict student performance. However, the results are paradoxical: although the student-level measure of victimization predicts lower test scores, as would be expected, more student victimization at the school level predicts *higher* test scores (holding constant individual victimization). Finally, frequency of classroom disruption negatively predicts test score, although the effect is only marginally significant. Model 3 also suggests that the other school-level variables have very small or nonsignificant effects. In sum, although we have to be cautious about the causality between disciplinary climate and academic performance, it is noteworthy that the two are related in the Netherlands.

Among the student-level variables, school track continues to exert a significant effect on test scores, and the addition of the disciplinary measures decreases the coefficients only minimally. This suggests that disciplinary climates are not strong mediators of school track effects. This is also supported by the small change in the percentage of unexplained variance across schools, which decreases only slightly, from 47 to 44 percent of the total unexplained variance.

### *TRAILS Data*

To supplement our analyses based on comparative international data provided by TIMSS, we conduct additional analyses focusing on the effects of social background on school achievement, as mediated by behavioral problems of children and their parents. TRAILS, being a prospective cohort study of Dutch preadolescents and following students every two to three years until they reach age 24, has a number of advantages over TIMSS. First, the TRAILS data include detailed information about misbehavior of students. Such information is important to ensure that a relationship between school-level disciplinary problems and academic achievement is not an aggregation of purely individual effects. Second, in addition to students' disciplinary problems, the data include information about parental behavior that may cause student disciplinary problems and lowered achievement, including parental drug use and psychological problems. Third, the longitudinal character of the data allows us to investigate more thoroughly the causal relationship between disciplinary problems and academic achievement.

The TRAILS target sample included 10- to 12-year-olds, drawn from five rural and urban municipalities in the north of the Netherlands (thus excluding the largest cities, in the west). For a detailed description of the sampling procedure and methods, see A. F. De Winter and colleagues (2005). Along with students, parents and teachers were asked to fill out questionnaires. For the purpose of our analysis we use data from the base (2001–2002) and second wave (2003–2004) of the survey. Students with missing values on any of the independent variables at the individual level (the two measures of parental disorders) and schools missing values on any of the school-level variables (disciplinary measures reported by teachers) are excluded from the sample, resulting in a final analysis sample of 1,977 out of the original 2,230.

## MEASURES, ANALYTIC STRATEGY, AND DESCRIPTIVE STATISTICS

### *Student-Level Measures*

We include three measures of student misbehavior in our analyses. General student misbehavior is defined as deviance that is not school related, from smoking and drinking to fighting on the street and starting fires. School-safety-related misbehavior consists of fighting at school and destroying school property. School-nonsafety-related misbehavior includes truancy and removal from the classroom by the teacher. For reasons of interpretation, we $z$ standardize all three measures of student misbehavior.

Other independent variables at the individual level include controls for gender and age and a standardized index of socioeconomic status comprising parental educational level and income, and two measures of parental disorders. These two measures were originally constructed by Ormel et al. (2005, 1828) and represent a count of the number of lifetime disorders within each domain as reported by respondents' biologic parents. Internal disorders include depression and anxiety, and external disorders include substance dependence and antisocial behavior. Factor analysis conducted on all reported behaviors confirmed the existence of two domains, highly similar to those constructed by the researchers. Finally, student academic performance is a scale combining teacher perceptions of the student's eagerness to learn; punctuality; and results on math, science, geography, and Dutch- and foreign-language tests.

### *School-Level Measures*

To create school-level variables, we aggregate measures of teacher estimates of the disciplinary climate at schools, using their judgment of the frequency of delinquency and the prevalence of aggressive behavior of individual students (ranging from 0 to 4, with higher scores indicating higher prevalence). The TRAILS questionnaire defines aggressive behavior as often being involved in fights, bullying other students, disrupting the class, and threatening others. Delinquent behavior includes lying or deceiving, skipping school, and using alcohol or drugs. We create school-level versions of the student misbehavior variables by calculating the mean of the student-level measures by school. Furthermore, we include the percentage of male students, the percentage of immigrants, and the percentage of students from economically disadvantaged backgrounds in the models. A student is assigned a low economic status if he or she scored 1 standard deviation or more below the average socioeconomic status.

### *Analytic Strategy*

We conduct two series of analyses, starting with a hierarchical linear model (HLM) with three types of student behavior as outcome variables: general misbehavior, school-safety-related misbehavior and school-nonsafety-related misbehavior. These models regress the student-level misbehavior measures from the second wave of data on student and school characteristics from the first wave of data. We follow these models with HLMs regressing academic performance from the second wave of data on student and school characteristics from the first wave of data. In both HLMs we use standardized measures for all scaled variables, including the student misbehavior variables and academic performance.

TABLE 6.4
*Descriptive statistics, Tracking Adolescents' Individual Lives Survey*

| | *Mean* | *SE* |
|---|---|---|
| BACKGROUND VARIABLES | | |
| Male | 0.484 | 0.499 |
| Age (t1) | 11.069 | 0.531 |
| Socioeconomic status | −0.065 | 0.801 |
| Parental disorder: depression and anxiety | 0.556 | 0.799 |
| Parental disorder: drug use and antisocial behavior | 0.142 | 0.424 |
| STUDENT BODY CHARACTERISTICS | | |
| Teacher estimates: aggressive behavior | 0.607 | 0.387 |
| Teacher estimates: delinquent behavior | 0.264 | 0.273 |
| Percentage of male students | 0.486 | 0.138 |
| Percentage of immigrant students | 0.125 | 0.132 |
| Percentage of economically disadvantaged students | 0.184 | 0.174 |
| STUDENT MISBEHAVIOR | | |
| General misbehavior (t1) | 0 | 1 |
| School-nonsafety-related misbehavior (t1) | 0 | 1 |
| School-safety-related misbehavior (t1) | 0 | 1 |
| General misbehavior (t2) | 0 | 1 |
| School-nonsafety-related misbehavior (t2) | 0 | 1 |
| School-safety-related misbehavior (t2) | 0 | 1 |
| ACADEMIC PERFORMANCE | | |
| Academic performance (t1) | 0 | 1 |
| Academic performance (t2) | 0 | 1 |

NOTE: SE = standard error. The first wave of data (t1) was collected in 2001–2002 (children ages 10–12). The first follow-up (t2) was two years later.

### *Descriptive Statistics*

Table 6.4 presents descriptive statistics for the TRAILS sample. The means suggest that, among parents, internal disorders such as depression and anxiety are more prevalent than parental misbehavior such as drug use and antisocial behavior. As one might expect, teachers report aggressive behavior, defined as fights, bullying, or class disruption, more often than delinquent behavior, which includes more serious misbehavior such as drug use and skipping class.

## DETERMINANTS OF DISCIPLINARY CLIMATE

Table 6.5 reports the effects of social background, parental disorders, and misbehavior and school characteristics on the three measures of student

TABLE 6.5

*Hierarchical linear models estimating the effects of student- and school-level characteristics on measures of misbehavior*

| | GENERAL MISBEHAVIOR | | | SCHOOL-SAFETY-RELATED MISBEHAVIOR | | | SCHOOL-NONSAFETY-RELATED MISBEHAVIOR | | |
|---|---|---|---|---|---|---|---|---|---|
| | *Model 1* | *Model 2* | *Model 3* | *Model 1* | *Model 2* | *Model 3* | *Model 1* | *Model 2* | *Model 3* |
| BACKGROUND VARIABLES | | | | | | | | | |
| Male | 0.392*** | 0.390*** | 0.403*** | 0.166*** | 0.168*** | 0.185*** | 0.479*** | 0.481*** | 0.495*** |
| | (0.048) | (0.048) | (0.050) | (0.047) | (0.047) | (0.048) | (0.046) | (0.046) | (0.048) |
| Age | 0.086 | 0.078 | 0.077 | 0.146** | 0.137* | 0.146** | 0.046 | 0.038 | 0.030 |
| | (0.048) | (0.048) | (0.050) | (0.055) | (0.054) | (0.054) | (0.048) | (0.047) | (0.046) |
| Socioeconomic status | −0.156*** | −0.141*** | −0.149*** | −0.079* | −0.053 | −0.069 | −0.114*** | −0.089** | −0.086* |
| | (0.035) | (0.035) | (0.038) | (0.035) | (0.035) | (0.037 | (0.033) | (0.034) | (0.036) |
| School track: general (HAVO) | −0.074 | −0.074 | −0.080 | −0.148* | −0.142* | −0.151* | −0.112 | −0.104 | −0.104 |
| | (0.064) | (0.064) | (0.066) | (0.064) | (0.064) | (0.064) | (0.062) | (0.062) | (0.062) |
| School track: university prep (VWO) | −0.184** | −0.177** | −0.169** | −0.157* | −0.146* | −0.152* | −0.152* | −0.143* | −0.138* |
| | (0.063) | (0.062) | (0.064) | (0.062) | (0.062) | (0.062) | (0.060) | (0.060) | (0.060) |
| Parental disorder: depression and anxiety | | −0.058 | −0.055 | | −0.033 | −0.032 | | 0.001 | 0.006 |
| | | (0.031) | (0.031) | | (0.030) | (0.030) | | (0.030) | (0.030) |
| Parental disorder: drug use and antisocial behavior | | 0.200** | 0.195** | | 0.294*** | 0.292*** | | 0.243*** | 0.235*** |
| | | (0.064) | (0.064) | | (0.061) | (0.061) | | (0.060) | (0.060) |
| STUDENT BODY CHARACTERISTICS (TEACHER ESTIMATES) | | | | | | | | | |
| Aggressive behavior | | | 0.143 | | | 0.057 | | | 0.060 |
| | | | (0.093) | | | (0.106) | | | (0.086) |
| Delinquent behavior | | | −0.033 | | | 0.078 | | | 0.130 |
| | | | (0.127) | | | (0.147) | | | (0.117) |
| Percentage of male students | | | −0.272 | | | −0.463 | | | −0.303 |
| | | | (0.210) | | | (0.241) | | | (0.191) |

*(continued)*

Table 6.5 *(continued)*

| | General misbehavior | | | School-safety-related misbehavior | | | School-nonsafety-related misbehavior | | |
|---|---|---|---|---|---|---|---|---|---|
| | *Model 1* | *Model 2* | *Model 3* | *Model 1* | *Model 2* | *Model 3* | *Model 1* | *Model 2* | *Model 3* |
| Percentage of students with immigrant status | | | 0.308<br>(0.227) | | | 0.121<br>(0.260) | | | 0.372<br>(0.209) |
| Percentage of economically disadvantaged students | | | −0.219<br>(0.196) | | | −0.325<br>(0.214) | | | −0.130<br>(0.180) |
| Intercept | −1.063*<br>(0.537) | −0.965<br>(0.535) | −0.910<br>(0.558) | −1.644**<br>(0.610) | −1.564**<br>(0.606) | −1.456*<br>(0.599) | −0.694<br>(0.529) | −0.639<br>(0.521) | −0.510<br>(0.517) |
| Pseudo $R^2$ | 0.096 | 0.102 | 0.094 | 0.091 | 0.096 | 0.097 | 0.096 | 0.097 | 0.098 |
| Proportion of variance between schools | 0.006 | 0.006 | 0.012 | 0.063 | 0.062 | 0.049 | 0.014 | 0.011 | 0.005 |
| *N* | 1,632 | 1,632 | 1,632 | 1,681 | 1,681 | 1,681 | 1,695 | 1,695 | 1,695 |
| Proportion of variance for intercept model | 0.007 | | | 0.058 | | | 0.014 | | |

NOTE: Standard errors are in parentheses.
* $p < .05$; ** $p < .01$; *** $p < .001$.

misbehavior, employing HLMs.[1] Children of lower socioeconomic status have higher levels of deviant behavior. Also, compared to students in the prevocational (VMBO) track, students in the university preparatory (VWO) track exhibit significantly lower levels of all types of misbehavior. This effect is echoed among students in the general (HAVO) track, who display significantly fewer school-safety-related misbehavior problems (the effect is also marginally significant for the variable measuring school-nonsafety-related misbehavior).

Model 2 adds parents' internal disorders and misbehavior to Model 1. As would be expected, there is a significant positive effect of parental misbehavior (e.g., drug use and antisocial behavior) on all measures of children's misbehavior. However, there is no systematic pattern in the results for parental internal disorders. It is, thus, predominantly the *actions* of parents, more than their psychological states, that seem to affect children's misbehavior.

Model 3 adds the school-level characteristics, including the measures of school discipline, to Model 2. Contrary to our expectations, the results indicate that none of the discipline measures are significantly associated with school characteristics or teacher reports on aggression and delinquency. Further, none of the coefficients for the background variables change much across models. Thus, on the basis of our sample of school children in the northern provinces of the Netherlands, we find little evidence that school-level indicators of disciplinary climates affect children's deviant behavior independent of their social background and parents' misbehavior. Looking at the proportion of variance across schools, one can see very little school-level variance.

### EFFECTS ON SCHOOL PERFORMANCE

Our next step is to examine the impact of individual- and school-level disciplinary problem indicators on student academic performance. As mentioned, we regress academic performance from the second wave of the study on student- and school-level characteristics obtained in the first wave of the study. We include first-wave academic performance as an independent variable in the last model, to see whether individual- or school-level, or both, disciplinary problem indicators affect academic performance independent of earlier performance. Including prior academic performance also allows for more confidence in isolating the causal direction of these relationships.

The proportion of the variance across schools is extremely low (around 0.06 in all models). This may be due partly to the way school performance is measured in the TRAILS dataset, with all students being tested according to the standards of the track they are attending, instead of being subjected to a standardized test as in the TIMSS survey.

Model 1 in Table 6.6 focuses on the relationship between performance and socioeconomic status, gender, and age. The results confirm well-known findings relating to effects of socioeconomic status, gender, and age. Although we use an unstandardized test score as a dependent variable, which standardizes performance mostly within classes, we do find track effects; students in the university preparatory track have a higher average test score than students in the other two tracks. Finally, similar to the results from Table 6.5, it is parental misbehavior, rather than internal disorders, that significantly and negatively affects children's outcomes.

In the second and third models, we add student- and school-level indicators of children's misbehavior. It appears that school-related misbehaviors affect academic performance negatively, albeit modestly. General misbehavior, indicating nonschool-related behaviors, has no effect on academic performance. These effects are similar across models. Contrary to our expectations at the start of this research project, none of the indicators of school-level disciplinary climate yield significant effects on school performance. However, the effect of being in the university preparatory (VWO) track decreases by 12 percent when these measures are included, suggesting that school disciplinary climates are slightly more positive in these schools. Importantly, given that the TIMSS data showed a negative impact of some indicators of disciplinary climate in schools, it is possible that these effects are aggregations of individual-level effects of misbehavior on performance. However, given the different measurements and research populations, this remains speculative.

Model 4 adds academic performance measured at the first wave of the panel study to Model 3. Adding this final control does not significantly alter the previous results. Although some coefficients decrease in size, it is still the case that individual misbehavior related to school (truancy, classroom removal) slightly decreases academic performance, and school-level disciplinary climate has no significant effect on school test results.

TABLE 6.6

*Hierarchical linear models estimating the effects of student- and school-level characteristics on test score*

| | *Model 1* | *Model 2* | *Model 3* | *Model 4* |
|---|---|---|---|---|
| BACKGROUND VARIABLES | | | | |
| Male | –0.399*** | –0.283*** | –0.278*** | –0.238*** |
| | (0.059) | (0.063) | (0.063) | (0.063) |
| Age | –0.066 | –0.032 | –0.071 | –0.061 |
| | (0.065) | (0.066) | (0.067) | (0.067) |
| Socioeconomic status | 0.135** | 0.133** | 0.138** | 0.106* |
| | (0.044) | (0.044) | (0.044) | (0.044) |
| School track: general (HAVO) | 0.033 | 0.017 | 0.027 | –0.067 |
| | (0.076) | (0.076) | (0.076) | (0.077) |
| School track: university prep (VWO) | 0.303*** | 0.290*** | 0.301*** | 0.100 |
| | (0.077) | (0.076) | (0.076) | (0.086) |
| Parental disorder: depression and anxiety | 0.009 | 0.012 | 0.010 | 0.005 |
| | (0.039) | (0.039) | (0.039) | (0.038) |
| Parental disorder: drug use and antisocial behavior | –0.237** | –0.204* | –0.203* | –0.184* |
| | (0.088) | (0.088) | (0.087) | (0.086) |
| STUDENT MISBEHAVIOR | | | | |
| *Student level* | | | | |
| General misbehavior | | –0.055 | –0.055 | –0.043 |
| | | (0.038) | (0.039) | (0.039) |
| School-nonsafety-related misbehavior | | –0.079* | –0.085* | –0.071 |
| | | (0.037) | (0.038) | (0.038) |
| School-safety-related misbehavior | | –0.054 | –0.069 | –0.066 |
| | | (0.037) | (0.038) | (0.038) |
| *School level* | | | | |
| General misbehavior | | | 0.071 | 0.046 |
| | | | (0.141) | (0.140) |
| School-nonsafety-related misbehavior | | | 0.086 | 0.066 |
| | | | (0.138) | (0.136) |
| School-safety-related misbehavior | | | 0.159 | 0.179 |
| | | | (0.144) | (0.143) |
| ACADEMIC PERFORMANCE | | | | |
| Academic performance (t1) | | | | 0.213*** |
| | | | | (0.043) |
| Intercept | 0.902 | 0.476 | 0.887 | 0.060 |
| | (0.721) | (0.729) | (0.747) | (0.759) |
| Pseudo $R^2$ | 0.120 | 0.221 | 0.222 | 0.272 |
| Proportion of variance between schools | 0.056 | 0.064 | 0.060 | 0.061 |
| *N* | 1,050 | 1,050 | 1,050 | 1,050 |

NOTE: Standard errors are in parentheses. The first wave of data (t1) was collected in 2001–2002 (children ages 10–12).

* $p < .05$; ** $p < .01$; *** $p < .001$.

## CONCLUSION

We have investigated the effect of school characteristics on a school's disciplinary climate and whether disciplinary climate affects the academic performance of students in the Netherlands. With regard to the relationship between school disciplinary climate and student performance, results based on the TIMSS are corroborated by those from the TRAILS. School disciplinary climates have few to no effects on student performance, independent of student- and school-level characteristics in both datasets. The longitudinal TRAILS dataset allowed for a more thorough investigation of disciplinary problems at the student and school level, enabling us to examine the impact of parental misbehavior on children's misbehavior and of a wide range of student disciplinary problems on academic performance. We found little evidence for any relationship between school-level disciplinary problems and children's misbehavior, independent of social background and parental deviance. Student misbehavior at the individual level, however, was significantly associated with academic performance, even after holding constant earlier academic achievement. Taken together, however, we conclude that we lack sufficient evidence to implicate school disciplinary climate as a factor in student performance.

One of the most consistent findings across the two datasets is that schools offering higher tracks have fewer disciplinary problems than schools that offer lower tracks. Data on the monitoring of school safety presented at the beginning of the chapter indicate that schools offering more academically oriented programs *but not offering the prevocational track* had higher levels of school safety (independent of school size). This may be interpreted as support for Coleman and Hoffer's (1987) thesis that (homogeneous) norm-enforcing networks surrounding schools lead to lower levels of deviant behavior. Norm-enforcing networks create social capital that promote academic achievement and reduce deviant behavior (see Dijkstra, Veenstra, and Peschar 2004).

What can we conclude about the distribution of disciplinary problems across different school tracks, the most important division in the Dutch educational system? Both the TIMSS and TRAILS analyses show that indicators of the level of disciplinary problems, ranging from truancy and smoking to fighting at school and classroom disruption, are significantly lower among students enrolled in the VWO university preparatory track than among students in the prevocational VMBO track. What does this finding say in the context of the contemporary discussions on early tracking in the Netherlands? Proponents of early tracking highlight the gains in academic performance of homogeneous schools. Yet these academic gains, which could be seen as an indicator of a school's efficiency in learning, are disputed (e.g., Hattie 2002; Thrupp, Lauder, and Robinson 2002; Van de Werfhorst and Mijs 2010). Opponents of early tracking point to increases in educational inequality in early-selecting systems (see Brunello and Checchi 2007; Van de Werfhorst and Mijs 2010) or to further inequality in terms of citizenship and active participation in society (Ten Dam and Volman 2003; Terwel 2005; Van de Werfhorst 2008). Our results complement these findings with evidence that individual problem behavior is more often encountered in prevocational tracks and that schools that offer higher-level tracks have fewer disciplinary problems than schools that offer only lower tracks, independent of the track of the individual student. Further research could examine track variations more thoroughly, by examining explanations for them, including differential selection or variations across tracks in friendship networks.

## NOTE

1. To maximize statistical power, the models predicting the three forms of misbehavior have different analytic sample sizes. The substantive findings are identical if we analyze exactly the same sample for all three forms of behavior. The aggregated teacher reports on delinquency and aggression are not included in the models predicting academic performance, as they had no significant effect.

## REFERENCES

Brunello, Giorgio, and Daniele Checchi. 2007. "Does School Tracking Affect Equality of Opportunity? New International Evidence." *Economic Policy* 22:781–861.

Coleman, James S., and Thomas Hoffer. 1987. *Public and Private High Schools: The Impact of Communities*. New York: Basic Books.

Crul, M., and J. Schneider. 2009. "Children of Turkish Immigrants in Germany and the Netherlands: The Impact of Differences in Vocational and Academic Tracking Systems." *Teachers College Record* 111 (6): 1508–27.

Crul, M., and H. Vermeulen. 2003. "The Second Generation in Europe. Introduction to the Special Issue." *International Migration Review* 37 (4): 965–86.

De Graaf, Nan Dirk, Paul M. De Graaf, and Gerbert Kraaykamp. 2000. "Parental Cultural Capital and Educational Attainment in the Netherlands: A Refinement of the Cultural Capital Perspective." *Sociology of Education* 73:92–111.

De Winter, A. F., A. J. Oldehinkel, R. Veenstra, J. A. Brunnekreef, F. C. Verhulst, and J. Ormel. 2005. "Evaluation of Non-response Bias in Mental Health Determinants and Outcomes in a Large Sample of Pre-adolescents." *European Journal of Epidemiology* 20:173–81.

Dijkstra, A. B., R. Veenstra, and J. Peschar. 2004. "Social Capital in Education. Functional Communities around High Schools in the Netherlands." In *Creation and Returns of Social Capital. A New Research Program*, edited by H. Flap and B. Völker, 119–44. London: Routledge.

Dronkers, J. 1995. "The Existence of Parental School Choice in the Netherlands." *Educational Policy* 9 (3): 227–43.

Entorf, H., and M. Lauk. 2008. "Peer Effects, Social Multipliers and Migrants at School: An International Comparison." *Journal of Ethnic and Migration Studies* 34 (4): 633–54.

Hattie, J. A. C. 2002. "Classroom Composition and Peer Effects." *International Journal of Educational Research* 37 (5): 449–81.

Hofman, R. H., and A. Hofman. 2001. School Choice, Religious Traditions and School Effectiveness in Public and Private Schools. *International Journal of Education and Religion* 2 (2): 144–64.

IRISvo. 2008. *Jaaranalyse 2007–2008 Incidenten Registratie in School.*

Janssens, Frans J. G., and Frans L. Leeuw. 2001. "Schools Make a Difference, but Each Difference Is Different: On Dutch Schools and Educational Equality: Trends and Challenges." *Peabody Journal of Education* 76 (3–4): 41–56.

Karsten, Sjoerd. 2010. "School Segregation." In *Equal Opportunities? The Labour Market Integration of the Children of Immigrants*, edited by OECD, 193–209. Paris: Organisation of Economic Cooperation and Development.

Karsten, Sjoerd, Charles Felix, Guuske Ledoux, Wim Meijnen, Jaap Roeleveld, and Erik Van Schooten. 2006. "Choosing Segregation or Integration? The Extent and Effects of Ethnic Segregation in Dutch Cities." *Education and Urban Society* 38:228–47.

Karsten, S., A. J. Visscher, A. B. Dijkstra, and R. Veenstra. 2010. "Towards Standards for the Publication of Performance Indicators in the Public Sector: The Case of Schools." *Public Administration* 88:90–112.

Ladd, Helen F., Edward B. Fiske, and Nienke Ruijs. 2009. "Parental Choice in the Netherlands: Growing Concerns about Segregation." Working paper SAN10-02. Duke University, Durham, NC. Available at http://sanford.duke.edu/research/papers/SAN10-02.pdf.

Luyten, H., and R. J. Bosker. 2004. "Hoe meritocratisch zijn schooladviezen?" *Pedagogische Studiën* 81:89–103.

Micklewright, John, and Sylke V. Schnepf. 2007. "Inequality of Learning in Industrialized Countries." In *Inequality and Poverty Re-examined*, edited by S. P. Jenkins and J. Micklewright, 129–45. Oxford: Oxford University Press.

Mullis, I. V. S., M. O. Martin, E. J. Gonzalez, and S. J. Chrostowski. 2004. *Findings from IEA's Trends in International Mathematics and Science Study at the Fourth and Eighth Grades*. Chestnut Hill, MA: TIMSS and PIRLS International Study Center, Boston College.

Ormel, J., A. J. Oldehinkel, R. F. Ferdinand, C. A. Hartman, A. F. De Winter, R. Veenstra, W. Vollebergh, R. B. Minderaa, J. K. Buitelaar, and F. C. Verhulst. 2005. "Internalizing and Externalizing Problems in Adolescence: General and Dimension-Specific Effects of Familial Loadings and Preadolescent Temperament Traits." *Psychological Medicine* 35:1825–35.

Schaapman, Karina. 2000. *Schoolstrijd. Ouders op de bres voor beter onderwijs.* Amsterdam: BV Uitgeverij SWP.

Schütz, G., H. Ursprung, and L. Wössmann. 2008. "Education Policy and Equality of Opportunity." *Kyklos* 61:279–308.

SCP Office. 2009. *Jaarrapport Integratie 2009*. The Haag: Social and Cultural Planning Office.

Ten Dam, Geert T. M., and Monique L. L. Volman. 2003. "A Life Jacket or an Art of Living: Inequality in Social Competence Education." *Curriculum Inquiry* 33:117–37.

Terwel, J. 2005. "Curriculum Differentiation: Multiple Perspectives and Developments in Education." *Journal of Curriculum Studies* 37 (6): 653–70.

Thrupp, M., H. Lauder, and T. Robinson. 2002. "School Composition and Peer Effects." *International Journal of Educational Research* 37 (5): 483–504.

Van de Werfhorst, Herman G. 2008. *Leren of Ontberen? Over onderwijsinstituties en ongelijkheid*. Inaugural lecture, University of Amsterdam. Amsterdam: Vossius.

Van de Werfhorst, Herman G., and Jonathan J. B. Mijs. 2010. "Achievement Inequality and the Institutional Structure of Educational Systems: A Comparative Perspective." *Annual Review of Sociology* 36:407–28.

Van de Werfhorst, Herman G., and Frank Van Tubergen. 2007. "Ethnicity, Schooling, and Merit in the Netherlands." *Ethnicities* 7:416–44.

CHAPTER SEVEN

# School Discipline, Math and Science Achievement, and College Aspirations in Contemporary Russia

*Theodore P. Gerber*

Although a rich scholarly literature examines trends and consequences of school disciplinary issues in the United States (e.g., Metz 1978; Arum 2003), these topics have received virtually no systematic attention from researchers studying education in contemporary Russia. This is somewhat surprising, because the Russian educational system has experienced a litany of widely discussed problems that may be expected to worsen the disciplinary climate within schools. Some of the problems date back to the late Soviet era, but many of them either emerged with considerable force or substantially worsened after the collapse of the Soviet Union at the end of 1991. These include a legacy of overcentralized administration; lack of innovation in teaching methodology and curricula; severe budget cuts; deteriorating infrastructure; shortages of textbooks, equipment, and computer technology; low morale, bad pay, declining status, and wage arrears for teachers; growing regionally based inequalities in school conditions; and a general sense of chaos in the face of widespread economic crisis, political instability, and a flurry of confused educational reform efforts (see OECD 1998; Sutherland 1999; Webber 2000). Moreover, in the post-Soviet era, Russian society experienced a surge in juvenile delinquency and other problems afflicting young people, such as drug abuse, alcoholism, poor physical and mental health, divorce and single parenthood, child poverty and homelessness, and lack of leisure opportunities (Pridemore 2002; Kerr 2005a).

It seems only logical that these developments would produce an increase in the frequency and severity of disciplinary breakdowns in Russian classrooms. Apart from the massive problems in the educational sector and among Russia's youth during the 1990s, in education as in Russian society, reformers in the 1990s urged rejection of authoritarian practices and the celebration of individualism and human rights, potentially paving the way for challenges to the traditional culture within Russia's schools (Karpov and Lisovskaya 2005; Kerr 2005b; Muckle 2005). Indeed, some authors casually mention that disciplinary problems have been on the rise in Russia's schools, but they seldom produce any evidence showing that this is the case. Perhaps the lack of scholarly attention to school discipline in Russia reflects the belief that it is such an obvious problem that it scarcely requires research. Alternatively, it might be construed as a mere minor symptom of the deeper and more drastic problems befalling Russian educational institutions and society.

However, there are grounds for considerable skepticism that school discipline has become a major problem in contemporary Russia, despite the litany of issues and challenges confronting Russian schools. Consider, for example, the following passage by a seasoned English observer of Russian schools:

> With regard to matters of discipline and stress-related problems, too, some comparative perspective is required, although in the absence of in-depth comparative studies I must again revert to anecdotal evidence and impressions gained from observation in Russia. Many of the Russian teachers interviewed during this research remarked on what they see as the rapidly declining standards of discipline among pupils and the lack of interest that many pupils show towards their studies. Furthermore, teachers complain that they are having to contend with the social problems that have worsened in society in recent years, ranging from drug and alcohol abuse, to hooliganism and criminal activities. I do not contest these claims, for it is clear that they have increased. Further, it is clear that Russian teachers have struggled to deal with these issues, owing both to the speed and intensity with which such problems have grown, and to the lack of training and advice given to the profession on how to face such new challenges. . . . Yet if we compare objectively the problems of Russian teachers with those which many of their colleagues in England have to face, then, to a degree, some of the more desperate conclusions made on the Russian situation are tempered somewhat. . . . Many [Russian teachers I talked to] professed to being surprised, even shocked, to hear of the discipline problems that English teachers encounter, the stress that pupils and parents can place teachers under, and the potential threat of dismissal, even prosecution, that can occasionally arise in extreme cases of teacher-pupil conflict. . . . I am confident that the discipline problems of the English school, and the related issues of drug abuse, juvenile crime, and so on, are still worse than those found in Russia. (Webber 2000, 87–88)

As this passage implies, anecdotal statements about increasing disciplinary issues in Russia must be viewed against the perspective of the previous legacy. In fact, the culture of Russian classrooms has historically emphasized respect for authority and the constructive development of moral virtue and good citizenship, tendencies that were only reinforced during the Soviet era (Holmes, Read, and Voskresenskaya 1995). Russian schools took responsibility not only for education (*obrazovanie*, or imparting knowledge and skills) but also for upbringing (*vospitanie*, or general character building and maturation). Although Russian and Soviet pedagogy has often been criticized—justifiably—for overemphasizing memorization and factual knowledge while suppressing critical thinking and creativity, scholars also note that Russian teachers typically are genuinely maternal and supportive to their students and students themselves cultivate a strong sense of commitment toward the class collective and mutually enforce norms of conduct (Muckle 2005).[1]

A joint study of Russian schools by Russian and American education researchers observed that the atmosphere in Russian classrooms is considerably more formal than in typical American classrooms: children rise when the teacher enters and sit only when told to, they speak only when the teacher gives permission, they do not slouch, and they calmly raise their hands by resting an elbow on the desk (Kourova and Ashmore 2004, 23). Students receive large quantities of homework (at least three to four hours daily for ninth graders), which is expressly intended (in part) to occupy time that they might otherwise devote to mischief. Teachers maintain order in the class through normative exhortations: "anti-social behavior and poor grades are equivalent to letting the team down" (24). Teachers also draw on parents to assist in working with especially recalcitrant students, which usually resolves matters effectively. However, in extreme cases students with severe disciplinary problems are expelled from school.

An anthropologist who spent time in three Russian high schools as part of a broad study of how Russian teens responded to the sweeping changes of the 1990s suggests that the new emphasis on individuality within schools led to some tentative experimentation by students and teachers that did not alter the fundamental authority structure within schools (Markovits 2000, chap. 5). Although Markovits found that students were pleased with the decision to do away with mandatory school uniforms, she nonetheless concluded,

> Teenagers in the last grades of Russian schools do not have a "high school" experience. They remain children who are simultaneously coddled and prodded by teachers, the objects of both affection and contempt. Schools are squarely under the control of teachers and administrators, "houses of knowledge" where children are to learn what their adult teachers prepare for them. Yet in this atmosphere, under difficult physical and economic conditions, teachers are trying out their newly gained mandate to encourage pupils' creativity and critical-thinking skills. It is shaky, untested ground, and often both students and teachers retreat to the known territory of the past. . . . The teachers' agendas are not secure, and neither are the students'. Both are not completely certain that things have changed—and perhaps unwilling for them to change as much as they might. Perhaps that is why the ringleaders at [the schools I studied] enjoy good-natured relationships with their teachers. They are . . . negotiating change in a structure that continues to decree that adults are in charge and teenagers are not autonomous. (92)

As this passage indicates, according to Markovits, reform in the direction of greater individual freedom within schools did not undermine the control of teachers and administrators.

An observational study of practices in Russian classrooms presents an idyllic picture of a complex pedagogical nexus of incentives and sanctions that motivate students to take learning seriously, do their work, and cooperate with their peers and teachers (Hufton and Elliott 2000). This is further evidence that Russian eighth graders are probably less exposed to the disciplinary climate issues that are the focus of this volume. Finally, from the perspective of the late 2000s we now see that the fervid celebration of individual rights and criticism of authority in Russian society during the early 1990s was short lived: partly in response to the harsh economic crisis and anomie associated with the heady reforms of the Boris Yeltsin era, in the last 10 years the watchwords have been a return to discipline, authority, and tradition, in education and other areas of social life (Karpov and Lisovskaya 2005). Cultural legacies change slowly, and schools have proved to be especially resilient institutions in many societies, perhaps even more so in Russia (Kerr 2005b). In contemporary Russia schools may well be, as Neil Hufton and Julian Elliott (2000) argue, "acting as enclaves for the preservation of at least a measure of familiar normality both for their pupils and in their communities" (116).

In short, there are ample grounds to doubt that school discipline has become as significant a problem in Russia as it is in the United States and other countries. As a British newspaper article quotes a teacher from St. Petersburg who taught for a year in an inner-city school in London, "In our [Russia's] system, we have obedience. . . . It is preferable. We don't have behavioural problems. We do not have behaviour management at all" (Ward 2002). Consistent with the view that Russian schools today are characterized by relatively positive disciplinary climates despite the array of significant challenges they face, an Organization for Economic Cooperation and Development (OECD) evaluation team observed no "significant discipline problems" or "signs of defacement or vandalism" in any of the schools it visited in the course of its extensive assessment of the Russian educational system in 1996. Instead, the reviewers "were impressed with the neatness and good order observable within the schools . . . [and] the sense of the school as a harmonious community existed at the sites they visited" (OECD 1998, 19).

Ultimately, only systematic empirical research can shed light on the extent and nature of school disciplinary issues in Russia today. This chapter is an initial attempt to do so within the framework of the project's broader comparative agenda. Using the 2003 TIMSS data, I examine school-level correlates of several measures of disciplinary problems in Russian schools. I then use multilevel models to assess whether disciplinary problems at both the school level and the individual level are related to performance on the TIMSS math and science tests and whether they affect the odds that Russian eighth graders expect to graduate university. In Russia as elsewhere a key question is whether the severity and consequences of school disciplinary issues are related to differences in the socioeconomic background of students or to other aspects of schools: because poor disciplinary climates are more often experienced by students from less advantaged backgrounds, origin-based inequalities in educational attainment or achievement may be mediated or exacerbated by school disciplinary problems. Previous research has demonstrated that origin-based inequalities in educational attainments were fairly pronounced in Soviet-era Russia and may have increased after the Soviet collapse (Gerber and Hout 1995; Gerber 2000, 2007).

As discussed in the introduction, research based in the United States has shown that school disciplinary climate can influence achievement and aspirations through both social control (administrative regulation) and the quality of the peer environment produced by disciplinary problems or lack thereof (Metz 1979; DiPrete, Muller, and Shaeffer 1981; Coleman and

Hoffer 1987; Arum 2003). No research on Russia has explored whether disciplinary climate plays these roles there, nor has any examined whether it mediates the effects of social background on these outcomes. Apart from shedding light on the role that school discipline plays in shaping academic achievement and inequality in contemporary Russian schools, this chapter breaks new ground as the first (to my knowledge) study to examine the role of social background and other individual- and school-level factors related to achievement and expectations in Russian schools.

## RUSSIAN SCHOOL DISCIPLINARY CONTEXT

### *Population Heterogeneity*

The main sources of population heterogeneity in Russia that might affect school disciplinary context are socioeconomic, ethnolinguistic, and nativity differences. As noted, previous research has shown that the educational and class origins of parents affected the educational attainments of students throughout the Soviet era and that the magnitude of these effects increased following the Soviet collapse at the end of 1991 (Gerber and Hout 1995; Gerber 2000, 2007). Little is known about whether class-based peer cultures play a role in generating these disparities in Russia, but it is certainly possible that they do and that disciplinary climates in schools both reflect and reinforce them. Russia is a multiethnic society: according to its 2002 population census (see http://www.perepis2002.ru, in Russian, source of the following figures) 79.8 percent of its 145 million population consists of ethnic Russians. Tatars, Ukrainians, Bashkirs, Chuvash, Chechens, and Armenians each total at least 1 million. All told, over 180 distinct ethnic groups and indigenous peoples live in Russia. In spite of this ethnic diversity, the vast majority of the population (98.2 percent) speaks Russian, according to self-reports on the census. Nevertheless, in some communities with high concentrations of non-Russians (particularly in the southern regions and parts of Siberia) a language other than Russian is the primary language spoken. Having a "first" language other than Russian is a reasonable proxy for a distinctive ethnic culture that might have consequences for school disciplinary climate. The TIMSS data provide a measure of how frequently the student respondents speak Russian at home, which I use as such a proxy. Finally, although there are no official figures, Russia clearly has a sizable foreign-born population. The World Bank's World Development

Indicators database puts migrants in Russia at 8.4 percent in 2005. Many immigrants are ethnic Russians who moved to Russia from other former Soviet republics, where they felt unwelcome after the breakup of the former Soviet Union. Culturally, they probably have more in common with the dominant native-born ethnic Russian population than immigrants typically have with the native-born populations in other countries. However, recent years have also seen the influx of labor migrants from abroad.

### *Structure of the Educational System*

In Russia today, educational enrollment (in first grade) begins at age 6 and is compulsory through age 15. This represents an official retreat from Soviet-era policies, when in principle all students were supposed to attain a complete secondary education, though in practice this goal was never reached. A secondary degree is generally awarded to students upon completion of the 11th grade. The basic structure of the Russian school system has changed little since the Soviet period. Most students attend unified institutions that provide instruction at all grade levels, and they remain in a class with the same classmates throughout their educational careers. However, some schools provide instruction only through grade 8 (known, somewhat incongruously, as the grade marking the completion of "incomplete secondary" education) and, correspondingly, others provide only the advanced secondary grades (9–11).

Apart from a small number of special schools that cater to the athletically, artistically, or intellectually gifted, Russian schools traditionally have not tracked students according to ability or academic performance. However, the Russian system does include vocational institutions, often known by their Russian initials, PTU, that emphasize cultivation of manual skills rather than academic preparation. Students who enter such institutions, many of which are run by large enterprises, usually do so after completing eighth grade. Although the Soviet regime attempted to bolster the reputation of PTUs in the late 1970s by awarding secondary degrees to many students who graduated from these institutions, they have long been the preserve of less advantaged students, particularly males, who struggle academically. In addition to the PTUs, there is another, somewhat more prestigious, vocational track in the so-called specialized secondary instructional institutions (SSUZ), also known as *tekhnikumy* ("technical colleges").

Roughly half these institutions provide training in auxiliary professions (librarians, nurses, paramedics, airline pilots, lab technicians) along with a standard academic secondary curriculum, while others focus exclusively on professional preparation and require matriculants to have a secondary degree before admission. Thus, Russian students can choose between three types of institutions after the eighth grade: PTUs that train them for skilled manual trades, SSUZs that prepare them for semiprofessional careers, and general secondary institutions (which may be in the same building or complex where they finished eighth grade or, in larger cities, may be separate institutions) whose purpose is to prepare them academically for university-level study.

The Soviet educational system was highly centralized: national ministries chose a uniform curriculum, pedagogical approach, and standard for the entire country, and federal and regional authorities dispersed financing. Administration was organized along strict hierarchical lines within institutions and between institutions and local, regional, and national educational authorities. This structure left little room for autonomy, experimentation, or the cultivation of policies or approaches to meet local needs and respond to changing times. Many of the reform efforts dating back to the 1980s sought to decentralize the system to combat inertia and promote innovation (see Holmes et al. 1995; Webber 2000; Kerr 2005b). Critics portrayed pedagogical practices as overly rigid and tradition bound, encouraging a shift to new approaches that emphasized cultivation of critical thought rather than inculcation of facts and correct answers.

When the Soviet system collapsed at the end of 1991, the moment seemed ripe for these objectives to be realized. However, the initial enthusiasm of reformers quickly turned to desperation, as the economic and political crisis unraveled the system of financial support for schools. Government support for schools fell dramatically; facilities and equipment deteriorated, teacher salaries plummeted (and often were not paid on time), and money for textbooks and instructional technology disappeared. Many schools were forced to raise money on their own to pay their bills. By most accounts, the financial and material problems were most pronounced in rural areas and in poorer cities (OECD 1998). A small sector of private, tuition-charging schools slowly developed, but it has yet to become a substantial institutional fixture.

### *Legal Context and Administration of School Discipline*

Laws meant little during the Soviet era, and Russians are widely understood to have little trust or faith in legal institutions (see, e.g., Gerber and Mendelson 2008). It was not possible for citizens to sue government officials in Soviet times, and as a result Russian citizens have little experience with this mechanism for seeking redress, including in educational settings. Although the practice slowly grew more common as the 1990s progressed, lawsuits against government officials remain rare (see Hendley 2002; Javeline and Baird 2007). A top expert on Russian litigation cannot recall ever hearing of a teacher or school official being sued by parents or students (Katherine Hendley, personal communication). Therefore, it is doubtful that the legal context of school discipline plays any role at all in Russia; the cultural, normative, and material factors just discussed are far more likely to be relevant.

In terms of the administration of school discipline, corporal punishment is illegal in Russian schools, and I have not found any accounts that suggest that this proscription is routinely or even occasionally violated. On the other hand, it seems highly unlikely that teachers or administrators balk at applying harsh disciplinary measures out of fear of being sued by students.

Traditionally, students in Russian schools were required to wear uniforms. Mandatory uniforms were officially banished in 1992, but they have remained the norm in many schools. Principals play an active role in Russian schools: they frequently observe classes, assess the behavior of students and the effectiveness of teachers, and report to authorities on the performance of their schools; moreover, they bear ultimate responsibility for dealing with children who misbehave (Kourova and Ashmore 2004, 21). In the classroom teachers are responsible for maintaining law and order, but in doing so they rely extensively on peer pressure to correct infractions. In rare cases teachers and principals will report especially defiant or recalcitrant students to their parents and enlist their support in curbing the problematic behavior. In still rarer ("extreme") cases schools will expel students with "severe discipline problems," and they are sent to boarding schools (Kourova and Ashmore 2004, 22). The concept of due process rights is generally unfamiliar to Russian society, and it is inconceivable that Russian students would sue their school or their teachers for having taken disciplinary actions.

## STUDY DESIGN

### *Research Questions*

This chapter addresses the same research questions as the other chapters in this book: (1) What school-level variables are associated with school disciplinary climate, as measured by principal, teacher, and student reports? (2) How, if at all, does school disciplinary climate affect individual math and science achievement and college expectations, through both school-level disciplinary environment and individual experiences of disciplinary infractions by other students? (3) Does school disciplinary climate mediate the effects of other school-level characteristics (in particular, the socioeconomic composition of schools) in Russia?

### *Data and Methods*

I use data from the 2003 Trends in International Mathematics and Science Study (TIMSS) survey to address the empirical questions that motivate this chapter and the comparative project. As described in detail in the introduction, TIMSS surveyed eighth graders and collected school-level data from principals and classroom-level data from teachers. Its rich set of measures at the individual, classroom, and school levels makes it ideal for analyzing the correlates and effects of school disciplinary climate in Russia. The only other Russian dataset suitable for addressing the issue of school discipline is the Program for International Student Assessment (PISA) study, and a useful next phase of this research would be an exploration of whether the results based on the TIMSS data can be replicated using the PISA data.

In addition to the standard variables used throughout this book (see introduction), I create several measures specifically for the Russian context. I supplement the standard school disciplinary climate measures with an alternative measure of student- and school-level victimization. At the student level, the measure is whether respondents experienced violence (kicked, hurt, or punched by other students) or coercion (forced by other students to do something they did not want to). At the school level, the measure is the proportion of students sampled within the school who reported being victims of violence or coercion. I create this measure because violence and coercion are particularly extreme forms of disciplinary violations in schools; therefore, I suspect that this measure identifies the most serious disciplinary problems more accurately than does the conventional student victimization index, which sums up the number of the following experiences that students report: encountering violence, being made fun of, and having something stolen. My measure has one item in common with the conventional measure (experience of violence), but mine incorporates an experience of being coerced to do something but not being made fun of or having something stolen.

I create additional school-level covariates that seem likely to be relevant in the Russian context of widespread material issues confronting schools. A scale measuring principal-reported economic difficulties is based on the principal's agreement with a series of questions pertaining to shortages of equipment, materials, facilities, and technology. This measure is designed to capture the material situation of the school itself, as opposed to that of its students. Second, a school-level measure of the percentage of students who speak Russian rarely or never at home is a proxy for the presence of a non-Russian peer culture in the school.

Following the mandate of the larger comparative project, I first examine the characteristics of Russian eighth grade students and schools, including their experiences of disciplinary problems, by analyzing descriptive statistics. Next, I examine how each measure of school-level disciplinary climate relates to other school characteristics using school-level regressions. I also explore models that regress school-level science and math performance and college expectations on school characteristics. Finally, I estimate a series of hierarchical linear and logistic regressions to identify individual- and school-level correlates of test performance and college expectations, with particular attention to the interplay between measures of school discipline and measures of social background in these models.

Because a large percentage of students are missing the parental education measure, I conducted all individual-level analyses using two missing-data strategies to assess the robustness of the results: mean substitution and listwise deletion. The two strategies yield very similar results. For the school-level analyses the loss of observations due to missing data on variables reported by principals is more serious because only 214 schools are in the sample. So I report the mean-substituted results for the school-level models. However, for the hierarchical models of individual outcomes I report the listwise missing results because sample size is less of a concern and they are more parsimonious (in the absence of nuisance parameters denoting mean substitutions).

## FINDINGS

### *Descriptive Statistics*

Table 7.1 presents descriptive statistics for the TIMSS individual- and school-level variables. Several means are worth noting. About 9 percent of the students were born outside Russia, and 3 percent can be classified as nonnative Russian speakers because they report speaking Russian rarely or never at home. In addition, the school-level descriptive statistics indicate that about one-third of the 214 schools sampled by the study have more than 10 percent immigrant students (based on the students included in the TIMSS). These variables may be aspects of social background that affect academic performance in Russia, but they have not been examined in earlier research. Further, among those who gave valid answers, three-quarters expect to finish university, making those who do not expect to do so a clear minority. Among those who provided valid answers, 16 percent of the TIMSS sample were victims of violence or coercion.[2] Altogether, the TIMSS data indicate that although direct encounters with disciplinary infractions are hardly uncommon in Russian schools, they are still far from majority or typical experiences, and the most serious infractions (violence or coercion) are the least widespread.

Given the ambiguity regarding the extent of disciplinary problems in Russian schools, it is worth noting how Russia compares to the other countries in this project on school-level disciplinary climate measures. Russia's interschool mean of 2.75 on principal reports of disciplinary disengagement is equivalent to the mean for all countries, suggesting that Russia is neither especially prone nor especially immune to this type of disciplinary violation. Russia's mean of 3.45 on the teacher-based measure of classroom disruptions is slightly above the mean for all countries (3.31). Comparing this average to the means from specific countries, based on the subjective assessments of teachers, indicates that Russian classrooms have substantially more disciplinary problems than classrooms in Canada, Japan, the United States, and the Netherlands; about the same as Italy; and fewer than Chile, Korea, and Israel. In other words, Russia does not stand out as notably high or low with regard to either principal or teacher reports of school disciplinary issues.

TABLE 7.1
*Descriptive statistics*

| | *Mean* | *SD* |
|---|---|---|
| STUDENT CHARACTERISTICS | | |
| Age | 14.172 | 0.531 |
| Male | 0.500 | |
| Immigrant status | 0.090 | 0.275 |
| Highest parental education | 5.540 | 1.434 |
| Number of books in household | 3.492 | 1.093 |
| Household size | 3.910 | 1.050 |
| Russian spoken rarely or never at home | 0.030 | 0.160 |
| Expect to attend university | 0.747 | 0.435 |
| SCHOOL AND COMMUNITY CHARACTERISTICS | | |
| *School and community variables* | | |
| School size (log) | 1.045 | 0.675 |
| School highest grade level | 10.890 | 0.452 |
| Community size (log) | 6.310 | 0.832 |
| *School-level student characteristics* | | |
| Male students | | |
| 46%–60% | 0.470 | 0.500 |
| >60% | 0.210 | 0.410 |
| Percentage male | 0.510 | 0.130 |
| Immigrant students | | |
| 1%–10% | 0.430 | 0.500 |
| >10% | 0.340 | 0.470 |
| Percentage immigrants | 0.090 | 0.080 |
| Average parental education | 5.438 | 0.690 |
| Variation in parental education | 0.239 | 0.050 |
| Material shortages reported by principal | 2.433 | 0.780 |
| School percentage non-Russian speakers at home | 0.040 | 0.130 |
| >10% non-Russian speakers | 0.080 | 0.270 |
| DISCIPLINARY CLIMATE | | |
| Principal reports: frequency of disciplinary disengagement | 2.748 | 0.930 |
| Teacher reports | | |
| Frequency of classroom disruption | 3.454 | 0.700 |
| Victim of violence or coercion at school | 0.165 | 0.371 |
| Student victimization index | 0.449 | 0.752 |
| Mean student victimization index | 0.444 | 0.210 |
| Proportion students victims of violence/coercion | 0.160 | 0.100 |
| COGNITIVE PERFORMANCE | | |
| Math and science test score (combined) | 100.430 | 18.520 |
| Math and science test score (combined), school average | 100.030 | 11.490 |
| *N* | 4,667 | |

NOTE: SD = standard deviation.

However, comparison of Russia's student-level reports of victimization to other countries indicates that it has the lowest school mean on the student victimization index. Thus, on the basis of what is probably the most accurate measure of disciplinary climate (assuming student-level reports of direct encounters with violence, coercion, theft, and mistreatment are more accurate than inherently more subjective reports by principals and teachers), it appears that Russia's schools are distinguished by exceptionally low levels of disciplinary problems. It would be interesting to examine how Russia compares to the other countries in regard to student reports of the various components of the student victimization index, but these measures were not broken out for the other countries.

*Analytic Results*

As seen in Table 7.2, the school-level measures of disciplinary climate are only weakly correlated with each other in Russia. The only exception is the strong correlation between the student victimization index and the school-level proportion of students who report violence or coercion, but this clearly reflects inclusion in the victimization index of variables measuring experiences of violence or coercion. The weak correlations among the school-level measures call for considerable caution in interpreting these as measures of overall or underlying disciplinary environments in the Russian schools in the TIMSS sample.

To assess how school-level factors relate to school disciplinary climate, I regress the four school-level measures on the other school-level characteristics (Table 7.3). The most striking finding is the overall weak and inconsistent associations between the measures of school discipline and the other variables. Principals report higher levels of disciplinary disengagement

TABLE 7.2

*Correlations among school-level measures of disciplinary problems*

| | *Teachers: disruption* | *Principal: disengagement* | *Student victimization index* | *Students: violence or coercion* |
|---|---|---|---|---|
| Teachers: disruptions | 1.000 | | | |
| Principal: disengagement | 0.171 | 1.000 | | |
| Student victimization index | 0.121 | 0.075 | 1.000 | |
| Proportion victims of violence/ coercion | 0.084 | 0.062 | 0.751 | 1.000 |

TABLE 7.3
*School-level regression models: measures of disciplinary climate*

| | *Disciplinary disengagement* | *Class-room dis-ruptions* | *Student victimiza-tion index* | *Students: violence or coercion* |
|---|---|---|---|---|
| SCHOOL AND COMMUNITY CHARACTERISTICS | | | | |
| *School and community variables* | | | | |
| Community size (log) | −0.014 | −0.075 | −0.009 | 0.007 |
| | (0.132) | (0.107) | (0.032) | (0.015) |
| School size (log) | 0.219* | 0.058 | −0.011 | 0.007 |
| | (0.117) | (0.095) | (0.028) | (0.013) |
| School highest grade level | 0.247 | 0.064 | 0.034 | 0.017 |
| | (0.152) | (0.123) | (0.037) | (0.017) |
| *School-level student characteristics* | | | | |
| Percentage male | 0.332 | 0.840** | 0.164 | 0.056 |
| | (0.484) | (0.397) | (0.117) | (0.054) |
| Non-Russian speakers >10% | −0.026 | 0.016 | −0.069 | −0.008 |
| | (0.236) | (0.196) | (0.057) | (0.026) |
| Average parental education | 0.030 | −0.016 | 0.078** | 0.020 |
| | (0.125) | (0.101) | (0.030) | (0.014) |
| Variation in parental education | 4.419** | 0.691 | 0.587 | 0.170 |
| | (1.495) | (1.207) | (0.360) | (0.166) |
| Report material shortages | 0.261** | 0.066 | 0.046** | 0.005 |
| | (0.079) | (0.064) | (0.019) | (0.009) |
| Immigrants | | | | |
| 1%–10% | 0.027 | 0.015 | −0.046 | −0.012 |
| | (0.160) | (0.130) | (0.039) | (0.018) |
| >10% | 0.007 | 0.138 | 0.005 | 0.001 |
| | (0.168) | (0.137) | (0.041) | (0.019) |
| Intercept | −3.337* | 1.743 | −0.577 | −0.259 |
| | (1.735) | (1.406) | (0.418) | (0.193) |
| $R^2$ | 0.184 | 0.073 | 0.095 | 0.067 |
| *N* | 214 | 211 | 214 | 214 |

NOTE: Dummy variables denoting missing-value substitution on community size, school size, school highest grade, and shortages are included but not shown. Standard errors are in parentheses.

* $p < .10$, two-tailed; ** $p < .05$, two-tailed.

in larger schools, schools with more variation in parental education, and schools with higher levels of reported material shortages. Teachers report more frequent classroom disruptions in schools with larger percentages of male students, which is in line with previous evidence suggesting that males are more likely to have disciplinary problems. Surprisingly, student-level reports of victimization are significantly higher in schools with higher average parental education but also in schools where principals report more material shortages. None of the other school-level variables has a statistically significant association with the school-level measure of violence or coercion.

The generally weak relationships between school socioeconomic composition (as measured by parental education) and level of disciplinary problems in Russia suggests that disciplinary issues are unlikely to mediate the effects of socioeconomic status on academic achievement and college expectations, such as they are. However, as Table 7.4 indicates, school-level parental education does have the expected direct effect on school average test scores and college expectations: schools with a higher proportion of well-educated parents have higher average test scores and elevated proportions of students who expect to finish college. Otherwise, few variables at the school level appear to have much influence on these measures. The only other variable that affects both outcomes in the simple school-level regressions is proportion of students reporting violence or coercion: this measure of disciplinary climate has the expected negative effects on both mean test scores and proportion planning to finish college. In contrast, the student victimization index has a negative effect on college aspirations but not on mean test scores. This is our first indication that the more precise measure of student-level reports of disciplinary issues performs better as a predictor of performance outcomes than the more aggregated student victimization index employed in this book's other chapters. Given these results, it is appropriate to consider both the student victimization index and the violence-coercion measure as alternatives in the hierarchical models for test scores and college expectations.

### *Individual-Level and School-Level Correlates of Test Scores and College Expectations*

To gain a sense of the overall contribution of school-level measures to variation in the test score outcome, it is useful to consider the residual variance components from a series of hierarchical linear regression models (Table 7.5). First, the table reports the results on the basis of the analyses of the entire sample using mean substitution to account for missing data. Following this, it reports the corresponding results for listwise models estimated on the subsample with valid data on all variables. However, because the latter yield the same conclusions and are more parsimonious than the mean substitution models, I focus my discussion on the listwise models

TABLE 7.4
*School-level regression models: outcome means*

| | MEAN TOTAL TEST SCORE | | PROPORTION EXPECTING COLLEGE | |
|---|---|---|---|---|
| | *Model 1* | *Model 2* | *Model 1* | *Model 2* |
| SCHOOL AND COMMUNITY CHARACTERISTICS | | | | |
| *School and community variables* | | | | |
| School size (log) | −1.745 | −1.606 | −0.029 | −0.025 |
| | (1.308) | (1.297) | (0.021) | (0.021) |
| School highest grade level | 0.876 | 0.990 | −0.025 | −0.025 |
| | (1.696) | (1.683) | (0.027) | (0.027) |
| Community size (log) | 0.945 | 1.109 | 0.024 | 0.027 |
| | (1.465) | (1.454) | (0.024) | (0.024) |
| *School-level student characteristics* | | | | |
| Percentage male | −6.680 | −6.586 | −0.188** | −0.192** |
| | (5.494) | (5.444) | (0.088) | (0.088) |
| Non-Russian speakers >10% | −1.118 | −1.021 | 0.037 | 0.042 |
| | (2.684) | (2.656) | (0.043) | (0.043) |
| Average parental education | 6.882** | 6.851** | 0.157** | 0.152** |
| | (1.408) | (1.380) | (0.023) | (0.022) |
| Variation in parental education | −46.262** | −46.202** | −0.320 | −0.352 |
| | (16.958) | (16.758) | (0.272) | (0.271) |
| Report material shortages | −1.075 | −1.206 | 0.016 | 0.010 |
| | (0.910) | (0.892) | (0.015) | (0.014) |
| Immigrants | | | | |
| 1%–10% | −2.535 | −2.502 | 0.019 | 0.022 |
| | (1.784) | (1.765) | (0.029) | (0.029) |
| >10% | −1.603 | −1.583 | 0.019 | 0.019 |
| | (1.871) | (1.856) | (0.030) | (0.030) |
| DISCIPLINARY CLIMATE | | | | |
| Principal reports: frequency of disciplinary disengagement | −0.571 | −0.537 | 0.016 | 0.017 |
| | (0.992) | (0.981) | (0.013) | (0.013) |
| Teacher reports: frequency of classroom disruption | −1.107 | −1.105 | −0.039** | −0.040** |
| | (0.794) | (0.788) | (0.016) | (0.016) |
| Student reports | | | | |
| Student victimization index | −4.094 | | −0.139** | |
| | (3.262) | | (0.052) | |
| Students: violence/coercion | | −15.199** | | −0.300** |
| | | (6.993) | | (0.113) |
| Intercept | 88.938** | 87.563** | 0.564* | 0.574* |
| | (19.639) | (19.461) | (0.315) | (0.315) |
| $R^2$ | 0.375 | 0.385 | 0.432 | 0.432 |
| *N* | 211 | 211 | 211 | 211 |

NOTE: Dummy variables denoting missing-value substitution on community size, school size, school highest grade, and shortages included but not shown. Standard errors are in parentheses.

* $p < .10$, two-tailed; ** $p < .05$, two-tailed.

TABLE 7.5

*Residual variance decomposition, selected hierarchical linear regressions for test score*

| Model | Description | L1 residual variance | L2 residual variance | L2 DF | % L2 variance |
|---|---|---|---|---|---|
| MODELS ESTIMATED USING MEAN SUBSTITUTION FOR MISSING DATA ON ALL VARIABLES | | | | | |
| 1 | Baseline (no covariates) | 224.27 | 119.99 | 213 | 34.9 |
| 2 | 7 student-level covariates, no victimization | 205.78 | 98.02 | 213 | 32.3 |
| 3a | Add school variables, no discipline | 205.74 | 77.33 | 199 | 27.3 |
| 3b | Trim school-level variables, no discipline | 205.75 | 75.87 | 206 | 26.9 |
| 4a | Add standard school-level discipline variables | 205.76 | 74.89 | 202 | 26.7 |
| 4b | Alternative specification of school-level student reports | 205.77 | 73.15 | 202 | 26.2 |
| 4c | Trim disaggregated school-level discipline variables | 205.76 | 73.13 | 203 | 26.2 |
| 5 | Add student-level victimization | 204.61 | 72.49 | 203 | 26.2 |
| MODELS ESTIMATED USING LISTWISE DELETION FOR MISSING DATA ON ALL VARIABLES | | | | | |
| *Model* | *Description* | *L1 residual variance* | *L2 residual variance* | *L2 DF* | *% L2 variance* |
| 1 | Baseline (no covariates) | 221.34 | 113.79 | 205 | 34.0 |
| 2 | 7 student-level covariates, no victimization | 207.52 | 94.20 | 205 | 31.2 |
| 3a | Add school variables, no discipline | 207.54 | 77.29 | 195 | 27.1 |
| 3b | Trim school-level variables, no discipline | 207.50 | 73.44 | 200 | 26.1 |
| 4a | Add standard school-level discipline variables | 207.50 | 72.91 | 197 | 26.0 |
| 4b | Alternative specification of school-level student reports | 207.51 | 71.16 | 197 | 25.5 |
| 4c | Trim school-level discipline variables | 207.51 | 71.01 | 198 | 25.5 |
| 5 | Add student-level report of violence/coercion | 207.53 | 70.99 | 198 | 25.5 |

NOTE: L1 = student level; L2 = school level; DF = degrees of freedom.

and present parameter estimates in subsequent tables based on them. According to the results for Model 1, the baseline model with no covariates, about 34 percent of the variance in student test scores is between schools. Introducing individual-level covariates in Model 2 reduces that proportion only slightly. Model 3a incorporates 10 school-level measures but excludes the disciplinary measures and reduces between-school variance by about 13 percent. Trimming in Model 3b the nonsignificant school-level effects decreases the between-school variance, leaving 26.1 percent of the variance in scores unexplained.

By next entering the school-level measures of disciplinary climate into a model in which I have already controlled for school-level factors that may be correlated with the disciplinary measures, I set the bar relatively high for demonstrating that disciplinary setting exerts an independent effect on test score. Despite this, the results clearly indicate that disciplinary context does matter for test performance, controlling for both school-level and individual-level variables that also affect test score. Model 4a, which adds the principal, teacher, and student assessments of disciplinary problems, reduces the residual school-level variance from 73.4 to 72.9. Using the violence-coercion measure in Model 4b in place of the standard student victimization index reduces school variance even further, to 71.2. Model 4c trims the nonsignificant measures of school disciplinary climate, with no increase in the level of remaining between-school variance. Comparing Model 4c to Model 3b, we can conclude on the basis of the optimal specification of school-level disciplinary climate that interschool variation in disciplinary problems accounts for about 2.5 percent of the interschool variation that remains once other school-level factors affecting mean test score are controlled.

When discipline-related measures are introduced only at the school level, it remains unclear whether their apparent effects operate at that level. More negative disciplinary settings may exert their effects solely by increasing the probability of individual-level encounters with disciplinary problems such as violence and disruption, but they may also undermine performance ecologically by creating an environment of tension, anomie, or general frustration. While it is not possible to say with certainty whether either of these mechanisms predominates, I assess in Model 5 the robustness of the contextual interpretation of the disciplinary effects by controlling for individual-level student victimization. This has little effect on the between-school variance explained, but we can tell whether individual victimization by disciplinary infractions account for the school-level effect of disciplinary climate only by inspecting the appropriate coefficients and standard errors, which I do later.

To understand what these results imply for the individual- and school-level factors associated with math and science tests in Russia, it is necessary to inspect the full sets of parameter estimates from four of the models described earlier. As mentioned, because the same substantive conclusions follow regardless of the strategy used to address missing data, I report the results on the basis of listwise deletion, since they do not include nuisance parameters. The results of Table 7.6 indicate that the individual-level covariates all have significant effects in the expected directions: age, household size, and immigrant status are negatively associated with test scores, while male gender, number of books in the household, and parental education have positive effects. An additional individual-level variable included for only this chapter, a dummy denoting nonnative speakers of Russian, has a significant negative effect on test scores. The large magnitude of this latter effect suggests its importance in the Russian context.

Model 3b also includes five school-level variables that affect the individual test-score intercept. Mean parental education of the school exerts a strong positive effect on test scores, controlling for the individual-level effect of parental education. Variation in parental education within the school is associated with lower test scores, as are the percentage of male students, the level of material shortages (as reported by the principal), and the size of the school. School-level variables that do not significantly affect test scores (and thus are omitted from Model 3b) include the two dummy variables characterizing the proportion of immigrants in the school, the logarithm of community size, the highest grade of instruction in the school, and the percentage of non-Russian speakers.

Models 4a and 4b add school-level measures of disciplinary climate to Model 3b. The only difference between them is how student-level reports are specified. If the student victimization index (Model 4a) is used, the effect is not significant. However, if the proportion of students who experienced violence or coercion is used, the effect is significant (Model 4b) and suggests that being in a school with more students who experience violence or coercion is associated with significantly lower math and science test scores. This supports the argument that it is worth distinguishing the

TABLE 7.6

*Hierarchical linear models estimating the effects of student- and school-level characteristics on math and science test scores (combined)*

| | *Model 3b* | *Model 4a* | *Model 4b* | *Model 5* |
|---|---|---|---|---|
| STUDENT BACKGROUND | | | | |
| Age | –2.811** | –2.811** | –2.841** | –2.856** |
| | (0.499) | (0.500) | (0.501) | (0.502) |
| Male | 2.393** | 2.396** | 2.399** | 2.399** |
| | (0.551) | (0.551) | (0.551) | (0.552) |
| Immigrant | –2.259** | –2.244** | –2.241** | –2.250** |
| | (0.887) | (0.889) | (0.888) | (0.885) |
| Non-Russian speaker | –6.789** | –6.906** | –6.944** | –6.914** |
| | (1.691) | (1.688) | (1.679) | (1.677) |
| Household size | –0.450* | –0.455* | –0.454* | –0.455* |
| | (0.235) | (0.235) | (0.235) | (0.235) |
| Highest parental education | 1.224** | 1.225** | 1.223** | –0.514 |
| | (0.196) | (0.196) | (0.196) | (0.674) |
| Number of books in household | 2.135** | 2.131** | 2.131** | 1.221** |
| | (0.263) | (0.263) | (0.263) | (0.196) |
| Victim of violence/coercion | | | | 2.137** |
| | | | | (0.263) |
| SCHOOL AND COMMUNITY CHARACTERISTICS | | | | |
| *School and community variables: school size (log)* | –2.012** | –1.678* | –1.460 | –1.461 |
| | (0.877) | (0.907) | (0.908) | (0.907) |
| *School-level student characteristics* | | | | |
| Percentage male | –8.166* | –6.603 | –6.204 | –6.777 |
| | (4.887) | (5.029) | (4.986) | (4.936) |
| Material shortages | –1.803** | –1.323 | –1.385 | –1.410 |
| | (0.818) | (0.854) | (0.854) | (0.856) |

| | | | | |
|---|---|---|---|---|
| Average parental education | 3.655** | 3.825** | 3.915** | 3.961** |
| | (1.386) | (1.426) | (1.407) | (1.400) |
| Variation in parental education | –55.534** | –48.209** | –47.812** | –47.862** |
| | (16.392) | (17.253) | (17.714) | (17.563) |
| DISCIPLINARY CLIMATE | | | | |
| Principal reports: frequency of disciplinary disengagement | | –1.166* | –1.169* | –1.251* |
| | | (0.703) | (0.702) | (0.702) |
| Teacher reports: frequency of classroom disruption | | –0.810 | –0.722 | |
| | | (0.990) | (0.991) | |
| Student reports | | | | |
| Student victimization index | | –2.337 | | |
| | | (3.276) | | |
| Students: violence/coercion | | | –14.291** | –14.235** |
| | | | (6.948) | (7.039) |
| COGNITIVE PERFORMANCE | | | | |
| Math and science test score (combined) | | | | |
| Intercept | 97.547** | 96.398** | 96.552** | 96.676** |
| | (2.420) | (2.442) | (2.459) | (2.471) |
| *N* | 3,894 | 3,894 | 3,894 | 3,894 |

NOTE: Standard errors are in parentheses.

* $p < .10$, two-tailed; ** $p < .05$, two-tailed.

most severe forms of student victimization from other, less serious forms in assessing the effects of school disciplinary climate on student achievement.

Across both models, principal reports of disciplinary disengagement also have a significant negative effect (using a one-tailed test, which seems appropriate because no theory or research suggests that test scores would be higher in more problematic disciplinary environments). Not only do two of the three measures of disciplinary climate exert the predicted negative effects on test score (according to Model 4b), but these factors appear to mediate to a considerable degree the effects of other school-level variables on test score: the negative effects of percentage of male students, material shortages, and logarithm of school size all decline in magnitude by at least 25 percent and become nonsignificant once school disciplinary measures are included in the model (compare Models 3b and 4b). School discipline does not, however, mediate the effects of parental background: the impact of parental education remains stable at the individual level and actually increases at the school level once the disciplinary measures are incorporated.

Finally, Model 5 indicates that introducing individual-level violence or coercion does not affect the estimates of school-level disciplinary effects. Moreover, the individual-level effect is counterintuitive: individual students who experience violence or coercion have higher predicted test scores than otherwise similar students who do not experience violence or coercion. Although it is risky to speculate, one plausible explanation for this surprising effect might be that high-performing students are most likely to be targeted by other students for violence and coercion.

I use the same basic modeling approach for the hierarchical logistic regressions for individual-level college expectations, and for simplicity I use the same specifications of individual- and school-level effects. For space considerations, I report only the results equivalent to those in Table 7.6. Table 7.7 suggests that the individual-level effects of age and socioeconomic background (as measured by parental education and number of books in the household) are consistent with their effects on test score. However, the remaining individual-level effects differ from the previous results: male students are less likely than females to expect to finish college, non-Russian speakers are more likely to expect to finish college than native Russian speakers, and neither immigrant status nor household size are significant predictors. At the school level, only percentage of male students and average parental education significantly affect college aspirations.

TABLE 7.7

*Parameter estimates, selected hierarchical logistic regressions for college expectations (3,518 students in 211 schools)*

| | MODEL 3B | | MODEL 4A | | MODEL 4B | | MODEL 5 | |
|---|---|---|---|---|---|---|---|---|
| | *B* | *SE* | *B* | *SE* | *B* | *SE* | *B* | *SE* |
| STUDENT-LEVEL VARIABLES | | | | | | | | |
| Age | −0.398** | 0.10 | −0.397** | 0.10 | −0.406** | 0.10 | −0.346** | 0.11 |
| Male | −0.724** | 0.09 | −0.725** | 0.09 | −0.726** | 0.09 | −0.845** | 0.10 |
| Immigrant | 0.001 | 0.16 | 0.014 | 0.16 | 0.010 | 0.16 | 0.064 | 0.17 |
| Non-Russian speaker | 0.652** | 0.33 | 0.641** | 0.32 | 0.636** | 0.32 | 0.848** | 0.33 |
| Household size | 0.008 | 0.04 | 0.006 | 0.04 | 0.007 | 0.04 | 0.015 | 0.05 |
| Highest parental education | 0.372** | 0.03 | 0.371** | 0.03 | 0.371** | 0.03 | 0.344** | 0.03 |
| Number of books in household | 0.197** | 0.05 | 0.200** | 0.05 | 0.201** | 0.05 | 0.132** | 0.05 |
| Victim of violence/coercion | | | | | | | −0.037 | 0.12 |
| Total test score | | | | | | | 0.037** | 0.00 |
| SCHOOL-LEVEL VARIABLES | | | | | | | | |
| Intercept | 1.587** | 0.21 | 1.553** | 0.21 | 1.602** | 0.21 | 1.608** | 0.25 |
| Percentage male | −1.147* | 0.59 | −0.974 | 0.59 | −0.998* | 0.58 | −0.701 | 0.69 |
| Material shortages | 0.057 | 0.08 | 0.074 | 0.08 | 0.055 | 0.08 | 0.121 | 0.09 |
| School size (log) | −0.131 | 0.10 | −0.162* | 0.09 | −0.135 | 0.09 | −0.063 | 0.10 |
| Highest parental education (mean) | 0.503** | 0.16 | 0.533** | 0.15 | 0.514** | 0.15 | 0.389** | 0.18 |
| Highest parental education (variation) | −2.919 | 2.19 | −3.035 | 2.04 | −3.431* | 1.97 | −1.793 | 2.47 |
| Principal: disengagement | | | 0.112 | 0.07 | 0.112* | 0.07 | 0.141* | 0.07 |
| Teachers: disruption | | | −0.170** | 0.07 | −0.183** | 0.07 | −0.151* | 0.08 |
| Student victimization index | | | −0.705** | 0.29 | | | | |
| Students: violence/coercion | | | | | −1.912** | 0.72 | −1.531* | 0.89 |

NOTE: SE = standard error.

* $p < .10$, two-tailed; ** $p < .05$, two-tailed.

For this outcome, unlike the test score outcome, both the model with the student victimization index (Model 4a) and the model with the violence-coercion measure (Model 4b) have significant negative effects, so neither can be deemed a more appropriate measure for predicting college aspirations. The effect of principal reports of disciplinary disengagement is marginally significant ($p < .10$) after controlling for the violence-coercion measure, but not controlling for the student victimization index, likely reflecting its slightly stronger correlation with the latter (see Table 7.2). However, this effect is counterintuitive: its positive sign implies that students are more likely to expect to finish college in schools where principals report higher levels of disciplinary disengagement. In contrast, the effect of teacher reports of classroom disruptions is significantly negative, as would be expected. Therefore, while all three components of school-level disciplinary climate appear to influence individual-level college aspirations controlling for a host of individual- and school-level factors, only two of the three have effects in the theoretically plausible direction. Finally, this pattern of school-level disciplinary effects is robust when including the individual violence-coercion measure and total test scores (Model 5).

## CONCLUSION

The results of the TIMSS analysis suggest that the disciplinary environments of Russian schools are important for academic achievement and college expectations: Russian students who attend schools with more disciplinary problems have lower combined math and science scores and are less likely to expect to finish college, even after controlling extensively for individual- and school-level variables related to these outcomes. These significant effects of school disciplinary context are robust when including individual-level experiences of victimization in the models. Moreover, school disciplinary context mediates the effects of other school-level characteristics, including school size, percentage of male students, and principal reports of material shortages. Larger schools, schools with more male students, and schools with more material shortages are associated with lower test scores largely because these factors are associated with more disciplinary problems, which in turn are associated with lower test scores. This mediating role of school-level disciplinary climate is somewhat surprising given the relatively weak relationships between measures of school discipline and other school-level variables in the school-level regressions. It should be noted, however, that the school disciplinary climate measures do not mediate the effects of school-level parental education. While the significant effects of the disciplinary measures indicate that there is considerable variation across Russian schools in the disciplinary environment, the variation is not correlated with differences in the socioeconomic makeup of the student body.

Of all the school-level disciplinary measures explored in this chapter, the one with the most consistent effects on student-level outcomes is the student victimization measure created specifically for this chapter. The proportion of students in a school who say they have been victimized by violence or coercion is negatively associated with both test score and college expectations, controlling for all the other individual- and school-level variables in both models, including individual-level victimization by violence or coercion. In contrast, principal reports of disciplinary disengagement exert a negative effect on test scores but also an implausible positive effect on college expectations. Teacher reports of classroom disruptions have no effect on test scores, but they have the predicted negative association with college aspirations.

The consistent effects of the school-level violence-coercion measure in Russia suggests that these forms of serious disciplinary infractions might measure the overall school disciplinary climate most accurately. It is worth noting that Russia scores distinctively low on the standard student victimization index, so perhaps violence and intimidation of students by other students is exceptionally rare in Russia compared to other countries. That would certainly be consistent with the studies by ethnographers and others that point to the uniquely supportive and orderly culture within Russian classrooms. However, if these reports are accurate, then why would Russia have a slightly higher mean on teacher reports of classroom disruptions, compared to other countries? One possibility is that Russian teachers hold their pupils to higher standards of behavior: they may consider slouching or speaking out of turn to be disruptive, while such behaviors might be tolerated or even ignored by teachers in countries where student violence, drug use, and more serious outbursts are more common in the classroom. As an inherently subjective measure, the teacher reports should probably be viewed as problematic for making international comparisons. The principal measures, on the other hand, are more objective by design, because they ask about both specific types of infractions and the frequency with which they occur. Thus, Russia's score at the mean for all countries poses a greater challenge to the optimistic views of the typical disciplinary climate in Russian schools. It would be an interesting exercise to break down the highly aggregated measure of principal reports of disciplinary disengagement into its discrete components and examine where Russia stands compared to the other countries in the TIMSS database with respect to the individual measures.

Taken together, the results of this chapter provide some quantitative evidence supporting the view that Russian classrooms have fewer disciplinary issues than typical classrooms in other countries. This is surprising given the trauma Russian schools and Russian adolescents experienced in the turbulent decades following the collapse of the Soviet Union in 1991. But it is not entirely unexpected given the findings of ethnographic studies and expert analyses that point to the durability of strong traditions of maternalism, collectivism, and order in Russian schools. Given the relative rarity of school disciplinary problems in Russia, the effects of such problems on test scores and college expectations are particularly noteworthy: perhaps school-level disciplinary problems are most likely to affect student outcomes in countries where they are more the exception than the rule.

## NOTES

1. As Muckle's use of "maternal" implies, most Russian teachers are female.

2. In preliminary analyses I also constructed two additional measures of individual-level victimization: one that measured reports of having something stolen (12 percent of students) and another that captured students who were victims of cruel but nonviolent treatment (made fun of or left out of activities; 29 percent of students). Because neither of these forms of victimization were related to student achievement or aspirations, I do not report them in Table 7.1; nor do I discuss them further.

## REFERENCES

Arum, Richard. 2003. *Judging School Discipline: The Crisis of Moral Authority.* Cambridge: Harvard University Press.

Coleman, James, and Thomas Hoffer. 1987. *Public and Private Schools: The Impact of Communities.* New York: Basic Books.

DiPrete, Thomas A., Chandra Muller, and Nora Shaeffer. 1981. *Discipline and Order in American High Schools*. Washington, DC: National Center for Educational Statistics.

Gerber, Theodore P. 2000. "Educational Stratification in Contemporary Russia: Stability and Change in the Face of Economic and Institutional Crisis." *Sociology of Education* 73:219–46.

———. 2007. "Russia: Growing Inequality, Institutional Change, and Economic Crisis." In *Stratification in Higher Education*, edited by Yossi Shavit, Richard Arum, and Adam Gamoran, 294–320. Stanford, CA: Stanford University Press.

Gerber, Theodore P., and Michael Hout. 1995. "Educational Stratification in Russia during the Soviet Period." *American Journal of Sociology* 101:611–60.

Gerber, Theodore P., and Sarah E. Mendelson. 2008. "Police Violence and Corruption in Russia: A Case of Predatory Policing?" *Law and Society Review* 42:1–43.

Holmes, Brian, Gerald H. Read, and Natalya Voskresenskaya. 1995. *Russian Education: Tradition and Transition*. New York: Garland.

Hufton, Neil, and Julian Elliott. 2000. "Motivation to Learn: The Pedagogical Nexus in the Russian School: Some Implications for Transnational Research and Policy Borrowing." *Educational Studies* 26:115–36.

Javeline, Debra, and Vanessa A. Baird. 2007. "Who Sues Government? Evidence from the Moscow Theater Hostage Case." *Comparative Political Studies* 40:858–85.

Karpov, Vyacheslav, and Elena Lisovskaya. 2005. "Educational Change in Time of Social Revolution: The Case of Post-Communist Russia in Comparative Perspective." In *Educational Reform in Post-Soviet Russia: Legacies and Prospects*, edited by Ben Eklof, Larry E. Holmes, and Vera Kaplan, 23–55. London: Frank Cass.

Kerr, Stephen T. 2005a. "Demographic Change and the Fate of Russia's Schools: The Impact of Population Shifts on Educational Practice and Policy." In *Educational Reform in Post-Soviet Russia: Legacies and Prospects*, edited by Ben Eklof, Larry E. Holmes, and Vera Kaplan, 153–75. London: Frank Cass.

———. 2005b. "The Experimental Tradition in Russian Education." In *Educational Reform in Post-Soviet Russia: Legacies and Prospects*, edited by Ben Eklof, Larry E. Holmes, and Vera Kaplan, 102–28. London: Frank Cass.

Kourova, Alla V., and Rhea A. Ashmore. 2004. *Russian Education Reconstructed: "Perestroika."* Bloomington, IN: Phi Delta Kappa Educational Foundation.

Markowitz, Fran. 2000. *Coming of Age in Post-Soviet Russia*. Urbana: University of Illinois Press.

Metz, Mary. 1978. *Classroom and Corridors: The Crisis of Authority in Desegregated Secondary Schools*. Berkeley: University of California Press.

Muckle, James. 2005. "The Conduct of Lessons in the Russian School: Is Real Change on the Way?" In *Educational Reform in Post-Soviet Russia: Legacies and Prospects*, edited by Ben Eklof, Larry E. Holmes, and Vera Kaplan, 322–33. London: Frank Cass.

OECD. 1998. *Reviews of National Policies for Education: Russian Federation*. Paris: OECD Center for Co-operation with Non-members.

Pridemore, William Alex. 2002. "Social Problems and Patterns of Juvenile Delinquency in Transitional Russia." *Journal of Research in Crime and Delinquency* 39:187–213.

Sutherland, Jeanne. 1999. *Schooling in the New Russia*. London: St. Martin's.

Ward, Stephen. 2002. "From Russia with Discipline." *Daily Telegraph*, January 19. http://www.telegraph.co.uk/education/educationnews/3292696/From-Russia-with-discipline.html.

Webber, Stephen L. 2000. *School, Reform and Society in the New Russia*. London: St. Martin's.

World Bank. 2005. *World Development Indicators*. Washington, DC: World Bank.

CHAPTER EIGHT

# School Disciplinary Climate and Consequences for Student Achievement in South Korea

*Hyunjoon Park*

In international comparative surveys of student achievement such as PISA (Program for International Student Assessment) and TIMSS (Trends in International Mathematics and Science Study), South Korean students in primary and secondary schools, along with other east Asian students, have consistently outperformed their peers from other parts of world (UNICEF 2002). The high performance of Korean students is often attributed to orderly school environments and disciplined student behavior. For example, one researcher notes, "Class skipping was . . . much lower in Japan and Korea and student discipline was better [than in other countries]. . . . Possibly this is the explanation for the remarkably high achievement levels of students in East Asia: students are more disciplined in class and study harder" (Bishop 2004, 10). Several indicators provide evidence of comparably high levels of discipline in Korean schools and students. For instance, the 2000 PISA asked high school principals whether learning in their schools was hindered by disciplinary problems such as student absenteeism, disruption of classes, class skipping, disrespect for teachers, intimidation and bullying of other students, and use of alcohol or illegal drugs (Organization for Economic Cooperation and Development [OECD] 2003, table 7.11). Among 39 countries with no missing data, Korea had the second-lowest number of school disciplinary problems, after Argentina. In the same PISA survey, students were asked to report the number of times in the last two weeks they skipped class and arrived late for school. Korean students, along with students from Japan and Hong Kong, reported the lowest levels of these behaviors (OECD 2003, table 4.2).

The orderly and disciplined environment of Korean schools is often attributed to influence from the society's traditional Confucian culture, which places a high value on education and hard work; emphasizes a hierarchical nature of human relationships, symbolized by respect for teachers and parents; and ranks the collective values and goals of the community over those of individuals (Paik 2001; Sorensen 1994). Although cultural influences likely play a role, very little attention has been paid to exploring how other structural factors of Korean schools contribute to their orderly and disciplined climate. What are the ecological and institutional environments of Korean schools that shape beliefs, values, norms, and behaviors of students, teachers, and administrators and enable them to maintain safe and disciplined climates conducive to academic achievement (see Arum 2000)? Understanding the linkages between structural features of the educational system and school discipline in the highly disciplined Korean context may help identify potentially important factors contributing to positive school disciplinary environments.

Another important, related question that has not yet received systematic investigation is how schools in Korea vary in disciplinary climates. Although cross-national comparative studies highlight that Korean schools generally have positive disciplinary climates, they usually do not examine whether Korean schools differ in this regard and what school characteristics account for the variation. The substantial influence of cultural factors related to Confucian attitudes and behaviors at the societal level might yield a comparably small degree of between-school differentiation in disciplinary climates. However, little research has specifically assessed the degree of variation in school discipline among Korean schools, especially in comparison to that in other countries. Moreover, additional research is needed to explore how various characteristics of schools, such as the social and economic composition of the student body and institutional characteristics, are related to between-school differences in disciplinary climates.

Effective school discipline is a critical institutional element that provides a safe and orderly learning and teaching environment, thus enhancing student outcomes. Several studies in the United States have found that stricter school disciplinary practices are associated with improved student achievement and behavior (Arum 2003; Barton, Coley, and Wenglinsky 1998). A study of eighth graders indicates that disruptive classroom climates are associated with poorer academic achievement (Ma and Willms

2004). Evidence also suggests that attending schools with positive school disciplinary climates may be particularly beneficial for disadvantaged students. For instance, in a study of U.S. high schools, Valerie Lee and Anthony Bryk (1989) found that the achievement gap between minority and white students was smaller in schools with fewer disciplinary problems. Although cross-national comparative studies have linked higher mean performance of Korean students to more positive school disciplinary climates at the country level, little research has systematically examined the association of school discipline with individual student outcomes, especially compared with other school-related and student-related factors.

To fill these gaps in the literature, this chapter examines the association of structural characteristics of schools, especially their socioeconomic and demographic characteristics, with school disciplinary environment in Korean middle and high schools. In addition, this study provides an empirical assessment of the effect of school disciplinary environment on student achievement in mathematics and science. Before moving into empirical analysis, however, it is useful to consider some ecological and institutional contexts of Korean schools, which will help explain how socioeconomic and demographic characteristics of schools relate to school discipline. Following the framework of the larger comparative project, I focus on four contextual factors: population heterogeneity, organizational structure, legal rights of students, and administration of discipline.

## CONTEXT OF SCHOOL DISCIPLINE

### *Population Heterogeneity*

Nations differ considerably in prevalence and composition of racial and ethnic minorities and immigrants. Depending on the depth of cultural and socioeconomic cleavages across lines of race/ethnicity and immigration, schools may face challenges in integrating students from different backgrounds. Although not always the case, the cultural or racial/ethnic heterogeneity of a student body may complicate student socialization and interactions between students and educators. This, in turn, can interfere with the creation of shared goals and norms among students, teachers, and administrators within schools. Moreover, in many contemporary societies, cultural or racial/ethnic minority students tend to be segregated into schools with a high concentration of minority students (Park and Kyei 2010). If minority students, who are more likely to be disadvantaged in economic resources, are associated with greater disciplinary problems, high concentrations of minority students may increase disparities in school disciplinary climates among schools.

In this regard, the extremely low population heterogeneity in Korean society is likely an important ecological factor that has contributed to positive school disciplinary climates. There have been no substantial racial or ethnic minority groups in Korean history. Korean society has long been characterized by its high degree of racial and ethnic homogeneity (see Han 2007). Moreover, despite slight variations by region, fundamentally the same language has been used throughout modern Korean history. In regard to immigration, only very recently has Korean society received inflows of migrant workers and marriage migrants, mostly coming from China and Southeast Asian countries (Kim 2007; Yoo et al. 2004). Reflecting the very recent history of migration, only a handful of immigrant students currently attend schools in Korea. The two data sources used in this study, for instance, include only a small number of immigrants among sampled students. In the Korean data from the 2003 TIMSS, only 1.3 percent of sampled eighth graders were born outside Korea. In the 2003 PISA, only 0.2 percent of sampled 15-year-old students were born outside Korea. In sum, Korean society is distinctive in its racial/ethnic, cultural, and linguistic homogeneity, a context that might help Korean schools maintain cohesive goals and norms among students, teachers, and administrators.

### *Organizational Structure*

The Korean educational system consists of six years of primary school, three years of middle school, three years of high school, and four years of university (or two at junior college). An important institutional feature of primary and secondary education in Korea is its high degree of standardization and centralization (Park 2007). Administered by the central government, curricula and instruction pace and methods are considerably uniform across schools. The state also tightly regulates and monitors teacher training, recruitment, and salary. The state even administers the college entrance examination that high school seniors take to apply for college.

The high level of standardization and centralization in Korean education, however, does not necessarily mean that most Korean schools are public. Although nearly all primary school students attend public schools, the share attending private schools for secondary education is considerable. A little less than 20 percent of middle school students attend private schools, in contrast to almost half of high school students (KEDI 2009). Compared to private schools in other countries, such as the United States, however, private schools in Korea are subject to considerable regulation by government. For instance, under the high school equalization policy, described later in more detail, private high schools cannot choose students on the basis of their own criteria but are instead subject to the same rules applied to public schools.

The high degree of educational standardization in Korea is also reflected in its placement of students within schools. Within-school differentiation in learning opportunities such as ability grouping or curriculum tracking has been rare in primary and secondary education, although its use has been increasing recently. In most schools in Korea, students are not retained or held back for poor academic performance but are automatically promoted to the next grade. Overall, the practice of within-school differentiation by student academic ability has been low. Instead, Korean schools mostly have mixed-ability classes in which students with a variety of academic abilities, motivations, and interests mingle. As mentioned, population homogeneity in regard to race/ethnicity and immigration is expected to provide conditions conducive to favorable disciplinary climates. However, the substantial heterogeneity in student academic ability and interests in mixed-ability classes presents teachers with pedagogical challenges in meeting each student's needs, achieving consensual goals, and ultimately maintaining a positive disciplinary climate.

On the other hand, it is also important to note that instead of moving from classroom to classroom for different subjects or courses, students in Korean schools generally stay in the same classroom for an entire school year. In primary schools, one homeroom teacher teaches different subjects in the same classroom and thus is fully in charge of classroom management. In secondary schools, different teachers come to the classroom to teach different subjects, and students remain in the same classroom, which is managed by a homeroom teacher. This setting, in which a homeroom teacher is responsible for the same students for an entire year, is conducive to establishing long-term relationships between the homeroom teacher and students and among classmates. In such a setting, the homeroom teacher can consistently monitor classroom disciplinary climate and students may feel a sense of belonging. Although improving overall academic achievement of students in the classroom is considered an important task of the homeroom teacher, a similarly critical job is "life guidance" (*seangwhal jido*). *Life guidance* is the responsibility that teachers have to monitor student class attendance and behavior, provide psychological counseling to students, and even help promote healthy lifestyles (Lee, Ryu, and Yun 2001; see Chapter 5 for Japanese homeroom teachers' lifestyle guidance).

An obvious indicator of the high degree of educational standardization and centralization in Korea is the policy of high school equalization. In 1974 the government implemented a new policy that distributed by lottery each school district's middle school graduates into high schools. In response to growing social concerns about significant differences among high schools in quality and resources, the policy abolished school-based entrance examinations (Byun 2008; Kim 2003). In other words, schools could no longer select students but had to accept students assigned by the lottery. Students could not choose their schools, either, but were subject to random assignment. Importantly, private schools were not exempt from the equalization policy (Kim and Lee 2002). Implemented in 1974 in the two largest cities (Seoul and Pusan), the equalization policy has since been expanded to many other areas across the nation and now affects 72 percent of all high school students (Byun 2008).

The random assignment policy mixes students from families with different socioeconomic backgrounds and students with different academic abilities. In other words, it tends to create greater heterogeneity in student body composition within a school than between schools. Along with the low level of curriculum differentiation, substantial diversity in socioeconomic status and ability among students within schools may challenge teachers' ability to maintain cohesive values and thus may have negative effects on disciplinary climate. Conversely, between-school differences in student body composition, and therefore between-school differences in school discipline, are expected to be relatively less pronounced. However, it is important to remember that the random assignment occurs within school districts. Because of residential segregation along socioeconomic lines, school districts vary significantly in their socioeconomic composition and student characteristics. Therefore, despite the random assignment, between-school differences in socioeconomic and academic backgrounds of students and hence disciplinary climate can be substantial.

Another structural element of school organization that likely increases between-school difference is the division between academic high schools and vocational high schools. Middle school education is comprehensive and compulsory, and between-school tracking does not begin until high school. Upon graduation from middle school, students can transition into either academic or vocational high schools. According to the most recent data for the 2008 academic year, about three-fourths of high school students attend academic high schools (KEDI 2009). The two types of schools differ considerably in their educational orientations, goals, and curricula. Although in later years a substantial number of vocational graduates have advanced to postsecondary education, this track mainly aims to prepare students for the labor market. Academic high schools prepare students to apply for college. The school admission process also differs between academic and vocational high schools. Because of the high school equalization policy, students who want to go to academic high schools are randomly assigned to academic high schools within their school districts. The equalization policy is not applied to vocational high schools; students apply to their preferred vocational schools and admission is determined on the basis of their middle school grades and other factors.

In general, academic high schools are considered more prestigious than vocational high schools, reflecting Korean society's traditional devaluation of vocational education and preference for a college education (Sorensen 1994; Park and Sandefur 2005). Some studies have shown that students with poorer academic and socioeconomic backgrounds are more likely to attend vocational high schools (Kim and Byun 2006; Kim 2004). Although little empirical research has systematically investigated differences in behavioral problems between academic and vocational high school students, the disadvantaged backgrounds of students attending vocational high schools suggest that behavioral problems may be more substantial in these schools (see Lee and Chang 2007; Lee, Park, and Jun 2009).

The last aspect of the organizational structure of Korean schools I discuss in relation to school discipline is the substantial number of single-sex schools. The high school equalization policy is applied to mixed-sex and single-sex schools. In other words, admission to mixed-sex and single-sex schools is entirely determined by lottery. The latest statistics for the 2008 academic year indicate that among a total of 1,493 academic high schools across the nation, there are 353 all-boy schools, 303 all-girl schools, and

837 mixed-sex schools (KEDI 2009). Thus, only 56 percent of academic high schools in Korea are mixed sex. Although the proportion of single-sex schools at the middle school level is much smaller than at the high school level, it is not trivial. In the 2008 academic year, all-boy schools and all-girl schools accounted for 14 percent and 12 percent, respectively, of all (3,077) middle schools across the nation.

The substantial role of Korean single-sex schools in educating middle and high school students deserves systematic discussion in regard to its implications for school discipline. On the one hand, single-sex schooling may enhance the disciplinary climate of schools by reducing the influence of adolescent culture, which often places emphasis on physical attractiveness and interpersonal relationships over academic activities (see Coleman 1961; Riordan 1990). On the other hand, putting boys together, who are more likely than girls to be involved in problematic behavior, may exacerbate their behavioral problems, which suggests that they would benefit from a mixed-sex setting (Dale 1971, 1974; Riordan 1990). However, some studies suggest that boys, as well as girls, have fewer disciplinary problems in single-sex schools compared to mixed-sex schools (Riordan 1990). If so, the high prevalence of single-sex schools may contribute to the generally favorable disciplinary environment in Korean schools.

### *Legal Context*

Although the Korean Constitution and the UN Convention on the Rights of the Child, which Korea signed in 1991, provide an overarching framework to protect student rights in schools, Korean educational laws and conventional practices in schools are considerably conservative in promoting student rights (Sohn 2006; Yun 2002). For example, although use of corporal punishment is restricted to occasions when it is "unavoidable for educational purpose," Korean educational laws do not prohibit its use. Because the definition of an "unavoidable" situation for educational purposes is so ambiguous, there is no clear-cut agreement on the conditions in which corporal punishment can be used. This ambiguity coincides with a cultural tradition that places great emphasis on the authority of teachers and has long accepted corporal punishment as a legitimate means for teachers to discipline students. In Korean culture the "stick of love" has been a symbol of teacher authority and responsibility for the discipline of students. It is difficult to precisely determine how common corporal punishment is in

Korean schools; systematic, nationwide surveys on the prevalence of corporal punishment are few. However, evidence suggests a considerable prevalence of corporal punishment in Korean schools. For instance, according to a nationally representative survey of middle school and high school students (i.e., 7th to 12th grade students) conducted in 2009, only 30 percent had never received corporal punishment (Mo and Kim 2009).

Although a series of incidents in which students were severely beaten by teachers and hospitalized outraged the public and motivated educational and political movements to ban corporal punishment in schools, that has not happened.[1] A large number of teachers view banning corporal punishment as an infringement of their rights and authority as teachers. According to a survey of 3,400 teachers, 86 percent opposed a proposal to ban corporal punishment and remove school regulations on student hairstyle (Kim 2006). The following statement by the spokesman of the Korean Federation of Teacher's Associations represents the view of teachers who consider corporal punishment an effective tool in maintaining classroom disciplinary climate:

> But if relations between students and teachers were defined by law, it would be difficult to create trust between them. Some violent students who harass their classmates and interrupt classes cannot be properly disciplined with gentle talk. We think limited levels of corporal punishment are necessary for the student's sake. I don't think making laws will help improve students' human rights. (Kim 2006)

The statement reveals Korean teachers' disinclination for relying on the legal system for educational matters. By emphasizing the separation between education and law, this viewpoint places great weight on teacher authority as a key element of education. Therefore, any legal restriction on teacher practices, such as corporal punishment, that have been traditionally granted to them is seen as a threat to their authority that would ultimately undermine student learning and discipline.

### *Administration of School Discipline*

Middle and high schools in Korea have highly detailed codes of conduct that affect many aspects of student life. Students have to wear school uniforms in the style and color specified by each school; schools regulate shoes, bags, and hair length and color. Further, in many schools students have to wear badges and name tags. Students are regularly inspected by teachers and administrators to ensure they meet all the requirements. An important effect of the dress code is that it makes students easily identifiable (Kim 2004), and their behavior outside school can be easily monitored and controlled.

Another mechanism that helps monitor and control student behavior is a long school day. In many academic high schools, students stay in school until late at night, often until 10 p.m. Although regular classes are finished by late afternoon, students are forced to stay late in schools for supplementary classes and self-study. Teachers rotate responsibility for monitoring students during this time. The long school day facilitates the separation of the school from the outside world and thus minimizes exposure of students to external events (Kim 2004). Moreover, during the school day entering and leaving school property is closely monitored, and special permission is required for students to leave, even for a short time.

Although the trend is toward its reduction, corporal punishment has traditionally been widely used in middle and high schools and the general public's attitude has been positive toward its use in schools. In a 2006 education poll that asked parents of primary or secondary school students about various educational issues, 66 percent believed that, if necessary, light corporal punishment is acceptable, and 8 percent felt that corporal punishment is always necessary (Kim and Kim 2006). Corporal punishment should be avoided if possible was the view of 21 percent, and 5 percent felt that no corporal punishment should ever be used. Having great concern for the prevalence of corporal punishment in Korean schools, the UN Committee on the Rights of the Child recommended that Korea modify legislation and regulations in order to prohibit corporal punishment (UN Office of the High Commissioner for Human Rights 2008).

The control mechanisms for school discipline described thus far are school initiated. However, there is another important source of control—peer groups. Korean education is highly competitive, especially in regard to college entrance. Academic pressure on students from parents and teachers is considerable. Because students compete with each other to gain admission into college, being together in the same classroom provides good motivation for students to work hard. Students often prefer to stay late at schools to study in a classroom with other classmates, not because they want to study together (group discussion and group projects are not used much in Korean schools), but because the presence of other students encourages them to focus (Kim 2004). Students exercise self-control and they do not disrupt class, because disruption would interfere with their academic goals.

## RESEARCH QUESTIONS

As a part of the larger project that examines school discipline in a cross-national comparative perspective, this study identifies factors associated with school discipline in South Korea and assesses consequences of school discipline for student academic performance. Specifically, on the basis of the preceding theoretical discussions about important structural features of Korean schools, I investigate how school socioeconomic and demographic compositions are associated with school discipline. Then I assess whether school disciplinary environment shapes individual students' scores on math and science tests, independent of other student- and school-level variables. I pay particular attention to the relationships between school socioeconomic composition, disciplinary climate, and student achievement to determine whether school-level socioeconomic status is related to disciplinary climate and whether disciplinary climate explains relationships between socioeconomic composition and student achievement.

In addressing these two questions, I examine two different age groups separately—8th grade students (mostly in their second year in middle school) and 15-year-old students (mostly corresponding to 10th graders, i.e., in their first year in high school). I use data from the 2003 TIMSS survey for the 8th graders and data from the 2003 PISA survey for the 15-year-old students. As reviewed in more detail in the introduction, TIMSS and PISA are international comparative surveys of student achievement that include student-level and school-level background information and math and science test scores.[2] Although school disciplinary climate and other major variables included in the two surveys are not identical, that does not prevent comparisons between the two data sources.

Assuming that students' behavioral problems increase as they get older, it is useful to compare two age groups. Moreover, in Korea, between-school tracking occurs at the high school level, resulting in potentially greater variation in test scores and discipline across schools compared to variation among middle schools, which are comprehensive and compulsory. Therefore, the levels of school discipline, the structural features of schools associated with school discipline, and how school discipline influences individual student outcomes may differ between the two groups. However, because of the cross-sectional design of TIMSS and PISA, it is difficult to explicitly model a life-course perspective. Despite this, comparison of the two age groups may still provide fruitful insights into how disciplinary environments vary with student age and institution.

## DATA AND METHODS

### *Data*

*TIMSS.* Analyses are based on Korean data from the 2003 TIMSS, an international survey of math and science achievement of eighth grade students in nearly 50 countries.[3] Following the standard sampling requirements of the international study, a two-stage sampling design was used that first selected schools and then selected classrooms within the selected schools.[4] In Korea one classroom per school was selected with equal probabilities, resulting in a total sample of 5,309 students across 149 schools. In addition to math and science test scores, TIMSS gathered information from students on their classrooms, schools, family background, learning attitudes, and learning experiences at home. TIMSS also asked school principals about school resources, curricula, organization, and climate. Math and science teachers of the sampled students provided information on their background, teaching practices, classroom disciplinary climate, and school safety.

*PISA.* I supplement the TIMSS analysis using data from the PISA, another major international survey of student achievement that Korea participated in and that was administered by the Organization for Economic Cooperation and Development (OECD). To allow comparison with the TIMSS, I use data only from the 2003 PISA, which administered math and science tests to all students who participated in the survey.[5] Although the PISA, like the TIMSS, used a two-stage sampling design, the second stage involved randomly sampling students with equal probabilities within selected schools, rather than sampling classrooms. Thus, PISA students could be drawn from different classrooms within schools. Other important differences between the PISA and the TIMSS are that (1) the PISA lacked a teacher questionnaire and (2) the TIMSS targeted eighth grade students, but the PISA surveyed 15-year-old students regardless of grade, school type, and part-time or full-time status. Thus, depending on the educational system, 15-year-old students in the PISA can be distributed into different grades. However, in Korea almost all respondents are 10th grade (i.e., first year in high school) students. Because of the way the Korean educational system is organized, PISA respondents, except for a negligible number of 15-year-olds in middle school, attend either academic or vocational high schools. The PISA sample for Korea consists of 5,444 students across 149 schools. Of these students, 73 are in middle schools and therefore excluded from this study. Students from two high schools missing school-level data are also excluded from the analysis. The final sample is of 5,298 students across 136 schools.

Measures created from the PISA data mirror as closely as possible those created from the TIMSS data (see the introduction for a detailed description). School disciplinary climate is measured by responses to principal and student questionnaires. PISA constructed an index of disciplinary disengagement using principal reports of the extent to which the following issues hinder student learning in their schools: student absenteeism, disruption of classes, class skipping, disrespect for teachers, use of alcohol or illegal drugs, and intimidation or bullying of other students. Higher values on this index indicate more negative disciplinary climates.[6]

A second school disciplinary climate measure, a negative classroom disciplinary climate index, is based on student reports of the frequency of the following occurring in their math classes: students not listening to what the teacher says, noise and disorder, the teacher having to wait a long time for students to become calm, students cannot work well, and students not starting working until well after the lesson begins. Higher values of the index indicate students' perception of more negative disciplinary climates in classrooms.[7] Because this index was constructed at the student level, I aggregate the student indices within a school to create a school-level variable of disciplinary climates.

Other school-level measures include school and community size, socioeconomic composition, and gender composition. School size is measured by the log of the number of students enrolled. The size of the community in which the school is located is divided into five categories (village of fewer than 3,000 people, small town of 3,000 to 15,000, town of 15,000 to 100,000, city of 100,000 to 1 million, large city of more than 1 million).

School socioeconomic composition is measured by the average of student socioeconomic status, an index provided by PISA that combines several measures of family socioeconomic background (discussed later). Heterogeneity in student socioeconomic background within schools is measured by the standard deviation of family socioeconomic status. Gender composition is based on principal reports of the total number of male and female students enrolled in the school.

To take into account the demographic characteristics of students and their families, I also create student-level measures for gender, household composition, and family socioeconomic status.[8] Gender is measured using a dummy variable to indicate male students, and household composition is measured using a dummy variable for a two-parent household. The PISA measure of family socioeconomic status is an index summarizing parental education, occupation, the number of books at home, and educational and cultural resources available at home. The variable is standardized with a mean of 0 and a standard deviation of 1. Using the composite measure of socioeconomic status instead of separate indicators helps assess the robustness of my conclusions compared with specific socioeconomic status measures.

*Methods*

Following the mandate of the larger project, my first aim in this chapter is to identify socioeconomic and demographic predictors of school-level discipline. Using school as the unit of analysis, I use ordinary least squares regressions to examine how schools vary in their disciplinary climates according to school size, community size, school average socioeconomic status, school socioeconomic status heterogeneity, and gender composition of schools. The second part of the analysis focuses on the association of school disciplinary environment with student achievement. I employ a two-level hierarchical linear model (HLM) technique (Bryk and Raudenbush 1992) in which all the student-level variables are centered on corresponding grand means to assess whether school discipline predicts student achievement in mathematics and science, after taking into account other school-level and student-level characteristics. Both TIMSS and PISA provide five plausible test values scaled by item response theory (IRT) methods for math and science tests. In both the TIMSS and PISA, test scores were scaled to have a mean of 500 and a standard deviation of 100.[9]

## ANALYSIS

Table 8.1 separately presents TIMSS and PISA descriptive statistics of all student- and school-level variables. One remark on the gender composition of schools is needed. As the table indicates, most students surveyed by PISA are enrolled in schools with 45 percent or less male students (of which the majority are all-girl schools) or more than 60 percent male students (of which the majority are all-boy schools). The distribution of schools by gender composition highlights the considerable share of single-sex high schools in Korea. Similarly, TIMSS includes substantial proportions of middle schools that are majority male or female. However, as mentioned, because TIMSS sampled only one classroom per school, the proportions might overestimate the number of single-sex schools if the selected classroom was a single-sex classroom within a mixed-sex school.

### *School-Level Analysis: Correlates of School Discipline*

Table 8.2 presents results of ordinary least squares regression analyses that predict school disciplinary climate by several school-level characteristics. In the TIMSS analysis three different indicators of school discipline are used, and for the PISA analysis two indicators are analyzed. Although the school-level variables used to predict school discipline are somewhat different between TIMSS and PISA, Table 8.2 indicates that the two sets of results have several commonalities. First, the association of school disciplinary climate with school socioeconomic composition seems fairly weak in Korea. Although the school average of parental education is negatively related to disciplinary disengagement as reported by school principals in the TIMSS, it has no relationship with classroom disruption as reported by teachers. Further, students in schools with higher levels of parental education report more, rather than fewer, victimization incidents. Intriguingly, the results also suggest that students in schools with more variation in parental education also experience more student victimization. The PISA analysis, on the other hand, indicates that neither school mean nor heterogeneity of socioeconomic status is associated with the disciplinary climate measures. The weak relationship between school socioeconomic composition and disciplinary climate suggests that affluent schools do not necessarily have more favorable disciplinary climates than poorer schools.

TABLE 8.1

*Descriptive statistics of student-level and school-level variables*

| | 8TH GRADERS, TIMSS 2003 | | 15-YEAR-OLDS, PISA 2003 | |
|---|---|---|---|---|
| | *Mean* | *SD* | *Mean* | *SD* |
| STUDENT BACKGROUND | | | | |
| *Background variables* | | | | |
| Male | 0.517 | 0.500 | 0.600 | 0.490 |
| Age | 14.601 | 0.309 | | |
| Highest parental education | 5.189 | 1.637 | | |
| Number of books in household | 3.193 | 1.284 | | |
| Socioeconomic status | | | 0.024 | 0.992 |
| Household size | 4.274 | 0.931 | | |
| Two parents (vs. others) | | | 0.724 | 0.447 |
| *Test scores* | | | | |
| Mathematics | 589.092 | 83.863 | 543.418 | 92.036 |
| Science | 558.399 | 69.582 | 539.776 | 100.079 |
| *N* | 5,309 | | 5,298 | |
| SCHOOL AND COMMUNITY CHARACTERISTICS | | | | |
| *School and community variables* | | | | |
| School size | 6.873 | 0.555 | 6.966 | 0.464 |
| Community size | 4.993 | 1.271 | 4.228 | 0.943 |
| Academic high school (vs. vocational) | | | 0.713 | 0.454 |
| *School-level student characteristics* | | | | |
| Average parental education | 5.158 | 0.691 | | |
| Variation in parental education | 0.295 | 0.043 | | |
| School mean socioeconomic status | | | 0.000 | 0.561 |
| School heterogeneity of socioeconomic status | | | 0.829 | 0.124 |
| Male students | | | | |
| 0–45% | 0.315 | 0.466 | 0.331 | 0.472 |
| 46%–60% | 0.362 | 0.482 | 0.235 | 0.426 |
| >60% | 0.322 | 0.469 | 0.434 | 0.497 |
| *Disciplinary climate* | | | | |
| Principal reports: disciplinary disengagement | 2.049 | 0.679 | –0.941 | 1.432 |
| Teacher reports: frequency of class-room disruption | 3.666 | 0.483 | | |
| Student reports | | | | |
| Victimization incidents, school level | 0.481 | 0.262 | | |
| Negative classroom disciplinary climates | | | 0.002 | 0.332 |
| *N* | 149 | | 136 | |

NOTE: SD = standard deviation.

## Table 8.2

*Regression models predicting school disciplinary climate*

| | 8th graders, TIMSS 2003 | | | 15-year-olds, PISA 2003 | |
|---|---|---|---|---|---|
| | *Disciplinary disengagement* | *Classroom disruption* | *Victimization incidents* | *Disciplinary disengagement* | *Negative classroom disciplinary climate* |
| SCHOOL AND COMMUNITY VARIABLES | | | | | |
| School size (log) | 0.199 | 0.070 | 0.001 | –0.310 | –0.102 |
| | (0.109) | (0.085) | (0.034) | (0.290) | (0.076) |
| Community size | 0.139** | 0.029 | –0.026 | –0.004 | 0.099* |
| | (0.051) | (0.039) | (0.015) | (0.148) | (0.039) |
| Academic high school (vs. vocational) | | | | –1.490*** | –0.204* |
| | | | | (0.299) | (0.078) |
| SCHOOL-LEVEL STUDENT CHARACTERISTICS | | | | | |
| Average parental education | –0.310* | –0.070 | 0.090* | | |
| | (0.118) | (0.091) | (0.037) | | |
| Variation in parental education | –2.112 | 0.722 | 1.483*** | | |
| | (1.138) | (0.878) | (0.109) | | |
| School mean socioeconomic status | | | | –0.075 | –0.069 |
| | | | | (0.294) | (0.076) |
| School socioeconomic status heterogeneity | | | | 0.217 | 0.425 |
| | | | | (0.890) | (0.232) |
| Male | | | | | |
| 46%–60% | 0.024 | 0.016 | 0.077* | 0.596* | 0.007 |
| | (0.123) | (0.095) | (0.038) | (0.276) | (0.072) |
| >60% | 0.088 | –0.144 | 0.388*** | 0.508 | 0.022 |
| | (0.133) | (0.103) | (0.041) | (0.271) | (0.071) |
| Intercept | 2.153** | 3.222*** | –0.442* | 1.743 | 0.075 |
| | (0.649) | (0.497) | (0.202) | (1.850) | (0.482) |
| $R^2$ | 0.166 | 0.042 | 0.496 | 0.310 | 0.176 |
| *N* | 149 | 147 | 149 | 136 | 136 |

NOTE: Standard errors are in parentheses.

* $p < .05$; ** $p < .01$; *** $p < .001$.

Second, compared to the weak relationship between school socioeconomic composition and disciplinary climate, the gender composition has a relatively substantial relationship with the outcome measures. In TIMSS schools, more victimization incidents are reported in schools where boys account for more than 45 percent of the student body than in schools that are 45 percent or less male. In PISA data, principals of schools with student bodies between 46 and 60 percent male report more disciplinary disengagement than those with 45 percent or less male. Schools with student bodies that are more than 60 percent male also have more disciplinary disengagement than schools that are 45 percent or less male (marginally significant at the $p = .1$ level). Given that all-girl schools represent the majority of schools with 45 percent or less males, the gender composition results suggest that all-girl schools have more favorable disciplinary climates than mixed-sex or all-boy schools.

Finally, the PISA analysis indicates that academic high schools have better school disciplinary climates than vocational high schools. For both outcomes, academic high schools show more positive disciplinary climates than vocational high schools, even after school mean socioeconomic status and other characteristics are held constant. The results suggest that vocational high schools suffer from poorer disciplinary environments because of not only their students' overall poorer socioeconomic backgrounds but also other student- and school-related factors.

### *Two-Level Hierarchical Linear Models: Student Achievement and School Discipline*

For the results of the two-level HLMs that assess the effects of school discipline on student achievement, Tables 8.3 and 8.4 present the results for the TIMSS and PISA math and science tests separately. Model 1 includes all student- and school-level variables except school discipline measures, and Model 2 adds school discipline variables to Model 1, thus showing the relationship between school discipline and student achievement, independent of other student- and school-level variables. Comparing Models 1 and 2 also helps assess whether relationships between school socioeconomic composition and student achievement are due to differences in school disciplinary environment between affluent and poor schools.

Beginning with the math outcome, Model 1 in Table 8.3 indicates that all the student-level characteristics except age are positively associated with

TABLE 8.3

*Hierarchical linear models estimating the effects of student- and school-level characteristics on test scores (8th grade, TIMSS 2003)*

| | MATHEMATICS | | SCIENCE | |
|---|---|---|---|---|
| | *Model 1* | *Model 2* | *Model 1* | *Model 2* |
| STUDENT BACKGROUND | | | | |
| Male | 7.320* | 7.653* | 13.742*** | 14.025*** |
| | (2.994) | (2.979) | (2.697) | (2.695) |
| Age | 2.768 | 2.952 | 6.530* | 6.643* |
| | (3.569) | (3.569) | (3.070) | (3.067) |
| Highest parental education | 6.761*** | 6.763*** | 4.609*** | 4.609*** |
| | (0.766) | (0.766) | (0.812) | (0.812) |
| Number of books in household | 20.493*** | 20.475*** | 16.914*** | 16.907*** |
| | (0.871) | (0.871) | (0.836) | (0.836) |
| Household size | -2.589* | -2.552* | -0.896 | -0.861 |
| | (1.182) | (1.182) | (1.041) | (1.038) |
| SCHOOL AND COMMUNITY CHARACTERISTICS | | | | |
| *School and community variables* | | | | |
| School size (log) | 6.828* | 5.457 | 3.043 | 2.128 |
| | (3.440) | (3.393) | (2.824) | (2.751) |
| Community size | 0.790 | 0.703 | 0.026 | -0.015 |
| | (1.363) | (1.327) | (1.132) | (1.106) |
| *School-level student characteristics* | | | | |
| Average parental education | 12.004*** | 14.013*** | 9.523** | 10.999*** |
| | (3.217) | (3.195) | (2.691) | (2.696) |
| Variation in parental education | -59.047 | -20.500 | -23.050 | 7.074 |
| | (44.215) | (44.305) | (34.869) | (34.964) |
| Male | | | | |
| 46%–60% | -0.386 | 2.030 | -1.965 | 0.006 |
| | (3.635) | (3.568) | (3.131) | (3.136) |
| >60% | -2.823 | 7.335 | -2.097 | 5.684 |
| | (4.336) | (5.188) | (3.700) | (4.264) |
| *Disciplinary climate* | | | | |
| Principal reports: disciplinary disengagement | | -1.541 | | -1.177 |
| | | (2.174) | | (1.824) |
| Teacher reports: classroom disruption | | -0.746 | | -2.501 |
| | | (2.890) | | (2.310) |
| Student reports: victimization incidents, school level | | -26.048** | | -20.515** |
| | | (7.077) | | (5.668) |
| Intercept | 588.499*** | 588.531*** | 558.210*** | 558.241*** |
| | (1.740) | (1.696) | (1.156) | (1.143) |
| Proportion of variance between schools explained | 0.576 | 0.663 | 0.420 | 0.550 |

NOTE: A total of 5,227 students across 147 schools were used for the analysis. Standard errors are in parentheses.

* $p < .05$; ** $p < .01$; *** $p < .001$.

TABLE 8.4

*Hierarchical linear models estimating the effects of student- and school-level characteristics on test score (15-year-olds, PISA 2003)*

| | MATHEMATICS | | SCIENCE | |
|---|---|---|---|---|
| | *Model 1* | *Model 2* | *Model 1* | *Model 2* |
| STUDENT BACKGROUND | | | | |
| Male | 15.742*** | 15.962*** | 10.135* | 10.456* |
| | (3.123) | (3.107) | (4.005) | (3.978) |
| Two parents (vs. others) | 3.239 | 3.141 | 0.444 | 0.357 |
| | (2.435) | (2.433) | (2.632) | (2.633) |
| Socioeconomic status | 10.949*** | 10.956*** | 8.999*** | 9.007*** |
| | (1.346) | (1.346) | (1.498) | (1.498) |
| SCHOOL AND COMMUNITY CHARACTERISTICS | | | | |
| *School and community variables* | | | | |
| School size (log) | 19.367* | 19.196** | 19.547* | 19.326* |
| | (8.116) | (7.055) | (9.176) | (7.836) |
| Community size | -6.334 | -4.162 | -6.678 | -4.064 |
| | (4.026) | (3.528) | (4.615) | (3.991) |
| Academic high school (vs. vocational) | 49.474*** | 34.002*** | 59.477*** | 41.162*** |
| | (8.130) | (7.695) | (9.465) | (8.922) |
| *School-level student characteristics* | | | | |
| School mean socioeconomic status | 46.190*** | 39.907*** | 41.496*** | 33.998*** |
| | (7.817) | (6.873) | (8.974) | (7.815) |
| School socioeconomic status heterogeneity | -33.020 | -18.043 | -42.325 | -24.600 |
| | (23.223) | (20.495) | (26.512) | (22.858) |
| Male | | | | |
| 46%–60% | -12.036 | -4.474 | -15.862 | -6.936 |
| | (7.466) | (6.649) | (8.847) | (7.768) |
| >60% | 0.473 | 5.165 | 0.202 | 5.675 |
| | (7.086) | (6.358) | (8.849) | (8.014) |
| *Disciplinary climate* | | | | |
| Principal reports: disciplinary disengagement | | -3.003 | | -3.435 |
| | | (2.002) | | (2.242) |
| School average of student reports: negative classroom disciplinary climates | | -49.965*** | | -59.767*** |
| | | (8.206) | | (9.290) |
| Intercept | 505.720*** | 516.759*** | 494.924*** | 507.992*** |
| | (6.450) | (6.055) | (7.467) | (6.930) |
| Proportion of variance between schools explained | 0.705 | 0.790 | 0.660 | 0.770 |

NOTE: A total of 5,298 students across 136 schools were used for the analysis. Standard errors are in parentheses.

* $p < .05$; ** $p < .01$; *** $p < .001$.

performance in math. Male students outperform female students, and students from affluent families, measured by parental education and the number of books in the household, perform better than students from less affluent families. In addition, students from larger families perform worse than their peers from smaller families. Among the school-level variables, the socioeconomic composition of the school, as measured by the school's average parental education, is significantly associated with student achievement. Further, school size is positively related to average math scores. Finally, the bottom of Table 8.3 provides information on variance components and indicates that school-level variables included in Model 1 explain 58 percent of the between-school variation in math scores.

Model 2 adds school discipline measures to Model 1 to see how school disciplinary environment contributes to student learning. First, the results indicate that schools with more victimization incidents have lower mean achievement than schools with fewer incidents. However, school discipline measures created from principal and teacher reports do not have significant relationships with student achievement. Second, including the school discipline measures accounts for an additional 8 percent of the between-school variation in math scores (i.e., total 66 percent). Third, addition of the school discipline measures results in few changes to the relationship between the socioeconomic composition of the student body and student achievement. Although the coefficient for the school's average parental education changes in the second model, it actually increases slightly after controlling for school disciplinary climate. This suggests that advantages associated with attending schools having more affluent students are not due to more favorable disciplinary climates in those schools. This result is in line with the finding in Table 8.2 that the relationships between school socioeconomic composition and disciplinary climate are fairly weak. Finally, adding school discipline measures in Model 2 hardly affects the relationships between student-level variables and student achievement.

The second set of results in Table 8.3 presents associations between student and school characteristics and science scores. The relationships between student-level characteristics and science scores are almost identical to those for math scores, with the exception that age is significantly associated with science scores and household size is not. The effects of school-level characteristics are also similar between math and science tests. Higher levels of average parental education are positively related to science achievement. Further, in Model 2 when the school disciplinary climate measures are included, schools with more victimization incidents have lower mean science achievement. Taking into account the school disciplinary climate measures increases the explained between-school variation by 13 percent, from 42 percent in Model 1 to 55 percent in Model 2. Again, similar to the results for math, including the school disciplinary measures hardly changes the relationship between average parental education and school mean science achievement.

The results for the PISA math and science score outcomes are presented in Table 8.4 and are consistent with the TIMSS results. First, schools in which students perceive more negative classroom disciplinary climates tend to have lower mean achievement for both math and science scores, although disciplinary disengagement as reported by principals is not related with school mean achievement. Second, the positive effect of attending schools having more students from affluent families is reduced after taking into account school disciplinary climates, but not by much. In the second model, the coefficient of school mean socioeconomic status decreases slightly, from 46 to 40 for math and from 41 to 34 for science. Third, the effects of the student-level variables are hardly affected by adding school discipline measures. It should also be noted that for the PISA there is a significant advantage associated with attending academic high schools. In Model 1, attending academic high schools has a significantly positive relationship with math and science scores even after school socioeconomic and demographic compositions are taken into account. Moreover, controlling for school discipline measures in Model 2 substantially reduces the effect of attending academic high schools: coefficients decrease from 50 to 34 for math and from 59 to 41 for science. In other words, a large part of the positive effects of attending academic high schools is attributable to academic high schools' more positive disciplinary climate compared to that of vocational high schools.

## CONCLUSION

International comparative studies have highlighted the outstanding performance of Korean students and attributed it, to some extent, to favorable disciplinary climates in Korean schools. Cultural explanations of the orderly and disciplined Korean school disciplinary climate often credit traditional Confucian culture, which emphasizes teacher authority and a subordinate relationship between student and teacher. In this study I have extended this perspective by examining school structural characteristics that are associated with school discipline. To provide context, I have also reviewed Korean population heterogeneity, the organizational structure of schooling, legal context, and administration of discipline in Korean schools.

One of the most interesting findings from the analyses is the weak relationship between school socioeconomic composition and school discipline. In other countries, such as the United States (see Chapter 9), schools with higher concentrations of economically disadvantaged students often exhibit more disciplinary problems. In other words, students from economically disadvantaged backgrounds may face a double disadvantage in the sense that they tend to be segregated into schools that are relatively poor and also problematic in terms of disciplinary climates. Interestingly, however, this is not necessarily the case among Korean schools. The weak relationship between school socioeconomic composition and school discipline may simply reflect a weak relationship between socioeconomic background and behavioral problems at the individual level. However, the weak relationship may also suggest that Korean schools are successful in disciplining students regardless of their socioeconomic background. By identifying factors that are conducive to a weak relationship between school discipline and socioeconomic composition of student body, future research can contribute to theoretical and policy efforts to enhance school disciplinary environments.

In contrast to the weak relationship between school socioeconomic composition and school discipline, school gender composition has a relatively substantial relationship with disciplinary climate. In both middle and high schools, all-girl schools have significantly more positive disciplinary climates than mixed-sex and all-boy schools. At the middle school level, all-boy schools in particular seem to have more victimization incidents, and at the high school level, mixed-sex schools and all-boy schools seem to have equally serious disciplinary problems. Taking into account the considerable share of single-sex schools in Korean secondary education, more systematic attention has to be paid to the relationship between single-sex schools, school discipline, and ultimately, student outcomes.

The school-level results are complemented by the student-level findings from the HLM analyses suggesting that school discipline is significantly associated with student achievement. Although not all indicators of school discipline show significant association with student achievement, schools with more victimization incidents in the TIMSS data and schools with more negative classroom disciplinary climates in the PISA data tend to have lower average test scores, even after taking into account other school- and student-level characteristics. It is interesting to note that of the three TIMSS school disciplinary measures, the school average of victimization incidents as reported by students is important for student achievement. Similarly, classroom disciplinary climate as reported by students is significantly associated with student achievement in the PISA. The significant relationship between student-reported school discipline and student achievement seems to suggest that students' own perceptions or experiences of school disciplinary climate, rather than principals' or teachers', may have more relevance to student achievement.

Finally, another important finding from the student-level analysis is that school discipline accounts for a small portion of the school mean socioeconomic status effect in Korea. This finding, along with the weak relationship between school socioeconomic composition and school discipline, suggests that schools with more poor students are not necessarily disadvantaged by worse school disciplinary climates. Considering that poorer schools often face more challenges in maintaining orderly and positive disciplinary climates in other nations, the Korean case raises an important question: How can schools, especially poor ones, enhance their disciplinary climates and thus aid student achievement, a connection found in this study? I have described the contexts in which disciplinary climates are created in Korean schools; future research should look more carefully at the roles of school principals, teachers, and students in affecting school disciplinary climates.

## NOTES

1. After this chapter was written, Seoul Metropolitan Office of Education prohibited corporal punishment in all primary and secondary schools in Seoul starting in the fall semester 2010.

2. PISA also administered a reading test. Because TIMSS did not test students' reading performance, however, I do not analyze reading achievement in this study.

3. See Mullis et al. (2004) for more information on the 2003 TIMSS math assessment and Martin et al. (2004) for more information on the 2003 TIMSS science assessment.

4. For more details on sampling procedures and other technical information on the 2003 TIMSS, see Martin et al. (2004).

5. For more information on the PISA surveys and basic findings of the 2003 PISA, see OECD (2004).

6. Originally, the index in the PISA school dataset was constructed to have a mean of 0 and a standard deviation of 1 for the OECD student population. I reverse coded the original scale so that higher values indicate more disciplinary disengagement. The national average of the index for Korea was –0.94 (see Table 8.1), which means that the level of disciplinary disengagement is lower than the OECD average.

7. This study reverse coded the original PISA index.

8. Because students were sampled on the basis of age, an age variable is not included as a student-level characteristic. In addition, unlike TIMSS, PISA did not ask students about the number of people in their household; thus, this measure is also excluded from the student-level characteristics.

9. However, the scaling had different reference groups. In the TIMSS, scores were scaled to have an average of 500 points and a standard deviation of 100 points for students from countries that participated in both the 1999 and 2003 surveys, while in PISA, scores were scaled for students from OECD countries.

## REFERENCES

Arum, Richard. 2000. "Schools and Communities: Ecological and Institutional Dimensions." *Annual Review of Sociology* 26:395–418.

———. 2003. *Judging School Discipline: The Crisis of Moral Authority*. Cambridge, MA: Harvard University Press.

Barton, Paul E., Richard J. Coley, and Harold Wenglinsky. 1998. *Order in the Classroom: Violence, Discipline, and Student Achievement*. Princeton, NJ: Educational Testing Service.

Bishop, John H. 2004. "Drinking from the Foundation of Knowledge: Student Incentive to Study and Learn—Externalities, Information Problems and Peer Pressure." Working paper 04-15. Ithaca, NY: Center for Advanced Human Resource Studies, Cornell University.

Bryk, Anthony S., and Stephen W. Raudenbush. 1992. *Hierarchical Linear Models: Applications and Data Analysis Methods*. Thousand Oaks, CA: Sage.

Byun, Soo-yong. 2008. "Assessing the Effects of the High School Equalization Policy on Shadow Education in South Korea: A Propensity Score Matching Approach." Paper presented at the ninth Educational Research Institute (ERI) International Conference on Educational Research, Seoul National University, Seoul, Korea, October 27–28.

Coleman, James S. 1961. *The Adolescent Society*. New York: Free Press.

Dale, Reginald R. 1971. *Mixed or Single-Sex Schools: Some Social Aspects*. Vol. 2. London: Routledge and Kegan Paul.

———. 1974. *Mixed or Single-Sex Schools: Attainment, Attitudes, and Overview*. Vol. 3. London: Routledge and Kegan Paul.

Han, Kyung-Koo. 2007. "The Archeology of the Ethnically Homogenous Nation-State and Multiculturalism in Korea." *Korea Journal* 47:8–31.

KEDI (Korean Educational Development Institute). 2009. Annual Educational Statistics 2008. http://cesi.kedi.re.kr/.

Kim, Hyun Mee. 2007. "The State and Migrant Women: Diverging Hopes in the Making of 'Multicultural Families' in Contemporary Korea." *Korea Journal* 47:100–122.

Kim, Jeong-Won. 2004. "A Meaning of School Discipline in Korean General High Schools." *Korean Journal of Sociology of Education* 14:53–79 [in Korean].

Kim, Kyung-keun. 2003. "Modifications of the Equalization Policy and Suggested Policy Measures." *Korea Journal* 43:200–214.

Kim, Kyung-keun, and Soo-yong Byun 2006. "The Impact of Family Background on Children's Educational Transition." *Korean Journal of Sociology of Education* 16:1–27 [in Korean].

Kim, Il-hyuk, and Yang-bun Kim. 2006. "KEDI (Korean Educational Development Institute) Poll 2006." Seoul: KEDI [in Korean].

Kim, Soe-jung. 2006. "'Ban the Rod, Spoil the Child' Is Widely Accepted." *Joongang Daily*, September 9. http://www.corpun.com/krs00609.htm#18444.

Kim, Sunwoong, and Ju-Ho Lee. 2002. "The Secondary School Equalization Policy in South Korea." Unpublished manuscript.

Lee, Hee-jung, and Yun-jung Chang. 2007. "Exploring Determinants of Disciplinary Punishment among Vocational High School Students." Paper presented at the annual conference of Korean Education and Employment Panel, Seoul, Korea, October 9 [in Korean].

Lee, Hee-jung, Hye-Sook Park, and Myong-Nam Jun. 2009. "Estimating Effects of Vocational High School Students' Changing Personal Characteristics on Experiencing Disciplinary Punishment." Paper presented at the annual conference of Korean Education and Employment Panel, Seoul, Korea, February 24 [in Korean].

Lee, Hye-Young, Bangran Ryu, and Yeo-Kak Yun. 2001. *Secondary School Teachers: Their Culture and Everyday Life*. Seoul: Korean Educational Development Institute [in Korean].

Lee, Valerie, and Anthony Bryk. 1989. "Multilevel Model of the Social Distribution of High School Achievement." *Sociology of Education* 62:172–92.

Ma, Xin, and J. Douglas Willms. 2004. "School Discipline Climate: Characteristics and Effects on Eight Grade Achievement." *Alberta Journal of Educational Research* 50:169–88.

Martin, Michael O., Ina V. S. Mullis, Eugenio J. Gonzalez, and Steven J. Chrostowski. 2004. *TIMSS 2003 International Science Report*. Chestnut Hill, MA: Boston College.

Mo, Sanghyun, and Heejin Kim. 2009. *Human Rights Condition of Korean Youth and Children: Right of Survival and Protection*. Seoul: National Youth Policy Institute [in Korean].

Mullis, Ina V. S., Michael O. Martin, Eugenio J. Gonzalez, and Steven J. Chrostowski. 2004. *TIMSS 2003 International Mathematics Report.* Chestnut Hill, MA: Boston College.

OECD. 2003. *Literacy Skills for the World of Tomorrow.* Paris: OECD.

———. 2004. *Learning for Tomorrow's World: First Results from PISA 2003.* Paris: OECD.

Paik, Susan J. 2001. "Introduction, Background, and International Perspectives: Korean History, Culture, and Education." *International Journal of Educational Research* 35:535–607.

Park, Hyeo-jung, and Eun-kyung Yeon. 2003. *An Analytic Study on the Life and Culture of Korean Secondary School Students.* Research report RR 2003-5, Korean Educational Development Institute. Seoul: KEDI [in Korean].

Park, Hyunjoon. 2007. "Inequality of Educational Opportunity in Korea: Gender, Socioeconomic Background, and Family Structure." *International Journal of Human Rights* 11:179–97.

Park, Hyunjoon, and Pearl Kyei. 2010. "School Segregation and the Achievement Gap between Immigrant and Native Students: A Comparative Study of 18 Countries." *Sociological Theory and Methods* 25:207–28.

Park, Hyunjoon, and Gary D. Sandefur. 2005. "Transition to Adulthood in Japan and Korea: An Overview." *Sociological Studies of Children and Youth* 10:43–76.

Riordan, Cornelius. 1990. *Girls and Boys in School: Together or Separate?* New York: Teachers College Press.

Sohn, Heekwon. 2006. "Is the Current Elementary, Middle, and High School Student Sanction System Constitutional?" *Journal of Korean Education* 33:199–226 [in Korean].

Sorensen, Clark W. 1994. "Success and Education in South Korea." *Comparative Education Review* 38:10–35.

UNICEF 2002. *A League Table of Educational Disadvantage in Rich Nations.* Innocenti Report Card no. 4. Florence: UNICEF Innocenti Research Centre.

UN Office of the High Commissioner for Human Rights. 2008. "Compilation Prepared by the Office of the High Commissioner For Human Rights, in Accordance with Paragraph 15(B) of the Annex to Human Rights Council Resolution 5/1: Republic of Korea." Geneva: United Nations.

Yoo, Kil-Sang, June J. H. Lee, and Kyu-Yong Lee. 2004. "Republic of Korea." In *A Comparative Study on Labor Migration Management in Selected Countries*, edited by Kil-Sang Yoo, June J. H. Lee, and Kyu-Yong Lee, 202–28. Seoul: Korea Labor Institute.

Yun, Yoong-Kyu. 2002. "A Study on the Justification of Corporal Punishment in Schools." *Journal of Comparative Criminal Law* 4:607–31 [in Korean].

CHAPTER NINE

# Class and Racial Differences in U.S. School Disciplinary Environments

*Richard Arum and Melissa Velez*

School discipline in the United States has been the subject of widespread public anxiety throughout the 20th century, especially since the increase of adolescents attending secondary education following the end of World War II. For example, nearly two-thirds of respondents to public opinion surveys in the 1950s reported that school discipline was not sufficiently "strict" or "severe" (Gallup 1972). In Gallop public opinion surveys conducted over the past three decades, school discipline has consistently been ranked as one of the top two educational concerns in the United States, with 50 percent of respondents reporting that school discipline is a "very serious problem" in the public schools in their community.[1] This public concern parallels government reports of relatively high levels of crime and violence in schools. For example, in 2004, 9 percent of secondary students reported being threatened or injured with a weapon on school property during the past year, 12 percent of urban secondary school teachers reported that they were threatened with injury by a student from school during the previous year, and 4 percent of urban secondary school teachers reported that they were physically assaulted (Dinkes, Cataldi, and Lin-Kelly 2007).

In response to these trends, over the past decades, school discipline has also been a reoccurring topic of investigation by social scientists (e.g., Coleman 1961; Metz 1978; DiPrete, Muller, and Shaeffer 1981; Coleman and Hoffer 1987; Arum 2003). Although 96 percent of U.S. teachers surveyed by the National Educational Association in 1956 reported that their students were either "exceptionally well behaved" or "reasonably well behaved," in recent decades the situation has changed significantly. Today, with fewer limits on expressions both of youthful exuberance and antisocial behavior, student disorder not only distracts from classroom instruction but at times has taken a particularly violent character. Recent national data from the U.S. Departments of Education and Justice's *School Crime and Safety* report provides a sense of the empirical dimensions of the current problem. At the end of the last century, approximately 30 students per year died of homicides committed on school grounds, 10 percent of public school teachers were threatened with injury by students, and 4 percent of teachers were physically attacked in the previous year. In urban public schools, these rates were even higher, with 14 percent of teachers threatened with injury and 6 percent physically attacked in the previous 12 months. More than 10 percent of high school males across all public and private schools reported carrying a weapon on school property over the past month, and 34 percent of urban high school seniors reported that street gangs were present in their schools (DeVoe et al. 2002).

Although many of these threats and incidents of student and teacher victimization were often minor, they have undermined individuals' sense of school safety and can create significant levels of school disorder that disrupt the educational process, particularly in high poverty urban settings (Gottfredson 2001; Gottfredson and Gottfredson 1985). Further, because of historical residential and school racial segregation in the United States, students are not sorted into schools by only socioeconomic background but also race. As a result, African American students are often overrepresented in high poverty urban settings, where they are particularly vulnerable to exposure to suboptimal school disciplinary environments (Coleman et al. 1966).

The prevalence of violence and disorder in many public schools has lowered teacher quality. In addition to deterring highly qualified people from seeking employment as teachers in settings where they are most needed, these problems have stimulated early and elevated rates of attrition from educational situations that are perceived as untenable. Richard Ingersoll's (2003) research on teachers has clearly identified the effect of disorderly school environments on teacher attrition in the United States. In high-poverty urban public schools, 15.2 percent of teachers leave their positions annually, a rate approximately 50 percent higher than the turnover rate in low-poverty public schools (10.5 percent) or employees generally (11 percent). While 45 percent of individuals who left the teaching profession because of job dissatisfaction cited low pay as one of the primary causes, 30 percent reported school discipline problems and 30 percent identified inadequate administrative support as reasons for their departure. In recent decades, similar trends have been found in other countries. In Sweden, for example, disorderly classrooms have increased teacher stress and lowered the quality of teachers (Bjorklund et al. 2005).

Research has also confirmed the importance of school discipline for cognitive outcomes. In the first study to systematically model the role of school discipline on student educational outcomes in the United States, Tom DiPrete, Chandra Muller, and Nora Shaeffer (1981) found that students with stricter discipline in 10th grade had lower rates of 12th grade misbehavior. In subsequent work, James Coleman and his colleagues (see, e.g., Coleman and Hoffer 1987) identified an association between student behavioral climates and cognitive performance. Specifically, their research demonstrated that behavioral climates had independent effects on 12th grade student performance, controlling for both social background and previous 10th grade test score performance.

Given the significant variation in cognitive outcomes by school disciplinary climate, researchers have begun to explore its potential for explaining differences in educational outcomes between students. In particular, differences between African American and white performance on standardized tests has been the focus of sociological and educational research for many decades (see, e.g., Coleman et al. 1966; Lee and Bryk 1989; Jencks and Phillips 1998). The gap between mean white and African American student test performance has ranged from about 1 standard deviation in the mid-1960s to approximately 0.70 standard deviation in more recent years (Hedges and Nowell 1999).[2] This racial difference is relatively large and implies that the typical African American scores at around the 30th percentile in test score distributions. Earlier research has also demonstrated that gaps between white and African American student performance are not fully accounted for by previous academic achievement; rather, close to 50 percent of the gap in 12th grade test performance occurs as a result of lower growth rate in the development of cognitive skills in elementary and secondary schools (Phillips, Crouse, and Ralph 1998).

Researchers have explored determinants for these differences between African American and white cognitive performance. Variation in social class, for example, has been demonstrated to account for approximately one-third of racial test score differences (Hedges and Nowell 1999). Other factors explored include variation in school resources (Coleman et al. 1966), teacher expectations (Ferguson 1989), peer composition (Hanushek, Kain, and Rivkin 2002), summer learning (Alexander, Entwisle, and Olson 2001; Entwisle and Alexander 1992; Entwisle and Alexander 1994; Heyns 1978), home and neighborhood environments (Halpern-Felsher et al. 1997; Phillips et al. 1998), family composition (Fischer et al. 1996), and social psychological factors associated with the test process itself (Steele and Aronson 1998). While many of these mechanisms have been demonstrated to play a role in explaining these differences, racial test score gaps have proved both hard to account for in full and also difficult to address in practice.

As a result, some researchers have increased focus on school disciplinary climate as a means of understanding black-white test score gaps. Meredith Phillips (2008) examines student reports of violent behavior among high school seniors using Monitoring the Future (MTF) data and finds an increase in the gap between white and African American student reports of violent behavior emerging in the early 1990s. Specifically, Phillips tracks the number of students reporting "at least two of the following violent acts in the previous twelve months: hitting an instructor or supervisor; getting into a serious fight at school or at work; taking part in a gang fight; hurting someone badly enough to need bandages or a doctor; and using a weapon to get something from a person" (267). In the early 1980s, white and African American students had comparable rates of self-reported violence (between 11.2 and 11.8 percent). By 1992–1994, 14.2 percent of white and 19.7 percent of African American high school seniors reported such incidents. African American high school students are also about twice as likely to report active gangs in their schools, to fear physical assault, or to witness another student carrying a gun (DeVoe 2002).

Phillips (2008) also explores the implication of family and school culture in the stalled progress in narrowing the black-white test score gap in the early 1990s. Phillips examines student reports of disciplinary problems from the National Assessment of Education Progress–Long Term Trend (NAEP-LTT) samples. Approximately 70 percent of African American students, compared to approximately 50 percent of white students, reported that they were sent to the principal's office, placed on probation, given detention, warned about attendance, or warned about behavior. While there were no trends over time in disciplinary problems reported by 13-year-old students, the gap between disciplinary problems reported by white and

African American 17-year-old students increased in the early 1990s, simultaneous with the stalled progress on reducing the black-white test score gap.

Bolstering Phillip's research that racial test score gaps coincide with increases in school disorder and violence, Valeria Lee and Anthony Bryk (1989) have argued that smaller gaps between the achievement of white and minority students occur in schools with orderly climates and with fair and effective disciplinary practices. They demonstrate that racial gaps in student performance are smaller in Catholic than public schools, after taking into account student- and school-level controls, "because the environments are more orderly and less disruptive" (185). In related work, Coleman and associates argue that students learned more in Catholic schools than in public schools, largely because of the improved student social behaviors found in those settings. Intriguingly, research on schools housed on U.S. military bases—schools that have been characterized as being orderly and possessing effective discipline—has also demonstrated that racial gaps in standardized tests are significantly lower in such settings (Smrekar and Owens 2003).

Thus, research exploring the relationship between test scores and disciplinary climate suggests that school environment may be a crucial factor in explaining learning differentials in U.S. schools. Despite this, relatively few have pursued a more nuanced evaluation of the schools economically disadvantaged or African American students attend with regard to their disciplinary climate and how that might relate to test score performance. Therefore, to add to this body of literature, in this study we examine the association between school background, school discipline, and academic performance. Using two national datasets, we provide a more detailed investigation of these relationships by examining student, teacher, and principal perceptions of school disciplinary climate. In doing so, we draw attention to one understudied factor associated with variation in test score and the gap between African American and white performance: school disciplinary climate. However, before moving into a more detailed examination of these relationships, we locate the topic in the larger context of U.S. school discipline.

## U.S. SCHOOL DISCIPLINARY CONTEXT

As organizations, schools are situated not only in ecological environments that produce variation in student demographic composition and related behavioral orientation but also in institutional environments (Arum 2000). These institutional environments are critical in shaping how school actors construct their taken-for-granted assumptions about how school practices should be structured. In defining the ecological and institutional characteristics associated with school disciplinary climate, we follow the comparative design of this book and focus on four areas: population heterogeneity, organizational structure, legal rights of students, and administration of discipline.

### *Population Heterogeneity*

One argument about cross-national variation in student performance is that population heterogeneity is a source of school differentiation related to school climate and student success (Schmidt et al. 1999, 163–165). Population heterogeneity can occur at two distinct levels. At the social level, patterns of immigration or ethnic and racial social cleavages can create pedagogical challenges, as well as public anxiety around assimilation, integration, and youth socialization. Earlier scholarship has suggested that student misbehavior potentially can emerge out of oppositional subcultures associated with such social differentiation in the United States (e.g., Ogbu 1978; Fordham and Ogbu 1986).

Population heterogeneity at the social level can also be associated with segregation and social isolation of disadvantaged youth. In the United States, for example, African American students are often concentrated in impoverished inner-city public schools where school discipline is often dysfunctional. Gary Orfield and Chungmei Lee (2006) document that in the 2003–2004 school year, 38 percent of African American students nationally attended schools with student compositions that were 90–100 percent nonwhite and 17 percent attended schools that were 99–100 percent nonwhite. Further, among the 14 percent of U.S. schools with student compositions that are 80–100 percent nonwhite, 77 percent have over half their student bodies qualifying for the federal government's free or reduced-price lunch program. Schools with concentrated poverty are often characterized by student peer environments with high levels of disciplinary problems. Schools that are segregated or predominantly nonwhite have also been shown to have lower rates of educational achievement (Coleman et al. 1966) and are associated with higher rates of subsequent adult incarceration (Lafree and Arum 2006).

Population heterogeneity can also exist at the school level. John Chubb and Terry Moe (1990) have argued that U.S. public schools become bureaucratic and organizationally inefficient when they are faced with diverse constituencies and high levels of social problems, such as in urban centers. "The nation's large cities are teeming with diverse, conflicting interests of political salience—class, race, ethnicity, language, religion," Chubb and Moe note. "Urban environments are heterogeneous and problem filled in the extreme (64)." Public authorities confront these social problems and diverse demands of constituencies, according to Chubb and Moe, by creating formal rules, procedures, and routines that institutionally insulate schools as organizations from an inhospitable environment but are dysfunctional in terms of school climate and student performance.

Given these theoretical considerations, researchers have pinpointed several concrete ways that population heterogeneity can affect student outcomes. Karolyn Tyson, William Darity, and Domini Castellino (2005), in an investigation of the importance of school organization and demographic content, find that African American students develop antiacademic achievement orientations—that is, Signithia Fordham and John Ogbu's postulated "acting white" rejection of academic performance—only in schools "in which socioeconomic status differences between blacks and whites are stark and perceived as corresponding to patterns of placement and achievement" (601). At the other extreme, Coleman and Thomas Hoffer (1987) have argued that integrated social communities that are cohesive in terms of a sense of norms and values around schools—such as Catholic schools—are associated with improved student outcomes.

### *Organizational Structure*

Elementary and secondary school education in the United States is highly decentralized and organized primarily as a public, state-controlled enterprise. In 2005, 89 percent of elementary and secondary students attended public schools (Snyder, Dillow, and Hoffman 2008). Private schools are largely unregulated and are not subject to either accountability or reporting mandates in the area of school discipline or student performance, although social science surveys have found that private schools in general have more positive disciplinary climates and higher student performance (Coleman, Hoffer, and Kilgore 1982; Coleman and Hoffer 1987). About half the students who attend private schools are enrolled in Catholic schools, although many of these schools are in urban areas where white middle-class Catholics have left and enrollments thus often also include nonwhite students from non-Catholic backgrounds. In addition to public and private schools, a relatively small but increasing number of parents are homeschooling their children (Stevens 2001).

Given the decentralized nature of education in the United States, various organizational configurations structure student progression through elementary and secondary education. Typically, however, U.S. students attend elementary schools that begin in kindergarten and continue through 5th (or occasionally 6th) grade. Students next generally move to middle school or junior high schools that span grades six through eight or seven through nine. Finally, students complete their secondary education in high schools that end in 12th grade. Following World War II, increasing numbers of students enrolled and completed high school. This increase was driven primarily by student demand for secondary education but was also supported and legally mandated by compulsory schooling laws that required students to enroll in schools through age 16 or older in many states (Toby 1995).

Prevalent until recent decades, historically separate vocational schools or tracks within larger comprehensive high schools often segregated students who were less academically motivated and prone to high levels of disciplinary problems into a distinct set of educational programs. These programs were designed to provide curriculum intended to be more relevant and engaging. Students in well-funded traditional vocational programs in the United States had increased likelihood of high school graduation and reduced likelihood of incarceration as young adults (Arum 1998; Arum and Beattie 1999). However, beginning in the 1980s with the Ronald Reagan administration, funding for these vocational programs was reduced and these programs were significantly cut back or eliminated.

Public schools in the United States have complex sources of oversight at local, state, and federal levels and from administrative, legislative, and judicial branches of government. Public schools are clustered into local school districts that typically are accountable to appointed administrative district officials and an elected school board. In some jurisdictions and in some areas of school governance, other local officials involved in school administration might include a local mayor, a city council, or other noneducation-related officials, such as a police department, which might be given responsibility for aspects of school security.

In recent decades, school discipline in many districts has been increasingly centralized and the professional discretionary authority traditionally afforded school-based educators has declined. Judith Kafka (2008) has examined historical changes in the administration of school discipline in Los Angeles, California. Kafka argues that the local school board created "new rules and procedures that expanded the role of the district in the administration of discipline and shifted the locus of control over many disciplinary decisions from school sites to district-level offices and procedures" (249). Kafka challenges Richard Arum's (2003) institutional emphasis on the role of court cases in producing this organizational transformation of school disciplinary practices by arguing that local actors—including administrators, teachers, parents, students, and community organizations—exerted grassroots pressure, for complex and contradictory reasons, that led to centralization of school discipline in the Los Angeles Unified School District.

While Kafka's (2008) emphasis on the role of local actors in shaping historical changes at the district level is refreshing and illuminating, the administration of school discipline was also being transformed by state and federal government actions. Schools and local school districts report to state governments that include state-level departments of education. Local and state units are accountable and regulated at the federal level by the U.S. Department of Education. While federal involvement in public education is weak in many areas of organizational practice, all three branches of the federal government have actively and repeatedly involved themselves in matters of school discipline in recent decades. This includes legislation and administrative regulations governing the use of school discipline, reporting requirements on racial disparities in the administration of school sanctions by the U.S. Department of Education's Office of Civil Rights, and court decisions defining the legal rights and entitlements of students. Over the past two decades, policies and administrative regulations have been mandated at the state and federal level that include zero tolerance—that is, mandatory sanctions for drug and weapon offenses—and special protections for disabled or handicapped students. In the United States, students who manifest behavioral problems are often classified as disabled (e.g., those with a diagnosis of attention deficit hyperactivity disorder or another pathology recognized by the American Psychiatric Association's *Diagnostic and Statistical Manual of Mental Disorders*) and granted special legal protections that limit the ability of schools to administer discipline.[3]

*Legal Context*

Historically, case and statutory laws changed the formal parameters in which rights afforded to individuals in schools were defined. For example, in the late 1960s and 1970s, a dramatic increase in educational litigation expanded student and employee rights in many domains (see, e.g., Tyack, Benavot, and James 1987; Kirp and Jensen 1986). While the volume of educational litigation has subsided and courts have grown more conservative in constraining student rights in recent decades (Adams 2000; Zirkel 1997), earlier established legal precedents continue to shape school practices and state regulation of the workplace in general has continued to expand (Arum and Priess 2009; Arum 2003; Edwards 1993).

The broad outlines of U.S. Supreme Court decisions in some domains—such as school discipline, student freedom of expression, and search and seizure—are fairly well known: *Tinker v. Des Moines Independent Community School District*[4] (1969) expanded students' rights to free expression in public schools and *Goss v. Lopez*[5] (1974) extended the right of due process to public school students in unprecedented ways. In a related decision, *Wood v. Strickland* (1975) held administrators personally liable for damages if they knowingly violated students' constitutional rights.[6] Subsequent to *Wood v. Strickland*, Supreme Court decisions became more conservative. In *Ingraham v. Wright* (1977), the Court held that the use of corporal punishment in public schools was not "cruel and unusual punishment" and thus could be appropriately used in schools.[7] *New Jersey v. T. L. O.* (1985) defined student privacy rights in public schools by permitting school officials to conduct searches when "reasonable" grounds were met.[8] Specifically, the legality of a student search depended on "whether the action was justified at its inception" and "whether the search, as actually conducted, was reasonably related in scope to the circumstances that justified the interference in the first place."

Law on the books, however, varies from law in action. Specifically, individual perceptions and mobilization of law are partially independent from formal legal mandates and can have consequences on organizational function. In the case of U.S. education, teachers and administrators report high levels of contact with and fear of legal challenges even though courts have made moves to restrict student rights. In a recent survey of educators, fear of legal challenge was measured by a battery of six questions given to teachers and principals.[9] These educators were asked whether fear of legal challenge affected their ability to perform a number of duties, ranging from maintaining order to creating a good learning environment.[10] For the questions related specifically to school discipline, 51 percent of teachers reported that fear of legal challenges affected their willingness or ability to maintain order in the classroom either “a little” or “a lot” (38 percent and 13 percent, respectively); 52 percent of administrators reported fear of legal challenges affected their willingness or ability to deal with student discipline (41 percent reported “a little” and 11 percent “a lot”).

Intriguingly, teacher and principal reports of fear of legal challenges were significantly higher in predominantly nonwhite urban public schools. In urban schools with more than 70 percent nonwhite students, 77 percent of teachers reported that fear of legal challenges affected their willingness or ability to maintain order in the classroom (37 percent reported this affected them “a lot”). In contrast, only 47 percent of teachers in nonsegregated, nonurban schools reported that this was an issue. Similarly, 73 percent of principals in urban schools with more than 70 percent nonwhite students reported that fear of legal challenges impeded their ability to deal with student discipline, versus only 48 percent of principals in nonurban, nonsegregated settings.

Although teachers and principals working in urban predominantly nonwhite schools report more fear of legal challenge, reports of actual contact (i.e., being sued or knowing somebody who was sued by a student or parent) with legal challenges suggest that educators have the greatest likelihood of adversarial contact with the legal system if they are located in suburban schools where white students are prevalent. While 43 percent of the sample as a whole reported personal contact with legal challenges (38 percent of teachers and 51 percent of principals), educators in suburban schools with less than 70 percent nonwhite students have a 47 percent probability of having experienced contact with legal challenges compared to 40 percent of educators in all other schools ($t = 1.65$; $p < .10$).[11] Although much of the development of student rights emerged from nonwhite students in urban areas (e.g., *Goss v. Lopez* originated from students being disciplined for protesting against the lack of African American curriculum in Central High School in Columbus, Ohio), where teachers and principals report more fear of legal consequences, educators in those settings had only a 41 percent probability of contact with legal challenges.

Thus, whereas educators report more contact with students and parents who have resorted to legal mechanisms to alter school decisions and practices in predominantly white suburban schools, educators in urban public schools where nonwhite students are concentrated have more fear and concern over these issues. This fear and concern potentially translates into a reluctance to act decisively, proactively, and appropriately to address student misbehavior and disorder and raises the possibility that legal challenges to school discipline have had disparate impact—negatively affecting in particular nonwhite students concentrated in high-poverty urban U.S. public schools.

Just as educators have responded to the expansion of student legal rights, students have responded to shifts in their legal entitlements by seeing school discipline as less fair (i.e., having less moral authority or legitimacy). Arum (2003) demonstrates that as courts in a state became less sympathetic to schools that had been sued over the use of discipline, student perceptions of fairness of discipline declined. Similarly, surveys of more than 5,000 U.S. students in the School Rights Project by Lauren Edelman, Calvin Morrill, Karolyn Tyson, and Arum have indicated robust associations between student reports of increased perceptions of legal entitlements and diminished perceptions of the fairness of school discipline (see, e.g., Arum and Priess 2009). International comparative data from the Program for International Student Assessment (PISA) also show that U.S. student perceptions of the fairness of school discipline are particularly low relative to other countries in this comparative project. The diminished sense of fairness in school discipline is potentially implicated in lower U.S. results on these international assessments.

### *Administration of School Discipline*

Public schools in the United States have relied on a wide variety of methods to monitor, administer sanctions, and control student misbehavior. In the 2005–2006 school year, 85 percent of public schools monitored or locked doors during school hours, 48 percent required faculty and staff to wear badges or picture identification, and 43 percent used security cameras. Public schools also often resorted to more invasive measures: 23 percent implemented "random dog sniffs" to check for drugs, 13 percent adopted other noncanine forms of "random sweeps for contraband," 14 percent required students to wear uniforms, and 5 percent performed drug testing on athletes (Dinkes, Cataldi, and Lin-Kelly 2007, 58). Further, 68 percent of public school students ages 12–18 in 2005 reported that security guards or assigned police officers were in their schools, and 11 percent reported school use of metal detectors (61).

In addition to monitoring student behavior, public schools have resorted to various forms of sanctions when facing disciplinary problems (Dinkes, Cataldi, and Lin-Kelly 2007, 56). At least one serious disciplinary action against a student, defined as expulsion, long-term (more than five days) suspension, or transfer to a specialized school, was taken by 48 percent of public schools in the 2005–2006 school year. Schools reported physical attacks or fights as the most common cause for serious disciplinary action. Other causes included distribution, possession, or use of drugs (21 percent); possession of a weapon other than a firearm or explosive device (10 percent); and possession of a firearm or explosive device (5 percent).

States vary in the United States on whether corporal punishment is legally permissible and how much it is used in public schools. According to federal monitoring of the use of corporal punishment, 223,190 students received this form of discipline in the 2006–2007 school year. Corporal punishment use is most prevalent in the Deep South, where 4.5 percent of students were paddled in Alabama, 4.7 percent in Arkansas, and 7.5 percent in Mississippi. As in other forms of school discipline, boys and African American students are particularly likely to be subject to corporal punishment: 78.3 percent of students paddled are male, and nationally African American students are two times as likely as white students to receive corporal punishment (Human Rights Watch 2009).

In 2002–2003 the Department of Education reported that 3 million students were suspended and 89,000 expelled (UCLA Institute for Democracy, Education and Access 2002). African American students are 2.6 times as likely as white students to be suspended: between 1972 and 2000 the percentage of white students suspended rose from 3.1 to 5.1 percent, while the percentage of African American students suspended rose from 6.0 to 13.2 percent (Wald and Losen 2003). Research on disparate rates of African American school discipline suggest that racial differences are largely unrelated to differences in socioeconomic background but rather are "due primarily to prior differences in the rate of referral to the [principal's] office for black and white students" (Skiba et al. 2002, 333). In the district researchers examined, African American students in particular were likely to be sent to the office for "disrespect, excessive noise, threat and loitering" (334).

## COMPARATIVE PROJECT

Our study contributes to the comparative project and extends earlier research on school discipline in several ways. First, we use cross-sectional data to provide detailed descriptive information, contrasting students by race and school setting, with a particular focus on comparing African American and white gaps in cognitive performance with related differences in school disorder, violence, and disciplinary climate. Further, we locate these factors within the larger U.S. disciplinary context by emphasizing how they interact with the most salient characteristics of the schools that African American students attend—that is, examining these patterns by urbanicity and school economic disadvantage. Although most research attributes lowered educational outcomes for attending poor, urban schools, it is possible that these characteristics are partial proxies for more unstable disciplinary climates. Second, we explore whether differences in African American and white achievement vary significantly with respect to *school-level* disciplinary climate. Finally, we use supplemental U.S. longitudinal data, which include more detailed school climate measures, to model the association between school disciplinary climate and change in cognitive performance. These differences in school disciplinary climate and variation in cognitive skill acquisition are potentially implicated in later life-course outcomes, such as crime and incarceration.

## DATA AND METHODS

### *Analysis with International Comparative Data: TIMSS*

In support of the larger comparative project, we rely on data from eighth grade students, teachers, and principals that were collected as part of the Trends in International Mathematics and Science Study (TIMSS) in 2003. Conducted by an international organization of national research institutions and governmental research agencies (the International Association for the Evaluation of Educational Achievement) since 1995, TIMSS is an international comparative project providing data on mathematics and science achievement in approximately 50 countries. Sampling for the United

States followed the requirements of the larger international project and involved using a two-stage sampling design in which schools ($N = 301$) and then classrooms within the schools were selected. In addition to the measures used as part of the larger project, the U.S. analyses include race/ethnicity variables and principal reports of the percentage of economically disadvantaged students in their schools.[12] Race/ethnicity variables include dummies for white; African American; Hispanic; Asian; and American Indian, Native Hawaiian, and Pacific Islander students. The school economic disadvantage measure includes a series of dummy variables indicating the percentage of economically disadvantaged students (0–10 percent, 11–25 percent, 26–50 percent, or 51 percent or more). After excluding a handful of students missing race/ethnicity information and those missing key school disciplinary climate measures, our final analytic sample included 7,461 students, of which 5,029 were white and 944 were African American. School-level analyses included school weights that adjust for nonresponse and the probability of schools being selected for the study. Student-level analyses included weights to make the sample representative of eighth graders in the United States and adjust for nonresponse.

Table 9.1 provides descriptive statistics for the U.S. TIMSS analysis sample as a whole and for white and African American students separately. The two groups of students have a number of significant differences between them. For example, African American students in the sample are more likely to be immigrants and come from homes with less educated parents, with fewer books, and located in more urban communities. They are more likely to attend schools with higher numbers of immigrant students and more students with lower socioeconomic status and more diverse social backgrounds (as measured by the highest level of parental education in the school and its variation). Similar to previous research, African American students are also much more likely to attend high-poverty schools: 44.6 percent of African American students attended a school in which principals reported more than half of enrolled students were from "economically disadvantaged homes," compared with only 17 percent of white students. At the other extreme, 33.3 percent of white students attended schools with principals reporting 10 percent or less of students from economically disadvantaged homes, compared to only 10.4 percent of African American students attending such schools. The table also provides descriptive evidence that African American students attend schools with more discipline problems:

TABLE 9.1

*Descriptive statistics (TIMSS data)*

| | ALL STUDENTS | | WHITE STUDENTS | | AFRICAN AMERICAN STUDENTS | |
|---|---|---|---|---|---|---|
| | *Mean* | *SE* | *Mean* | *SE* | *Mean* | *SE* |
| STUDENT CHARACTERISTICS | | | | | | |
| *Race* | | | | | | |
| White (reference category) | 0.681 | 0.021 | | | | |
| African American | 0.131 | 0.016 | | | | |
| Hispanic | 0.144 | 0.013 | | | | |
| Asian | 0.031 | 0.004 | | | | |
| American Indian/Native Hawaiian/ Pacific Islander | 0.014 | 0.002 | | | | |
| *Background variables* | | | | | | |
| Male | 0.482 | 0.007 | 0.483 | 0.008 | 0.466 | 0.018 |
| Age | 14.229 | 0.011 | 14.223 | 0.011 | 14.274 | 0.026 |
| Immigrant status | 0.081 | 0.006 | 0.038 | 0.004 | 0.089*** | 0.011 |
| Highest parental education | 5.956 | 0.064 | 6.156 | 0.069 | 5.862** | 0.100 |
| Number of books in household | 3.239 | 0.042 | 3.475 | 0.040 | 2.732*** | 0.069 |
| Household size | 4.495 | 0.027 | 4.377 | 0.029 | 4.512 | 0.077 |
| SCHOOL AND COMMUNITY CHARACTERISTICS | | | | | | |
| *School and community variables* | | | | | | |
| School size (log) | 6.407 | 0.048 | 6.372 | 0.055 | 6.422 | 0.084 |
| School highest grade level | 8.225 | 0.059 | 8.259 | 0.069 | 8.161 | 0.087 |
| Community size | 3.286 | 0.110 | 3.007 | 0.109 | 4.013*** | 0.204 |
| *School-level student characteristics* | | | | | | |
| Male students | | | | | | |
| 0–45% (reference category) | 0.380 | 0.036 | 0.365 | 0.039 | 0.459 | 0.072 |
| 46%–60% | 0.529 | 0.037 | 0.545 | 0.040 | 0.418 | 0.071 |
| >60% | 0.092 | 0.021 | 0.091 | 0.022 | 0.123 | 0.048 |

*(continued)*

Table 9.1 *(continued)*

| | All students | | White students | | African American students | |
|---|---|---|---|---|---|---|
| | *Mean* | *SE* | *Mean* | *SE* | *Mean* | *SE* |
| Immigrant students | | | | | | |
| 0% (reference category) | 0.154 | 0.027 | 0.191 | 0.033 | 0.075** | 0.036 |
| 1%–10% | 0.562 | 0.037 | 0.585 | 0.040 | 0.604 | 0.068 |
| >10% | 0.284 | 0.033 | 0.224 | 0.032 | 0.321 | 0.064 |
| Average parental education | 5.935 | 0.062 | 6.056 | 0.066 | 5.751*** | 0.080 |
| Variation in parental education | 0.290 | 0.006 | 0.276 | 0.007 | 0.308*** | 0.006 |
| Economically disadvantaged | | | | | | |
| 0–10% (reference category) | 0.283 | 0.035 | 0.333 | 0.040 | 0.104*** | 0.048 |
| 11%–25% | 0.226 | 0.032 | 0.253 | 0.037 | 0.133** | 0.035 |
| 26%–50% | 0.247 | 0.033 | 0.244 | 0.035 | 0.317 | 0.067 |
| >50% | 0.244 | 0.032 | 0.170 | 0.029 | 0.446*** | 0.075 |
| *Disciplinary climate* | | | | | | |
| Principal reports: frequency of disciplinary disengagement | 3.060 | 0.074 | 2.997 | 0.077 | 3.263 | 0.151 |
| Teacher reports: frequency of classroom disruption | 3.367 | 0.047 | 3.284 | 0.048 | 3.679*** | 0.086 |
| COGNITIVE PERFORMANCE | | | | | | |
| Math and science test score (combined) | 1,039.375 | 7.142 | 1,080.217 | 5.880 | 915.543*** | 10.101 |
| Math test score | 508.149 | 3.610 | 526.458 | 3.138 | 451.026*** | 5.195 |
| Science test score | 531.227 | 3.599 | 553.759 | 2.833 | 464.517*** | 5.191 |
| *N* | 7,461 | | 5,029 | | 944 | |

NOTE: SE = standard error. Analyses are adjusted using weights provided by TIMSS. Standard errors are adjusted for clustering of students within schools.
* $p < .05$; ** $p < .01$; *** $p < .001$.

teachers in the schools that African American students attend are more likely to report that disruptive students limit how they teach their classes. Finally, similar to the larger national patterns, African American students have significantly lower test scores than whites (approximately 1 standard deviation on the math test and 1.17 standard deviations on the science test).

As discussed earlier, one of the most prominent features of the schools many African Americans attend is their tendency to have high levels of concentrated poverty. Given that our sample of African American students follows this pattern, in Table 9.2 we attempt to better understand how school economic disadvantage interacts with cognitive test scores and disciplinary climate. The results indicate that teacher reports of classroom disruptions are particularly pronounced for African American students attending schools described by their principals as enrolling predominantly economically disadvantaged students. Specifically, almost half the African American students in our sample attended the most economically disadvantaged schools, where teacher reports of classroom disruption are 1 standard deviation higher than the mean from the overall sample.

Because previous research finds that African American students are segregated into schools with concentrated poverty and attend more urban schools, we restrict the sample to urban schools with predominantly economically disadvantaged students to highlight schools that are a focus of public policy concern. In these schools—attended by approximately one-quarter of African American students in the country—the reports of disciplinary problems are even greater: 1.23 standard deviations higher on teacher reports of classroom disruption. We find similar patterns among principal reports of disciplinary disengagement (e.g., being late).[13] Principals in urban schools where over half the students are economically disadvantaged report 0.50 standard deviation higher levels of disciplinary disengagement. Finally, African American students in urban schools with predominantly economically disadvantaged students score 1.24 standard deviations lower on combined math and science test scores than the overall sample.

To better understand how economic disadvantage and disciplinary climate are related, we run a series of school-level regressions that examine the institutional predictors of principal- and teacher-reported discipline issues. The regressions presented in Table 9.3 indicate that larger school size is associated with more teacher and principal reports of disciplinary problems. In addition, schools located in larger communities are associated with

TABLE 9.2

*Descriptive statistics by percentage of economically disadvantaged students in schools (TIMSS data)*

| | | DISCIPLINARY CLIMATE | | | | COGNITIVE PERFORMANCE | | | | | |
|---|---|---|---|---|---|---|---|---|---|---|---|
| | | PRINCIPAL REPORTS OF FREQUENCY OF DISCIPLINARY DISENGAGEMENT | | TEACHER REPORTS OF CLASSROOM DISRUPTION | | MATH AND SCIENCE TEST SCORE (COMBINED) | | MATH TEST SCORE | | SCIENCE TEST SCORE | |
| | *N* (*students*) | *Mean* | *SD* | *Mean* | *SD* | *Mean* | *SD* | *Mean* | *SD* | *Mean* | *SD* |
| ALL STUDENTS | | | | | | | | | | | |
| All schools combined | 7,461 | 3.060 | 1.009 | 3.367 | 0.632 | 1,039.375 | 144.546 | 508.149 | 75.990 | 531.227 | 76.015 |
| AFRICAN AMERICAN STUDENTS | | | | | | | | | | | |
| Economically disadvantaged | | | | | | | | | | | |
| 0–10% | 90 | 2.612 | 0.712 | 3.583 | 0.540 | 952.376 | 151.823 | 464.145 | 82.883 | 488.231 | 75.433 |
| 11%–25% | 137 | 3.239 | 0.949 | 3.504 | 0.368 | 948.989 | 125.550 | 464.776 | 65.874 | 484.214 | 67.843 |
| 26%–50% | 270 | 3.233 | 1.025 | 3.446 | 0.476 | 922.888 | 116.987 | 454.791 | 65.142 | 468.098 | 63.058 |
| >50% | 392 | 3.589 | 0.995 | 4.014 | 0.603 | 878.322 | 115.212 | 435.337 | 64.615 | 442.985 | 60.803 |
| Urban and >50% disadvantaged | 243 | 3.567 | 1.088 | 4.146 | 0.557 | 859.572 | 115.386 | 425.467 | 65.082 | 434.105 | 60.908 |

NOTE: SD = standard deviation. Analyses are adjusted using weights provided by TIMSS. Sample sizes for African American student means by economic disadvantage are smaller than the overall sample because of missing principal reports of school economic disadvantage.

TABLE 9.3

*Regression models predicting principal and teacher reports of school disciplinary climate (TIMSS data)*

| | *Principal report of frequency of disciplinary disengagement* | *Teacher report of classroom disruption* |
|---|---|---|
| SCHOOL AND COMMUNITY CHARACTERISTICS | | |
| *School and community variables* | | |
| School size (log) | 0.383*** | 0.239** |
| | (0.085) | (0.077) |
| School highest grade level | –0.028 | 0.090 |
| | (0.059) | (0.054) |
| Community size | 0.107** | –0.002 |
| | (0.036) | (0.032) |
| *School-level student characteristics* | | |
| Average parental education | –0.040 | –0.020 |
| | (0.187) | (0.159) |
| Variation in parental education | –1.104 | –0.367 |
| | (1.612) | (1.418) |
| STUDENT BODY CHARACTERISTICS | | |
| *Male* | | |
| 46%–60% | 0.404** | 0.172 |
| | (0.145) | (0.128) |
| >60% | –0.145 | 0.455** |
| | (0.162) | (0.150) |
| *Immigrants* | | |
| 0–10% | –0.186 | 0.078 |
| | (0.149) | (0.136) |
| >10% | 0.062 | 0.200 |
| | (0.166) | (0.148) |
| *Economically disadvantaged* | | |
| 11%–25% | –0.277 | –0.302 |
| | (0.191) | (0.171) |
| 26%–50% | 0.245 | 0.213 |
| | (0.212) | (0.195) |
| >50% | 0.431* | –0.059 |
| | (0.214) | (0.189) |
| Intercept | 0.687 | 1.001 |
| | (1.825) | (1.573) |
| $R^2$ | 0.424 | 0.256 |
| N | 200 | 215 |

NOTE: Standard errors in parentheses are adjusted for clustering of students within schools. Analyses are adjusted using weights provided by TIMSS. Missing covariates are mean substituted; missing dummy covariates are coded to 0. Dummy variables flagging missing covariates are included in the analyses but not shown.

* $p < .05$; ** $p < .01$; *** $p < .001$.

more principal reports of disciplinary disengagement. The gender composition of the student body is also positively associated with teacher and administrator reports of disciplinary climates, albeit in slightly different ways. While having a student body that is 46–60 percent male significantly predicts more disciplinary disengagement, it is schools with more than 60 percent males that are significantly associated with classroom disruption. Importantly for our study's focus, the set of regressions also shows that disciplinary problems are perceived more acutely in schools that cater predominantly to economically disadvantaged students. Specifically, schools with more than 50 percent of students from economically disadvantaged homes have significantly higher levels of principal reports of disciplinary disengagement. The explained variance in these regressions ranges from .26 to .42 $R^2$, indicating that while student composition, grade-level range, and school and community size together predict a significant portion of school disciplinary climate, other factors—such as variation in site-based policies, local administrative practices, and institutional environmental factors—are responsible for an even greater share of school-level differences.

The results of our analyses thus far suggest that African American students score lower on cognitive tests but are concentrated in economically disadvantaged schools with more discipline problems. To explore how these school-level factors predict student-level outcomes, Table 9.4 presents findings from a hierarchical linear model of student- and school-level characteristics on the combined math and science test score measure. We examine these relationships using three models: the first includes only student characteristics, the second adds school characteristics to Model 1, and the third adds the measures of disciplinary climate to Model 2. In addition to presenting these results for the full sample, we also divide the sample by white and African American students to explore how disciplinary climate affects the two groups.

As the table indicates, students' racial backgrounds are strongly associated with test score performance, and these differences are largely unaffected by the addition of school characteristics in general and disciplinary climates in particular. As found in previous research (see, e.g., Coleman et al. 1966; Lee and Bryk 1989; Jencks and Phillips 1998), the difference between African American and white test scores are particularly pronounced. After controlling for social background and school characteristics, African American students are still predicted to have a score approximately

TABLE 9.4

*Hierarchical linear models estimating the effects of student- and school-level characteristics on combined math and science test score (TIMSS data)*

| | ALL STUDENTS | | | WHITE STUDENTS | | | AFRICAN AMERICAN STUDENTS | | |
|---|---|---|---|---|---|---|---|---|---|
| | *Model 1* | *Model 2* | *Model 3* | *Model 1* | *Model 2* | *Model 3* | *Model 1* | *Model 2* | *Model 3* |
| STUDENT BACKGROUND | | | | | | | | | |
| *Race* | | | | | | | | | |
| African American | −85.026*** | −85.396*** | −85.012*** | | | | | | |
| | (4.440) | (4.408) | (4.402) | | | | | | |
| Hispanic | −40.007*** | −37.489*** | −37.380*** | | | | | | |
| | (3.968) | (3.960) | (3.956) | | | | | | |
| Asian | 17.739** | 17.231* | 17.021* | | | | | | |
| | (7.085) | (7.073) | (7.071) | | | | | | |
| American Indian/ Native Hawaiian/ Pacific Islander | −52.323*** | −51.657*** | −51.845*** | | | | | | |
| | (9.962) | (9.951) | (9.949) | | | | | | |
| *Background variables* | | | | | | | | | |
| Male | 25.794*** | 25.737*** | 25.738*** | 28.855*** | 29.009*** | 28.981*** | 16.439** | 15.216* | 16.087** |
| | (2.301) | (2.303) | (2.302) | (2.779) | (2.778) | (2.777) | (6.539) | (6.526) | (6.503) |
| Age | −24.691*** | −24.161*** | −24.137*** | −24.883*** | −23.533*** | −23.459*** | −28.357*** | −28.263*** | −28.564*** |
| | (2.626) | (2.621) | (2.620) | (3.355) | (3.342) | (3.339) | (6.260) | (6.231) | (6.207) |
| Immigrant status | −47.369*** | −46.649*** | −46.629*** | −56.166*** | −55.035*** | −55.091*** | −59.210*** | −60.313*** | −61.097*** |
| | (4.448) | (4.450) | (4.450) | (7.280) | (7.269) | (7.265) | (11.856) | (11.818) | (11.758) |
| Highest parental education | 7.487*** | 6.909*** | 6.912*** | 9.120*** | 8.173*** | 8.139*** | 7.281*** | 5.906** | 5.735** |
| | (0.766) | (0.769) | (0.769) | (0.975) | (0.979) | (0.978) | (2.106) | (2.112) | (2.102) |
| Number of books in household | 20.957*** | 20.640*** | 20.660*** | 22.730*** | 22.339*** | 22.402*** | 18.395*** | 17.391*** | 17.087*** |
| | (0.980) | (0.980) | (0.979) | (1.191) | (1.189) | (1.188) | (2.767) | (2.763) | (2.752) |
| Household size | −3.752*** | −3.770*** | −3.767*** | −3.337** | −3.432** | −3.401** | −3.337 | −3.394 | −3.308 |
| | (0.890) | (0.888) | (0.888) | (1.150) | (1.147) | (1.146) | (2.252) | (2.235) | (2.224) |

(*continued*)

Table 9.4 *(continued)*

| | All students | | | White students | | | African American students | | |
|---|---|---|---|---|---|---|---|---|---|
| | *Model 1* | *Model 2* | *Model 3* | *Model 1* | *Model 2* | *Model 3* | *Model 1* | *Model 2* | *Model 3* |
| School and community characteristics | | | | | | | | | |
| *School and community variables* | | | | | | | | | |
| School size (log) | | 1.527 | 6.348 | | −3.320 | 1.302 | | 25.847 | 28.294 |
| | | (6.567) | (6.508) | | (6.652) | (6.602) | | (15.956) | (14.887) |
| School highest grade level | | 4.679 | 3.510 | | 4.084 | 2.954 | | 6.980 | 5.540 |
| | | (4.395) | (4.226) | | (4.272) | (4.119) | | (9.842) | (9.407) |
| Community size | | −1.158 | 0.091 | | −1.091 | −0.140 | | −1.189 | 6.562 |
| | | (2.759) | (2.668) | | (2.884) | (2.796) | | (5.619) | (5.473) |
| *School-level student characteristics* | | | | | | | | | |
| Male students | | | | | | | | | |
| 46%–60% | | −3.190 | −2.063 | | −0.618 | 0.295 | | 20.213 | 18.449 |
| | | (8.121) | (7.810) | | (8.236) | (7.969) | | (15.716) | (14.765) |
| >60% | | −12.791 | −10.976 | | −7.341 | −5.120 | | −30.847 | −54.003* |
| | | (13.306) | (12.770) | | (13.333) | (12.847) | | (25.676) | (24.354) |
| Immigrant students | | | | | | | | | |
| 1%–10% | | −15.042 | −17.006 | | −9.238 | −11.243 | | −37.834 | −23.049 |
| | | (10.854) | (10.402) | | (10.699) | (10.276) | | (28.236) | (26.508) |
| >10% | | −36.023** | −34.088** | | −39.200** | −37.566** | | −48.411 | −29.809 |
| | | (12.277) | (11.766) | | (12.174) | (11.696) | | (28.942) | (27.382) |
| Average parental education | | 31.610** | 30.373** | | 37.448*** | 36.567*** | | 24.716 | 25.105 |
| | | (10.435) | (10.017) | | (10.792) | (10.423) | | (19.815) | (18.471) |
| Variation in parental education | | −174.050 | −182.110 | | −137.190 | −145.700 | | −218.940 | −225.710 |
| | | (100.160) | (96.161) | | (102.520) | (98.930) | | (202.060) | (188.510) |

| | | | | | | | | | |
|---|---|---|---|---|---|---|---|---|---|
| Economically disadvantaged | | | | | | | | | |
| 11%–25% | | 3.266 (10.910) | 5.290 (10.443) | | 9.850 (10.658) | 12.632 (10.238) | | −53.545* (25.485) | −41.748 (24.069) |
| 26%–50% | | −1.913 (11.453) | 7.807 (11.229) | | 6.768 (11.418) | 17.443 (11.273) | | −33.645 (25.084) | −21.073 (23.939) |
| >50% | | −23.252 (13.571) | −11.943 (13.293) | | −14.676 (13.891) | −4.234 (13.613) | | −58.623* (28.182) | −32.239 (27.331) |
| *Disciplinary climate* | | | | | | | | | |
| Principal reports: frequency of disciplinary disengagement | | | −2.475 (3.860) | | | −2.271 (3.908) | | | −4.308 (7.072) |
| Teacher reports: frequency of classroom disruption | | | −25.241*** (5.967) | | | −25.062*** (6.011) | | | −57.280*** (13.195) |
| Intercept | 1,306.310*** (38.276) | 1,150.010*** (114.920) | 1,220.640*** (111.850) | 1,291.830*** (48.653) | 1,105.750*** (119.590) | 1,174.040*** (117.010) | 1,277.480*** (92.073) | 1,059.750*** (250.500) | 1,223.200*** (239.760) |
| Pseudo $R^2$ | 0.034 | 0.037 | 0.037 | 0.014 | 0.018 | 0.019 | 0.019 | 0.034 | 0.037 |
| Proportion of variance across schools[a] | 0.328 | 0.191 | 0.176 | 0.317 | 0.175 | 0.161 | 0.346 | 0.265 | 0.221 |
| *N* | 7,461 | 7,461 | 7,461 | 5,029 | 5,029 | 5,029 | 944 | 944 | 944 |

NOTE: Analyses are adjusted using weights provided by TIMSS. Missing covariates (with the exception of race/ethnicity) are mean substituted; missing dummy covariates are coded to 0. Dummy variables flagging missing covariates are included in the analyses but not shown.

[a] Proportion of variance across schools for the intercept model is 0.443 for all students, 0.374 for white students, and 0.380 for African American students.

* $p < .05$; ** $p < .01$; *** $p < .001$.

85 points (0.59 standard deviation) lower on the combined math and science test score. Highest level of parental education, number of books in the household, and male gender are also positively associated with student test score, while age, immigrant status, and household size (for the full sample and for white students) are negatively associated with cognitive performance.

More critically in terms of our focus on school discipline, we observe in Model 2 that for African American students, attending schools with students who are predominantly economically disadvantaged is negatively associated with student test score performance. Further, the association between attendance at a predominantly economically disadvantaged school and test scores is particularly strong: the coefficient for a school with 51 percent or more economically disadvantaged students is –58.6 relative to –23.3 for the sample as a whole. Interestingly, adding the school disciplinary measures to the regression in Model 3 decreases the coefficient for predominantly economically disadvantaged schools by 45 percent for African Americans and becomes nonsignificant. Thus, a large and significant component of the negative effects of attending economically disadvantaged schools on test score performance is associated with the dysfunctional disciplinary climates that exist there. In terms of the disciplinary measures in Model 3, teacher reports on the frequency of classroom disruptions are a consistent predictor of test score performance. This effect is particularly strong for African American students (the coefficient is –57.3, compared to –25.1 for white students).

Finally, we present the proportion of variance across schools for each model and note that the addition of school characteristics to Model 1 decreases the proportion of variance across schools by 42 percent for the full sample, suggesting that much of the similarity among students in schools is accounted for by our institutional measures. For white students, the proportion of variance between the first and second models decreases by about the same amount, but for African American students the addition of school characteristics in Model 2 decreases the proportion of variance across schools by only 23 percent. Thus, for these students, school variables are less successful in accounting for the similarities among students in schools.

In sum, the results from the TIMSS data indicate that African American students attend schools with more economic disadvantage and disciplinary problems than white students. Further, these differences in school climate have powerful impacts on math and science test scores. Most important, however, is the finding that for African American students the negative effect of economic disadvantage on test scores works through the disciplinary climate, allowing us to better understand what happens inside disadvantaged schools that produces negative student outcomes. While this finding is illuminating, it also suggests that we need further investigation into the school disciplinary climates associated with different types of schools. A large component of school climate is peer environment and student perceptions of discipline. A limitation of the TIMSS, however, is that in the United States students were not asked questions that could tap into these perceptions and that teachers and principals were not asked about the administration of school discipline. In addition, because the TIMSS is cross-sectional, we cannot explore how disciplinary climate affects students over time. Therefore, to capture the crucial component of student observations about their school environment, including teacher and principal reports of the administration of school discipline, and to examine longitudinal relationships, we turn to supplementary analyses using a national longitudinal dataset that includes student and educator assessments about school discipline.

### *Supplementary U.S. Analysis: NELS*

In addition to our analysis based on comparative international data drawn from TIMSS, we present supplementary analyses focusing on school discipline and racial differences in longitudinal modeling of test score performance with data drawn from the 1988, 1990, and 1992 restricted files of the U.S. Department of Education's National Education Longitudinal Survey (NELS). This survey gathered longitudinal data on a nationally representative sample of 8th graders in 1988, following them at two-year intervals: as 10th graders in 1990 and 12th graders in 1992. The dataset has the advantage of allowing longitudinal modeling of academic achievement and including detailed information about school discipline and student backgrounds. The 1988 base survey was administered to 8th graders selected in a two-stage stratified sampling design in which schools and then students within those schools were sampled. Subsequent waves were administered using the same two-stage stratified sampling design to select a subset of students from the previous waves and refresher students to compensate for attrition and maintain a nationally representative sample. In addition to student surveys, questionnaires were administered to parents, teachers, and principals.

To establish longitudinal relationships between students and schools, we restrict the sample in our analysis to those students with data in all three years who did not change schools between the 10th and 12th grades.[14] Students missing a 12th grade test score or racial identification are also excluded from the analysis.[15] Additional students are excluded from the final analysis sample ($N$ = 9,241) because of missing values on key school climate and behavioral variables. Weights provided by NELS and scaled for use in this sample are used to make the sample nationally representative.

Table 9.5 presents descriptive statistics of the analysis sample. Because of the richness of the student, teacher, and principal reports about the school climate, we are able to create more detailed school climate measures than were available in the TIMSS dataset. Specifically, we divide school climate and behavioral variables obtained from the 1990 wave of data into five categories consisting of discipline, violence, student disobedience, educational commitment, and school safety measures. Within these categories, variables were created to measure principal, teacher, and student responses and perceptions.[16] Student- and school-level controls (e.g., school location) are obtained from all three waves of data. The key outcome measure, a composite of scores from reading and math cognitive tests administered by NELS researchers, is obtained from the 1992 wave of data.[17]

In addition to reporting the means for the full sample, Table 9.5 also provides means (and tests for differences in means) for African American and white students to highlight the often large differences between the samples, including for the outcome variable (white students' mean, 0.23; African American students' mean, −0.53). Before examining the school climate measures, we note that African American students in our sample are less likely to be male, to live in a two-parent household, and to be in an academic track. Conversely, they are more likely to come from a disadvantaged background, have more siblings, and be enrolled in a vocational track. Finally, the schools they attend tend to be larger, have higher student-teacher ratios, be in urban areas, and contain more dropouts, nonwhite students, nonwhite teachers, and poor students.

Focusing on the school climate measures, we see numerous significant differences between the samples. Among the disciplinary climate variables, we note that the principals in schools that African American students attend

Table 9.5

*Descriptive statistics (National Education Longitudinal Survey [NELS] data)*

| | ALL STUDENTS | | WHITE STUDENTS | | AFRICAN AMERICAN STUDENTS | |
|---|---|---|---|---|---|---|
| | *Mean* | *SD* | *Mean* | *SD* | *Mean* | *SD* |
| STUDENT CHARACTERISTICS | | | | | | |
| *Race (white = reference category)* | | | | | | |
| African American | 0.11 | 0.31 | | | | |
| Hispanic | 0.07 | 0.26 | | | | |
| Other[a] | 0.05 | 0.21 | | | | |
| *Background variables* | | | | | | |
| Male | 0.50 | 0.50 | 0.50 | 0.51 | 0.45* | 0.50 |
| Student socioeconomic status | 0.10 | 0.90 | 0.22 | 0.86 | −0.38*** | 0.92 |
| Number of siblings | 2.47 | 1.99 | 2.30 | 1.86 | 3.28*** | 2.71 |
| Two-parent family | 0.79 | 0.41 | 0.84 | 0.38 | 0.51*** | 0.50 |
| Vocational track | 0.12 | 0.32 | 0.10 | 0.31 | 0.20*** | 0.40 |
| Academic track | 0.47 | 0.50 | 0.49 | 0.51 | 0.38*** | 0.49 |
| Non-English-speaking home | 0.07 | 0.25 | 0.02 | 0.14 | 0.02 | 0.14 |
| SCHOOL AND COMMUNITY CHARACTERISTICS | | | | | | |
| *School and community variables* | | | | | | |
| School size | 6.81 | 0.70 | 6.74 | 0.71 | 7.03*** | 0.60 |
| Student-teacher ratio | 4.05 | 0.67 | 4.00 | 0.66 | 4.10* | 0.57 |
| Urban location (suburban = reference category) | 0.24 | 0.43 | 0.18 | 0.40 | 0.44*** | 0.50 |
| Rural location (suburban = reference category) | 0.35 | 0.47 | 0.38 | 0.50 | 0.30* | 0.46 |
| *School-level student characteristics* | | | | | | |
| Poor students (%) | 0.20 | 0.19 | 0.17 | 0.17 | 0.30*** | 0.22 |
| Average student SES | 0.10 | 0.57 | 0.16 | 0.54 | −0.19*** | 0.59 |
| Dropout rate (%) | 0.07 | 0.09 | 0.06 | 0.08 | 0.10*** | 0.10 |
| African American 12th grade students (%) | 0.12 | 0.21 | 0.07 | 0.13 | 0.48*** | 0.32 |
| Hispanic 12th grade students (%) | 0.07 | 0.15 | 0.04 | 0.09 | 0.06* | 0.12 |
| Other 12th grade students[a] (%) | 0.04 | 0.09 | 0.03 | 0.07 | 0.02* | 0.04 |

*(continued)*

Table 9.5 (continued)

| | All students | | White students | | African American students | |
|---|---|---|---|---|---|---|
| | *Mean* | *SD* | *Mean* | *SD* | *Mean* | *SD* |
| *School-level teacher characteristics* | | | | | | |
| African American teachers (%) | 0.06 | 0.11 | 0.03 | 0.08 | 0.22*** | 0.19 |
| Hispanic teachers (%) | 0.02 | 0.07 | 0.01 | 0.03 | 0.02** | 0.03 |
| Other teachers[a] (%) | 0.01 | 0.03 | 0.00 | 0.01 | 0.01 | 0.01 |
| SCHOOL CLIMATE MEASURES | | | | | | |
| *Disciplinary climate* | | | | | | |
| Principal reports | | | | | | |
| Discipline emphasized at school | 0.01 | 0.98 | 0.00 | 1.00 | 0.13 | 0.90 |
| School rules | 0.02 | 0.99 | -0.01 | 1.05 | 0.28*** | 0.74 |
| Severity of discipline index | 0.00 | 1.00 | -0.05 | 1.04 | 0.21*** | 0.91 |
| Teacher reports: rules for student behavior enforced | 0.02 | 0.99 | 0.04 | 1.01 | -0.01 | 1.05 |
| Principal and teacher reports: discipline index | 0.05 | 2.26 | -0.01 | 2.34 | 0.62*** | 2.04 |
| Student reports | | | | | | |
| Strictness perception, individual level | 2.76 | 0.73 | 2.75 | 0.74 | 2.83* | 0.81 |
| Strictness perception, school level | 2.78 | 0.31 | 2.77 | 0.32 | 2.81 | 0.32 |
| Fairness perception, individual level | 2.63 | 0.76 | 2.64 | 0.77 | 2.48*** | 0.83 |
| Fairness perception, school level | 2.67 | 0.24 | 2.67 | 0.24 | 2.61* | 0.29 |
| *Violence measures* | | | | | | |
| Principal reports: degree physical conflicts a problem | 1.81 | 0.63 | 1.76 | 0.63 | 2.03*** | 0.64 |
| Teacher reports: degree physical conflicts a problem | 1.89 | 0.47 | 1.82 | 0.45 | 2.24*** | 0.51 |
| Student reports | | | | | | |
| Student fighting, individual level | 0.13 | 0.39 | 0.11 | 0.39 | 0.20** | 0.46 |
| Student fighting, school level | 0.20 | 0.15 | 0.20 | 0.15 | 0.21 | 0.17 |
| Student self-reported arrest, individual level | 0.04 | 0.27 | 0.04 | 0.29 | 0.03 | 0.17 |

| | | | | | | |
|---|---|---|---|---|---|---|
| Student self-reported arrest, school level | 0.04 | 0.09 | 0.04 | 0.10 | 0.03 | 0.07 |
| *School safety measures: student reports* | | | | | | |
| Safe school, individual level | 0.91 | 0.28 | 0.93 | 0.27 | 0.85*** | 0.36 |
| Safe school, school level | 0.93 | 0.09 | 0.94 | 0.08 | 0.87*** | 0.11 |
| *Disobedience measures* | | | | | | |
| Principal reports: disobedience index | 1.33 | 0.36 | 1.31 | 0.34 | 1.47*** | 0.42 |
| Teacher reports: disobedience index | 1.57 | 0.35 | 1.53 | 0.32 | 1.81*** | 0.46 |
| Student reports | | | | | | |
| Disobedience index, individual level | 0.00 | 0.67 | 0.00 | 0.69 | 0.04 | 0.65 |
| Disobedience index, school level | 0.00 | 0.26 | 0.01 | 0.26 | −0.03 | 0.30 |
| *Educational commitment measures* | | | | | | |
| Principal reports: educational commitment index | 2.72 | 0.69 | 2.79 | 0.69 | 2.46*** | 0.63 |
| Teacher reports: educational commitment index | 2.49 | 0.56 | 2.56 | 0.54 | 2.22*** | 0.62 |
| Student reports | | | | | | |
| Educational commitment index, individual level | 0.58 | 3.32 | 0.64 | 3.38 | 0.56 | 3.23 |
| Educational commitment index, school level | 0.30 | 1.38 | 0.37 | 1.39 | 0.17 | 1.35 |
| COGNITIVE PERFORMANCE | | | | | | |
| Test score (10th grade) | 0.17 | 0.92 | 0.29 | 0.91 | −0.43*** | 0.87 |
| Test score (12th grade) | 0.10 | 0.94 | 0.23 | 0.92 | −0.53*** | 0.88 |
| *N* | 9,241 | | 6,919 | | 791 | |

SOURCE: NELS 1988, 1990, 1992.

NOTE: SD = standard deviation. Analyses are adjusted using weights provided by NELS.

[a] "Other" refers to Asian Americans and American Indians.

* $p < .05$; ** $p < .01$; *** $p < .001$.

report significantly more rules[18] (0.28 standard deviation higher) and more severe administration of discipline[19] (0.26 standard deviation higher). Similarly, a discipline index combining teacher and principal measures of the disciplinary climate indicates that there are significantly more rules, rule enforcement, emphasis on discipline, and severe discipline at schools African American students attend.[20] Echoing educator reports, African American students indicate that rules for behavior are stricter in the schools they attend. Interestingly, however, when asked if discipline at their school is fair, their responses both individually and at the school level are significantly lower than those of white students. Given previous research on the importance of perceived fairness in schools, this marked difference between African American and white reports on this measure may prove particularly important for explaining test score gaps between the two groups of students.

In addition to creating school disciplinary climate indices, we use reports from principals, teachers, and students on violence in their schools, and students are asked about school safety. According to principals, teachers, and students alike, the schools African American students attend are more violent. Principals and teachers note that the degree to which physical conflicts between students are a problem is significantly higher in the schools African American students attend than in schools that white students attend (0.42 standard deviation and 0.88 standard deviation higher, respectively). Likewise, African American students are more likely to self-report getting into a physical fight in school and to report, or be in schools where other students report, concerns about safety. Finally, twice as many African American students as white students report that they "don't feel safe at this school" (15 percent compared to 7 percent).

It is worth noting that there are no significant differences between African American and white student self-reported arrests, even though criminal justice figures suggest wide disparities, with African American youth experiencing much greater police enforcement. This finding foreshadows other student self-reported measures of disobedience and educational commitment discussed later; teachers and principals identify significant differences between schools that white students and African American students attend, whereas student self-reports do not show significant racial differences. The possibility of African American youth underreporting delinquent behavior has been previously identified in criminological literature (see, e.g., Hindelang, Hirschi, and Weis 1981; Huizinga and Elliot 1986), although the matter is subject to ongoing debate (Farrington et al. 1996; Thornberry and Krohn 2000).

Just as the schools African American students attend have more discipline, violence, and safety problems, principal and teacher reports indicate that these schools are subject to more disobedience issues. According to the teacher and principal disobedience indices, measured by asking about verbal and physical abuse of teachers, the schools that African Americans attend have greater disorder.[21] Specifically, principals report disobedience levels 0.46 standard deviation higher than white students, and teachers report disobedience levels 0.83 standard deviation higher. On the other hand, the student-level disobedience index, created by asking students and the students' teachers about how disruptive they are, indicates no significant difference between white and African American students.[22]

Finally, the descriptive analysis suggests that the students in the schools that African Americans attend have significantly different levels of educational commitment. Principal and teacher educational commitment measures are created by asking them whether class cutting and absenteeism are problems in their school.[23] African American students attend schools with significantly lower levels of principal- and teacher-reported student educational commitment (0.48 and 0.61 standard deviation lower than white students, respectively). Similar to the disobedience index, although principals and teachers find educational commitment to be lower in schools African Americans attend, student self-reports of educational commitment show no significant differences when compared to schools whites attend.[24]

In sum, our descriptive findings based on the NELS dataset illustrate how African American and white students differ in their test score results and disciplinary experiences in school. The schools that white students attend have significantly fewer violence, disobedience, and safety problems. White students are in schools for which principals report almost half a standard deviation less violence compared to principal reports of the schools African Americans attend. Similarly, teachers report almost a full standard deviation less violence in schools that white students attend. In addition to reporting less violence, principals and teachers in white students' schools report significantly fewer disobedience problems. White students corroborate these reports by indicating that their schools are perceived to be almost 1 standard deviation less unsafe than African American students' schools.

Although our findings indicate that African American students—with the exception of some of the measures based on student self-reported misbehavior—attend schools with notably more misbehavior and disorder (recall that many of the gaps in violence and disorder approach 1 standard deviation), our results also suggest that U.S. schools have only partially adjusted to this pattern with corresponding changes in the administration of school discipline (note how our measures of the administration of school discipline in general have smaller differences in terms of standard deviations). Principals in African American students' schools report only moderately higher levels of sanctions and rules. Further, African American students and other students in the schools they attend report only moderately higher levels of strictness, while white students report higher perceptions of disciplinary fairness. Even more critically, however, teachers in the schools African American students attend report no greater enforcement of rules. These differences are potentially related to the finding discussed earlier that teachers and principals working in urban schools with high concentrations of African American students are much more likely than other educators to fear adversarial legal challenges when considering responding to youth misbehavior.

To explore how these differences might be related to the observed black-white test score gap, we turn to multivariate models that examine relationships between 10th grade school climate and behavioral measures and 12th grade test scores. In our analysis, we combine white and African American samples to focus on the association of differences in test score with school discipline. Our multivariate analyses consist of five models that attempt to pinpoint fluctuations in the black-white test score gap.[25] Model 1 includes only student- and school-level institutional covariates. Model 2 adds the discipline indices to Model 1. Model 3 adds the violence and disobedience indices to Model 1. Model 4 adds school safety measures, discipline measures, and the violence and disobedience indices to Model 1. Finally, given our particular interest in understanding the differences between white and African American students and the consequences of variation in school discipline for African American students, Model 5 adds an interaction between African American students and the principal and teacher discipline index to Model 4.[26]

Table 9.6 indicates that although each model contains different covariates, the African American coefficients remain almost completely constant

TABLE 9.6

*Regression of 12th grade test score on individual and school characteristics (National Education Longitudinal Survey [NELS] data)*

| | *Model 1* | *Model 2* | *Model 3* | *Model 4* | *Model 5* |
|---|---|---|---|---|---|
| STUDENT CHARACTERISTICS | | | | | |
| *Race* | | | | | |
| African American | −0.08** | −0.07** | −0.08** | −0.07** | −0.08*** |
| | (0.03) | (0.03) | (0.03) | (0.03) | (0.03) |
| Hispanic | −0.04 | −0.03 | −0.04 | −0.03 | −0.04 |
| | (0.03) | (0.03) | (0.03) | (0.03) | (0.03) |
| Other[a] | 0.06* | 0.06* | 0.06* | 0.06* | 0.06* |
| | (0.03) | (0.03) | (0.03) | (0.03) | (0.03) |
| *Background variables* | | | | | |
| Male | −0.01 | −0.01 | 0.01 | 0.01 | 0.01 |
| | (0.01) | (0.01) | (0.01) | (0.01) | (0.01) |
| Student socioeconomic status | 0.05*** | 0.05*** | 0.05*** | 0.05*** | 0.05*** |
| | (0.01) | (0.01) | (0.01) | (0.01) | (0.01) |
| Number of siblings | 0.00 | 0.00 | 0.01* | 0.01 | 0.01* |
| | (0.00) | (0.00) | (0.00) | (0.00) | (0.00) |
| Two-parent family | 0.00 | 0.00 | 0.00 | 0.00 | 0.00 |
| | (0.02) | (0.02) | (0.02) | (0.02) | (0.02) |
| Vocational | −0.01 | −0.01 | −0.01 | −0.01 | −0.01 |
| | (0.02) | (0.02) | (0.02) | (0.02) | (0.02) |
| Academic | 0.12*** | 0.12*** | 0.12*** | 0.12*** | 0.12*** |
| | (0.01) | (0.01) | (0.01) | (0.01) | (0.01) |
| Non-English-speaking home | 0.05 | 0.05 | 0.05 | 0.05 | 0.05 |
| | (0.03) | (0.03) | (0.03) | (0.03) | (0.03) |
| Test score (10th grade) | 0.84*** | 0.84*** | 0.83*** | 0.83*** | 0.83*** |
| | (0.01) | (0.01) | (0.01) | (0.01) | (0.01) |

(*continued*)

Table 9.6 *(continued)*

| | *Model 1* | *Model 2* | *Model 3* | *Model 4* | *Model 5* |
|---|---|---|---|---|---|
| SCHOOL AND COMMUNITY CHARACTERISTICS | | | | | |
| *School and community variables* | | | | | |
| School size | 0.02 | 0.02 | 0.02 | 0.02 | 0.02 |
| | (0.01) | (0.01) | (0.01) | (0.01) | (0.01) |
| Student-teacher ratio | −0.03** | −0.03** | −0.03*** | −0.03*** | −0.04*** |
| | (0.01) | (0.01) | (0.01) | (0.01) | (0.01) |
| Urban location | 0.02 | 0.02 | 0.02 | 0.03 | 0.03 |
| | (0.02) | (0.02) | (0.02) | (0.02) | (0.02) |
| Rural location | 0.01 | 0.01 | 0.01 | 0.01 | 0.01 |
| | (0.02) | (0.02) | (0.02) | (0.02) | (0.02) |
| *School-level student characteristics* | | | | | |
| Poor students (%) | −0.03 | −0.03 | −0.03 | −0.02 | −0.03 |
| | (0.04) | (0.04) | (0.04) | (0.04) | (0.04) |
| Average student socioeconomic status | 0.04* | 0.04* | 0.03* | 0.03* | 0.03* |
| | (0.02) | (0.02) | (0.02) | (0.02) | (0.02) |
| Dropout rate (%) | | | −0.12* | −0.10 | −0.10 |
| | | | (0.06) | (0.06) | (0.06) |
| African American 12th grade students (%) | −0.04 | −0.05 | −0.04 | −0.04 | −0.04 |
| | (0.07) | (0.07) | (0.07) | (0.07) | (0.06) |
| Hispanic 12th grade students (%) | 0.07 | 0.06 | 0.05 | 0.05 | 0.06 |
| | (0.06) | (0.06) | (0.06) | (0.06) | (0.06) |
| Other 12th grade students[a] (%) | −0.04 | −0.04 | −0.04 | −0.04 | −0.04 |
| | (0.07) | (0.06) | (0.06) | (0.06) | (0.06) |
| *School-level teacher characteristics* | | | | | |
| African American teachers (%) | 0.01 | 0.00 | 0.01 | 0.01 | −0.01 |
| | (0.11) | (0.11) | (0.11) | (0.10) | (0.10) |
| Hispanic teachers (%) | −0.08 | −0.09 | −0.07 | −0.07 | −0.08 |
| | (0.10) | (0.11) | (0.11) | (0.11) | (0.11) |
| Other teachers[a] (%) | −0.13 | −0.16 | −0.19 | −0.22 | −0.22 |
| | (0.16) | (0.16) | (0.15) | (0.16) | (0.15) |

| | | | | |
|---|---|---|---|---|
| SCHOOL CLIMATE MEASURES | | | | |
| *Disciplinary climate* | | | | |
| Principal and teacher reports | | | | |
| Discipline index (×100)[b] | −0.05 | | −0.16 | −0.31 |
| | (0.31) | | (0.33) | (0.35) |
| Discipline index, African American interaction (×100) | | | | 2.04* |
| | | | | (1.04) |
| Student reports | | | | |
| Strictness perception, individual level (×100) | −1.13 | | −1.16 | −1.17 |
| | (0.79) | | (0.80) | (0.80) |
| Strictness perception, school level (×100) | −0.55 | | −1.03 | −1.03 |
| | (2.48) | | (2.46) | (2.51) |
| Fairness perception, individual level (×100) | 3.54*** | | 2.64*** | 2.65*** |
| | (0.77) | | (0.77) | (0.78) |
| Fairness perception, school level (×100) | −3.70 | | −3.90 | −3.43 |
| | (3.11) | | (3.12) | (3.12) |
| *Violence measures* | | | | |
| Principal reports: degree physical conflicts a problem (×100) | | 0.85 | 0.82 | 0.70 |
| | | (1.30) | (1.31) | (1.30) |
| Teacher reports: degree physical conflicts a problem (×100) | | 2.80 | 3.29 | 3.25 |
| | | (2.31) | (2.31) | (2.28) |
| Student reports | | | | |
| Student fighting, individual level (×100) | | −7.50*** | −6.64*** | −6.53*** |
| | | (1.69) | (1.69) | (1.68) |
| Student fighting, school level (×100) | | −8.83 | −8.11 | −8.15 |
| | | (4.87) | (4.78) | (4.78) |
| Student self-reported arrest, individual level (×100) | | −9.53** | −8.60** | −8.67** |
| | | (3.46) | (3.40) | (3.40) |

*(continued)*

TABLE 9.6 *(continued)*

| | *Model 1* | *Model 2* | *Model 3* | *Model 4* | *Model 5* |
|---|---|---|---|---|---|
| Student self-reported arrest, school level (×100) | | | 17.48** | 16.15* | 16.21* |
| | | | (6.87) | (6.86) | (6.95) |
| *School safety measures* | | | | | |
| Student reports | | | | | |
| Safe school, individual level | | | | 0.09*** | 0.09*** |
| | | | | (0.02) | (0.02) |
| Safe school, school level | | | | −0.02 | −0.02 |
| | | | | (0.09) | (0.08) |
| *Disobedience measures* | | | | | |
| Principal reports: disobedience index (×100) | | | −0.91 | −0.56 | −0.49 |
| | | | (2.24) | (2.23) | (2.22) |
| Teacher reports: disobedience index (×100) | | | −5.45 | −6.05* | −5.65* |
| | | | (2.84) | (2.89) | (2.90) |
| Student reports | | | | | |
| Disobedience index, individual level (×100) | | | −1.03 | −0.48 | −0.51 |
| | | | (1.06) | (1.07) | (1.07) |
| Disobedience index, school level (×100) | | | −3.81 | −4.35 | −4.20 |
| | | | (3.06) | (3.05) | (3.04) |
| *Educational commitment measures* | | | | | |
| Principal reports: educational commitment index (×100) | | | −0.02 | 0.02 | 0.00 |
| | | | (1.22) | (1.22) | (1.21) |

| | | | | | |
|---|---|---|---|---|---|
| Teacher reports: educational commitment index (×100) | | | 0.15 | 0.70 | 0.58 |
| | | | (1.91) | (1.98) | (1.96) |
| Student reports | | | | | |
| Educational commitment index, individual level (×100) | | | −0.26 | −0.30 | −0.30 |
| | | | (0.20) | (0.20) | (0.20) |
| Educational commitment index, school level (×100) | | | −0.87 | −0.77 | −0.78 |
| | | | (0.56) | (0.56) | (0.56) |
| Intercept | −0.09 | −0.04 | −0.01 | −0.02 | −0.03 |
| | (0.08) | (0.15) | (0.12) | (0.19) | (0.19) |
| $R^2$ | 0.81 | 0.81 | 0.81 | 0.81 | 0.81 |
| *N* | 9,241 | 9,241 | 9,241 | 9,241 | 9,241 |

SOURCE: NELS 1988, 1990, 1992.

NOTE: Analyses are adjusted using weights provided by NELS. Standard errors adjusted for clustering at the school level and strata sampling are in parentheses. Mean substitution is used for missing individual and school-level continuous covariates. Missing individual- and school-level dummy covariates are coded to 0. Dummy variables flagging all missing individual- and school-level covariates are included in analyses but not reported.

[a] "Other" refers to Asian Americans and American Indians.

[b] Because of the small size of the coefficients and standard errors of standardized variables, these are multiplied by 100 as noted.

* $p < .05$; ** $p < .01$; *** $p < .001$.

in a manner similar to our earlier TIMSS cross-sectional analysis. On average, African American students score between 0.07 and 0.08 standard deviation lower than white students on the 12th grade test after controlling for previous test score performance and a large number of student- and school-level covariates. Student socioeconomic background is also strongly associated with 12th grade test score performance at both the student and school level, although these differences are also not affected by adding school disciplinary climate measures into the model. Likewise, previous test score and being in an academic track positively predict 12th grade test score consistently across models. In terms of school-level characteristics associated with 12th grade test score, higher student-teacher ratios are associated with lower scores, and there is some evidence that higher student-dropout rates at the school are negatively associated with student achievement.

School climate measures are strongly associated with student academic achievement, after taking into account social background, previous test score performance, and other factors. Student perceptions of fairness of school discipline, consistent with earlier research (Arum 2003), are strongly associated with academic achievement, with more fairness predicting higher test scores. Student reports of fighting or arrest are negatively associated with 12th grade performance. Interestingly, school-level average self-reports of student arrests are positively associated with test scores—that is, social contexts in which other students attending the same school have experienced more police enforcement are associated with higher individual academic achievement after taking into account our other controls. Therefore, this measure may actually be a proxy for a stricter school environment. Finally, student perceptions of safe learning environments are associated with higher 12th-grade test scores, and similar to the results from the TIMSS data, teacher reports of student disobedience are negatively associated with student achievement.

Model 5 in Table 9.6 supports earlier findings from the TIMSS analysis indicating that African American students are particularly sensitive to disciplinary climates. The results suggest that there is an interaction between African American students and the principal and teacher discipline index (which sums the three principal indices and the teacher index measuring the administration of school discipline). For African American students, each unit increase in the discipline index increases tests scores by 0.02 standard deviation, suggesting that African American students' test scores are more sensitive to disciplinary climates than white students' test scores. Thus, although African American students score lower on the cognitive tests, the results of Model 5 suggest that this varies with respect to whether students attend schools with more or less administration of school discipline.

Because results of the previous models suggest that African American students perform better in schools with greater discipline, we examine descriptive statistics and run multivariate tests by discipline index quintile.[27] Our descriptive statistics, available upon request, indicate that African American students are approximately equally distributed across these five quintiles. While most of the student- and school-level characteristics are also fairly equally distributed across these types of disciplinary settings, there is one intriguing difference. As schools go from lower to higher school discipline, white students have higher socioeconomic status than white students in other settings. However, as schools go from lower to higher school discipline, African American students have lower socioeconomic status than African American students elsewhere.

To further examine the relationship between discipline quintiles and test scores, we run Models 1 and 3 by these divisions. Model 1 provides a baseline with no school climate or behavioral controls and Model 3 adds violence, disobedience, and educational commitment measures to Model 1. Results of these models are presented visually in Figure 9.1 and suggest that as discipline increases, the gap between African American and white test scores decreases. Notably, the gap is diminished to nearly zero for both models in the fourth and fifth quintiles. Table 9.7 presents a truncated table of these findings. Results are similar for both models and indicate that there are large and significant black-white test score gaps in the first through third quintiles that decrease to nonsignificance (and zero magnitude) by the fourth and fifth quintiles. Thus, expanding on the interaction found in Model 5 (see Table 9.6), these results support the idea that greater disciplinary administration may be beneficial for African American students.

## CONCLUSION

School discipline is a necessary institutional component that allows youth socialization to occur, facilitates cognitive development, and permits educators to teach in settings that are safe and professionally attractive in terms of recruitment and retention. Although discipline has long been recognized

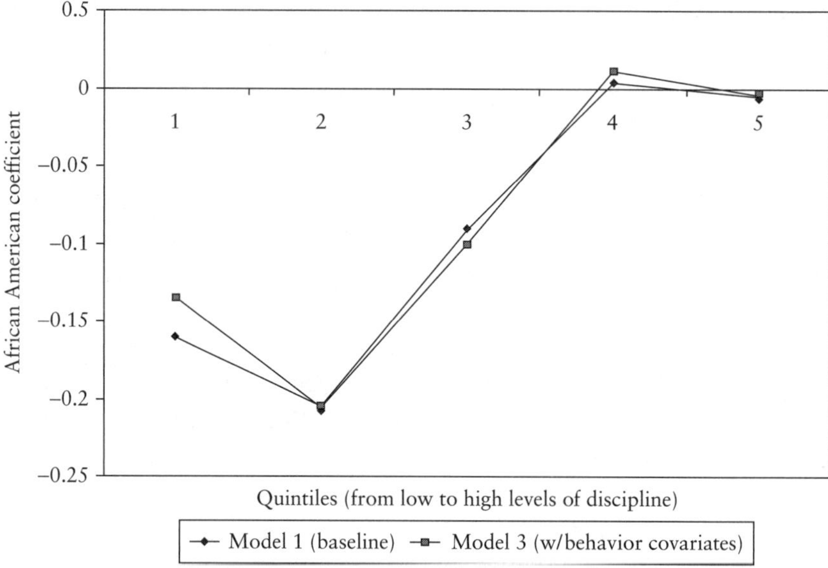


*Figure 9.1.* African American regression coefficients by teacher-principal discipline index quintile

as a central feature of successful schools, researchers in recent decades have given relatively scant attention to this critical topic. Our research attempts to address this scholarly shortcoming.

Our study demonstrates that in the United States the association between social background and school discipline often operates more strongly in terms of race than class. African American and white students face significantly different school contexts in terms of exposure to disorder, violence, and disciplinary climate. Not only do African American students attend schools with more economically disadvantaged students and disciplinary issues, our results suggest that the negative effect of economic disadvantage is mediated by the disciplinary climate. Whereas we found no effect of the school's economic composition on white students' test scores, there were significant negative effects of school economic composition for African American students until disciplinary climate was controlled for. Further, although African American students are in schools with more violence and disorder, the administrative disciplinary responses to these conditions are more similar to other schools than one might expect. Indeed, there was no

## Table 9.7

*Regression of 12th grade test score on individual and school characteristics, by administrator and teacher discipline index quintile (National Education Longitudinal Survey [NELS] data)*

| | Model 1[a] | | | | | Model 3[b] | | | | |
|---|---|---|---|---|---|---|---|---|---|---|
| | *Quintile 1* | *Quintile 2* | *Quintile 3* | *Quintile 4* | *Quintile 5* | *Quintile 1* | *Quintile 2* | *Quintile 3* | *Quintile 4* | *Quintile 5* |
| African American | −0.16** | −0.20*** | −0.09* | 0.00 | 0.00 | −0.13* | −0.21*** | −0.10* | 0.01 | −0.01 |
| | (0.06) | (0.06) | (0.05) | (0.04) | (0.04) | (0.06) | (0.06) | (0.05) | (0.04) | (0.04) |
| Intercept | −0.06 | −0.08 | 0.25 | −0.43** | −0.25 | 0.06 | −0.01 | 0.15 | −0.45 | −0.11 |
| | (0.16) | (0.13) | (0.16) | (0.15) | (0.14) | (0.19) | (0.19) | (0.20) | (0.29) | (0.24) |
| $R^2$ | 0.80 | 0.81 | 0.81 | 0.82 | 0.82 | 0.81 | 0.82 | 0.81 | 0.83 | 0.83 |
| African American students (%) | 0.07 | 0.10 | 0.11 | 0.12 | 0.14 | 0.07 | 0.10 | 0.11 | 0.12 | 0.14 |
| *N* | 2,039 | 1,870 | 1,733 | 1,773 | 1,826 | 2,039 | 1,870 | 1,733 | 1,773 | 1,826 |

SOURCE: NELS 1988, 1990, 1992.

NOTE: Covariates outlined in Table 9.6 were run but are not shown. Analyses are adjusted using weights provided by NELS. Standard errors adjusted for clustering at the school level and strata sampling are in parentheses. Mean substitution is used for missing individual- and school-level continuous covariates. Missing individual- and school-level dummy covariates are coded to 0. Dummy variables flagging all missing individual and school-level covariates are included in analyses but not reported.

[a] Model 1 includes individual background characteristics and school-level covariates.

[b] Model 3 adds violence, disobedience, and educational commitment measures to Model 1.

* $p < .05$; ** $p < .01$; *** $p < .001$.

detectable difference in teacher reports about student behavior enforcement between schools whites and African American students attend. According to results of the reviewed teacher survey responses, this may be because educators in these schools are more fearful of legal consequences and thus less effective in administering disciplinary action.

Although disciplinary climate is not clearly associated with overall aggregate differences in test score performance across racial groups in the United States, they are implicated significantly in explaining individual African American and white student gains—that is, in explaining patterns of within-group variance. Specifically, in the 40 percent of schools that have greater levels of discipline, African American students learn at rates comparable to whites (as assessed through longitudinal modeling of test score performance). Further, this occurs despite African American students' socioeconomic status being on average lower as levels of discipline increase. Racial differences in test scores that control for previous performance and social background are the result solely of the 60 percent of schools that are characterized by teachers and principals as having lower levels of discipline.

While earlier social science research has highlighted how school discipline has disproportionately subjected African American students to disciplinary sanctions (Skiba et al. 2002; Wald and Losen 2003), our research both confirms and challenges this previous work. We have highlighted disparate patterns in administration of disciplinary regulation, but we also have noted that African American students are exposed to school environments with high levels of disorder, violence, and concern over safety—that is, African American students also face the disparate impact of inadequate and ineffective discipline in U.S. schools. Significantly, in schools with more disciplinary administration, we also have found that the gap between African American and white student test performance does not exist. While greater disciplinary administration in other schools may be warranted on the grounds of increasing both overall achievement and equity across racial groups, policy makers and practitioners should know that perceived fairness of school discipline is a necessary element of effective authority relationships in schools (Gottfredson et al. 2005; Arum 2003; Welsh 2000). To improve the school's ability to contribute to youth socialization and student internalization of positive social norms and values, any changes in school disciplinary administration must not be just more responsive to behavior problems but also work to enhance the legitimacy and moral authority of school actors that underpin effective school discipline.

## NOTES

1. See the annual Phi Delta Kappa–Gallup "Poll of the Public's Attitudes toward the Public Schools." Respondents were asked about the seriousness of problems in 1998. From the first poll in the series in 1969 through 2008, lack of school discipline emerged as one of the most common responses to an open-ended question on the most important problem facing the public schools; drug abuse and lack of financial support have also been primary public concerns. School discipline has repeatedly been in the top of these rankings, even though responses are separately coded for "fighting/violence/gangs," crime and vandalism, drug use, lack of respect, and other responses related to school discipline.

2. Alternative tests, such as that from the National Assessment of Education Progress, indicate that the black-white achievement gap in reading and math has moved from 1.25–1.33 standard deviations in 1971 to 0.69–0.89 standard deviations in 1996 (Jencks and Phillips 1998, 3).

3. The U.S. Department of Education notes, "Two important federal mandates protect the rights of eligible children with ADHD—the Individuals with Disabilities Education Act (IDEA) and Section 504 of the Rehabilitation Act of 1973 (Section 504). The regulations implementing these laws are 34 CFR sections 300 and 104, respectively, which require school districts to provide a 'free appropriate public education' to students who meet their eligibility criteria. Although a child with ADHD may not be eligible for services under IDEA, he or she may meet the requirements of Section 504" (U.S. Department of Education 2003, 9).

4. 393 U.S. 503.

5. 419 U.S. 565.

6. 420 U.S. 308.

7. 430 U.S. 651.

8. 469 U.S. 325.

9. Data for examining educators' fear of legal challenge across individuals and schools were drawn from two sources. First, measures concerning legal issues in public schools were obtained from a restricted dataset of responses to a survey conducted by Harris Interactive. The survey, funded by the Common Good organization, was conducted during the 2003–2004 school year and asked 801 public school teachers and principals about their fear of legal challenges to public schools. Second, demographic measures of student composition for the schools in the survey were obtained from the Common Core of Data (CCD) of the National Center for Education Statistics. Because Arum, the first author, was a consultant on the Harris Interactive survey, we were granted access to restricted information about the identity of the respondents' schools. This information allowed us

to match the identifiers from the survey dataset with corresponding identifiers on the CCD dataset. Because of the centrality of school demographic information to our research questions, analysis was restricted to survey data for which we were able to find an appropriate CCD match. Merging the two datasets yielded a total sample of 633 respondents consisting of 343 teachers and 290 principals.

10. Specifically, teachers were asked, "To what extent does fear of legal challenge affect your willingness or ability to . . . participate in extracurricular activities, comfort or console students, maintain order in the classroom, give honest and candid evaluations of students, deal with unreasonable demands by parents, and create a good learning environment?" Principals were asked, "To what extent does fear of legal challenge affect your willingness or ability to . . . fire a bad teacher, deal with unreasonable demands by parents, deal with student discipline, create a good learning environment, try new reforms or ideas, and maintain order in your school?" Answers were recorded on a three-point scale (a lot, a little, not at all).

11. Educators in suburban public schools with 50 percent or more white students reported a 48 percent probability of contact with adversarial legal challenge compared to a 40 percent probability in other settings ($t = 1.91$; $p < .10$).

12. Principals were asked, "Approximately what percentage of students in your school come from economically disadvantaged homes?"

13. The index of disciplinary disengagement was created by averaging principal responses to questions about the frequency of students being late, being absent, and skipping class if respondents answered at least two of the questions ($\alpha = .80$).

14. Although our sample restrictions aim to be as inclusive as possible, we ran sensitivity tests to ensure that our results were not driven by a systematic exclusion of certain students in the analysis. Of greatest concern was that by restricting the sample to students in the same school in both the 10th and 12th grade we lost transfer and dropout students. Thus, it is possible that our results are a function of the type of student who remains in the same school for two years. To examine this possibility, we eased our sample restriction requiring that students remained in the same school in 10th and 12th grade (thus allowing for the inclusion of transfer and dropout students with a 12th grade test score). We then reran Model 5 in Table 6 and the quintile models in Table 3. Results of these models are nearly identical to the originals, indicating that our results are not driven by excluding students who were not in the same school in the 10th and 12th grades. Examining Model 5 in Table 2 we see that the effect of being African American is significantly negative (−0.09; $p < .001$) but accompanied by a marginally significant positive effect of the interaction between being African American and the discipline index (0.02; $p = .09$). In the quintile analysis, results of Model 1 and Model 3 are nearly identical, thus only the latter are presented. The African American coefficient is significant in quintiles 1 (−0.13; $p < .05$) and 2 (−0.19; $p < .001$) but insignificant in subsequent quintiles.

15. We were also concerned that our results might be driven by the type of student who has a 12th grade test score available, but supplementary analyses found little evidence supporting this possibility. Specifically, it is possible that those students missing a 12th grade test score were systematically different from those with a nonmissing score. More troubling, however, is that these systematic differences might stem from our variable of interest, discipline. Less able students in schools with high levels of discipline might be more likely to drop out or transfer schools, making it more difficult for researchers to administer a 12th grade test, and this might vary by race. If this is the case, then results may be generalizable only to the type of student willing to stay in a school with increased discipline. Our results, then, might overstate a positive effect of increased discipline. To test this idea, we ran a logistic regression of missing 12th grade test score on all of the 10th grade covariates. Results of this regression indicate that rather than increasing the likelihood of having a missing 12th grade test score, more discipline actually *decreases* the likelihood of having a missing test score (–0.09; $p < .001$). Given these results, it is unlikely that our findings are being driven by the types of students who remain in schools with high levels of discipline.

16. For all measures created from the teacher questionnaire (unless otherwise noted), aggregated school-level data was generated by taking the average of all teachers surveyed in a particular school; the measure was then standardized to a mean of 0 and a standard deviation of 1 for the full sample.

17. Before averaging the math and reading sections to create the composite score, NELS standardized each test to a mean of 50 and a standard deviation of 10. For the purposes of this study, the composite test score variable was then standardized to a mean of 0 and a standard deviation of 1 for the full sample. Note that standardized values were calculated for the *full* sample; thus, the *analysis* sample means reported in Table 9.5 may not have a mean of 0 and a standard deviation of 1 for this and subsequent standardized variables.

18. Principals were asked to indicate if school rules within four categories were present: hall passes, dress code, closed-lunch campus, and smoking. The presence of *any* school rule within each of the four categories was flagged with a dummy variable equaling 1 and summed to create the school rules index. The index ranges from 0 (no rules present in any of the categories) to 4 (at least one rule in each of the categories; a = .45). For comparative purposes, the measure was standardized to a mean of 0 and a standard deviation of 1 for the full sample.

19. The severity of discipline in the school was measured by asking principals about the punishment for an array of infractions. Specifically, principals were asked about the penalty for "cheating on tests," "skipping classes," "skipping school for one or two days," "skipping school for three or more days," "physical injury to another student," "possession of alcohol," "possession of illegal drugs," "selling illegal drugs," "possession of weapons," "use of alcohol at school," "use of illegal drugs at school," "verbal abuse of teachers or staff members," "physical

injury to a teacher or staff member," "theft of school property," "classroom disturbance," and "use of profanity in class." For each infraction principals noted the severity of the punishment as from 0 (no punishment) to 5 (expulsion). To create the severity of discipline index, we calculated the average of the most severe punishments noted within each category (a = .87). For comparative purposes, the measure was standardized to a mean of 0 and a standard deviation of 1 for the full sample.

20. The combined teacher and principal discipline measure was created by summing the three principal discipline variables (discipline enforcement, presence of school rules, and severity of discipline index) and the teacher discipline index (a = .28). Although the alpha for this index is low, suggesting that principals and teachers often disagree in their perception of discipline and with the official school regulations, we proceeded with its use because the components are conceptually related.

21. Answers to these questions were recorded on a 1 to 4 scale, with higher numbers indicating more of a problem. The average of the principal responses to the two questions were calculated to create the principal disobedience index (a = .38). Again, although the alpha for this index is low, we proceeded with its use because the components are theoretically related. The teacher responses to the two questions were also averaged, creating the teacher disobedience index (a = .57).

22. Individual student disobedience was measured using an index consisting of four questions. Students were asked if they "feel it's ok to disobey school rules," if they "feel it's ok to abuse teachers," and how often they "feel it's ok to talk back to teachers." Responses to the three questions could range from 1 (never) to 4 (often). Finally, up to two of the students' teachers were asked, "How often is the student disruptive in class?" Their responses could vary from 1 (never) to 5 (all of the time). If more than one teacher of a particular student was asked the question, responses were averaged. Each of the student and teacher responses were standardized to a mean of 0 and a standard deviation of 1 for the full sample and then averaged to create a student disobedience index (a = .57) that applied to the specific student. A school-level version of this measure was also created by averaging student responses by school.

23. Responses were averaged to create the principal index (a = .73) and the teacher index (a = .90).

24. Students' individual educational commitment was measured by creating an index made up of several questions. Students were asked, "How often do you go to class without: pencil/paper, books, your homework done." Students could respond on a scale from 1 (usually) to 4 (never). Students were also asked, "How many times were you absent from school for any reason?" Responses were measured on a scale from 1 (none) to 7 (21 days or more). Finally, students were asked how many times they were "late for school" and "cut or skipped classes."

Responses were recorded on a scale from 1 (never) to 4 (over 10 times). Because of the differing scales used to measure each question, responses were standardized to a mean of 0 and a standardized deviation of 1 for the full sample before being summed to create the educational commitment index (a = .66). A school-level index of this measure was also created.

25. Student-level covariates were obtained from all three waves of NELS data. Dummy variables were created to indicate male, African American, Hispanic, and other students (Asian Americans and American Indians). Dummy variables were also created to flag students living in two-parent households, living in non-English-speaking homes, enrolled in a vocational program, or enrolled in an academic program. The student's 10th grade test score, standardized to a mean of 0 and standard deviation of 1 for the full sample, was obtained from the 1990 wave of data. Finally, additional individual controls were included for the number of siblings in a student's household and household socioeconomic status. This composite socioeconomic status variable was created by NELS and comprised mother and father's education level, mother and father's occupation, and family income. Before summing each component, the variables were standardized to a mean of 0 and a standard deviation of 1.

School level covariates were also obtained from all three waves of NELS data. Dummy variables were created to indicate a school's urban or rural location. Additional variables measured the dropout rate, the number of poor students (measured by those receiving free or reduced-price lunch), African American students in the 12th grade, Hispanic students in the 12th grade, and other students in the 12th grade. Teacher composition is captured by measuring the percentage of African American teachers, Hispanic teachers, and other teachers. Additional school variables measure the student-teacher ratio (using its square root to adjust for skewness in the distribution), and the school size (logged to adjust for outliers). Finally, the average school socioeconomic status is calculated from the average student socioeconomic status in the school and standardized to a mean of 0 and a standard deviation of 1 for the full sample.

Missing data was substituted only for student- and school-level covariates; cases with missing data on either 12th grade test score or school discipline measures were dropped from the analysis. Missing data from *continuous* measures were mean substituted using means from the full sample with dummy variables added to indicate observations in which the mean substitution was made. The missing-data dummy variables were included in all statistical analyses to control for the mean-substitution assumption but results are not reported in the tables (full results available upon request).

26. In addition to weighting the analyses, we adjusted standard errors for the models for strata and school-level clustering.

27. It would have been optimal to conduct these analyses by segregating the school as well; however, sample sizes did not permit this additional subdivision.

REFERENCES

Adams, A. Troy. 2000. "The Status of School Discipline and Violence." *Annals of the American Academy of Political and Social Science* 567:140–56.

Alexander, Karl L., Doris R. Entwisle, and Linda S. Olson. 2001. "Schools, Achievement, and Inequality: A Seasonal Perspective." *Educational Evaluation and Policy Analysis* 23:171–91.

Arum, Richard. 1998. "The Effects of Resources on Vocational Student Educational Outcomes: Invested Dollars or Diverted Dreams." *Sociology of Education* 71:130–51.

———. 2000. "Schools and Communities: Ecological and Institutional Dimensions." *Annual Review of Sociology* 26:395–418.

———. 2003. *Judging School Discipline: The Crisis of Moral Authority.* Cambridge, MA: Harvard University Press.

Arum, Richard, and Irenee Beattie. 1999. "High School Experience and the Risk of Adult Incarceration." *Criminology* 37:515–39.

Arum, Richard, and Doreet Priess. 2009. "Still Judging School Discipline." In *From Schoolhouse to Courthouse: The Judiciary's Role in American Education*, edited by Joshua Dunn and Martin West, 238–60. Washington, DC: Brookings Institution Press.

Chubb, John E., and Terry M. Moe. 1990. *Politics, Markets, and America's Schools.* Washington, DC: Brookings Institution Press.

Coleman, James. 1961. *The Adolescent Society: The Social Life of the Teenager and Its Impact on Education.* New York: Free Press of Glencoe.

Coleman, James, Ernest Campbell, Carol Hobson, James McPartland, Alexander Mood, Frederic Weinfeld, and Robert York. 1966. *Equality of Educational Opportunity.* Washington, DC: Government Printing Office.

Coleman, James, and Thomas Hoffer. 1987. *Public and Private Schools: The Impact of Communities.* New York: Basic Books.

Coleman, James S., Thomas Hoffer, and Sally Kilgore. 1982. *High School Achievement: Public, Catholic, and Private Schools Compared.* New York: Basic Books.

DeVoe, J. F., K. Peter, P. Kaufman, S. A. Ruddy, A. K. Miller, M. Planty, T. D. Snyder, D. T. Duhart, and M. R. Rand. 2002. *Indicators of School Crime and Safety: 2002.* NCES 2003–009/NCJ 196753. Washington, DC: U.S. Departments of Education and Justice.

Dinkes, Rachel, Emily Forrest Cataldi, and Wendy Lin-Kelly. 2007. *Indicators of School Crime and Safety: 2007*, tables 4.1, 5.1, 5.2. NCES 2008-021/NCJ 219553. Washington, DC: National Center for Education Statistics, Institute of Education Sciences, U.S. Department of Education, and Bureau of Justice Statistics, Office of Justice Programs, U.S. Department of Justice.

DiPrete, Tom, Chandra Muller, and Nora Shaeffer. 1981. *Discipline and Order in American High Schools*. Washington, DC: National Center for Educational Statistics.

Edwards, Patricia A. 1993. "Before and After School Segregation: African American Parents' Involvement in Schools." *Educational Policy* 7 (3): 340–69.

Entwisle, Doris, and Karl Alexander. 1992. "Summer Setback: Race, Poverty, School Composition, and Mathematics Achievement in the First Two Years of School." *American Sociological Review* 57:72–84.

———. 1994. "Winter Setback: The Racial Composition of Schools and Learning to Read." *American Sociological Review* 59:446–60.

Farrington, David P., Rolf Loeber, Magda Stouthamer-Loeber, Welmoet B. Van Kammen, and Laura Schmidt. 1996. "Self-Reported Delinquency and a Combined Delinquency Seriousness Scale Based on Boys, Mothers, and Teachers: Concurrent and Predictive Validity for African-Americans and Caucasians." *Criminology* 34 (4): 493–517.

Ferguson, Ronald. 1989. "Teachers' Perceptions and Expectations and the Black-White Test Score Gap." In *The Black-White Test Score Gap*, edited by Christopher Jencks and Meredith Phillips, 273–317. Washington, DC: Brookings Institution Press.

Fischer, Claude, Michael Hout, Martin Sanchez Jankowski, Samuel Lucas, Ann Swidler, and Kim Voss. 1996. *Inequality by Design: Cracking the Bell Curve Myth*. Princeton, NJ: Princeton University Press.

Fordham, Signithia, and John U. Ogbu. 1986. "Black Students' School Success: Coping with the 'Burden of "Acting White."'" *Urban Review* 18:176–206.

Gallup, George. 1972. *The Gallup Poll: Public Opinion, 1935–1971*, pp. 1281, 1587. New York: Random House.

Gottfredson, Denise. 2001. *Schools and Delinquency*. New York: Cambridge University Press.

Gottfredson, G. D., and D. C. Gottfredson. 1985. *Victimization in Schools*. New York: Plenum.

Gottfredson, Gary D., Denise C. Gottfredson, Allison Ann Payne, and Nisha C. Gottfredson. 2005. "School Climate Predictors of School Disorder: Results from a National Study of Delinquency Prevention in Schools." *Journal of Research in Crime and Delinquency* 42:412–44.

Halpern-Felsher, Bonnie L., James P. Connell, Margaret B. Spencer, J. Lawrence Aber, Greg J. Duncan, Elizabeth Clifford, Warren E. Crichlow, et al. 1997. "Neighborhood and Family Factors predicting Educational Risk and Attainment in African American and White Children and Adolescents." In *Neighborhood Poverty*, vol. 1, edited by J. Brooks-Gunn, G. Duncan, and J. L. Aber, 146–73. New York: Russell Sage Foundation.

Hanushek, E. A., J. F. Kain, and S. G. Rivkin. 2009. "New Evidence about Brown v. Board of Education: The Complex Effects of School Racial Composition on Achievement." *Journal of Labor Economics* 27 (3): 349–83.

Hedges, Larry, and Amy Nowell. 1999. "Changes in the Black-White Gap in Achievement Test Scores." *Sociology of Education* 72:111–35.
Heyns, Barbara Lee. 1978. *Summer Learning and the Effects of Schooling*. New York: Academic Press.
Hindelang, Michael J., Travis Hirschi, and Joseph G. Weis. 1981. *Measuring Delinquency*. Beverley Hills, CA: Sage.
Huizinga, David, and Delbert S. Elliot. 1986. "Reassessing the Reliability and Validity of Self-Report Delinquency Measures." *Journal of Quantitative Criminology* 2 (4): 293–327.
Human Rights Watch. 2009. *A Violent Education: Corporal Punishment in U.S. Public Schools*. New York: Human Rights Watch.
Ingersoll, Richard. 2003. *Who Controls Teachers Work? Power and Accountability in America's Schools*. Cambridge, MA: Harvard University Press.
Jencks, Christopher, and Meredith Phillips. 1998. *The Black-White Test Score Gap*. Washington, DC: Brookings Institution Press.
Kafka, Judith. 2008. "'Sitting on a Tinderbox': Racial Conflict, Teacher Discretion, and the Centralization of Disciplinary Authority." *American Journal of Education* 114:247–70.
Kirp, David L., and Donald N. Jensen. 1986. *School Days, Rule Days: The Legislation and Regulation of Education*. Philadelphia, PA: Falmer Press.
Lafree, Gary, and Richard Arum. 2006. "The Impact of Racially Inclusive Schooling on Adult Incarceration Rates Among U.S. Cohorts of African Americans and Whites Since 1930." *Criminology* 44:73–103.
Lee, Valerie, and Anthony Bryk. 1989. "Multilevel Model of the Social Distribution of High School Achievement." *Sociology of Education* 62:172–92.
Metz, M. 1978. *Classroom and Corridors: The Crisis of Authority in Desegregated Secondary Schools*. Berkeley: University of California Press.
National Educational Association. 1956. "Teacher Opinion on Pupil Behavior, 1955–56." *NEA Research Bulletin* 34 (2): 51–107.
Ogbu, John U. 1978. *Minority Education and Caste: The American System in Cross-Cultural Perspective*. New York: Academic Press.
Orfield, Gary, and Chungmei Lee. 2006. *Racial Transformation and the Changing Nature of Segregation*. Cambridge, MA: Civil Rights Project, Harvard University.
Ortiz, Flora I. 2002. "Essential Learning Conditions for California Youth: Educational Facilities." Los Angeles, CA: UCLA Institute for Democracy, Education and Access, Williams Watch Series: Investigating the Claims of Williams v. State of California.
Phillips, Meredith. 2008. "Culture and Stalled Progress in Narrowing the Black-White Test Score Gap." In *Steady Gains and Stalled Progress: Inequality and the Black-White Test Score Gap*, edited by Katherine Magnuson and Jane Waldfogel, 250–85. New York: Russell Sage Foundation.

Phillips, Meredith, Jeanne Brooks-Gunn, Greg J. Duncan, Pamela K. Klebanov, and Jonathan Crane. 1998. "Family Background, Parenting Practices, and the Black-White Test Score Gap." In *The Black-White Test Score Gap*, edited by C. Jencks and M. Phillips, 103–45. Washington, DC: Brookings Institution Press.

Phillips, Meredith, James Crouse, and John Ralph. 1998. "Does the Black-White Test Gap Widen after Students Enter School." In *The Black-White Test Score Gap*, edited by Christopher Jencks and Meredith Phillips, 229–72. Washington, DC: Brookings Institution Press.

Schmidt, William H., Curtis C. McKnight, Leland S. Cogan, Pamela M. Jakwerth, and Richard T. Houang. 1999. *Facing the Consequences: Using TIMSS for a Closer Look at U.S. Mathematics and Science Education.* New York: Springer.

Skiba, Russell J., Robert S. Michael, Abra Carroll Nardo, and Reece L. Peterson. 2002. "The Color of Discipline: Sources of Racial and Gender Disproportionality in School Punishment." *Urban Review* 34 (4): 317–42.

Smrekar, Claire, and Debra Owens. 2003. "It's a Way of Life for US: High Mobility and High Achievement in Department of Defense Schools." *Journal of Negro Education* 72:165–77.

Snyder, T. D., S. A. Dillow, and C. M. Hoffman. 2008. *Digest of Education Statistics 2007.* Washington, DC: National Center for Education Statistics, Institute of Education Sciences, U.S. Department of Education.

Steele, Claude, and Joshua Aronson. 1998. "Stereotype Threat and the Test Performance of Academically Successful African-Americans." In *The Black-White Test Score Gap*, edited by Christopher Jencks and Meredith Phillips, 401–27. Washington, DC: Brookings Institution Press.

Stevens, Mitchell. 2001. *Kingdom of Children: Culture and Controversy in the Homeschooling Movement.* Princeton, NJ: Princeton University Press.

Thornberry, Terence P., and Marvin D. Krohn. 2000. "The Self-Report Method for Measuring Delinquency and Crime." *Measurement and Analysis of Crime and Justice* 4:33–83.

Toby, Jackson. 1995. "The Schools." In *Crime*, edited by James Wilson and Joan Petersilia, 141–70. San Francisco: Institute for Contemporary Studies.

Tyack, David, Aaron Benavot, and Thomas James. 1987. *Law and the Shaping of Public Education: 1785–1954.* Madison: University of Wisconsin Press.

Tyson, Karolyn, William Darity Jr., and Domini R. Castellino. 2005. "It's Not 'A Black Thing': Understanding the Burden of Acting White and Other Dilemmas of High Achievement." *American Sociological Review* 70 (4): 582–605.

U.S. Department of Education. 2003. *Identifying and Treating Attention Deficit Hyperactivity Disorder: A Resource for School and Home.* Washington, DC: Government Printing Office.

Wald, Johanna, and Daniel J. Losen. 2003. "Defining and Redirecting a School-to-Prison Pipeline." In *Deconstructing the School-to-Prison Pipeline: New Directions for Youth Development, Number 99*, edited by Johanna Wald and Daniel J. Losen, 9–15. Oxford: Jossey-Bass.
Welsh, Wayne N. 2000. "The Effects of School Climate on School Disorder." *Annals of the American Academy of Political and Social Science* 567:88–107.
Zirkel, Perry A. 1997. "Tipping the Scales." *American School Board Journal* 184 (10): 36–38.

# INDEX

*Italic page numbers indicate material in tables or figures.*

STUDIES IN SOCIAL INEQUALITY

*Broke: How Debt Bankrupts the Middle Class*
EDITED BY KATHERINE PORTER
2012

*Making the Transition: Education and Labor Market Entry in Central and Eastern Europe*
EDITED BY IRENA KOGAN, CLEMENS NOELKE, AND MICHAEL GEBEL
2011

*Class and Power in the New Deal: Corporate Moderates, Southern Democrats, and the Liberal-Labor Coalition*
BY G. WILLIAM DOMHOFF AND MICHAEL J. WEBBER
2011

*Social Class and Changing Families in an Unequal America*
EDITED BY MARCIA J. CARLSON AND PAULA ENGLAND
2011

*Dividing the Domestic: Men, Women, and Household Work in Cross-National Perspective*
EDITED BY JUDITH TREAS AND SONJA DROBNIČ
2010

*Gendered Trajectories: Women, Work, and Social Change in Japan and Taiwan*
BY WEI-HSIN YU
2009

*Creating Wealth and Poverty in Postsocialist China*
EDITED BY DEBORAH S. DAVIS AND WANG FENG
2008

*Shifting Ethnic Boundaries and Inequality in Israel: Or, How the Polish Peddler Became a German Intellectual*
BY AZIZA KHAZZOOM
2008

*Boundaries and Categories: Rising Inequality in Post-Socialist Urban China*
BY WANG FENG
2008

*Stratification in Higher Education: A Comparative Study*
EDITED BY YOSSI SHAVIT, RICHARD ARUM, AND ADAM GAMORAN
2007

*The Political Sociology of the Welfare State: Institutions, Social Cleavages, and Orientations*
EDITED BY STEFAN SVALLFORS
2007

*On Sociology, Second Edition*
*Volume One: Critique and Program*
*Volume Two: Illustration and Retrospect*
BY JOHN H. GOLDTHORPE
2007

*After the Fall of the Wall: Life Courses in the Transformation of East Germany*
EDITED BY MARTIN DIEWALD, ANNE GOEDICKE, AND KARL ULRICH MAYER
2006

*The Moral Economy of Class: Class and Attitudes in Comparative Perspective*
BY STEFAN SVALLFORS
2006

*The Global Dynamics of Racial and Ethnic Mobilization*
BY SUSAN OLZAK
2006

*Poverty and Inequality*
EDITED BY DAVID B. GRUSKY AND RAVI KANBUR
2006

*Mobility and Inequality: Frontiers of Research in Sociology and Economics*
EDITED BY STEPHEN L. MORGAN, DAVID B. GRUSKY, AND GARY S. FIELDS
2006

*Analyzing Inequality: Life Chances and Social Mobility in Comparative Perspective*
EDITED BY STEFAN SVALLFORS
2005

*On the Edge of Commitment: Educational Attainment and Race in the United States*
BY STEPHEN L. MORGAN
2005

*Occupational Ghettos: The Worldwide Segregation of Women and Men*
BY MARIA CHARLES AND DAVID B. GRUSKY
2004

*Home Ownership and Social Inequality in Comparative Perspective*
EDITED BY KARIN KURZ AND HANS-PETER BLOSSFELD
2004